9844

MUSIC and the ARTS in the COMMUNITY:

The Community Music School in America

by
ROBERT F. EGAN

The Scarecrow Press, Inc.
Metuchen, N.J., & London
1989

British Library Cataloguing-in-Publication data available

Library of Congress Cataloging-in-Publication Data

Egan, Robert F., 1924-
   Music and the arts in the community : the community music
school in America / by Robert F. Egan.
      p.   cm.
   Bibliography: p.
   Includes index.
   ISBN 0-8108-2117-6 (alk. paper)
   1. Music--Instruction and study--United States--History.
2. Community music--United States--History and criticism.
I. Title.
MT3.U5E36   1989
780'.71'073--dc20   89-30492

Dedicated

to

Ruth

CONTENTS

ACKNOWLEDGMENTS

The author is indebted--for assistance and expertise--to the following organizations whose contributions made this book possible:

The National Endowment for the Humanities for a Travel to Collections Grant that allowed the author to travel to Minneapolis to do research at the Social Welfare History Archives at the University of Minnesota in Minneapolis.

The Social Welfare History Archives Center, University Libraries, University of Minnesota at Minneapolis, for the invaluable assistance given during the preparation of this book, especially the expertise and kindness of David Klaassen, curator of the archives.

Duquesne University in Pittsburgh, Pennsylvania, and its School of Music for granting the author a sabbatical leave to complete necessary research and assemblage of materials for this book.

The National Guild of Community Schools of the Arts for its assistance and for making its records and materials available for the author's use. A special thanks to the guild's National Office and to Lolita and Azim Mayadas.

The University of Illinois at Chicago, The University Library, the Jane Addams Memorial Collection, for making photographs of Jane Addams and various pictures of Hull-House and its Music School available for publication in this book.

Ulrich Franzen & Associates, Architects, for making the picture of the Harlem School of the Arts available for publication in this book.

The Member Schools of the National Guild of Community
Schools of the Arts, which made unusual efforts and contribu-
tions of materials from their early records to contemporary
files, especially the Brooklyn Music School, Cleveland Music
School Settlement, Harlem School of the Arts, Henry Street
Settlement and its Abrons Arts for Living Center, Manhattan
School of Music (which began as the Neighborhood Music
School, New York City), Peabody Preparatory, School for
Strings (New York City), Settlement Music School (Philadel-
phia), Third Street Music School Settlement, and the Green-
wich House Music School (New York City), and the many
other guild schools which completed questionnaires and sent
additional materials. The list is too long to be itemized:
Thank you to all schools affiliated with the National Guild of
Community Schools of the Arts.

To Monroe Levin, past president of the National Guild,
who while in the office of president managed and presented
the fiftieth anniversary of the National Guild of Community
Schools of the Arts with help from his loyal member schools
and chapters.

To the many individuals, including Betty Allen (Harlem
School of the Arts), Louise Behrend (School for Strings),
George Bennette (Lighthouse Music School), Dr. Catherine
M. Campbell (Turtle Bay Music School), Robert Capanna
(Settlement Music School, Philadelphia), Dean Eileen Cline
(Peabody Preparatory), Barbara Field (Third Street Music
School Settlement), Emily Franz (Roosa School of Music), Jean
Whitlock Freifeld (Mannes College of Music), Annetta Kaplan
(Metropolitan School for the Arts), Daniel Kronenfeld (Henry
Street Settlement), David Lapin (Community Music Center of
Boston), Hadassah B. Markson (YM/YWHA School of Music),
Stowe C. Phelps (Third Street Music School Settlement), Ilse
Sass (Manhattan School of Music), Dr. Stephen Shapiro (Com-
munity Music Center, San Francisco), Barbara Tate (Henry
Street Settlement Abrons Arts for Living Center), and Jose-
phine Whitford (Manhattan School of Music)--all of whom made
special efforts to send accurate information and materials.

For permission to use selected quotations from contemporary literature, the author is indebted to the following.

From The Damrosch Dynasty by George Martin. Copyright

PREFACE

The United States of America can readily boast of its contributions to the world of the arts and arts education. Until the recent past, however, this country's accomplishments in the arts have been underrated or overlooked. Indeed, this had been a nation recognized for great achievements in exploring and settling new territories, of emerging strongly during the Industrial Revolution, and for the development and expansion of the social settlement movement begun in England during the late nineteenth century.

From the last of the three came the idea that the art of musical performance and its related areas--music theory, ensemble playing, composition, and teaching--should be available to all regardless of age, nationality, or cultural or religious background, and that no one should be denied music study only for the want of money to pay the cost of instruction. The spark of inspiration caught fire in America and spread throughout the land. So much so that musical instruction, in the lap of the social settlement houses, became an important issue at national and international conferences of social work and other fields during the first quarter of the twentieth century.

The result of this was the formation of the community music school--an institution that offers music instruction of the highest quality for those who desire it, regardless of ability to pay. As one examines music education and its development in the United States, one discovers that many nationally and internationally known music performers had their early training in community music schools under the tutelage of outstanding musicians who had come to these shores to find artistic freedom and escape political or religious persecution.

This book attempts to show the development of musical instruction given with the stated philosophy from the 1890s to the present, and the willingness of other art forms to accept that pattern and philosophy. The early part of the book purports to present a brief glimpse of music and art history to show that music and the other arts have existed healthily in civilized communities for centuries, but that the philosophy of the community music school urges the artistic development of the indigenous population in communities that are urban, suburban, or rural.

The community music school recognizes the need for the student to be keenly aware of historical events, past and present, exhilarating and tragic, artistic or humanistic, that can affect the lives of individuals. But most of all, it is important for the various arts to recognize and accept each other and to understand the intrinsic value of other art forms--music, dance, drama, painting, sculpture, poetry, prose, etc. For this reason the book identified outstanding artists, such as recitalists, theatrical performers, operatic performers, playwrights, composers, at specific periods during the late nineteenth century and most of the twentieth, at least to the 1980s. To identify the unanimity of thought, the term "community music school" has become "community school of the arts" in the United States and Canada. Actually, all forms of arts education can coexist under one roof.

Occasional use in the book of masculine grammatical forms ("he," "himself," etc.) reflects the present scarcity of alternative terms for third person singular construction, rather than any intended bias in perspective.

It is hoped that many community schools of the arts throughout these two great nations on the North American continent will become inspired and encouraged to write their own historical documents showing their unique struggles to develop programs of artistic and educational value. Their efforts to work together resulted in the formation of the National Guild of Community Music Schools in the 1930s, later to have the name altered to the National Guild of Community Schools of the Arts, of which many schools are members, and the development of which is traced throughout the book. Let the communities share their successes and failures so that others may learn and grow. Let arts education flourish throughout the land.

1

A HISTORICAL GLANCE AT THE PAST AND EARLY AMERICAN MUSICAL LIFE

A little more than a decade ago, the United States of America celebrated its bicentennial. During the many events organized and presented for that two hundredth anniversary, music and all the arts--dance, drama, theatre, photography, painting and design, etc., were called upon to assist in the many gala celebrations and festivities to be presented to the American people, and, indeed, to the world.

The arts were taken for granted by a very large percentage of our population. The arts were here, available, abundant, and in highly sophisticated form. There were theatres, opera companies and houses, dance companies, skilled writers and dramatists, actors and actresses, dancers, instrumentalists, singers and performers of all kinds ready and willing to use their various artistic abilities to acknowledge the auspicious occasion. And there were museums of all kinds--historical and artistic--anxious to participate in the festivities with special displays and exhibitions.

States, counties, parishes, cities, towns, and villages, all prepared to spend tremendous energy and much money to accomplish this goal. The arts were needed by all.

In tracing the steps of artistic progress in this country, one first finds it difficult to imagine what daily existence was like three hundred sixty-eight years ago when the Pilgrims landed at Plymouth. The grim matter of self-preservation was immediately present in a wilderness with no houses, no farms and gardens, no cities or city dwellers as they are now known, no form of government yet organized to help the new arrivals to settle and live, no paved streets or signposts, no public transportation of any kind as yet, and, in reality, nothing in the way of creature comforts which three

1

hundred and sixty-eight years later had become a way of life
and readily expected from birth to adulthood.

And, intentionally saved until last, no telephone, no
radio, no television! No method of easy communication!
Succinctly, there was no way to summon help or relief from
any kind of natural disaster. There was no way to predict
or announce the coming of hurricanes, tornadoes, forest
fires, earthquakes, of the presence of some form of human
foe--advancing armies or marauding enemies, for example.
Life itself was arduous and unpredictable.

The implication of the previous statements is that artistic endeavors were non-existent during this period of American history. But could this be true? Does this then mean
that the new arrivals to America had lost or never had the
spirit to express themselves in non-verbal terms? No one
hummed a simple tune which he remembered from his earlier
life in another country and which was, perhaps, his favorite?
No young people ever had the urge to move feet and bodies
in simple dance steps? In the praise of God in whom so
many of the early settlers believed fervently, no one raised
his voice in song and praise? Was folk music non-existent
to the newcomers? Had none of them heard any of the great
choral works performed in the churches of England or Holland?

It would seem that the many questions deserve reasonable responses. It is necessary then to investigate the
earliest available records to determine thoughtful and accurate
answers.

THE COMMUNITY AND ITS COMPOSITION

It behooves the reader to consider the kinds of musical
and artistic masterpieces which were in existence and established as venerable works of art even prior to the birth
of those who were later to be known as the Pilgrims in the
New Land. While the average citizen may not have had daily
acquaintance with great works of art, many were exposed,
at least, to some of the recognized masterpieces of the world,
many of which still exist today, especially in the forms of
literature, painting, sculpture and, of course, music.

Since the emphasis of this book is on the arts in the

community, it is important to determine a reasonable definition of the term "community." It is also necessary to consider the amount of influence a community must exert to produce an outstanding composer or a performing musician, a playwright or an actor, a painter or a sculptor, a choreographer or a professional, performing dancer, and most important of all, an intelligent, receptive, and appreciative audience.

The seeds of creativity and ambition must exist within the potential artist himself. If, as is believed today, environment strongly influences the artistic development of an individual, it must be made clear that in the past such influence did exist within the communities of distinctly talented young people.

While over the years some individuals may have achieved recognized greatness in spite of difficult surroundings, they were perhaps the few in number. The majority received help from the Church, a king's court, or a wealthy and generous benefactor. The inherent abilities of the potential artists were, indeed, recognized.

Training and encouragement were available. Whether the exposure was to great music, paintings, sculpture or writings for theatre, or dance, is not important. The ground was fertile in given locations, such as Italy, France, England, Holland, and other European countries, and the arts flourished.

It is now essential to define the word "community." The first community in which a person finds himself is usually a family where he initially experiences acceptance, assistance, love, and where he receives encouragement and earns recognition. It is here that he acquires self-confidence, learns to accept recognition from other people, to join and comply with others, to enjoy camaraderie, and to move within society and the surrounding culture.

A community school of the arts should create an atmosphere of love, help, encouragment, and correction, never forsaking the required conditions in an acceptable community school--quality and standards in performance in whatever area it might be, and in the skill of teaching, which is in itself an art. Also the conditions of the student's first community should be reflected within the institution.

Community, therefore, is simply the place, spot, or atmosphere in which one is. The community school of the arts has a responsibility to create and preserve the most enriched environment conducive to creativity and learning as it can. The school must further be available for those who can afford to pay the full fee and for those who can pay very little of it--an awesome task, indeed!

It is safe to say that each individual finds himself in a community. It is from his community that he receives inspiration, encouragement, and training. Ultimately he presents a performance for the public in whatever form he finds at his command--music (performance or composition), sculpture, painting, dance or drama, poetry or prose. The very name of the National Guild of Community Schools of the Arts reflects the recognition and acceptance of the multiplicity of art forms available to communities today.

For purposes of reflection and study, it is wise to adopt a focal point or date in history from which examination can extend. The year of the Pilgrims' landing was 1620, 368 years prior to the present year, 1988. Let that be the focal point to peruse the events, historical and artistic, that illuminate the time period of 368 years both prior to and after 1620.

This will allow a time span of approximately 730 years to be investigated that will present a picture of how a community school of the arts evolved, and what is necessary in the future for such a school to grow and to be supported within its community--urban, suburban, or rural.

BRIEF HISTORICAL OVERVIEW

Three hundred sixty-eight years before the landing of the Pilgrims brings the reader to the date of 1252, or roughly mid-thirteenth century. Historically this was a productive period for the arts in the countries that later were most likely to send settlers to the New World. They were Italy, France, England, Holland, and the area now known as Germany. (In later times Poland, Russia, and several East European nations will deserve special consideration, perhaps in a different study.)

During the mid-thirteenth century the world was beginning to hear the words of Thomas Aquinas (1225-1274),
an Italian scholastic philosopher who pre-dated Dante by some
forty years, and who was canonized as a saint in the Roman
Catholic Church in 1323. Shortly thereafter followed Dante
(1265-1321), born Durante Alighieri, an Italian poet whose
masterpieces, Divine Comedy (1307) and Inferno (1321), are
still read today by students of the classics and English literature. (In this country few read them today in their original
Latin.)

In France, Philippe de Vitry (c. 1285 to 1295, d. 1365),
a poet-composer and theorist, was well respected in his own
day and was strongly influential in identifying the heavily
contrapuntal musical period of his time as Ars Nova. He was
a contemporary of Guillaume de Machaut (c. 1300-1377), a
French poet-composer, and like him became a priest at an
early age. De Machaut was considered to be one of the finest
composers of his time who wrote in the contrapuntal style
using a cantus firmus often constructed from a phrase of
Gregorian chant.

Two more Italian authors were prominent during this
period for their abilities in writing both prose and poetry.
The first was Francesco Petrarca (1304-1374)--known as Petrarch in English--who, while also involved in political missions,
earned a reputation for himself writing in both literary forms.
The second was Giovanni Boccaccio (1313-1375), who, though
he was to become known as an Italian writer of prose and
poetry, was actually born in Paris, France. At the young
age of ten, he was sent to Italy to study accounting. He
became a friend of Petrarch whom he met around 1350. He
accepted diplomatic missions to Florence in 1353, 1354, 1365,
and 1367. Later in 1375, he was appointed lecturer on Dante
also in Florence. He was considered the father of Italian
prose because of his celebrated collection of one hundred
novellas and his Decameron, first published in 1353. His
writings have been used as source books by many subsequent
writers, including Chaucer, Shakespeare, and others.[1]

During the first quarter of the 14th century the Pope
forbade the use of counterpoint in the writing of church
(liturgical) music, an action that is very difficult for us to
understand, after having had the opportunity to study the
beautiful choral music of the period. Fortunately, it would

seem that the edict was not enforced for a very long period
(if at all), or the church composers ignored the order, which
does not seem very likely.

From England one finds the great poet Geoffrey Chaucer
(1340-1400), born in London. His father was a wine merchant.
Chaucer himself was employed for ten years on diplomatic
missions to Italy, Flanders, and Lombardy, where he met
Boccaccio and possibly Petrarch. He was appointed comptroller
of petty customs in London in 1382, and later he was made
deputy (1385), allowing him to have more time to write. His
Canterbury Tales consist of 23 stories of pilgrims assembled
at Tabard Inn in Southwark, a splendid fragment of the projected scheme of two stories each from 29 pilgrims.[2]

During the latter part of the Middle Ages and as early
as the 12th century, the appearance of the minstrel was
recognized, particularly in France where he might have been
a poet, singer, or musician who traveled from place to place
singing and reciting, usually to the accompaniment of the lute
or the harp. He was similar to his counterpart in Germany,
the Minnesinger. Minstrels also seemed to have been engaged
by troubadours to supply musical accompaniment for the lyric
poet and poet-singers who lived in France and Northern Italy.
While the names of 460 troubadours are recorded, only 269
of the melodies they used or composed are preserved, but
over 2,500 of their song-poems are extant.[3]

This is a shining example in history of music and the
arts in the community. One sees the use of literature (poetry
or possibly prose), instrumental music, and vocal performance
carried from one section of a country to another. While a
community school of the arts did not exist per se, instructions
and training had to take place to encourage poets and performers, and to prepare others to learn a skill in the arts,
possibly functioning as apprentices. This may even be the
forerunner of teaching graduate assistants as we know them
today.

Minne is the German word for love, and therefore a
Minnelied is a love song, and a Minnesinger is a singer of
love, or perhaps more accurately, a singer of love songs.
A Minnesinger was one of any number of German lyric poets
and singers from the 12th to the 14th centuries, all of whom
were of nobility and similar to the minstrels and troubadours.

Developing from the Minnesinger in the 14th, 15th, and 16th centuries came what was known as the Meistersinger-- by simple translation from the German, the master singer. Die Meistersinger (pl.) were members of one of the craft guilds, who were primarily workingmen organized in the principal cities of Germany with the purpose of cultivating music and poetry.[4]

Enough inspiration came from stories about these people to encourage the 19th century German composer Richard Wagner (1813-1883) to write his only comedy, Die Meistersinger von Nüremberg. Wagner, of course, functioned as librettist as well as composer, a pattern he followed most of his life. The story included the character of Hans Sachs, who actually was a shoemaker and Meistersinger in the 16th century. This music drama was first performed in America at the Metropolitan Opera House in New York City on January 4, 1886. (It is interesting to note that 1886 is the same year in which Stanton Coit founded the Neighborhood Guild, later to be called the University Settlement, the first settlement house in the United States.) More information is given about this organization in a later chapter.

About the middle of the 14th century (1347-1351) a disaster struck Europe and Asia. It was a deadly disease known as the Black Death (probably Bubonic Plague) which ruthlessly claimed the lives of an estimated 75 million people, thus reducing the world's population considerably. It is significant to recognize this devastating event when one stops to speculate how many who lost their lives might have become musicians, writers, painters, etc., of world-wide fame and recognition. The possible loss to the world of the arts is impossible to measure.

And yet during this same period, musically speaking, one finds records of the development of the clavichord and cembalo (actually forerunners of the pianoforte), and in 1348, Giovanni Boccaccio produced his much heralded and remembered Decameron. Slightly more than a decade later in 1364, having been one of the fortunate ones to survive the plague, Guillaume de Machaut (1300-1377) composed his famous Mass for Four Voices, which was entitled the Mass of Our Lady (Messe de Notre Dame), reportedly composed in honor of the coronation of Charles V at Rheims.

The development of major institutions of higher education, though different in administrative style from today's educational structures and different in the methods of faculty selection, was impressive and significant in the 14th century. Records reveal that the following colleges and universities began in the years indicated:

Institution	Founding year	Country
University of Prague	1348	Czechoslovakia
Gonville and Caius College of Cambridge University	1348	England
Corpus Christi College of Cambridge University	1352	England
University of Vienna	1365	Austria
Heidelberg University	1386	Germany
Cologne University	1388	Germany

At this time the brilliance and popularity of Geoffrey Chaucer was recognized in England. Within a span of six years, Chaucer's prolific writing included House of Fame (1381), Parlement of Foules (1384), Troilus and Cryseide (1385), and The Canterbury Tales (1387). This was an accomplishment seldom achieved by the most erudite and distinctive authors.

One can readily see that education and the arts were becoming more and more available to the general public, though certainly not to the entire citizenry. The enrichment of educational and artistic backgrounds of the ancestors of the hardy settlers who were to come to American shores in the 17th century was increasing steadily. This growth was to continue during the 15th, 16th, 17th, 18th, and 19th centuries.

The 15th century began on a rather sad note for the literary and artistic worlds, because it was in the year 1400 that the death of Geoffrey Chaucer was reported in England.

Another unhappy occurrence was the burning at the stake of
Jeanne d'Arc (Joan of Arc) at Rouen in France in 1431. On
a brighter side the Gutenberg Bible, which was a Latin bible
produced in Mainz, Germany c. 1455, was regarded as the
earliest book ever printed by the use of movable metal type.
It was created by Johannes Gutenberg and financed by Johannes
Fust. Probably the greatest achievement in this century was
the discovery of the New World, actually Watling Island in
the Bahamas, by Christopher Columbus and his adventurous
crew in 1492. This event led the way to establishing this
country as we know it today.

Some outstanding choral composers of the polyphonic
period produced their masterpieces during this century.
These include Guillaume Dufay (c. 1400-1474), who with Gilles
Binchois lead the first Dutch School of contrapuntal choral
composition; Johannes Okeghem (1430-1495) was an excellent
composer and an outstandingly successful teacher whose pupils
influenced the compositional styles in Italy, France, and Germany; Josquin des Pres (c. 1445-1521) was a great composer
of both secular and church music. He, like Dufay, was Dutch;
a contemporary of des Pres was Heinrich Isaac (c. 1450-1517),
a German-Dutch composer of note whose choral compositions
strongly influenced the church musicians of his day.

There were many distinguished writers and statesmen
during the 15th century, and the world of art produced many
fine painters and sculptors during this prolific period. They
are represented by the Italian painters Fra Filippo Lippi
(1406-1468), Sandro Botticelli (1447-1510), and Leonardo da
Vinci (1452-1519), who was considered to be the universal
genius because of his multiplicity of talents and abilities. He
invented the parachute in 1480, drew a picture of a flying
machine in 1492 (the same year as Columbus's first trip to
the New World), completed his Madonna of the Rocks in 1494,
some eleven years after having started it, and produced one
of his most celebrated paintings, The Last Supper, in 1495.

Another Italian sculptor should be mentioned before
leaving this period, Donatello (1386-1466), whose meticulous
and prolific statues are still recognized for their intrinsic
value by connoisseurs throughout the world of art. It is
amazing to realize that Donatello produced figures of David
and St. John, both in 1408, and in 1412 he sculpted his St.
Peter, St. George, and St. Mark, all three in one year.

At this time in history, Martin Luther (1483-1546) was born, who was to become the leader of the Reformation.

Educational institutions were established rapidly during the 15th century when some 15 colleges and universities are readily known to have been founded throughout the European continent. They are as follows:

1409 Leipzig University, Leipzig, Germany
1411 St. Andrews University, Edinburgh, Scotland
1426 Louvain University, Belgium
1427 Lincoln College, Oxford University, England
1431 University of Caen, France
      University of Poitiers, France
1437 All Souls College, Oxford University, England
1438 Eton College, England
1441 Kings College, Cambridge University, England
1447 Palermo University, Palermo, Italy
1451 Glasgow University, Glasgow, Scotland
1479 Copenhagen University, Copenhagen, Denmark
1495 Kings College, Aberdeen, Scotland
1496 Jesus College, Cambridge University, England
1499 University of Alcala, Spain

In 1499, Oxford University in England established degrees in music. A special note should also be made that in 1455 Cosimo de' Medici, the Elder founded the Medicean Laurenziana Library in Florence, Italy. Education and the arts were flourishing in the countries of Europe from which our early explorers and eventual settlers were to come.

Classes in music history take up the identification of the various musical periods roughly placing them into categories of 150 years in length (with generous overlapping on either end of periods). They are generally classified as follows:

Pre-1300s: Monophonic   1600-1750: Baroque
1300-1450: Polyphonic   1750-1900: Romantic
1450-1600: Renaissance   1900-   : Modern

While it is not my intention in this chapter to present a detailed history of music, the names of prominent composers, artists, writers, etc., and events are presented for the convenience of the reader to make further investigations on topics of special interest to him.

The 16th century proved to be a lively and active period in the arts. In 1505 the Dutch composer Jacob Obrecht, who was born in 1430, died, and in the same year, Thomas Tallis, the English composer, was born and lived to be 80 years old. Heinrich Isaac (1450-1517) became a well-known and respected German choral composer.

Giovanni Pierluigi da Palestrina (1512-1594) became one of the most gifted Italian composers whose great works are still performed frequently today. His use of vocal counterpoint was extremely skillful causing his music to be studied carefully for its masterful structure. Theoreticians and composers to this day marvel at his creativity and the copious quantity of his beautiful choral music.

The Italian school held reign in the Renaissance period of musical composition. In addition to those already mentioned, Italy boasted of producing the following composers: Giulio Caccini (1550-1618), Giovanni Gabrielli (1557-1612), Jacopo Peri (1561-1633), Girolamo Frescobaldi (1583-1643), and Claudio Monteverdi (1567-1643). During this century, Italy also produced the famous Amati family known throughout the musical world for making some of the finest violins available. Andrea Amati (1530-1598) was the founder of the violin-making family. It was Nicola Amati (1596-1684), who, born at the very end of the 16th century, was to become the most widely known of all of that famous family.

The Netherlands were proud of Orlando de Lassus (1532-1618) and Jan Sweelinck (1583-1621), who like Frescobaldi was a prominent organist as well as a composer. The English also had an organist and composer in the figure of Orlando Gibbons (1583-1625) and the theorist and composer Thomas Morley (1557-1603); and the Germans presented Michael Praetorius (1571-1621), author and composer, and Heinrich Schütz (1585-1672), the most recognized pre-Bach composer in that country.

The Italian school of art was predominant in the 16th century with Raphael's Marriage of the Virgin in 1504; Triumph of Galatea in 1510; and his painting, The Sistine Madonna, in 1516; his death was a great loss in 1520. In 1508, Michelangelo began to paint the Sistine Chapel in Rome which he completed in 1512. Born in 1475, his full name was Michelangelo Buonarroti. He became known as a sculptor, painter,

and architect. At the early age of 27, he created his statue,
Bacchus, and at 28 he did his famous statue Pietà. In 1500
he painted his Madonna and Child, and in 1501 he sculpted
his statue David.

A man of many distinctive talents (similar to Leonardo
da Vinci, though not the genius of that earlier artist), Michelangelo proved himself to be outstanding in his paintings,
sculptures, as well as his architectural undertakings. He
will long be remembered, particularly for his work done in
the Sistine Chapel.

Titian (1477-1576) whose full name was Tiziano Vecelli,
completed many familiar paintings in his ninety-nine years.
His works include The Gypsy Madonna in 1510, The Tribute
Money in 1514, Flora in 1515, and many other masterpieces
including portraits of Cardinal Ippolito de Medici, Charles V,
King Francis I, Pietro Aretino, Pope Paul III and his Nephews,
his own daughter, Lavinia, Philipe II, and a Self-portrait.
His last painting was done in 1567 when he was eighty-nine.
It was entitled Jacopo de' Strade.

Albrecht Dürer (1471-1528), the German artist, though
having a considerably shorter life than Titian, was prolific
in his output of portraits and paintings. His early works
included two self-portraits in 1484 and 1498. In 1501 he
painted Life of the Virgin and in 1504 Nativity. He, too,
was known for his portrait painting, and in 1522 he produced
a design of a Flying Machine for War. He painted his picture
The Four Apostles in 1526, and died in 1528.

Germany also produced two other painters who gained
considerable prominence. Hans Holbein the Elder (1465-
1524) and his son Hans Holbein the Younger (1497-1543),
who was far more prominent and prolific than his father and
who was appointed painter to the court of Henry VIII of
England in 1536. His paintings included, in addition to the
Portrait of Henry VIII, Thomas More and His Family in 1527,
The Artist and His Family in 1528, The Ambassadors in 1533,
and Anne of Cleves in 1539. Henry VIII's portrait was completed in 1535. In the next year, Holbein was appointed
court painter by Henry VIII.

As might be expected, the desire and need for additional
education and higher learning was felt throughout the civilized

world, and European countries responded accordingly.   A
partial list of new institutions founded in the 16th century is
presented here (In this century, the Jesuit Order was founded
by Ignatius Loyola, 1491-1556):

1500   University of Valencia, Spain
1509   Brasenose College, Oxford University, England
1511   St. John's College, Cambridge University, England
1517   Corpus Christi College, Oxford University, England
       founded by Richard Fox
       Collège des Trois Langues, Louvain, Belgium
1527   First Protestant University, Marburg, Germany
1529   College of France, Paris
1531   University of Granada, Spain
1542   Magdalene College, Cambridge University, England
1543   University of Pisa, Italy, refounded by Cosimo I de'
       Medici, originally founded in 1338
1554   Trinity College, Oxford University, England
1559   University of Geneva, Switzerland
1567   University of Helmstedt, Brunswick
1571   Jesus College, Oxford University, England founded by
       Hugh Price
1574   University of Berlin, Germany
1576   University of Warsaw, Poland
1582   University of Edinburgh, Scotland
1585   Jesuit University, Graz, Austria
1592   Trinity College, Dublin, Ireland founded by Elizabeth I
       of England
1596   Sidney Sussex College, Cambridge University, England

     The 16th century was one which saw many, continuous,
and bitter battles and wars, not desired by anyone, but unending struggles between large and smaller countries and
territories.   Religious differences raged between the established Roman Catholic Church and the zeal of Martin Luther
(1483-1546) and John Calvin (1509-1564).   In all the religious
fervor a bitterness infested any philosophical disputation that
still exists today in the minds of some.   Nonetheless, it was
a century which enjoyed the more flexible techniques of printing, so that books were far more plentiful and accessible
than ever before.   Education and the arts were again working
together for a more advanced knowledgeable society.   Exploration continued into the areas of previously unknown sections
of the globe, adding, of course, to the increased knowledge
of mankind.   Progress was continuing for man to understand

himself and his neighbors by extending forms and methods
of education for all. Expression through the arts, music,
drama, poetry and prose, painting and sculpture, offered
greater recognition and acceptance of aesthetic values which
are today readily accepted in our civilization. Great strides
were made for man to understand and appreciate the various
communities in which he exists.

The 17th century was to bring equally exciting advances
and events, especially in artistic development. In the year
1600 the Italian composers were inspired by the development
of opera and operatic form. They seemed to be enamored of
the tale of Orpheus and Eurydice, for both Giulio Caccini
(1550-1618) and Jacopo Peri (1561-1633) chose that theme to
set to music, and each chose the title Euridice. In 1607
Claudio Monteverdi (1567-1643) used the same tale for his
opera Orfeo. More than a century and a half later (in 1762),
the French composer Christoph Willibald Gluck (1714-1787), a
great reformer of opera, chose the theme once again for his
opera Orfeo ed Euridice.

The recorder became a very popular instrument in England in the early part of the 17th century. Today it is used
frequently as a beginning instrument for children in elementary
music education programs throughout the United States. There
are also many recorder clubs, societies, associations, and organizations that perform as recorder ensembles using recorders
of all sizes and ranges. The year 1600 saw the publication
of The First Book of Ayres by Thomas Morley (1557-1603).

In this time period William Shakespeare (1564-1611)
became prominent as an actor in London, England, but more
importantly as a playwright. Between 1595 and 1602 he completed Romeo and Juliet, A Midsummer Night's Dream, Henry
V, Julius Caesar, and Hamlet--an unusually large output.

The famed Fortune Theatre in London, England, opened
and the telescope was invented in Holland, both in 1600.
The Italian painter Michelangelo da Caravaggio (1573-1610),
completed his Doubting Thomas in 1600 and one year later his
Conversion of St. Paul in 1601. In 1609 Henry Hudson
(?-1611) explored the Delaware Bay and the Hudson River.

It was in 1620 that the Mayflower left Plymouth, England,
to sail West until it landed in the New World at New Plymouth
in what is now the State of Massachusetts. With the passen-

gers was Miles Standish who was the most experienced leader
among them, but it was John Carver who was to become the
first Governor of this colony. From this point, one finds
firm growth and strength in the development of this new,
fledgling country, as well as the acceptance and expansion of
the arts, slowly but steadily.

So much advancement in civilization and artistic understanding was made thereafter that only highlights of specific
examples will be cited from this point on. The previously
mentioned materials have been presented only for the purpose
of having the reader understand some of the steps and developments of world cultures and civilization in the past seven
centuries leading to the establishment of social settlements
in England which led directly to the formation of community
music schools in what is now the United States of America, with
its sister country, Canada.

Two English composers/musicians lived into the first
quarter of the 17th century. They were William Byrd (1543-
1621) and Orlando Gibbons (1583-1625).

The year 1640 saw the publication of the first book of
sacred music materials produced in the colonies. It was The
Bay Psalm Book, which in this printing gave the words but
not the music for use by the new settlers in their church
services. There were indications as to which familiar tunes
were to be used for specific psalms.

One might wonder about the musical abilities of the
settlers, particularly if there were those who could be leaders
in training the congregation to sing the psalms correctly.
It is known that one of the congregation who sailed from
Holland to England and then to the New World made a comment,
"many of our congregation (are) very expert in music."[5]
This is, indeed, one of the few references made about the
musical abilities and skills of the Pilgrims.

A most important occurrence came at the mid-17th century which was the development of harmonic procedures (the
use of four-part harmony) in contrast to the renaissance
and baroque use of contrapuntal linear procedures. This
was to become a pattern to be followed for the next two centuries progressing to diatonic harmony and ultimately chromatic harmony in the romantic period.

Henry Purcell (1659-1695) the outstanding English composer was born in the same year as Alessandro Scarlatti (father of Domenico) who lived until 1725. Heinrich Schütz composed his Johannes Passion after having composed his Christmas Oratorio just the year before.

Thirty-six percent of the territories on the North American continent now known as states of the United States of America were settled during the 17th century. Listed in chronological order they are as follows:

No.	Year	State	No.	Year	State
1	1605	NM	10	1638	DE
2	1607	VA	11	1650	NC
3	1614	NY	12	1664	NJ
4	1620	MA	13	1668	MI
5	1623	NH	14	1670	SC
6	1624	ME	15	1682	PA
7	1634	MD	16	1690	LA
8	1635	CT	17	1691	TX
9	1636	RI	18	1699	MS[6]

The latter part of the 17th century saw the exploration of the territories touched by the mighty Mississippi River by the French explorers Jacques Marquette (1637-1675) and Louis Joliet (1645-1700), both of whom made enormous contributions to the knowledge and understanding of little known territories in this vast country.

In 1666 Puritans from Connecticut settled in Newark, New Jersey; it was also the year in which Antonio Stradivari began to put labels in the violins of his making. John Milton (1608-1674) wrote his famous work, Paradise Lost, in 1667, the same year in which the British author Jonathan Swift was born. His most memorable work was Gulliver's Travels, written in 1726. This English writer was actually born in Ireland and died in 1745.

In 1674 the opera of Jean Baptiste Lully (1632-1687) entitled Alceste was written and performed in Paris. Shortly before this, France was privileged to have another native son born, François Couperin (1668-1733), widely recognized for his keyboard compositions which were highly ornate and delicate. A contemporary of Lully's was the Danish composer Dietrich Buxtehude (1637-1707)--known for his fine choral

music--who outlived his French contemporary some twenty
years.

Italy was also able to boast of Antonio Vivaldi (1675-
1741), whose chamber music and choral music are still performed frequently today. And in England, Christopher Wren
(later Sir Christopher Wren--1632-1733) was a most respected
and admired architect. His contributions included work on
St. Paul's Cathedral in London, the Trinity College Library,
and the Tom Tower of Christ's Church in Oxford. The
French painter Jean Antoine Watteau (1684-1721) had his works
recorded and recalled by William Gilbert and Sir Arthur Sullivan in their light opera Trial by Jury.

The year 1685 will be remembered by the musical world
for many generations to come, since it was the year in which
three outstanding musical geniuses were born in three different
countries. They were, of course, Johann Sebastian Bach
(1685-1750), who was born in Germany where he spent his
life dedicated to his church and music and who was strongly
impressed and moved by his short period of study with Buxtehude; George Frederic Handel (1685-1759), who can be
classified as a German-English composer who had been strongly
influenced by his study and work in Italy; and Domenico
Scarlatti (1685-1757--son of Alessandro Scarlatti), whose keyboard sonatas are heard frequently in the recital world today.
These three masters set a pattern and direction for much of
the musical period to follow. Though immersed in contrapuntal
writing, these contemporaries showed the path to the field
of harmonic procedures that were to become so prominent in
the early romantic period, often identified as the classical
period. And so dawned the 18th century.

As we approach the beginning of the 18th century, one
which was destined to become the most important period for
a new country to be born in the western hemisphere, we are
aware that special materials and historical events become more
carefully recorded. Because they are more readily available
as we move forward to more contemporary times, selection of
materials and events are narrowed considerably. Since this
brief chapter is in no way intended to be a history of the
world, nor a history of the musical and artistic worlds, but
rather a cursory observation of trends in society and musical
and artistic developments, it is hoped the reader will understand and accept them as such. Where specific examples are

stated, they are given to help the reader to seek further information on a topic of interest to him and to supply a starting
point, at least, for his convenience.

The records reveal that the first pipe organ was brought
to America in the year 1700. Lahee tells us that it was
placed in Port Royal, Virginia, and that it was later moved
to Hancock.[7] Just two years later the French established a
settlement in what is now the State of Alabama. In 1704,
J. S. Bach wrote his first cantata entitled Denn Du wirst
meine Seele, and G. F. Handel composed his St. John Passion,
written while he was still in Hamburg. It was in 1707 that
Handel and Scarlatti met in Venice, Italy during the period
of time that Handel was studying, composing and performing
in that country. Lahee further reports that in 1712 the first
singing instruction book was published in Newbury, Massachusetts by John Tufts. In 1713, the first pipe organ in New
England was installed in King's Chapel in Boston.[8] In that
same year, a School of Dance was established at the Paris
Opera in France.

In the year 1716, the first record of importing instruments appeared with a bill stating that the order included
flageolets, hautbois (oboes), and other instruments which were
shipped to Edward Enstone in Boston.[9] 1720 was the year
in which singing societies were established in New England.
In his excellent book A History of Music Education in the
United States, James A. Keene gives a remarkable and clear
description of "The Singing School" and the "Tune Books"
used by the teachers and students.[10] This scholarly report
is of value to all engaged in the teaching of music.

One must pause momentarily here, even though the
presentation is discussing the development and expansion of
a new country, to comment on the amazing number of distinguished compositions of Johann Sebastian Bach between
1721 and 1725. The major ones are as follows:

1721 All of The Brandenburg Concertos
1722 The Well-Tempered Clavier, Vol. I
1723 The Passion according to St. John
1725 The Anna Magdalena Bach Notebook

Many of these well recognized compositions of J. S.
Bach are regularly studied and heard still today. Nearly

every piano student will have been acquainted with some of
this standard repertoire, perhaps having started with The
Anna Magdalena Bach Notebook and progressed to The Well-
Tempered Clavier with its beautiful preludes and well constructed fugues in every major and minor key. The amazing
musical output of this composer staggers the minds of many
musicians. Just contemplating the difficulty of writing the
manuscripts alone astonishes many. It is equally interesting
to note that Bach finished his St. Matthew Passion in 1729.

The records also show that the first concert given in
Boston was during the month of December in 1731, and in
1732 a concert was recorded in Charleston, South Carolina,
a city which enjoyed music and theatre and other cultural
affairs. The first song recital given in America was also presented in Charleston, as well as the first ballad opera, Flora
or Hob in the Well.

The first Playhouse known to have existed in America
was in Williamsburg, Virginia, in 1722. In 1733, a pipe organ
was put into Trinity Church at Newport, Rhode Island--the
second organ to exist in New England. It was in the same
year that the Italian composer Giovanni Battista Pergolesi
(1710-1736) completed his opera La Serva Pedrona, which is
an opera-buffa in true Italian style, and it was performed
in Naples. It became so popular that at one time it was referred to as the oldest opera in the standard repertoire.

Pergolesi is a musician of particular interest to this
study since he at one time attended the Conservatorio dei
Poveri di Gesu Christo when he was 16 years old. This, of
course, took him to the City of Naples. This institution was
established for the poor children of Jesus Christ, as its name
indicates, to give them training in religion and music. There
were four such conservatories in Italy at the time. The
other three were the Collegio di San Onofrio a Capuana, the
Collegio de Santa Maria di Loreto, and the Collegio de la
Pietà de Turchini. [11]

When Romain Rolland (1866-1944), the French critic,
novelist, and biographer who received a Nobel prize in 1915,
wrote his book The Musical Tour through the Land of the Past,
he made the following statement about these schools:

> ...and here we see what artistic institutions may
> do, not indeed to transform a race, but to make it

produce what it has in reserve, and what, but for
them, would probably never have sprung from the
soil.
   These institutions, in the case of Naples, were
its famous conservatories for the musical training of
poor children. An admirable idea, which our modern
democracies have neither conceived nor revived.[12]

   Janet D. Schenck in her book Music, Youth and Opportunity, retorted in this fashion:

   The development of the Music School Settlement
   idea is our reply to Romain Rolland. A democracy
   is meeting here and now, the same need felt and
   answered in Italy many years ago.
      A Music School Settlement aims to put the
   highest musical education within reach of serious
   students whose circumstances do not allow them to
   pay professional rates.[13]

   While there are some similarities between the plan used
in the 17th century in Italy and the plan used in the United
States in the 20th century, there are also many differences.
The plan in the earlier times benefitted primarily orphans
and in some cases, very few cases, the talented students
who were not orphans but whose abilities were such that the
musical program would be helped by their presence.

   The 20th century plan came to the assistance of families
and kept their children in the home situation. One can understand Mrs. Schenck's attitude in response to Romain Rolland.
In America the communities supported the music schools and
the children in them. Each student of community music schools
needed only to give evidence of his interest in musical study.
The philosophies of the two plans are vastly different.

   At the turn of the 18th century, there was a flowering
of efforts in the arts as well as the development of a new
country and the birth of its leaders who were to become responsible for the independence and security of the United
States of America. The French philosopher François Marie
Arouet Voltaire (1694-1778) was also a historian, dramatist,
and poet. His works and writing were to have a profound
effect on his native country and the world at large. One
still finds many quotations of his writings in the literature of

the world. He was preceded by six years by the English
poet and critic Alexander Pope (1688-1744), whose couplets
are still quoted today, and his contemporaries included
Henry Fielding (1707-1754), the English novelist, and also
the English lexicographer and writer Samuel Johnson (1709-
1784). Thomas Gainesborough (1727-1788), the English painter, painted his masterpiece, The Blue Boy, in 1770, just six
years before the American Revolution in 1776. J. S. Bach
continued his remarkable record by completing his St. Matthew
Passion in 1729.

        In 1731, the building known as the State House was
built in Philadelphia. Its name was later changed to Independence Hall which still stands at the time of this writing.
During this decade, several important musical compositions
were written which are familiar today. G. F. Handel composed
six Concerto Grossi (1734), and J. S. Bach completed the
full version of his famous B-minor Mass (1738), and Handel
wrote two of his oratorios, Saul and Israel in Egypt.

        America welcomed two who were to make unusual con-
tributions to the musical world with the birth of James Lyon
(1735-1794), who was known as a psalmodist, preacher, and
patriot. Two years later was born Francis Hopkinson (1737-
1791), who identified himself as the first American poet-
composer. In Sonneck's book Francis Hopkinson and James
Lyon, a most enlightening section occurs in the introduction
by Richard A. Crawford of the University of Michigan. He
gives us the following information:

        A member of the Class of 1759 at Princeton, Lyon
        began his career as an active musician while a college
        student, and seems to have abandoned it some time
        before his ordination as a Presbyterian minister in
        1764. ...his importance to the history of American
        music lies in the fact that he compiled Urania, the
        prototype of the eighteenth-century American tunebook.
            Urania, ... modeled after the English collections,
        was not the first book of tunes printed in America.
        It was preceded by two small instructional manuals
        which included some music--the first by the Rev.
        John Tufts, the second by the Rev. Thomas Walter,
        both initially published in Boston around 1720 ...
        Urania dwarfed these tiny collections in every way.
        Oblong in shape, a bulky 198 pages in length, Lyon's

work began with a detailed set of instructions about
note reading and singing.... Though Urania might
appear to be a self-instruction book, it enjoyed most
of its sale as a textbook for use in singing schools.
...Urania stands at the beginning of this period of
burgeoning musical activity ... And it should not be
forgotten that Urania established a healthy precedent
by including, together with the compositions taken
from European sources, six of the compiler's own
tunes.[14]

In the same introduction, Crawford tells an interesting
bit of information about Francis Hopkinson, a signer of the
Declaration of Independence and the one indicated as the
first American poet-composer:

Francis Hopkinson is remembered as one of America's
founding fathers, a man of wide-ranging interests
and considerable ability who claimed to have been
America's first composer. ...According to Sonneck's
interpretation, Hopkinson's claim rests on the song,
"My days have been so wondrous free," which he
wrote in 1759 ... Sonneck contends that Hopkinson
must have "been aware of the fact that James Lyon
was a dangerous competitor for the title of first native
of the United States who produced a musical composition." ..."From all we know of Hopkinson's character, I doubt not that he himself investigated the
correctness of his claim and found his earliest compositions to antedate those of James Lyon." ...That
Francis Hopkinson, active in both art music and psalmody and by no means contemptuous of the latter,
considered "composition" a term inapplicable to psalmody is an indication of the gulf which separated the
traditions of art music and psalmody in eighteenth-
century America.[15]

Mr. Crawford sheds further informaiton about the position of musical composition in the life styles of eighteenth-
century Americans when he says:

...Though there are some notable exceptions, most
tunebooks printed after the Revolutionary War contain
at least a sampling of works by Americans, and by the
mid-1780's a group of composers centered in New

England were writing a style of sacred music differing
substantially from anything produced by their European
contemporaries. These Yankee musicians, including
William Billings (1746-1800), Daniel Read (1757-1836),
Justin Morgan (1747-1798), Supply Belcher (1751-1836),
Lewis Edson (1748-1820), and Timothy Swan (1758-
1842), among others, represent the first school of
indigenous American composers. Their compositions,
printed in tunebooks and carried southward from New
England by itinerant music masters, were sung in
churches, meetings, and singing schools throughout
the young United States.[16]

It is now evident that music played an important role
in the lives of early Americans and that many of them were
creative in their own right, actually constructing a compositional style recognizable as their own. All of this was immediately after the Revolutionary War won in 1776. Music
and the arts were developing and spreading in the various
communities in the country--north, south, and west.

The religious zeal of the people and their desire to include music in their worship services are evidenced by the
fact that in 1737 the first pipe organ completely constructed
in America was built by John Clemm and was placed in Trinity
Church in New York City, so that organs were being built
and placed in more heavily populated areas. This also indicates that there were musicians who could play these instruments and who could train others to do the same.

In 1737 Thomas Paine (1737-1809), the English-American
author, was born, Handel's opera Berenice was first performed
at Covent Garden in London, Rameau composed his opera
Castor and Pollux, and Antonio Stradivari died in Italy.

By 1750 America had seen the Moravian Settlement established in Bethlehem, Pennsylvania; the Moravians had
placed two organs in their church in Philadelphia, and began
to use stringed instruments, Flutes, and French horns in
their church for the first time. The first pipe organ completely planned, designed and built in New England was done
by Edward Bromfield in the City of Boston. Mr. Bromfield
did not live to see the completion of his instrument.

A most enlightening and scholarly doctoral thesis has

been written by Lucy Ellen Carroll entitled, "Three Centuries of Song: Pennsylvania's Choral Composers 1681 to 1981."[17] Dr. Carroll presents materials dating from the early seventeenth century to contemporary times in the State of Pennsylvania. Her examples are well chosen, and she included a detailed chronology. For those who might wish to write about the arts in a different state or location, this is an excellent example to follow.

Other books written about specific geographic territories, periods, or topics concerning North American musical contributions include the following: Hill Country Instrumental Folk Music of Southwestern Pennsylvania by Samuel Preston Bayard;[18] Old Philadelphia Music by Jane Campbell;[19] Notes on Music in Old Boston by William Armes Fisher;[20] Music in Philadelphia by Robert A. Gerson;[21] Orpheus in the New World: The Symphony Orchestra as an American Cultural Institution by Philip Hart;[22] Music in Canada by Ernest MacMillan;[23] Rhode Island Music and Musicians 1722-1850 by Joyce Ellen Mangler;[24] The House Music Built--Carnegie Hall by Ethel Peyser;[25] Music in New Hampshire by Louise Pichierri;[26] Music and Musicians of Pennsylvania by Gertrude Martin Rohrer;[27] The Ballad of America: The History of the United States in Song and Story by John A. Scott;[28] Community of Sound--Boston Symphony and Its World of Players by Louise Snyder;[29] Music at Harvard by Walter Spalding;[30] Frontier Musicians on the Connequenessing, Wabash and Ohio by Richard D. Wetzel;[31] and Song in America from Early Times to about 1850 by Grace D. Yeabury.[32]

These represent only a few of the books available today for study and inspiration. Music and the arts existed in many locations and communities then. One sees that music has been present in various forms for a long time, though not in forms as sophisticated as might be desired. The arts were alive and well in mid-eighteenth-century America, but without the benefit of recordings, radio, or television.

Higher education became a priority in the minds of many. One speculates on the state of the country during this early period as a nation with very small settlements of people scattered around the land. Coastal cities perhaps drew larger numbers of people, but the countryside was literally marked by winding trails and little more. Yet during

the period from 1620 to 1800, some sixteen major institutions
of higher education were founded, all of which still exist at
the time of this writing. In chronological order those institutions were as follows:

Year	College or University	City and State
1636	Harvard Univ.	Cambridge, MA
1693	William and Mary Coll.	Williamsburg, VA
1701	Yale Univ.	New Haven, CT
1740	Univ. of Pennsylvania	Philadelphia, PA
1746	Princeton Univ.	Princeton, NJ
1749	Washington and Lee Univ.	Lexington, KY
1754	Columbia Univ.	New York City, NY
1764	Brown Univ.	Providence, RI
1766	Rutgers Univ.	New Brunswick, NJ
1770	Coll. of Charleston	Charleston, SC
1780	Transylvania Coll.	Lexington, KY
	Washington and Jefferson Coll.	Washington, PA
1787	Univ. of Pittsburgh	Pittsburgh, PA
1789	Georgetown Univ.	Washington, DC
1794	Bowdoin Coll.	Brunswick, ME
	Univ. of Tennessee	Knoxville, TN

A simple perusal of the above information reveals that
ten of these colleges and universities were established and
functioning before the Revolutionary War (1775-1783) and the
Declaration of Independence (1776). Two more were founded
while the war was still in progress, and four were started
within eleven years after the war was over. Obviously,
much preparation and planning had been done earlier.

Education and the arts were clearly becoming significant
factors in the lives of those who had come to this land for
a permanent home. Opportunities were becoming available
to them and to their children to study and participate in the
arts as they so desired.

George Washington, the American general and first
president of the United States, and Franz Joseph Haydn, the
Austrian-born composer and musician, had many things in
common. They were, of course, contemporaries. Each was
born in 1732, and they both lived for approximately the same
period, Washington having died in 1799 and Haydn in 1809.
Washington was called the "Father of his country," and

Haydn was known as "Papa Haydn" by the men who played
in the orchestra he conducted in the house of Esterhazy because of his kindness and consideration. Each left his mark
in the community in which he lived, and, indeed, the world
at large. Haydn kept music flowing for Prince Esterhazy,
and Washington was known to support musical events and
concerts avidly.

In 1931, the United States George Washington Bicentennial Commission assembled a book entitled The Music of
George Washington's Time.[33] The American musical historio-
grapher John Tasker Howard gathered materials and stories
about the music, songs, dances, marches, etc. prominent
in the days of George Washington, and in his preface, Howard
made the following statement:

> In publishing and distributing this booklet it is our
> aim to give correct and interesting information, not
> only on the origin of our first national airs, but also
> on musical conditions in early America, the influences
> that shaped our musical life, and most important, the
> relation of music to the events of the period.[34]

Fortunately, Mr. Howard was quite successful in the
task set before him. He states information about early concerts in this country:

> The first public concert in America, of which we have
> record, was held in Boston. This was in 1731, at
> a time when the New England ban against secular
> music was gradually being lowered. The affair, "a
> Concert of Music on sundry instruments", was held
> in "the great room" at Mr. Pelham's, an engraver,
> dancing master, instructor in reading and writing,
> painting upon glass, and a dealer in the "best Vir-
> ginia tobacco".[35]

As can well be imagined, the need for diversion and
entertainment was felt by many of the citizens at the end of
the eighteenth century, particularly in the larger cities.
Howard continues when he states:

> If contemporary records are to be trusted, Philadel-
> phia heard its first advertised concert in 1757, when
> John Palma offered an affair "at the Assembly Room

in Lodge Alley", January 16th. Yet it seems altogether likely that there were concerts in the Pennsylvania city before this time, for Philadelphians were
cultured, and except for the Quakers, fond of amuse-
ment. There was a dancing master in the city in
1710, and dancing was taught in the boarding schools
as early as 1728. [36]

    Programs took a very different format in those days
from their present-day cousins. The evening's concert often
appeared in the programs in the same manner as a theatrical
presentation.

    Typical programs of the period show a variety of
    compositions. In 1769 an Italian resident of Philadel-
    phia, John (Giovanni) Gualdo offered this character-
    istic list:

ACT I

Overture composed by the Earl of Kelly.
'Vain is beatuy, [sic] gaudy flower' [sung] by
    Miss Hallam.
Trio composed by Mr. Gualdo, first violin by Master
    Billy Crumpto.
'The Spinning Wheel' by Miss Storer.
A German flute concert, with Solos, composed by
    Mr. Gualdo.
A new symphony after the present taste, composed
    by Mr. Gualdo.

ACT II

A new Violin concerto with solos, composed by Mr.
    Gualdo.
A Song by Mr. Wools.
A Sonata upon the Harpisichord, by Mr. Curtz.
Solo upon the Clarinet, Mr. Hoffman, junior.
Solo upon the Mandolino, by Mr. Gualdo.
Overture, composed by the Earl of Kelly. [37]

    Some of the programs presented compositions by com-
posers who are still known and recognized today, such as
a Haydn Symphony, a Sinfonia by Johann Christian Bach and
music by Reinagle. Other composers who were represented

include Stamitz, Gretry, Boccherini, Pleyel, Martini, and
Handel.

It is interesting to note that the name of Wolfgang
Amadeus Mozart (1756-1791) does not appear in the programs
nearly as frequently as that of his illustrious teacher, Papa
Haydn.

The efforts of John Tasker Howard are commendable,
indeed, in his writing of The Music of George Washington's
Time for the Bicentennial Commission. Much factual and accurate information is available in this report. It also clarifies
the need for and use of the arts in early America--the communities provided the opportunities for the use of music and
the arts at celebrations and special events.

From the middle of the 18th century through to the
19th century, there was a flurry of activity throughout
Europe in the musical arts. Names of composers and musicians
from that period are well-known today. Muzio Clementi
(1752-1832) was recognized as an Italian composer and pianist.
His music composed for keyboard instruments is still
used frequently. Wolfgang Amadeus Mozart, considered
one of the greatest geniuses of the musical world, wrote
prolifically in this period in history. He is known for his
compositions for piano, violin, voice, chamber music, orchestra, and operatic compositions. During his short life he
composed for nearly every medium of musical expression in
great quantity and with great rapidity. In some 35 years, he
etched his mark in the history of music.

While such musical activity was in progress in Europe
with much word of mouth information coming to this country
by those who crossed the Atlantic to secure a position for
themselves in America, many institutions of higher education
were being established in many parts of this newly forming
nation. In addition to those already mentioned, the following
institutions were founded: Colgate University was founded
in Hamilton, New York; in 1821 George Washington University
opened its doors in Washington, D.C.; in 1826 Western Reserve University began its long history in Cleveland, Ohio;
in 1834 Tulane University in New Orleans, Louisiana offered
classes; Duke University in Durham, North Carolina, started
in 1838; Boston University began in 1839; Fordham University
in New York City was founded in 1841; down in Waco, Texas,

Baylor University formed in 1845; and in 1846 both Bucknell
University in Lewisburg, Pennsylvania, and Buffalo University
in Buffalo, New York, opened for the first time.

During 1847, Verdi's opera Macbeth, based on Shakespeare's play of the same name, was first performed in Florence,
Italy, while in this country Lawrence College was founded
in Appleton, Wisconsin. In 1849, New York state had one
more school, Syracuse University, in the city of the same
name.

In the state of Ohio two institutions were started in
1850, Capital University in Columbus and the University of
Dayton in Dayton. During this year Jenny Lind, the Swedish
Nightingale, toured the United States under the management
of P. T. Barnum. Her successes were continuous and remarkable. One of her most popular songs was "Home, Sweet
Home," which she performed frequently. The citizens of this
country wanted music and musical entertainment. Her stunning
voice pleased audiences around the country. While these
performances were being presented in this country, in Weimar,
Germany, Wagner's opera Lohengrin was given its first performance. Not to be outdone, in 1851 Verdi's opera Rigoletto
was presented for the first time in Venice. Two of his operas
were to be performed for the first time in 1852, La Traviata
was done in Venice, while Il Trovatore was given in Rome. In
America in 1853, Henry Steinway and his sons began to manufacture pianos in New York City. His company has become
one of the most renowned in the country and competes with
the finest names in piano manufacturing anywhere in the
world.

The Te Deum composed by the French composer Hector
Berlioz (1803-1869) was performed in Paris first in 1855.
In America the University of California at Berkeley was founded in the same year, as was Butler University in Indianapolis,
Indiana. Robert Schumann, the German composer who had
unsuccessfully attempted suicide in 1854, died in 1856. In
1857 Hans von Bülow, the conductor, pianist, and music
critic, married Cosima Liszt, the daughter of Franz Liszt.
Edward Elgar (1857-1934) was born in England. In America
the Chicago Conservatory of Music was established, and the
Peabody Institute of the City of Baltimore was founded. And
in 1858 the New York Symphony gave its first concert under
the leadership of Theodore Thomas. In Italy the composer

Giacomo Puccini was born. He had a distinguished career
composing some of the most popular operas accepted in the
standard operatic repertoire. His most successful operas
include La Bohème, Madama Butterfly, Tosca, and Turandot.
Puccini died in 1924.

In 1859 the song, "Dixie" was composed by Daniel D.
Emmett. It was to become a favorite song of the Confederacy,
and its lively tune is still heard frequently at the time of this
writing. Gounod's opera Faust, which was to become so
enormously popular that it became a regular member of the
standard operatic repertoire was first performed in Paris in
1863. Verdi's Un Ballo in Maschera earned a similar reputation
after its first performance in Rome. Adelina Patti, the Italian
soprano, made her New York debut in Donizetti's opera Lucia
di Lammermoor. Cooper Union was built in New York City.
Its architect was far-sighted enough to plan for space for
the installation of an elevator, even before the elevator had
been invented.

Ignace Jan Paderewski (1860-1941) was born in Poland
and became internationally known as a pianist, composer, and
statesman. In 1861, Nellie Melba, the Australian soprano (1861-
1931), was born. She was to become one of the truly great
singers of her day, and Wagner's music drama Tannhäuser,
with its famed Venusberg Scene, was to create a scandal in
Paris.

The period from 1861 to 1865 was to be one of great
anguish, desperation, violence, and hardship for this country
which was not yet one hundred years old. It was the time
of the Civil War in the United States. The southern states
and the northern states fought each other over the issue of
freedom for all men in this nation with the abolition of slavery
throughout the country. The effects of that war, though
perhaps more subdued and quiet now, are still felt today.
This internal turmoil resulted in the assassination of Abraham
Lincoln (1809-1865), the 16th president of the United States,
who earned for himself the title of "Great Emancipator." On
January 1, 1863, Lincoln issued the "Emancipation Proclama-
tion" freeing all those held in the bonds of slavery. His
assassination occurred on April 14, 1865, and the war ended
in May of that year.

In 1861 Vassar College (for women) opened in Poughkeepsie, New York, and also in 1861 Edward MacDowell was

born on the Lower East Side of New York City. His home
was at 220 Clinton Street, very near the area served by the
Third Street Music School Settlement and where the Henry
Street Settlement and its Music School were to exist. He
became the first internationally recognized, American born
concert pianist and composer. He was invited to perform extensively in Europe as well as in this country.

He was appointed to the chair of music at Columbia
University in New York City in 1896. His was the first such
appointment ever to the chair of music at this University.
At this time in history, the recognition of the significance
of music as an art was of great importance. Harvard, University of Pennsylvania and now Columbia had all moved in
the same direction. MacDowell remained at Columbia until
January, 1904 and then left after a serious disagreement with
Nicholas Murray Butler who was then president of the University. He deserves great credit for being so erudite and
dedicated to the musical art as he was, and for earning his
international reputation as a pianist/composer. MacDowell
was the first American to do so.

England and France both were to produce musicians who
were to make favorable reputations for themselves as composers.
Each was born in the very next year, 1862. Frederick Delius
(1862-1934) and Edward German (1862-1936) were the English
composers of distinction. Probably the best known of the
three born in 1862 was Claude Debussy (1862-1918), the
French impressionist composer who undoubtedly was the most
influential composer/musician of his time. His piano, vocal,
and orchestral works are heard frequently in the concert
world today.

In the same year, 1862, the ever musically productive
Giuseppe Verdi had his opera La Forza del Destino performed
for the first time in St. Petersburg in Russia. Another important event took place in this year when Ludwig Köchel
began to catalog all the musical compositions of Wolfgang
Amadeus Mozart, hence giving us Köchel numbers rather than
opus numbers to identify properly the music of Mozart.

Swarthmore College was founded in Swarthmore, Pennsylvania, in 1862.

During the year in which Abraham Lincoln was assassi-
nated, 1865, three composers of note were born, each in a

different country. They were as follows: Paul Dukas (1865–
1935), the French composer; Alexander Glazunov (1865–
1936), the Russian composer; and Jean Sibelius (1865–1957),
the Finnish composer. Two operas of importance were performed for the first time which proved to have lasting success.
They were L'Africaine by Giacomo Meyerbeer (1791–1864),
performed posthumously in Paris, and Richard Wagner's Tris-
tan and Isolde, presented in Munich. The Symphony No. 8
("Unfinished") by Franz Schubert (1797–1828), composed
in 1822, received its first public performance in Vienna in
1865. Four more institutions of higher education were opened.
They were Cornell University in Ithaca, New York; Purdue
University in Lafayette, Indiana; the University of Maine in
Orono; and the University of Kentucky in Lexington.

From this time period (1866 on), the musical world in
Europe abounded in the development and composition of new
works with greater creativity and imagination, and the quan-
tities of new music were being composed and presented to the
general public. Much of it was filtering across the Atlantic
to America, and composers, conductors, performers and teachers were coming to this country to find new ways and opportunities to use their musical gifts. New York City, Boston,
Charleston, South Carolina, Philadelphia and many other areas
were opening their doors to accept new opportunities in the
art forms now available to them. America was becoming culturally alive!

Operas by Smetana, Ambroise Thomas, Gounod, Verdi,
Wagner, and music of Brahms were arriving and were beginning
to be performed in this country. The Chicago Musical College
opened in 1867 along with the Cincinnati Conservatory of
Music. Music Education––music taught in public schools in
the classroom––had become more and more evident, and instrumental instruction in public schools was also starting.

The development of public school music programs was
largely due to the efforts of Lowell Mason (1792–1873) who
was brilliant in this management of school music programs in
the Boston area. He had been known for his musical publications as early as 1829 when he produced his Juvenile Psalmist.
He later became interested in the educational theories of
Johann Heinrich Pestalozzi (1746–1827), the Swiss educational
theorist. This information is clearly documented by James A.
Keene in his History of Music Education in the United States.

> ...He (Lowell Mason) became the country's most import-
> ant leader in the discussion of his understandings of
> Pestalozzianism. The ninth or 1811 edition of The
> Boston Handel and Haydn Society Collection of Church
> Music begins to show his conversion. The introductory
> rules were rewritten, demonstrating his newly acquired
> affinity for the form of question and answer.
>   Three years later Mason published his famous
> Manual of the Boston Academy of Music, for Instruction
> in the Elements of Vocal Music on the System of Pes-
> talozzi.[38]

Several points of emphasis for the teaching of singing
were somewhat new and previously unknown. Keene identifies
them in concise statements:

> ...The essence of this new system was that each
> thing would be taken up one at a time and thoroughly
> examined and practiced before another would be com-
> menced. The knowledge was to be acquired by the
> pupils themselves and not from the dictation and
> direction of the teachers. The teacher must lead the
> students to the desired information, excite their curi-
> osity, and "fix their attention". The system precluded
> the teacher from singing continuously with the schol-
> ars in the hope that the children would be "guided
> by their own ear and skill". Mason stated that his
> sources were "various; but always derived from per-
> sonal experience, or the written experience of others,
> and never from mere theory". ...The system must be
> traced to Pestalozzi, a Swiss Gentleman of wealth and
> learning, who devoted his life and fortune to the
> improvement of the young.[39]

The classroom approach began to be used with time
periods of musical instruction similar to some still in use
today:

> The regular classes were to begin with the formal
> instruction in vocal music "occupying two or three
> hours in the week." The areas of rhythm, melody,
> and dynamics were to be treated separately, although
> Mason informs us that in practice they could be pur-
> sued together. One-fourth of each meeting "should
> be occupied in lessons for tuning and giving flexibility

to the voice, and the rest of the time divided between
Rhythm, Melody, and Dynamics." Mason suggested
that melodies with appropriate words be sung. They
could be learned entirely by imitation "without books
or notes." Mason had no aversion to rote singing
at this time and his reasons demonstrate a sensitivity
to a practical classroom environment.

There is no objection at all, to learning tunes
by rote, under the direction of a judicious teacher.
It is only objectionable when in consequence of singing
the syllables appropriate to solmization, the pupil
is led to suppose that he is singing by note, while
his voice is guided solely by others. Mason valued
rote singing as a device to "enliven the mind, to
strengthen and improve the voice, and cultivate the
ear."[40]

Simple observation reveals that the cultural development
of this new country was growing from several viewpoints.
As cities became more heavily populated and new communities
were settled, public education became a more valued asset.
Not only the area of education for children was noticeably
increased, but the institutions of higher education were established under private and public auspices. The formal
study of the arts, particularly music, did not enter the curriculum until a century or more later in most colleges and
universities. In fact, music played a much more important
role far earlier in European institutions as mentioned by
Walter Spalding in his book, Music at Harvard: A Historical
Review of Men and Events, when he states in his preface:

Of all the arts about which to speak or write, music
is the most baffling. This statement is true because
the component factors of music, rhythm and sound,
are intangible, even mysterious; and because its
message is suggestive rather than definite as is the
case with literature, painting, architecture and sculpture. Music, however, has its history like any other
human activity, for there have been mighty achievements in this art, e.g., the Niebelungen dramas of
Wagner; great characters have thereby expressed
themselves--Palestrina, Bach, Handel, Haydn, Beethoven and Brahms. Musicians have been associated
for several centuries with kings, potentates, men of
affairs, and have played their part in important historical events. ...As to length of existence, it is

true that Harvard University, although about to celebrate its three-hundredth anniversary, is very young
in comparison with Oxford, Cambridge, the Sorbonne,
Upsala, Padua and Bologna. Oxford asserts that its
department of music was founded in the 9th Century
by Alfred the Great. Looking at the matter, however,
from the standpoint of our own country, the Harvard
University Orchestra, originally called the Pierian
Sodality, has had an unbroken existence since 1808.
The Glee Club was founded in 1858; and the teaching
of theoretical music has had the highest official recognition since 1862. Courses in Music are counted
toward degrees on a parity with any other courses
in the curriculum. As things move very rapidly in
our country, these dates prove that we have passed,
at any rate, the period of infantile ailments.[41]

Spalding states in a later section of his book that it
had been difficult to produce hard, cold facts regarding the
availability of music and musical training for the earlier Harvard students:

To trace the origin and development of music in New
England, especially in connection with Harvard University, the prominent manifestation of the New England
spirit, we must often rely upon conjecture and assump-
tion. Authentic data are few. It is certain, however,
that neither the early settlers nor the college students
were deaf or dumb. The elemental factors in music
are rhythm and sound. All human beings by the gift
of nature are potential musicians, for they are born
with a sound producing instrument, the voice, and
their whole bodily activity--heart-beat, gait, and
gestures--is on a rhythmical basis. Since physical
energy and vocal utterance are natural means for
emotional expression, we may be sure that music in
some form has always existed at Harvard. Academic
conditions, however, in our young country were so
different from those in England and on the Continent
that during Harvard's first century and a half (1636-
1786) we find but rudimentary symptoms of musical
life, and meager historical records. It is comparatively
recent times that music has gained recognition as a
fine art and as an educational subject of the highest
value. Little systematic instruction was given at
Harvard until 1862.[42]

The New York/New England area became well known
for its establishment of colleges for women. It was with pride
that residents of this territory saw the founding of Wellesley
in 1870 in Wellesley, Massachusetts; Smith College in 1871
in Northampton, Massachusetts; Radcliffe College in 1879 in
Cambridge, Massachusetts; Bryn Mawr in 1885 over in the
State of Pennsylvania at Bryn Mawr; and Barnard College
in New York City in 1889. Thus with the inclusion of Vassar
there was a healthy complement of colleges to educate women.
This is important to remember, for it was to be many of these
educated women who were later to help to establish settlement
houses in America, and subsequently community music schools.

Progress of all kinds was being achieved in the civilized
world during the decade from 1870-1880 which included the
following:

In 1871

The musical world heard the first performance of Verdi's
opera, Aida, in Cairo, Egypt near the site of the famed
Suez Canal which was opened in 1869, extending some
103 miles connecting the Mediterranean Sea with the Red
Sea.

P. T. Barnum opened his circus which he termed The
Greatest Show on Earth, in Brooklyn, New York.

The great Chicago Fire occurred on October 8th causing
an estimated $196,000,000 in damage and killing some
250 people. The fire raged for three days.

The Italian Law of Guarantee allowed the Pope to have
full possession of the Vatican (situated in Rome).

In 1872

The Brooklyn Bridge was opened spanning the East
River (which is not really a river at all) connecting
Brooklyn and Manhattan at the lower end of Manhattan
Island.

Alexander Scriabin (1872-1915), the Russian composer,
was born in Moscow on January 10th.

Georges Bizet (1838-1875), the French operatic composer,
wrote his incidental music to Daudet's L'Arlésienne,
now most frequently heard on orchestral programs entitled L'Arlésienne Suite.

Lowell Mason, the American music educator who was
born in 1792, died.

In 1873

Enrico Caruso, the famed Italian operatic tenor, was
born. He died in 1921.

Feodor Chaliapin, internationally acclaimed Russian
Basso, was born. He lived until 1938.

Sergei Rachmaninoff, the Russian composer/pianist was
born. He died in 1943.

Nikolai Rimsky-Korsakov (1844-1908), the Russian composer completed his opera, Ivan the Terrible.

Max Reger, the German composer, was born in 1873
and died in 1916.

In 1874

Modeste Mousorgsky (1839-1881), the Russian composer,
heard his opera, Boris Godunov, performed for the
first time in St. Petersburg.

Bedrich Smetana (1824-1884), the Bohemian composer,
completed his Ma Vlast, (My Fatherland), a group of
four symphonic poems, one of which, "Vlatava", is the
most familiar in this country.

Johann Strauss II (1825-1899), the Austrian composer,
had his opera, Die Fledermaus, first performed in Vienna,
Austria.

Verdi's Requiem was first performed in Milan, Italy.

In 1875

Georges Bizet, the French composer, died in the same

year that his opera, <u>Carmen</u>, was first performed in
Paris.

In England, Gilbert and Sullivan collaborated to produce
<u>Trial by Jury</u>, which was their first effort together.

Maurice Ravel (1875-1937), the French composer was
born.

Tschaikovsky's <u>Piano Concerto No. 1</u> was performed
for the first time in this country in Boston conducted
by Benjamin Lang with the Boston Orchestra.   The
first New York performance was conducted by Leopold
Damrosch with Hans von Bulow as soloist.

The Shenandoah Conservatory of Music was founded
in Dayton, Virginia.

Brigham Young University was established in Provo,
Utah.

In 1876

The world renowned Bayreuth Festspielhaus opened
which would feature the music of Richard Wagner since
it was built to his specifications.   The first complete
presentation of Wagner's <u>Der Ring des Nibelungen</u> with
its four music dramas, <u>Das Rheingold</u>, <u>Die Walküre</u>,
<u>Siegfried</u>, and <u>Götterdämmerung</u>. (This was the first
performance of <u>Siegfried</u>.)

Johannes Brahms (1833-1897), the German composer,
completed his <u>Symphony No. 1</u>, in C minor, Op. 68.

Two Spanish composers of international recognition were
born in the same year, 1876.   They were Pablo Casals,
violoncellist/composer, and Manuel De Falla, who died in
1946.   Casals lived to the age of 97 and died in 1973.

Bruno Walter (1876-1972), the German conductor known
and loved throughout the musical world, was born in
this year.

Amilcare Ponchielli (1834-1886) had the premier of his
opera, <u>La Gioconda</u>, at La Scala in this year with great

success. The success was to continue when La Gioconda
was performed again in 1883 at the Covent Garden in
London, England.

In 1877-1880

Brahms composed his Symphony No. 2, in D Major, Op.
73; Ernst Dohnanyi (1877-1960), the Hungarian pianist
and composer was born; the opera, Samson et Delila
by Camille Saint-Saëns was performed for the first time
at Weimar; Gilbert and Sullivan produced their comic
opera, H.M.S. Pinafore.

In 1878 George Grove began one of the most valuable
projects to be created for the musical world. He began
work on his first edition of Grove's Dictionary of Music
and Musicians. The most recent edition of this is The
New Grove Dictionary of Music and Musicians edited
by Stanley Sadie, in twenty volumes, 1980.

Creighton University in Omaha, Nebraska and Duquesne
University in Pittsburgh, Pennsylvania were each established in 1878, as well as the Cincinnati (Ohio) College
of Music.

Eighteen seventy-nine was the year in which Tschaikovsky
had his opera, Eugen Onegin, performed in Moscow.

Ernst Bloch (1880-1959), the Swiss-American composer,
was born in 1880, and it was that year in which the
Case School of Applied Science was founded in Cleveland,
Ohio. It was later known as the Case Institute of
Technology, and is now part of the Case-Western Re-
serve University complex.

Historically, the decade from 1880-1889 was to be one
of much immigration to the United States of America and one
of considerable social reform in this country and in Europe,
particularly England. Our country faced increased development and considerable cultural growth.

This decade was to see the culmination of many projects,
goals and developments which were to make the country more
productive, successful and strong in matters of satisfactory
solutions to social problems, educational goals and cultural

achievements. First it should be noted that the United States
had successfully survived a major internal struggle that
wracked the entire nation. The Civil War had tested the lives
and souls of every citizen in both the North and the South.
Yet the nation was to rebound and emerge stronger with a
greater feeling of brotherhood and willingness to accept others
as equals, with consideration for the thoughts and ideas of
each man or woman.

Despite the argumentation that must have existed, progress continued to be made in matters of education in nearly
all the states. With varying degrees of success, different
parts of the country made education available in most communities. While during the 19th century the education of
children or young people became more and more needed and
expected, communities solved their local problems of bringing
educational skills to the masses.

Studying a pattern set by the European countries, we
learn of as many as six institutions of higher education which
were established in the 14th century in England, Austria
and Germany. Still observing the European trend we learn
that in the 15th century an additional fifteen major institutions were founded in Germany, Scotland, Belgium, England,
France, Italy, Denmark and Spain. Between 1500 and 1599,
twenty more were added in many of the same countries and in
a few new ones--Spain, England, Belgium, Germany, France,
Italy, Switzerland, Poland, Brunswick (a former division or
district of Germany), Scotland, and Ireland.

Beginning in the 17th century slowly the North American
continent began to find institutions of higher education scattered throughout the country. From 1636 to 1800, several
such institutions were founded in areas that were to become
states of the United States of America. They were in the
following locations: Massachusetts, Virginia, Connecticut,
Pennsylvania, New Jersey, South Carolina, Kentucky, Maine,
Tennessee, and the District of Columbia. Geographically,
then, the trend was nationwide. By 1865 four more institutions of this kind were added in New York, Indiana, Maine
and Kentucky with two conservatories established in Illinois
and Ohio. By 1880, three more universities had been founded
in Utah, Nebraska and Pennsylvania, and another conservatory
started in Virginia.

The Industrial Revolution, which had begun in England during the 18th century, spread throughout Europe and the United States. This caused radical and unprecedented social and economic changes throughout the country, but it also opened the door for continued expansion and development of this country.

The introduction of power tools and larger industrial growth forced a restructuring of occupational skills and elimination of some forms of production which had relied primarily on the skills of individuals alone. Now mechanical tools could more effectively and more economically produce what the earlier artisan had done. It was a similar period in history to that which the world faces today with the introduction of the use of computers. Daily life may become somewhat easier, but social unrest and discontent can emerge as a result of many unemployed and currently unskilled workers who may be unwilling or unable to become reskilled or retrained. Such a disturbing situation existed in this country then, and at the same time many immigrants came to these shores in droves, creating unusual congestion and some deprivation, as new workers attempted to find employment in this country.

Andrew Carnegie (1837-1919), who was born in Scotland, came to America to become one of the giants of industry and manufacturing in America. He made many generous contributions to this nation in the form of donations for construction of libraries, museums, and especially the magnificent concert hall which bears his name still, standing majestically at the southeast corner of Seventh Avenue and 57th Street in New York City. Carnegie Hall today has some of the finest acoustics found anywhere in the world. The need for the Hall and its value to New York City were envisioned, discussed and planned during the 1880s. It was Walter Damrosch, the German born conductor and son of Leopold Damrosch, who urged Andrew Carnegie to build the stunning edifice in Manhattan.

To hear orchestral music was desired by many people in the 19th century, those who were immigrants and native-born. There was, of course, no radio or television nor recordings. The only possibility to hear good orchestral music was to attend an actual, live performance.

The oldest regular and established performance organization which presented orchestral programs was the Philharmonic Symphony Society of New York. The New Grove
Dictionary of Music and Musicians (1980) gives the following
description of the Philharmonic Society:

> The Philharmonic Symphony Society of New York
> dates from 1842 and is the oldest orchestra in con-
> tinuous existence in the USA. ...The first organiza-
> tional meeting of the Philharmonic Society was called
> by (U.C.) Hill on 2 April 1842. ...The first concert
> was held in the Apollo Rooms on 7 December 1842,
> and featured an orchestra of 63 players; they per-
> formed Beethoven's Fifth Symphony under Hill, who
> had introduced the work in America on 11 February
> 1841. ...The first season comprised three concerts;
> the second (18 February 1843) included the American
> première of Beethoven's Third Symphony. During
> the next sixteen seasons the orchestra gave four
> concerts annually; in 1859-60 they gave five, and
> a decade later six. During its first ten years the
> orchestra numbered between 50 and 67 players.
> Various conductors, usually members of the orchestra,
> shared the podium, often during the same concert;
> ...Later on one or two conductors assumed the res-
> ponsibility, beginning with Theodore Eisfeld who was
> elected director in 1852 and served until 1865.
> Other conductors included Carl Bergmann (1855-76),
> Theodore Thomas (1877-91) and Anton Seidl (1891-98).
> Under the presidency of R. G. Doremus, the number
> of players increased to 100 in 1867, and the orchestra
> moved to larger quarters at the Academy of Music.[43]

Therefore, it is accepted that a firmly established
orchestra existed in New York City on the eastern seacoast
of the United States from the mid-19th century on. Important
figures of that period helped to organize and support the
Philharmonic Society, and at least acceptable performers and
conductors were available at that time to meet the needs of
a professional performing ensemble which grew in size and
quality over the ensuing years. The proof lies in the fact
that the New York Philharmonic Orchestra exists today as
one of the outstanding orchestras in the world.

Grove gives further information about other orchestras

that had been heard in New York but indicates that earlier
ones were mostly amateur groups which began to appear in
the late 18th century. The Brooklyn Philharmonic, founded
in 1857, was similar to its New York counterpart and among
its conductors were some familiar names--Eisfeld, Bergmann,
and Thomas. [44]

The records will also show that Theodore Thomas formed
his own 60 to 80 piece orchestra in 1867 which performed
in New York and on national tours until 1891 when he moved
his activities to Chicago. The music he performed with his
own orchestra included works of J. S. Bach to then contemporary European composers including Brahms and Wagner.
It is fascinating to note that Thomas was conductor of the
Philharmonic Society at the same time as he was conducting
his own orchestra. Stiff competition existed between him and
Leopold Damrosch who formed his own orchestra, The New
York Symphony, in 1878. His son, Walter, was to assume
the responsibility for the New York Symphony after his
father's death in 1885.

In 1891 Theodore Thomas organized the Chicago Orchestra whose name was changed to the Theodore Thomas
Orchestra for a period of fifteen years. In 1912 the orchestra's name was changed officially to the Chicago Symphony
Orchestra, which it still bears today.

The City of Boston, Massachusetts, has been a cultural
leader and supporter of the arts and education from its very
early days. Renowned for its establishing of music in the
curriculum of its public schools, its unusual contribution to
the advancement and development of church music, its many
musical organizations of great distinction such as the Handel
and Haydn Society, and the contributions in the arts by its
institutions of higher education, since 1881 Boston has possessed an excellent, musically sensitive symphony orchestra,
having engaged the most skillful performers available at that
time.

The Boston Symphony Orchestra was established and
endowed by Henry Lee Higginson, a prominent Boston banker.
His goal was to bring good musical performances to the residents of Boston at a very low fee. This was to be for the
enjoyment and cultural development of the local citizenry
(perhaps Mr. Higginson was a bit ahead of the times in his
recognition of the cultural needs of his community).

Higginson engaged Georg Henschel as the first conductor of the Boston Symphony Orchestra as well as 68 performing musicians. The first concert was given on 22 October 1881, and in that first season, 83,359 attendees heard the 24 pairs of concerts. During its long and impressive history, many distinguished conductors have appeared with the orchestra including Wilhelm Gericke, Arthur Nikisch, Emil Paur, and much later Koussevitzky, Charles Munch, Erich Leinsdorf, William Steinberg, and Seiji Ozawa.[45]

In New York City the now world famous Metropolitan Opera House opened on 22 October 1883 (exactly two years after the date of the first concert of the Boston Symphony Orchestra) with a presentation of Gounod's opera Faust, and in reality the Metropolitan Opera has far surpassed the early expectations of its founding fathers. It has become the major opera house in the United States, and it equals or surpasses opera houses in other countries, though some of them may be older than the Metropolitan. Today it presents its annual series of performances at its new home in the Lincoln Center of New York City.

Historically it is interesting to note that Leopold Damrosch was engaged to manage the second season of the Metropolitan Opera and to present a year entirely devoted to the performances of German opera. The fairly large German population in New York City must have been delighted. A more complete explanation of this is given in George Martin's book The Damrosch Dynasty.

It is clear that in the years from 1880 to 1893 many categories of the human condition converged at one time in this country. They were the social, industrial, cultural, and educational needs of people, each requiring special attention and satisfactory solutions to the problems it presented. In addition there was a tremendous influx of immigrants from Europe, particularly from Poland, Russia, and the Eastern European countries. Many of them remained in the major port cities along the Atlantic coast to take up residence. A large portion of them stayed in New York City (especially on the Lower East Side). Others remained in Boston or Philadelphia, while some ventured as far west as Cleveland, Pittsburgh, and Chicago. Each community struggled to solve the problems of so many human beings--men, women, and children-- living within its confines.

As a part of the large group of Russian immigrants,
there came to this country a child born in Russia in 1888,
whose father, a Jewish cantor, brought him to this country
in 1893, the same year in which the Henry Street Settlement
was founded, and the same year that the Hull-House Music
School opened in the City of Chicago.

The youngster's name was Israel Balin, and at a very
young age, he worked as a street singer on the Lower East
Side of New York, and later as a singing waiter in a Chinatown
Cafe. He began writing lyrics to songs in 1907, the first of
which was a success in that year. He then began writing his
own lyrics and music.

His first outstanding success was the song "Alexander's
Ragtime Band," to which he wrote both the words and music.
Through a printer's error on the cover of his first published
song, his name appeared as Berlin, and so he was known
thereafter. He is, of course, Irving Berlin, the beloved and
prolific composer of popular songs, musical shows and music
for motion pictures. This Russian born, truly American genius
is still living at the time of this writing, and is recognized
professionally and fondly in this country and around the world.[46]

The indigenous riches of this country, the wealth of
opportunities for success, the encouragement for those willing
to make the effort to achieve, all were undeniably present
in this young nation, only slightly more than 100 years old
in the late 19th century. Also buried in the hearts and minds
of the human beings who came to the land of opportunity was
the urgent need for artistic expression. The scene was set.
The time was ripe for the creation of a path or channel to
give the opportunity to all, young and old alike, to develop
a mode of artistic expression for themselves.

The first realization of this quest was the establishment
of the Music School Settlement or Settlement Music School.
Later these schools were called Community Music Schools.
These were a uniquely American innovation which led to the
expansion of artistic education into many different media--
dance, drama, visual arts, etc. Ultimately these schools led
to the formation of the National Guild of Community Music
Schools, later to become the National Guild of Community
Schools of the Arts. This organization celebrated its fiftieth
anniversary in the Fall of 1987.

   The beginnings of the National Guild of Community
Schools of the Arts are rooted in the late 19th century.
America absorbed the talents of those who came to these shores
seeking freedom of expression both socially and artistically.
Americans dared to dream for themselves! Let us trace the
origin and development of a Community School of the Arts.

2

AMERICAN SETTLEMENT HOUSES AND
THEIR ENGLISH ORIGINS

The movement for establishing settlement houses in America
came directly from England at the end of the 19th century.
At the time when America was becoming more settled, greater
in size and more culturally minded, social problems arose in
America similar to those in England, particularly in large
coastal cities. Overcrowded conditions, which resulted in both
health and educational problems, became serious conditions
in both countries.

Middle income families in England began to see their
sons attending the Universities, both Oxford and Cambridge.
In America the college-aged sons began to attend Harvard,
Yale, Princeton and Columbia, while daughters were enrolling
at Smith College, Wellesley, Vassar, and Barnard. Social
consciences were being developed in the minds of college
students.

In London living areas for the poor were squalid hovels
ridden with rats and roaches. Educational opportunities were
slim for the youngsters because children were sent to work
as soon as any reasonable opportunity presented itself for
them to be employed. Children in Boston, Chicago, New
York City, and Philadelphia faced similar educational limitations.

Many children never went beyond the beginning elementary grades in either country. Frequently, examples were
related telling of as many as nine children sleeping in one
bedroom, and families reluctantly renting precious space to
boarders in order to gain enough money to feed and clothe
the family members in addition, of course, to paying the
rent. Similar situations existed in the major cities of both
America and England.

As early as 1856, a strong group of serious-minded, dedicated graduates of Cambridge University organized the Working Men's College in London led by Frederick Denison Maurice. Here is an example of community action which reveals a realization of the problems that existed in the community and also an attempt to find satisfactory solutions for the betterment of all.

The joint efforts of workingmen who were prominent and responsible people in their trade unions and cooperative societies, and men led by Charles Kingsley, who were affiliated with the Church of England and with the Universities (Oxford and Cambridge) helped to solve difficult social problems. Each group worked to improve the living conditions of the general public, but especially the conditions of the poor and downtrodden.

Edward Denison, an Oxford man, lived in Stepney, East London, for a relatively short period of time from August, 1867 to March, 1868, and worked with John Richard Green who was then the vicar of the parish. They developed a plan for having a group of young college men join Mr. Denison to continue to improve the living conditions in East London.

At this point in history, 1873, the Reverend Samuel A. Barnett appeared on the scene. His contributions were destined to make history. He was then Canon of Westminster, and he and his wife, Henrietta, began to work at St. Jude's in Whitechapel and its surrounding neighborhoods. They both told of the needs and conditions in East London by frequently making visits to lecture at Oxford and Cambridge. This was the start of apprising the young, college-trained men of the conditions that existed then, and to encourage them to work against these terrible social evils.

During the summer months of 1875 Mr. Arnold Toynbee, an Oxford tutor, lived in Whitechapel and worked under the direction of Reverend Barnett. After this experience, Toynbee frequently spoke to working men on topics of ethics and economics. Seven years later, Reverend Barnett proposed to a group of Oxford men that a house be established in East London which would be similar to the college missions[1] which were already in existence. He recommended that the men should live at the house in order to provide responsible leadership, both social and civic. The next year, 1884, saw the

opening of Toynbee Hall, Whitechapel, and the Reverend
Barnett was appointed as warden,[2] a position he held for
twenty-five years.[3] Henrietta Barnett explained how the
first settlement was named:

> On the 10th of March, 1883, Arnold Toynbee had
> died. He had been our beloved and faithful friend.
> ...The 10th of March, 1884, was a Sunday, and on
> the afternoon of that day Balliol Chapel was filled
> with a splendid body of men who had come together
> from all parts of England in loving memory of Arnold
> Toynbee, on the anniversary of his death. ...We
> had often chatted...as to what to call it. ...As I
> sat on that Sunday afternoon in the chapel, ...the
> thought flashed to me, "Let us call the Settlement
> Toynbee Hall." To Mr. Bolton King, the honorary
> secretary of the committee...had come the same idea
> ...and our new Settlement received its name before
> a brick was laid or the plans concluded.[4]

It is difficult to imagine the impact that the work done
at Toynbee Hall had on social workers around the world. In
America, many who were aware of the social problems that
existed in this country spent time in London visiting Toynbee
Hall and observing the work being done by Reverend and
Mrs. Barnett. Word travelled rapidly of the successes in
England, and the desire to visit seemed impossible to resist.

Space allows listing only a few of the prominent social
workers from this country who made the pilgrimage to London.
One of the first was Stanton Coit who spent but a brief period
at Toynbee Hall, but who found the program so impressive
that he returned home to establish the first settlement house
in America. It was called the Neighborhood Guild, later to
become the University Settlement, which was founded in 1886
on the Lower East Side of New York City. Many settlement
houses were to be founded in that heavily populated area in
a very short period of time, including the famed Henry Street
Settlement.

Most impressed of all, perhaps, was Jane Addams, who
with her friend and companion, Ellen Starr, worked diligently
to form and establish Hull-House in Chicago. In her book
Twenty Years at Hull-House, Miss Addams related her experience as follows:

...So that it finally came about that in June, 1888,
five years after my first visit in East London, I
found myself at Toynbee Hall equipped not only with
a letter of introduction from Canon Fremantle, but
with high expectations and a certain belief that whatever perplexities and discouragement concerning the
life of the poor were in store for me, I should at
least know something at first hand and have the
solace of daily activity.[5]

The inspiration she received in Whitechapel was of such
strength that she further relates:

The next January (1889) found Miss Starr and myself in Chicago, searching for a neighborhood in which
we might put our plans into execution. In our eager-
ness to win friends for the new undertaking, we
utilized every opportunity to set forth the meaning
of the settlement as it had been embodied in Toynbee
Hall.[6]

Jane Addams had a very clear picture of what it was
she wished to bring to the people in the neighborhood. With
her strong cultural background and education, she included
the arts in her program immediately. In his preface to the
reprint of the Woods and Kennedy book, Zone of Emergence,
Sam B. Warner, Jr. states the following:

...When Jane Addams moved her family furniture into
an old farm house on Halstead Street, Chicago, hers
was not an attempt to insinuate herself into the
neighborhood mores, but rather to offer a model of
middle class home life to any who wished to avail
themselves of her hospitality and teaching. The
settlement movement's battery of child groups, night
education meetings, art shows, craft and athletic
facilities was conscious presentation of the tools of
the middle class morality.[7]

Her interest in the arts is expressed in Twenty Years
at Hull-House, when she relates that the first building erected
for Hull-House contained an art gallery and that as early as
1891, the first art exhibit of pictures on loan was opened by
Reverend and Mrs. Barnett of London.[8]

In a later paragraph in the chapter, "Arts at Hull-House," she comments on the use of music in the settlement's program:

> From the beginning we had classes in music, and the Hull-House Music School, which is housed in quarters of its own in our quieter court, was opened in 1893.* The school is designed to give a thorough musical instruction to a limited number of children.[9]

The last quotation from Jane Addams' book, "to give a thorough musical instruction to a limited number of children" suggests the reason that Hull-House is not a member of the National Guild of Community Schools of the Arts, nor, perhaps, considered a true community music school. The elitist attitude suggested by this phraseology would eliminate the Hull-House Music School from becoming a Guild member because it is against the Guild's philosophy that would allow any child to attend regardless of his musical ability. Janet D. Schenck addressed the subject when she stated:

> The majority of schools are committed to the doctrine that any child who desires to study music should have the opportunity whether or not he has unusual talent. ...Hull-House Music School is an exception. Its founder and director, Miss Eleanor Smith, receives only talented children who expect to become professionals.[10]

Schenck further presents the director's opinion when she quotes:

> ...The Hull House [sic] Music School was founded in 1892 [see footnote below] by Miss Eleanor Smith. "Miss Hannig and I," writes Miss Smith, "had

---

*It is curious that Janet D. Schenck repeatedly refers to the opening date of the Hull-House Music School as 1892. Jane Addams in her first book, Twenty Years at Hull-House, gives the date as 1893 (p. 378). It is even more curious to note that in the Tables presented in her two books, Schenck uses 1893. This will, therefore, be the accepted date for the beginning of the Hull-House Music School.

made the plan for the Music School in Germany some
years before we returned and put it into effect."[11]

This topic is more throughly discussed in the next
chapter when the philosophy of a community school of the
arts is presented and examined.

Boston, Massachusetts, was a city with similar social
problems as those found in Chicago and New York City, also
with cultural and artistic leanings. In December of 1891,
Andover House was established by William J. Tucker who was
a professor at the Andover Theological Seminary and who was
later to become the president of Dartmouth College.   Robert
A. Woods, who had studied social work in England and while
there spent six months at Toynbee Hall, was appointed head
of the house. Mr. Woods was to become the "unofficial philosopher" for social work in America. In 1895, the name of
the settlement house was changed to South End House which
it bears today, and in 1896 its own philosophical statement
was made:

> ...The house aims to bring about a better and more
> beautiful life in its neighborhood and district and to
> develop new ways (through study and action in this
> locality) of meeting some of the serious problems in
> society.[12]

Two years after the founding of Andover House, now
South End House, Lillian D. Wald with her friend, Mary
Brewster, opened what was to become the Henry Street Settlement, originally designed as a visiting nurse program. The
first site chosen by the nurses to open their doors was on
the top floor of a tenement house on Jefferson Street on the
Lower East Side of New York City. The only point of distinction in the apartment was that it had its own bathroom.
The program flourished so that in two years it moved into a
house of its own at 265 Henry Street. The acquisition of the
house was made possible through the generosity of Mr. Jacob
Schiff who was to remain a life-long friend of Lillian D. Wald
and of the Henry Street Settlement. The building at 265
Henry Street has been declared an historical landmark which
is announced by a plaque on the front of the building today.

It may have been difficult at first for the neighbors
in any of the major cities to understand the terminology when

the word "settlement" was used to describe the building or
the program and organization housed within it. A simple
perusal of a good dictionary would give a variety of definitions.
Twelve or thirteen meanings can be found for the same word.
For a clear explanation one can turn to Warner's statement
in his preface to Zone of Emergence by Woods and Kennedy,
when he states:

> ...The principal type of settlement house was a
> commons, in America a residence of young, educated
> middle class men and women who lived together in a
> poor district and helped the people there cope with
> the problems of everyday life. Their special concerns
> were the care of children and the aged, and the im-
> provement of housing and sanitation and the aug-
> menting of public facilities for education and culture.[13]

A further explanation of the term "settlement" comes from
Gaylord S. White in his chapter entitled "The Settlement
Problems of a Changing Neighborhood," in Readings in the
Development of Settlement Work, edited by Lorene M. Pacey:

> A social settlement presupposes neighbors. It is
> essentially a neighborhood institution. But it is not
> concerned primarily as to the particular kind of neigh-
> bors who surround it. All it demands as a condition
> of its work is that living about it shall be people--
> men, and women and children, who need help in working
> out the social, industrial, civic and moral problems
> which confront them.[14]

Mary K. Simkhovitch was the founder and first director
of the Greenwich House Settlement in New York City. In
her book Neighborhood: My Story of Greenwich House, she
gives her own philosophical statement:

> I have never ceased to believe that the settlement
> ought to be the matrix of a more adequate under-
> standing of what goes on, and that its permanent
> value is not so much in the rendering of specific
> services (which necessarily change with a changing
> environment) as in the fruitful knowledge obtained
> through firsthand contact with the people of the
> neighborhoods. To voice their wrongs, to understand
> their problems, to stand by their side in their life

struggles, to welcome their own leadership, to reveal
to others who have not had this opportunity of direct
contact the inner character of situations that arise,
is the primary task of the settlement.[15]

Her simplistic explanation of what a settlement is, is
undoubtedly the most effective of all:

The Settlement was really another home for the neighbors who met there, a place where the needs and
desires of each were sympathetically considered.[16]

In the Fall of 1887, four graduates of Smith College
met by chance and began to discuss the emergence of social
consciousness in this country. They also made reference to
the work being done at Toynbee Hall in England. The four
women recognized their own responsibilities to organize similar
programs in this country. As they parted company, each
promised faithfully to do her utmost in establishing an organization which would assume the task of forming a strong program to be nationally supported somehow, which would allow
settlement houses to become realities wherever they might be
needed. Thus, the College Settlements Association was started.

During the next year, an appeal for support was sent
out which resulted in the Association's being financially able
to take a house at 95 Rivington Street on the Lower East Side
of New York City. In the Fall of 1889, the first College
Settlement was opened with Jean G. Fine appointed headworker.
In 1890, the College Settlements Association was formally organized with chapters at Smith College, of course, and at Bryn
Mawr, Vassar, and Wellesley.

It was the College Settlement in New York City which
offered space to Emilie Wagner at the Rivington Street address
to let her music program expand, which ultimately led to the
formal establishment of the Third Street Music School Settlement.

The following chart shows the names of the organizations established between 1886 and 1909 in New York City, the
dates when they were founded, and the location in Manhattan
where they were.*

---

*East Side--from the East River to Fifth Avenue above 14th

In the list of settlement houses that were founded between 1886 and 1909, one particular settlement deserves special
consideration at this point. It is the Music School Settlement,
now known as the Third Street Music School Settlement, begun
in 1894 by Miss Emilie Wagner. One very significant fact is
that this organization has never dropped the term "settlement"
from its title, nor has it failed to act as a genuine settlement.
At the same time, it has succeeded in being one of the outstanding music schools in this country.

From its earliest days, the Third Street Music School
Settlement has maintained a music library and a book library.
Its curriculum included private lessons in piano, violin, cello,
and voice. Group instruction offered orchestra, junior orchestra, choral work and theory. More will be said about
its expanded curriculum and its growth later in this study.

The social work program included much neighborhood
visiting, a Penny Provident Bank (very common in settlement
houses during this period), medical work employment possibilities, and clubs interested in debating, city history, civics,
art and literature, dance and socials. A variety of activities
were carried on in the summertime.

Some of the early directors of the school were Emilie
Wagner from 1894 to 1904, and subsequently Mary Wines, and
Eleanor J. Crawford, all of whose titles officially were Head
Residents. In 1907, the Music Director was Thomas Tapper,
and he was succeeded by David Mannes, who was musical
director from 1910 to 1916* and was later to establish and
head the Mannes College of Music on the Upper East Side

(cont. from p. 54) Street.
Lower East Side--South of 14th Street to the Battery East of
    the Bowery (Third Avenue).
West Side--entire West Side from the Hudson River East to
    Fifth Avenue.

*In his book Music Is My Faith, David Mannes states: "In
1916, after 15 years, I finally resigned as director of the
Music School Settlement." This is somewhat misleading. Mr.
Mannes taught at Third Street for 15 years from 1901 to 1916,
but he was the director for only six years.

SETTLEMENT HOUSES ESTABLISHED IN NEW YORK CITY (MANHATTAN) 1886-1909

	East Side	Lower East Side	West Side
1886		Neighborhood Guild (later to become The University Settlement)	
1889		The College Settlement	
1891	East Side House		
1892		Jacob Riis Neighborhood Settlement	Riverside House
1893		The Henry Street Settlement	
1894		Music School Settlement of Third Street (The first Music School in America organized initially as a Community Music School)	
1895			Hudson Guild
1896	Uptown Nurses Settlement (Branch from Henry Street Settlement)		
1897		Christadora House Gospel Settlement	Hartley House
1898	Warren Godard House (formerly Friendly Aid Settlement)	Downtown Ethical Society	

Year			
1899		Alfred Corning Clark Neighborhood House Recreation Rooms and Settlement	
1900			Richard Hill House
1901		Hamilton House	
1902			Greenwich House Speyer House
1904		China Town Settlement and Recreation Room	Do Ye Nexte Thynge Society
1905		Edward Clark Club House	
1906			Kennedy House Stillman Branch for Colored People (Branch of Henry Street Settlement)
1907		People's Three Arts School	Bloomingdale Guild
1909	Homemaking Settlement		

of New York City. (This School has recently moved to a new
location on the Upper West Side of Manhattan.)*

The dedicated and indefatigable Emilie Wagner began her
distinguished career in 1894 by teaching children piano on the
Lower East Side of New York City in rooms supplied by a
Bowery Mission. It is reported that she charged 10 cents per
lesson. Her immediate success attracted the attention of some
of the women of the College Settlement, which had been established in 1889 by the College Settlements Association (see
p. 54) at 95 Rivington Street. This organization offered
Miss Wagner space in order to teach music in their building.
Woods and Kennedy are most anxious to indicate the following:

> Although Miss Wagner's classes bore the name Music
> School of the College and University Settlements, they
> were at no time maintained by these settlements. As
> the work outgrew the rooms provided by the two settle-
> ment committees, the committees united in 1900, es-
> tablishing the classes in a small house at 31 Rivington
> Street. In 1902, the work still growing and expenses
> increasing, it seemed best to sever all connection with
> the two settlements and to form a separate board of
> management. This was done and the society of the
> Music School was incorporated in 1903.[17]

In the first annual report of the Music School of the
University and College Settlements, Alice M. Ditson (Mrs.
Charles Healy Ditson), chairman of the Music School Committee,
reveals additional pertinent information about the Music School:

> ...The present number of pupils is 140 (varying in
> age from 5 to 16). These receive instruction on the
> violin and the piano at the rate of 50 cents an hour.
> The daily attendance is about 60, this being the
> greatest number that can be properly taken care of
> under the present conditions. The waiting list amount-
> ed, at latest reports, to about 200.[18]

It is interesting to note information about the finances
to operate the Music School from the same report:

---

*Woods and Kennedy give the year as 1909 when Mannes be-
gan his directorship, but reports from the files of the Third
Street Music School Settlement indicate 1910.

...The school is under the control of a committee
consisting of 40 members contributing $25 a year.
There are 20 associate members contributing $5 and
upwards, and one patron who gives $100 a year.
These, with the average from the children of $50 a
month, yield an income of about $1,700 a year--$800
more being required, as will appear.[19]

Figures such as these are difficult to accept in today's
world, yet the national economy was considerably different
at the turn of the 20th century. Further information is
presented:

I may say in passing that the Music School, being
outside of the Settlement Building, is obliged to pay
a large rent. Through the generosity of Mr. and
Mrs. Speyer this expense has been met for the present
year.
    The cost of maintaining the school, allowing $1,000
for rent, $1,000 for salaries, and about $500 for current expenses, is at least $2,000; this does not include
various payments to the pupils who teach--an excellent
system of fitting them for their work in the future,
as teaching is the ultimate aim of many, the talented
ones who are to make their mark as performers being
more rare.[20]

It was also stated in the report that there were 13
teachers who kindly donated their services. "Especial thanks
are due to Mr. David Mannes, who has arranged to devote
one evening a month to the little orchestra of about a dozen
children, who rehearse in the meantime under Miss Wagner."[21]
Several statements or points regarding the philosophy of such
a school as she envisioned them were included in the report of
Mrs. Ditson.

Mention should be made of those schools which have
only recently become members of the National Guild of Community Schools of the Arts whose dates of origin seem to pre-
date that of the Third Street Music School Settlement. The
list below includes those schools in chronological order with a
brief descriptive statement about each. The information about
them comes from the 1985 Directory of the National Guild of
Community Schools of the Arts:

NAME OF THE SCHOOL	DESCRIPTIVE STATEMENT

Lawrence University Conservatory Preparatory Department

Location: Appleton, Wisconsin
Founding date: 1847
First Guild Membership date:
    1983

The Department provides voice,
theory and instrumental instruction to all residents of
the Fox Valley. The faculty
consists of artist-teachers
from the Lawrence University
School of Music.

University of Cincinnati
College, Conservatory of Music
Preparatory Department

Location: Cincinnati, Ohio
Founding date: 1867
First Guild Membership date:
    1983

The Preparatory Department
traces origins to 1867, with
the founding of the Cincinnati
Conservatory of Music. The
Department now offers a full
program of private lessons,
classes, and ensembles in
music, dance and drama for
students of all ages and levels
of advancement. The program
prepares students for ad-
missions to professional schools,
while at the same time developing their knowledge and enjoyment of music.

Shenandoah College and
Conservatory Community Arts
Program

Location: Winchester, Virginia
Founding date: 1875
First Guild Membership date:
    1984

Community Arts Program provides professional instruction
in private music lessons and
classes for adults and children
...in piano, voice, organ,
band and orchestra instruments, Suzuki violin, guitar,
banjo, jazz improvisation,
music theory and composition
...Art instruction is offered
in drawing, art history, painting, water color, acrylics,
clay modeling, sculpture and
portrait painting.

Converse College Department
of Pre-College and Adult
Music

The Pre-College and Adult
Music Department has enjoyed
the support of the South
Carolina Community for 40

Location: Spartenburg,
    S. Carolina
Founding date: 1890
First Guild Membership date:
    1984

years...Students in music
and dance currently number
about 600 and range from pre-
schoolers to senior citizens.
The Department has its own
large building and shares
four other facilities on campus.
The Department inaugurated
a creative drama program for
children as well as new evening classes in music for adults.

Hartford Conservatory of Music and Dance

Location: Hartford, Connecti-
    cut
Founding date: 1890
First Guild Membership date:
    1982

The Conservatory was organized as The Seminary School
for Church Musicians by the
Founder/President of the
Hartford Seminary. The name
was changed to the Hartford
School of Music in 1895. Incorporated as a non-profit
institution in 1905, the name
was changed in 1959 to the
Hartford Conservatory, and
in 1981 to the present name.
The School offers professional
instruction in music and dance
at all levels and all ages
through three basic programs:
the Diploma Program, ...the
General Enrollment Division,
and the Outreach Program.

Peabody Institute of the Johns Hopkins University Preparatory Division

Location: Baltimore, Maryland
Founding date: 1894*
First Guild Membership date:
    1983

The Preparatory Division offers instruction in music, dance,
drama, early childhood and
adult education to a student
body of 1,700. Certification
Programs are available in the
music and dance divisions.
A full array of repertoire
classes for instrumental students, a full orchestra, wind

---

*The same year, the Third Street Music School Settlement
began.

and brass ensembles, and
chamber music are also offered.[22]

Before the turn of the century, three other schools
were founded which are the Sherwood Conservatory of Music:
Community Music School, Chicago, Illinois in 1895; the Brooklyn Conservatory of Music, Brooklyn, New York in 1897; and
the Wisconsin Conservatory of Music, Milwaukee, Wisconsin in
1899.

It is significant that of the six schools having been established prior to 1894 or actually in 1894, all were or subsequently became part of larger organizations, either a college,
conservatory, university or seminary.

From the larger institutions developed preparatory departments or pre-college training schools, or, as in the case
of Peabody, they were annexed to the larger school.

Also in the case of the Peabody Preparatory there is
evidence of a different, but equally successful, kind of community development. In 1894 in Baltimore, Maryland, an adventurous and courageous young woman, May Garrettson Evans
resigned her position as a reporter for the Sun papers. She
envisioned a cultural program which she chose to call the
People's Music School,* and she launched a school that was to
receive considerable recognition both in Baltimore and in the
surrounding areas. By 1898 the school was thriving and was
formally annexed to the Peabody Conservatory of Music of the
Johns Hopkins University and had its name changed officially
to the Peabody Preparatory. It still functions as such at the
date of this writing.[23]

Here we see a clear example of the development of a
school because the community recognized or stated the need
for such a cultural organization, and aroused the imagination
of one of its members who started the school by her own initiative. The early development of the school was so great
a success that within four years, it was made part of the

---

*A title to be used again by the school founded in Chicago
in 1976.

prestigious university in its community. Thus, the cycle was completed.

While each of these schools obviously served its community well, it did not originate from the Settlement House movement in America, but rather from independent musical organizations per se that reflected the need for such professional training within the existing community.

In the year that Stanton Coit returned to this country to establish the first settlement house in America (1886), much was happening throughout the world in the fields of music, art, literature, science, sports and the betterment of conditions for mankind.

It proved sadly to be the year in which the internationally known Hungarian pianist/composer, Franz Liszt, died. Born in 1811, Liszt gave spectacular piano performances at a very early age. His piano technique astounded many distinguised musicians of the day, including Ludwig van Beethoven (1770-1827), as well as the general public. Liszt admired the works of Wilhelm Richard Wagner (1813-1883), and his own daughter, Cosima, was to leave her first husband, Hans von Bulow, the conductor, pianist and critic, to marry the German composer, better known as simply Richard Wagner. Liszt left a wealth of his musical compositions which require such pianistic dexterity that only the most outstanding pianists plan carefully to perform his music today.

As if to replace one musical genius with another, 1886 is also the year that Wilhelm Furtwangler was born (d. 1963). His conducting technique and musicality ranked him with such conductors as Arturo Toscanini (1867-1957), George Szell (1897-1970), and Leopold Stokowski (1882-1977).

The literary world recognized the novel The Bostonians by Henry James (1843-1916), the American novelist and brother of William James (1842-1910), the American philosopher and psychologist; Robert Louis Stevenson (1850-1894), the Scottish author, penned his famous and terrifying novel Dr. Jekyll and Mr. Hyde; and the American author Frances Hodgson Burnett, wrote her book Little Lord Fauntleroy. One might not think of the American steel manufacturer and philanthropist, Andrew Carnegie (1837-1919), as an American author, yet in 1886 his book, Triumphant Democracy, appeared. This

was also the year when Das Kapital, the "communist manifesto"
written by the German socialist journalist Karl Marx (1818-
1883), was published for the first time in English.

In the world of art, notice must be given to Auguste
Rodin (1840-1917), the French artist, whose sculpture The
Kiss was completed in 1886. He is also the sculptor of the
famous statue The Thinker.

Probably the single, most important event for American
labor in 1886 was the establishment of the American Federation
of Labor, led by a sincere and dedicated leader, Samuel Gompers (1850-1924). Gompers was born in England but became
an American labor leader and was president of the A F of L
from 1886 to 1924, except for the year 1895.

> ...The fact that organized labor as it exists in the
> late Twentieth Century is largely the product of the
> A F of L and its leaders obscures the Federation's
> recent and inauspicious beginnings. What became the
> keystone of the modern American labor movement em-
> erged from a tiny conclave of skilled tradesmen who
> met in Columbus, Ohio in 1886 and founded the
> American Federation of Labor. [24]

Harold Livesy states in his book, Samuel Gompers and
Organized Labor in America:

> ...They designed the A F of L as an agency to co-
> ordinate the activities of existing craft unions through-
> out the United States of America under the trade-
> union banner and lead them to dignity and prosper-
> ity. [25]

Gompers' efforts were, indeed, to place the workingman
in a position where he could realize self-respect and personal
dignity in his community.

> ... Gompers and his colleagues watched its [the
> Knights of Labor] growth with a suspicion that
> ripened into hostility. In 1886 the Knights so threat-
> ened the preeminence of trade unions in organized
> labor that Gompers helped junk the enfeebled Federa-
> tion of Organized Trades and Labor Unions and joined

those who replaced it with a leaner, harder instrument, the American Federation of Labor.[26]

International relations between the United States of America and France improved immensely in 1886 when the Lady with the Torch, the Statue of Liberty, was presented to the American people by the citizens of France.

> The largest and best-known statue in America towers over Liberty Island in the Upper Bay of New York, a symbol of welcome to returning Americans and to thousands of immigrants who have come to the New World. It is the classically draped figure of a woman, 151 feet high, holding a torch high in her right hand and a tablet in the left bearing the inscription "July 4, 1776". The upheld arm is forty-two feet long and twelve feet in diameter at its thickest. Energetic young people like to climb a circular stairway of 168 steps leading from the top of the 152-foot pedestal to the spiked crown; others may take an elevator.
>   The Statue of Liberty designed by Frédéric Auguste Bartholdi, was a gift of the French people to celebrate "the alliance of the two nations in achieving the independence of the United States of America, and attests their abiding friendship." It was formally presented to the United States in Paris on July 4, 1884, was shipped to New York in 234 cases, and was dedicated by President Cleveland two years later (1886)*.[27]

After major repairs and refurbishing, this magnificent statue was re-dedicated on July 4, 1986 by President Ronald Reagan.

The world of science proudly boasted of the founding of the Pasteur Institute in Paris in that same year, 1886. In that same period, Ernst von Bergmann was successful in demonstrating the sterilization of surgical instruments by the application or use of steam. In the United States, the first installation of a hydro-electric power plant was begun in Niagara, New York, while in England, sports enthusiasts

---

*In the same year that Stanton Coit founded the University Settlement, the first settlement house in America.

learned of the foundation of the English Lawn Tennis Association. This year also recorded the birth of David Ben-Gurion
who was born in Poland and was later to become the Prime
Minister of Israel from 1946-1953, and again from 1955 to 1963.
He died in Israel in 1973.

In the higher education field, music and the arts were
not being overlooked. As early as 1835, Oberlin College
(Oberlin, Ohio) offered courses in Sacred Music, and by 1865,
the Conservatory of Music was established. Two years later
it was included as part of the College. It should be noted
that, when Fenelon B. Rice became the director in 1871, Oberlin College began to develop an excellent reputation throughout the country.[28]

In 1875, two major institutions brought musical study
into their academic programs. Harvard University (Cambridge,
Massachusetts) appointed John Knowles Paine (1839-1906),
the American organist and composer, to a full professorship,
which firmly planted music in the University's curriculum.
Not to be outdone, the University of Pennsylvania in Philadelphia appointed Hugh A. Clarke to a full professorship also.
By this time, both Vassar and Smith Colleges had included
music in their programs.[29]

Between 1877 and 1889, the following institutions established music departments, or at least included music in
their curricula:

> ... University of Illinois (Urbana), Ohio Wesleyan
> (Delaware), University of Michigan (Ann Arbor), Knox
> College (Galesburg, Illinois), the Missouri Valley Col-
> lege and the Missouri Industrial Institute and College,
> University of Colorado (Boulder), Amherst College
> (Amherst, Massachusetts), Augustana College (Sioux
> Falls, South Dakota), and both Wellesley College
> (Wellesley, Massachusetts) and Mount Holyoke College
> (South Hadley, Massachusetts) in 1889.[30]

The year, 1887, was a lively one for both musical composition and literary successes. London-born Sir John Stainer
(1840-1901) composed his most popular work, The Crucifixion,
an oratorio. He is also remembered for his Sevenfold Amen.
German composer Richard Strauss (1864-1949) completed his
Symphonic Fantasie Aus Italien, and the highly successful

team of William (Schwenck) Gilbert (1836-1911), the English
librettist and poet, and Sir Arthur (Seymour) Sullivan, the
popular English composer, collaborated once again to produce
Ruddigore in London. Also, the prominent Italian opera composer Giuseppe Verdi (1813-1901) saw his opera Otello performed on February 5, 1887, in Milan. It was based, of
course, on Shakespeare's play Othello, which was one of
several Shakespearean plays that inspired Verdi to put them
into operatic form.

This was also the year that the internationally known
Polish pianist and statesman, Ignace Jan Paderewski (1860-
1941), performed his first formal public recital in Vienna. He
received such acclaim that he was requested to play in all
parts of the world. In his book, Music in Harvard, Walter
R. Spalding relates a rather humorous episode relating to
Paderewski that took place at a meeting regarding the activities of the Harvard Pierian Sodality:

> February 27, 1893. There was a discussion as to
> whether it might be possible to arrange in Sanders
> Theatre a concert by the pianist, Paderewski, visiting
> this country for the first time. Later, Mr. Frothing-
> ham said that President Eliot refused to let Sanders
> be used for a public entertainment to which admission
> was charged, explaining the exception made in favor
> of the Boston Symphony Orchestra because it was
> "educational" (an early use of this overworked term!).
> Why, inquired the Sodality records, would not Pierian-
> cum-Paderewski be educational?[31]

During 1887, Queen Victoria (1819-1901) celebrated her
Golden Jubilee as Queen of England, and Sir Thomas More
(1478-1535) was beatified by Pope Leo XIII. Vincent Van
Gogh, the Dutch painter (1853-1890), completed his painting
called Moulin de la Galette.

One of the most interesting contributions to international
relations was the devising of Esperanto by Dr. L. L. Zamenhof
(1859-1917). Esperanto is an artificial language of international
use, chiefly European, based on words common to the main
European languages; it has self-evident parts of speech in
which all nouns end in "o", all adjectives in "a", etc., a
single and regular conjugation of verbs, a few simplified in-
flections, phonetic spelling and accented penults, etc.[32]

Unfortunately, this invention has not received the wide usage that was initially envisioned for it.

The literary world welcomed the first Sherlock Holmes mystery, A Study in Scarlet, written by Sir Arthur Conan Doyle (1850-1920), who was a British physician as well as a novelist and detective story writer. Many Sherlock Holmes stories were to follow such as The Sign of Four (1890) and The Hound of the Baskervilles in 1902, much to the delight of the reading public.

Another British author, both novelist and poet, Thomas Hardy (1840-1928), published his book The Woodlanders, which was preceded by his Far from the Maddening Crowd in 1874 and The Return of the Native in 1878. (Johan) August Strindberg (1849-1912), the Swedish novelist and playwright, produced Fadren in 1887, The Father in 1899, and Miss Julie in 1912. His dramas were widely acclaimed by the theatre-going public.

In the year 1888, H. Benjamin Harrison (1833-1902), son of William Henry Harrison, American general and ninth president of the United States, and grandson of Benjamin Harrison, a signer of the Declaration of Independence, was, himself, elected twenty-third president of the United States of America, and served as such from 1889* to 1893. That was the same year that the Henry Street Settlement House began in its first quarters on Jefferson Street on the Lower East Side of New York City.

Many musical events occurred in 1888, particularly in the European sector. Two Russian composers received important first performances of their works. The first was Peter Ilich Tschaikovsky (1840-1893) whose Symphony No. 5 in E minor was presented in St. Petersburg, as was "Scheherezade" from The Arabian Nights, Op. 35, a Symphonic Suite by Nicholas Andreievich Rimsky-Korsakov (1844-1908). This was also the year when Gustav Mahler (1860-1911) the Czech-born composer became the musical director of the Budapest Opera.

---

*The same year in which the College Settlement in New York City and Hull-House in Chicago were founded within a few days of each other.

At this period in American history, George Eastman (1854-1932) perfected the "Kodak" box camera, the manufacture of which was to grow to become the Eastman Kodak Company in Rochester, New York. Through the cultural leaning and the generosity of Mr. Eastman, the world-renowned Eastman School of Music was established in Rochester where it is now a professional school within the University of Rochester.

> It was George Eastman's love for the arts in Rochester and his desire to improve the use of leisure time by Americans generally that led him in 1918 to propose a school of music within the University of Rochester. The Eastman School of Music formally opened in 1921, becoming the first professional school of the University.
>
> The Eastman School was established at an opulent time in America, and school facilities such as the 3094-seat Eastman Theatre, the 459-seat Kilbourn Hall, and practice rooms numerous enough to be available without scheduling remain clear evidence of George Eastman's resources and of his dream for music and the arts in this country. [33]

George Eastman proved himself to be not only an inventor of great genius, but also an enormously generous philanthropist who clearly demonstrated his personal love for the arts and for his city, state and country.

Newspapers around the world reported that the first of all beauty contests was held in Spa, Belgium, and that "Jack the Ripper" horrified the civilized world by murdering six women in London. It was also the year in which Jim Thorpe was born. He died in 1953, but before his death, Thorpe had earned himself the reputation of being the world's greatest all-around athlete of all time. This country boasted that the American Lawn Tennis Association was founded, as was the first Football League.

In the year when Jane Addams revisited Toynbee Hall in London, 1888, three men were born to become internationally-known in the field of the arts. The first was the French entertainer Maurice Chevalier (1888-1972), who appeared as an actor, singer and dancer, and who was equally at home on

the stage, in radio and on television, as well as being a recording artist. He was internationally recognized and brought
his sophisticated entertainment to countless thousands world-
wide. He continued to perform until his death in 1972.

The literary community welcomed the writing of the
Anglo-American poet T. S. Eliot (1888-1965), whose works included Murder in the Cathedral (1935), Family Reunion (1939),
and The Cocktail Party (1949).

The American-born and -bred, and prolific author Eugene (Gladstone) O'Neill (1888-1953) wrote many plays which
included Emperor Jones (1920), The Hairy Ape (1922), Desire
Under the Elms (1924), The Great God Brown (1926), Strange
Interlude (1928), Mourning Becomes Electra, a Trilogy (1931),
The Iceman Cometh (1946), and Moon for the Misbegotten
(1957). Eugene O'Neill will be a long-remembered playwright
in the annals of American theatre and literature.

From the visual arts sector one finds that Vincent van
Gogh completed his painting The Yellow Chair, and the French
painter and lithographer Henri de Toulous-Lautrec (1860-
1901) finished his painting Place Clichy.

The evidence makes it abundantly clear, as we approach
a most significant era in the United States, that the world
was ready for and needed the courageous people in the arts
and in social services who were to become leaders in America's
movement to bring the arts to all!

The year 1889 was to prove to be a banner year for
this country. First the United States added four states to its
growing list. North and South Dakota each became a state
on November 2; Montana joined on November 8, 1889, and
Washington became a state on November 11 of that year.
Oklahoma became open territory for non-Indian settlers, but
was not to become a state until 1907.

Two more settlement houses were to be founded, the
College Settlement on the Lower East Side of New York City
and Hull-House in Chicago.

Established September 1, 1889 by the College Settlement Association with Jean G. Fine (Mrs. Charles
B. Spahr) as head worker with the purpose of

"establishing a home in a neighborhood of working people in which educated women might live, in order to furnish a common meeting ground for all classes for the mutual benefit and education."[34]

And in another section of the Woods and Kennedy book, one learns that the College Settlement has been located in many different places:

95 Rivington Street (1889); 188 Ludlow Street (1902-); 84-86 First Street (1907-); Summer Home, Mount Ivy, New York (1900-).

Activities: I. Investigations. The house has for many years carried on a series of sociological studies; largely into aspects of women's and children's life and labor; ...III. Local Institutional Improvement. Provided public baths for women; maintains a private playground in its yard; a library service, and for some years, a visiting library service; started a music school which later developed into the Music School Settlement.[35]

Daniel Levine in his book Jane Addams and the Liberal Tradition, differs slightly with Woods and Kennedy when he states:

...Three years after the opening of the Neighborhood Guild, two of Coit's associates founded America's second settlement, College Settlement, also in New York. A few months later Hull House [sic] became the third.[36]

Woods and Kennedy state that the founding of Hull-House was only a matter of seventeen days after the College Settlement opened.

Established September 18, 1889 by Jane Addams and Ellen Starr. "Hull-House was opened by two women backed by many friends, in the belief the mere foothold of a house, easily accessible, ample in space, hospitable and tolerant in spirit, situated in the midst of the large foreign colonies which would be in itself a serviceable thing for Chicago."[37]

Later in the Woods and Kennedy book is a description
of the art program as it was operated then at Hull-House:

> Art Work--Art Gallery (1891) with loan exhibits of
> pictures, engravings, etc.; cooperation in the move-
> ment to open the Art Institute Sunday afternoon;
> leadership in the Public School Art Society; Studio
> and classes in the arts of line and form; headquarters
> of the Chicago Arts and Crafts Society; Bookbindery;
> and studios of resident artists, shops for metal and
> other crafts. Good pictures have been hung in the
> various rooms for their educational effect. The thea-
> tre is frescoed. Music School (1893-); memorial
> organ; chorus; concerts, etc.; prizes for labor songs.
> Theatre; dramatic presentations of classic and modern
> plays by Hull-House and other companies; national
> plays by Greeks, Italians, Lithuanians, Bohemians,
> etc., moving picture show (1908).[38]

In her book Twenty Years at Hull-House, Jane Addams
recalls the first art exhibit when her London friends came to
open the exhibit.

> The first building erected for Hull-House contained
> an art gallery well lighted for day and evening use
> and our first exhibit of loaned pictures was opened
> in June, 1891, by Mr. and Mrs. Barnett of London.
> It is always pleasant to associate their hearty sym-
> pathy with that first exhibit, and thus to connect
> it with their pioneer efforts at Toynbee Hall to secure
> for working people the opportunity to know the best
> art, and with the first permanent art gallery in an
> industrial quarter.[39]

In a later comment about the arts in the Hull-House
program, Jane Addams made the following statement:

> The arts have, I think, always been embodied in
> the ultimate aim of Hull-House. From time to time in
> moments of depression or at exhilaration over some
> public undertaking to which the residents were com-
> mitted, we have urged Miss Smith to phrase in music
> the social compunction which at the moment it seemed
> impossible to express in any other way.[40]

Thus, one sees clearly that the Settlement House Movement carried with it the genuine, almost spiritual meaning of ventures into the world of the arts. Though the founders of the outstanding settlement houses of the nation may not have been performing or practicing artists in their own rights (though some of them have been), there was within each of them the concept of beauty and the need to express that understanding.

The appreciation for the arts was growing among the people throughout the world. International travel was more and more common, and crossing the Atlantic was becoming readily possible. In 1889 Cesar Franck (1822-1890) had his Symphony in D minor performed for the first time; Richard Strauss' Symphonic Poem Don Juan had its premier performance in Weimar; and Gilbert and Sullivan collaborated once again, this time to present The Gondoliers in London.

The theatrical world marks 1889 as an important year, since both Jean Cocteau, the French writer, artist, stage designer and producer, and George S. Kaufman, the brilliant American playwright were born. Cocteau (1889-1963) lived to the age of 74, and Kaufman (1889-1961) died at age 72. It was also the year in which Robert Browning died. He was born in 1812 and became an internationally recognized English poet who married Elizabeth Barrett (Browning) (1806-1861), the recognized British poetess. In this year, Robert Louis Stevenson completed his novel The Master of Ballantrae, and Vincent van Gogh produced his painting called Landscape with Cypress Tree. The educational world welcomed the opening of the Catholic University of America in Washington, D. C. The ominous event of the year was the birth of Adolph Hitler, who was to become the German Nazi dictator.

The dawn of the decade known as the Gay Nineties was welcomed with enthusiasm. The United States of America accepted two more states into its inner circle as Idaho became the forty-third state of the Union on July 3, and Wyoming became the forty-fourth on July 10, 1890, each accepting the responsibility of becoming part of this great nation in the first year of the last decade of this century.

Three internationally known and recognized statesmen, each from a different country, were born in 1890:

From America: Dwight D. Eisenhower, who became an American
          general, the thirty-fourth president of the United States
          of America from 1953 to 1961, and supreme Allied com-
          mander in Europe in World War II.

From France: Charles DeGaulle, who became a French general,
          a statesman, premier from 1958-1959, and president
          from 1959 to 1969.

From Russia: Vyacheslav Molotov, who became a Russian
          statesman, and foreign minister from 1939 to 1949 and
          from 1953 to 1956.

Each of these men was to become a figure of political power
and strength in his own country, as well as a recognized leader with whom the entire world would have to reckon.

The opera Prince Igor by the Russian scientist and
composer Alexander Porphyrievich Borodin (1834-1887), was
performed posthumously in St. Petersburg, and Richard
Strauss, the German composer and conductor, added to his
list of outstanding orchestral compositions with his Symphonic
Poem Tod und Verkärung (Death and Transfiguration). Another opera, Cavalleria Rusticana, by the Italian composer
Pietro Mascagni (1863-1945), received its first performance
in Rome. While this opera received literally wild acclaim, its
substance and charm were never again realized by Mascagni.
This was also the year in which the world mourned the death
of the French composer César Franck (1822-1890), who is
probably best remembered for his setting of the Panis Angel-
icus.

Heinrik Ibsen (1828-1906), the Norwegian poet and
dramatist, produced what has become one of his most important
plays, Hedda Gabler, in 1890. His works for the stage created much interest, particularly in his own native country and
included such plays as The Doll's House in 1883; Ghosts in
1888; The Master Builder in 1893; and The Wild Duck in 1905.
Several of his plays translated into English are studied and
performed at colleges and universities in this country today,
nearly one hundred years later. In Great Britain, Oscar
Fingall O'Flahertie Willis Wilde (1854-1900), better known simply as Oscar Wilde, wrote his novel The Picture of Dorian
Gray, which was later to have a motion picture adaptation
made in America with the same title.

The art community learned of the death of Vincent van Gogh who had been born in 1853. Paul Cézanne (1839-1906), the French post-impressionist painter, completed his painting The Cardplayers. By this time, Cézanne had become internationally known and recognized.

News from around the world carried the information of a devastating influenza epidemic spreading throughout the world. Eighteen ninety was also the year in which rubber gloves were used for the first time in surgery at the Johns Hopkins Hospital in Baltimore, Maryland.

The first moving picture show appeared in New York City launching the United States into an entertainment era previously never imagined for the common man. It was also the year when the Daughters of the American Revolution was founded in Washington, D. C.

By comparison, the year 1891 seems to have been one of less artistic significance. It is surrounded, however, by two years which were rich and plentiful in artistic development and world events. The records show that such authors as James Barrie, Sir Arthur Conan Doyle, Thomas Hardy, and Rudyard Kipling, all English, added much to the literary world. Global events noted the devastating results of 18 earthquakes in Japan which killed some ten thousand people. In America, W. I. Judson invented the zipper which revolutionized the clothing industry.

The year 1892 is distinctive in the history of the United States of America. It is the only election year in this country when a president was elected to his second, but non-consecutive, term of office. He was (Stephen) Grover Cleveland, who was elected in 1884 as the twenty-second president of the United States and served that term from 1885 to 1889, and as twenty-fourth president upon his election in 1892 to serve from 1893 to 1897.

Eighteen ninety-two saw the birth of two more settlement houses in New York City, one on the Upper West Side and the other on the Lower East Side, each including some forms of music and arts in its program. The first is the Riverside House on the West Side and the other is called Jacob Riis Neighborhood Settlement named after the famous American journalist, photographer and author. Riis wrote extensively on living conditions in the tenements. Among his books were <u>The Battle with the Slum</u>, <u>The Children of the Poor</u>, <u>The Children of the Tenements</u>, <u>How the Other Half Lives</u>, and <u>Theodore Roosevelt, the Citizen</u>.

The cultural life in this country was thriving. Literary works, artistic masterpieces, and musical compositions from Europe were finding their ways to America, much to the enjoyment of the populace. The country was maturing in economic, sociological and cultural ways considerably. A cursory glance at the world's enrichment in the area of the fine arts shows the following:

In literature <u>Mrs. Warren's Profession</u> was written by George Bernard Shaw (1856-1950), the Irish dramatist, who was later to receive the Nobel Prize in Literature in 1925.

<u>Barrack-Room Ballads</u> was completed by Rudyard Kipling (1865-1936), the English author who also wrote <u>Wee Willie Winkie and Other Child Stories</u> in 1888, <u>The Light That Failed</u> in 1890, and <u>The Jungle Book</u> in 1894, and many other books that became beloved around the world.

<u>Children of the Ghetto</u> was written by yet another English novelist and poet, Israel Zangwill (1864-1926).

Emile Zola (1840-1902), the French novelist, wrote <u>La Débâcle</u> and subsequently other well received novels. He is also well known for his book <u>The Dreyfus Case</u>.

Maurice Maeterlinck (1862-1949), the Belgian poet and dramatist, wrote his play <u>Pelléas et Mélisande</u>, which was later to be turned into operatic form by the French composer Claude Debussy (1862-1918). It was composed over a ten-year period and completed probably in 1902. It is more correctly called a lyrical drama.

The play <u>Lady Windemere's Fan</u> by the Irish dramatist and novelist, Oscar Wilde, was completed in 1892.

In Great Britain, Alfred, Lord Tennyson, the English poet-laureate, died; in America, Walt Whitman, the poet who is probably best known for his <u>Leaves of Grass</u>, also died.

In the year 1892, the French impressionist painter Claude Monet (1840-1926), began his series of paintings of the Rouen Cathedral.

The world of music was alive with activity. Anton
Bruckner, the Austrian composer, had his Symphony No. 8
performed for the first time in Vienna. Ruggiero Leoncavallo
(1858-1919), the Italian operatic composer, completed his
opera I Pagliacci, and like Richard Wagner, the German composer of music dramas, wrote his own libretto for his opera.
As Pietro Mascagni had done just two years earlier, Leoncavallo
received much critical acclaim for his opera, but none of his
other works achieved such success. It is interesting to observe today that Cavalleria Rusticana by Mascagni and I Pagliacci by Leoncavallo are frequently presented on the same
program as a double bill. Also in this exciting musical year,
the Russian composer, Peter Ilitch Tschaikovsky (1840-1893),
composed his ever popular ballet The Nutcracker.

At this time in the history of America's musical life, an
important event occurred which involved the Czech composer
Anton Dvorak (1841-1906), and is related in Grove's Dictionary
of Music and Musicians (Third Edition, 1935) as follows:

> Meanwhile the fame of Dvorak's name had reached
> overseas. A number of his more important works
> having found their way to various centres [sic] in
> America, American musical circles desired to follow the
> example of England and to make the personal acquain-
> tance of the great Czech musician.
> At the invitation of Mrs. Thurber, the foundress
> of the National Conservatory of Music in New York,
> Dvorak, in 1892, accepted the directorship of this
> institution, and having obtained leave from the Prague
> Conservatoire, migrated to America, where he met
> with a splendid reception and remained for three years,
> being greatly appreciated there as a teacher, a con-
> ductor of his own works, and, of course, as a com-
> poser. His aim of developing a national school of
> composition among his American pupils met--as may
> be well understood--with no success. [41]

The National Conservatory of Music had been founded
by Jeanette Thurber in 1885 (just the year before Stanton Coit
established the first settlement house in America), and it was
granted a national charter in 1891. In 1923 it was absorbed
by the New York College of Music, which was later taken over
by New York University in 1968.

At this period in the history of the United States,
Americans were only too willing to accept the advice, direction,
training and teaching of those artists who had come from
Europe, while they were not willing to recognize the developing
capabilities of America's own composers, conductors, and most
of all teachers and instructors. Our cultural advancement
had not yet been appreciated, correctly evaluated, or accepted by the people of our own nation.

Today it is with deep appreciation and gratitude that
Americans from all walks of life recognize and accept the idea
for the development of the Community Music School born during
this turbulent and difficult period in our history. The Community Music School is a uniquely American institution. This
American cultural brainchild has made a significant contribution to the world of music and music education in this country
for the past ninety years. It must also be realized that the
community music school is an inspirational and enthusiastic
cultural flame, burning brightly, spread to ignite the same
desire in the other arts--drama, dance, pottery, painting,
sculpture and literature. So strong was that burning need
that community music schools were urged to accept the responsibility of welcoming the other arts into their basic programs. Ultimately there developed a new organization--The
National Guild of Community Schools of the Arts. (There will
be more about this in a later chapter.)

Let us, then, give credit where credit is due! The
development of the community music school came directly from
the settlement house movement in America at the turn of the
century, which in turn had been inspired by the social work
done so successfully at Toynbee Hall in London. And it was
the American social workers who first adopted the early music
teachers giving them a place to function. Without the generosity of the College Settlement in New York City, Emilie Wagner might not have been able to persevere to establish the
Music School Settlement of Third Street. Thus it was the
settlement houses that saw the need for music and the other
arts in the community and began to include music in their
programs, particularly those organizations along the eastern
seaboard.

The community music school, per se, evolved initially
because there were those on staff who cared about the quality
and standards of the musical instruction given to those who

needed and requested excellent training, not necessarily for achieving professional performance careers, but that training, too, should have been available for outstandingly gifted students. It is fitting then, that the development of such schools should occur here, in America--a democracy, and the only country in the world to offer such an opportunity to its citizens, and especially to its young people. It is most important to note that the support of these schools comes from their local communities and their neighbors, not primarily from the state or large national government grants. It is with great pride that we should show this, one of our major musical contributions to the world-at-large. (Additional information will be presented in a later chapter on the structure of community music schools.)

In 1893 the Henry Street Settlement was begun on the Lower East Side of Manhattan. Its initial thrust was to help the newly arrived neighborhood members with their health problems in this teeming and polyglot city. Lillian D. Wald and her companion, Mary Brewster, were astounded at the squalid living conditions very much evident throughout the Lower East Side.

Reminiscent of the path followed by Emilie Wagner of the Music School Settlement of Third Street, Lillian Wald and Mary Brewster received assistance from the College Settlement on Rivington Street in lower New York. Through a friend, Miss Wald met two gentlemen who were very knowledgeable about real estate and living conditions in this highly populated section of the city.

> ...I soon learned, they were competent to speak with authority, they set out with me at once, in a pouring rain, to scout the adjacent streets for "To Let" signs. One which seemed to me worth investigating my newly acquired friends discarded with the explanation that it was in the "red light" district and would not do. Later I was to know much of the unfortunate women who inhabited the quarters, but at the time the term meant nothing to me.
> After a long tour one of my guides, as if by inspiration, reminded the other that several young women had taken a house on Rivington Street for something like my purpose, and perhaps I had better live there temporarily and take my time in finding satisfactory

quarters. Upon that advice I acted, and within a
few days, Miss Brewster and I found ourselves guests
at the luncheon table of the College Settlement on
Rivington Street. [42]

The two young nurses were to remain about two months
at the College Settlement, and Miss Wald further relates the
success of finding living quarters allowing them to begin their
work:

> Before September of the year 1893 we found a house
> on Jefferson Street, the only one in which our careful
> search disclosed the desired bathtub. ...Naturally,
> objections to two young women living alone in New
> York under these conditions had to be met, and some
> assurance as to our material comfort was given to
> anxious, though at heart sympathetic, families by
> compromising on good furniture, a Baltimore heater
> for cheer, and simple but adequate household appur-
> tenances. Painted floors with easily removed rugs,
> windows curtained with spotless but inexpensive scrim,
> a sitting-room with pictures, books and restful chairs,
> a tiny bedroom which we two shared, a small dining-
> room [sic] in which the family mahogany did not look
> out of place, and a kitchen, constituted our home for
> two full years. [43]

The problems the neighbors brought to the two nurses
far exceeded health problems alone, and the great needs of
the neighbors made Lillian Wald realize that it would be impossible for them to extend their efforts to other areas while
they were in such limited space. And so, through the generosity of Jacob Schiff, the well-recognized American philanthropist, the building at 265 Henry Street was purchased in
1895 to allow expansion of the program of the Nurses Settlement as Henry Street was often called. Many other buildings
were to be added in the future, but in 1895 Miss Wald grate-
fully stated, "From this first house have since developed the
manifold activities in city and country now incorporated as
the Henry Street Settlement." [44]

With her genuine interest in the arts, it was only a
short period of time before they permeated the Henry Street
program, and the organization grew to include a music school,
a theatre housing programs of dance and drama, a pottery,

a painting studio, an arts and crafts center primarily designed
for those in the geriatrics program, as well as a community
mental health center, and programs for young children, teenagers, and adults. Most of these programs began as clubs,
whether by design or accidental happening is not clearly known,
but clubs were the popular, functioning groups.

Lillian Wald recounts the use of clubs in the earliest
days of the Henry Street Settlement:

> I do not know who originated the idea of a "club"
> as a means of guidance and instruction for the young.
> Our inducement to organize socially came from a group
> of small boys in the summer of 1895, our first in the
> Henry Street house. We had already acquired a large
> circle of juvenile friends, and it soon became evident
> that definite hours must be set aside for meeting dif-
> ferent groups if our time was not to be dissipated in
> fragmentary visits. When these boys of eleven and
> twelve years of age, who had not up to that time,
> given any evidence of partiality for our society, called
> to ask if they could see me some time when I "wasn't
> busy". I made an appointment with them for the next
> Saturday evening, whereupon the club was organized.
> It is still in existence with practically the original
> membership [written in 1915]; and the relationship
> of the members of this first group to the settlement
> and to me personally has been of priceless value. [45]

Many years later, Miss Wald continued to comment on
the value of clubs.

> It would be all too easy to write an entire chapter
> about Henry Street Clubs. No two of them are alike
> in the circumstances of organization, the way they
> hold their meetings, their "rules", their programmes,
> their goals. And yet each one, almost always con-
> sciously, has functioned as a means of education,
> and as a source of mental and spiritual enrichment
> as well as of "good times".
> ...A group seldom rises above the stature of the
> leader, but an intelligent leader, unhampered by
> rules and routine, can bring the members to original
> thought and initiative. [46]

Though it is a simple task for the writer to regale the reader with a listing of the arts ultimately available at the Henry Street Settlement, it is far more significant to read the words of the first and most recognized headworker when she comments on them.

> ...Our experience on Henry Street show that outlets through the arts and crafts--music, painting, pottery, woodwork, and kindred projects--give more lasting satisfaction when they are shaped by teachers who, in their approach to both child and grown-up, recognize the high educational significance of these activities.
> Our pottery shop was organized by a talented teacher who is now the director of the art department in the Settlement. From it there went to the Century of Progress Exhibition a beautifully modeled representation of the back of the House on Henry Street, and the garden which converted into the first organized public playground in New York.[47]

Further words of Miss Wald tell of the work of the Music School and Playhouse of the Henry Street Settlement.

> Under the direction of a gifted woman [Hedi Katz] the music school now holds a distinguished place in our programme. It was established after many years of music in classes, in clubs, in orchestra, in balalaika ensemble, in glee clubs.[48]

She continued her statement, this time regarding the Playhouse.

> But none of our activities in the arts is to be compared with the contributions made by Alice and Irene Lewisohn through their inspired leadership in the theatre. ...They first came to Henry Street as young girls, and they brought with them rare gifts of personality and talent. They served a long apprenticeship with clubs and classes, but soon began to originate art forms through new combinations of the elements of the drama and of pageantry.[49]

In her book Unfinished Business, Helen Hall, the second director of the Henry Street Settlement from 1933 to 1967, comments also on the work of the Lewisohn sisters.

Miss Wald had been fortunate in having these young
girls come to work with her as she expanded her work.
Alice and Irene Lewisohn and Rita Wallach Morganthau,
who came as volunteers in 1904, were very young,
very spirited, and gifted in the arts, and Miss Wald
encouraged them in their enthusiasms as they took
a salient part in developing the arts in Henry Street's
program.[50]

Lillian D. Wald concludes her chapter on education and
the arts with these words:

Through the informal workshops and the studies,
through recreation as well as through the beautiful
festivals and the plays, through music and the opportunities that have presented themselves, intertwin-
ing education and the arts, it is impressed upon us
that the world has barely awakened to the force and
the importance that may be afforded to old and young,
to the happy, to the weary, and to the inhibited.
The writer has designedly emphasized the arts, the
influence of creative expression and the sense of new
powers, as an essential part of education. G.B.S.
[George Bernard Shaw], our modern stimulator, has
felt the urge of this: "Every device of art should
be brought to bear on the young, so that they may
discover some form of it that delights them naturally,
for there will come to all of them that period between
dawning adolescence and full maturity when the pleas-
ures and emotions of art will have to satisfy cravings
which, if starved or insulted, may become morbid and
disgraceful satisfactions, and, if prematurely gratified
otherwise than poetically, may destroy the stamina of
the race."[*]
    But long, long ago Confucius, out of his wisdom,
spoke thus: "Man has no place in society unless he
understands aesthetics."[51]

An energetic, well-educated, and attractive young woman
was to arrive on the scene who was to contribute much to the
social work field and to the development of yet another settlement house where music and the other arts were to thrive in

---

*From Bernard Shaw, by Frank Harris.

the programs of the institution. Her name was Mary M. Kingsbury, later to be known as Mary K. Simkhovitch, after having
married Professor Vladimir Simkhovitch, whom she had met
during the year she had spent in Europe. She had apparently
been doing much personal soul-searching in order to determine
what career path to follow during her European travels.

> ...Sociology and economics and history would surely
> turn out to have a reality and a validity for one if
> one could gain a wider personal experience. I was
> glad, therefore, when the opportunity now came for
> me to live at the College Settlement. I had given up
> the idea of a church settlement which I had vaguely
> thought of in Boston days, for I felt that there could
> hardly be such a thing.
> ...I was drawn to the idea of plunging into life
> where it was densest and most provocative. There
> was no longer the divided allegiance in my mind to
> the University and the City. The city's problems,
> and especially the life and fortunes of the great influx
> of Europeans to America, far outweighed in challenge
> and attraction the call to academic life.
> In the long summer holiday I returned to the British
> Museum for study. Then in September, 1897, I un-
> packed my trunk and hung up my hat and coat at
> 95 Rivington Street.[52]

As if following a prescribed path in the footsteps of
Emilie Wagner, Lillian D. Wald, and Mary Brewster, Mary
Kingsbury took up residence at the College Settlement in the
Lower East Side of New York which she described as follows:

> Rivington Street was crowded and noisy and rank
> with the smell of overripe fruit, hot bread and sweat-
> soaked clothing. The sun poured down relentlessly
> and welded the East Side together in one impress of
> fetid fertility. Neither in Phillips Street among my
> colored friends in Boston nor in the East End of Lon-
> don was there the vivid sense of a new and overpower-
> ing vitality such as emanated from the neighborhood
> of the College Settlement.[53]

Somewhat to her surprise she found action in the Settlement that she had not really anticipated.

...In the front basement Miss Emily [sic] Wagner
began the music school. It is said that one child
practiced on one end of the piano and another on the
other end. At any rate, violin lessons soon overflowed
into the basement half. To Sara's [the cook] patience
as well as to Miss Wagner's genius is due the immediate
success of the music lessons. The neighborhood avidly
responded to the opportunity; before my year was
up a floor was engaged in the wooden house opposite,
and the music school began to live its own life. Later
it combined with the University Settlement Music School
and then emerged into [sic] the Third Street Music
School Settlement with a house of its own.[54]

Simkhovitch further makes a brief comment about the human
products that arose from this overcrowded and difficult part
of the City known as the Lower East Side.

...From the slavery of the tenement sweatshop have
arisen leaders in industry, in education, in art and
in political life. Indeed, the old East Side was the
fertile producer of today's judges, teachers, actors,
musicians, playwrights and leaders in New York.[55]

After her year's introduction to the Lower East Side and
its social problems, Mary Kingsbury accepted a post at the
Friendly Aid House on East Thirty-fourth Street, a position
in which she remained for a three year period. Philosophical
differences between some of the board members and herself
made it impossible for her to remain in that position, though
the parting of the ways was very affable and friendly. Her
next step was of great importance!

In leaving the Friendly Aid House to found a society
in accordance with our own ideals, we had no regrets
for our happy years there, and only gratitude for the
opportunity of learning at firsthand those principles
of organization, growth and social adjustment which
no books can teach and only experience can convey.[56]

As a young, married woman whose career was only just
blooming, it took great courage to develop and plan her next
move carefully, but with her friends and colleagues the move
was made with much excitement.

> ...In 1901 we embarked upon an enterprise founded
> on the principles in which we believed, and endorsed
> by some of our friends in New York who were so gen-
> erous as to have confidence in us and our ideas.
> Thus Greenwich House came into being.[57]

The group of friends were certainly gentlemen of distinction and excellent reputation.

> The incorporators of the Cooperative Social Settlement
> Society, as we called our new organization, were
> Henry C. Potter, then Bishop of the Episcopal Diocese
> of New York, Eugene Philbin, a prominent Roman
> Catholic layman afterwards judge, Carl Schurz, Jacob
> Riis, Felix Adler, Robert Fulton Cutting, and myself.
>   This group represented a variety of approaches
> to the social problem. Bishop Potter had been a leader
> in the exposé of the red-light district; Dr. Adler was
> deeply involved in the improvement of tenements; as
> was Mr. Cutting; Jacob Riis was for slum clearance;
> Carl Schurz for civil service reforms; Judge Philbin
> was identified with movements for a better conduct
> of political life.[58]

Much like the experience of the Henry Street Settlement,
early appearance of music and the arts was in the group or
club situation, and Simkhovitch relates how the music school
came to be.

> This branch of our work began as an informal social
> interest on Jones Street, with the summer concerts
> on our front steps in 1903 and then taking pupils as
> they came to us for better musical training. Music
> in the public schools has been confined to the voice,
> with a few informal orchestras here and there. Music
> techniques, whether for piano or strings, have been
> regarded as matters of private education...we also
> never aimed to develop a conservatory whose object
> would be professional training or performance. We
> hoped to combine the merits of superior technical
> training with no illusion we were creating, unless as
> outstanding exceptions, professional artists. We hoped
> rather to create a musical center for interest, under-
> standing, performance and joint musical effort which
> would set afire the lukewarm, hearten the eager and
> praise that civilizing effect music uniquely conveys.[59]

As this statement explains, Mrs. Simkhovitch comes closest to the concept regarding the establishment of a community music school. The implications suggest enormous responsibility to be placed on the shoulders of the directors and staff members in performing their duties.

With all this genuine appreciation and understanding, Greenwich House did not have a formal music school until 1914 (the year of the outbreak of World War I), with Marion Rous as director. A twelve year span before the establishment of the Greenwich House Music School does not seem so long when one considers that it took the Henry Street Settlement thirty-four years to open the Henry Street Settlement Music School in 1927 with Hedi Katz as director. The organization which took its steps in reverse order is the Third Street Music School Settlement which began by giving lessons first, and as its enrollment grew and new space was found, began to undertake more of what might have been classified as "settlement responsibilities" as described earlier in this chapter. Hull-House in Chicago followed a path similar to Henry Street and Greenwich House, though it imposed more stringent entrance requirements for its newly arriving music students.

The establishment of each of the three schools mentioned above came about because there was an expressed need from the neighbors. It is undoubtedly true that the European immigrants brought with them an already ingrained love for music and the arts with great respect for serious musical and artistic training. The backgrounds of the three directors showed that they, too, recognized the need to be able to express one's self musically or artistically. They were not superimposing their own aims and goals upon the neighbors in the community, but rather were simply responding to the desires of those who came to their doorsteps.*

A genuine respect is reflected for these organizations and their counterparts in the recent edition of The New Grove

---

*It is a tribute to Settlement Music Schools that they were included in Grove's Dictionary of Music and Musicians in the Third Edition in 1935 with two separate entries. See Vol. III, p. 628, and the American Supplement of that Edition, Edited by Waldo Selden Pratt, pp. 301, 302. Each is under Music School Settlements.

Dictionary of Music and Musicians under the section dedicated
to the educational music institutions founded in New York City
when it says the following:

> ...The National Conservatory of Music in America
> founded by Jeanette Thurber in 1885, was granted
> a national charter in 1891. ...A Metropolitan Con-
> servatory, begun as a school of singing in 1886, be-
> came the Metropolitan College of Music in 1891 and the
> American Institute of Music in 1900. Both institu-
> tions survived at least 40 years but eventually suc-
> cumbed to financial troubles. Settlement schools found-
> ed from 1894 to provide musical training for under-
> privileged children fared better. The Henry Street,
> Greenwich House, Third Street and Turtle Bay music
> schools were among those that survive.[60]

One must notice continued insistence upon quality and
standards in the teaching of music and the arts within the
settlement structure. While formats and programs may remain
fundamentally similar, new aspects of programming are con-
tinously welcome in settlements. Change is not only accepted, encouraged, and welcome--as it should be--but it is
never feared. This writer well remembers a statement
that Helen Hall, director of the Henry Street Settlement from
1933 to 1967, made frequently to her staff members. It was
this: "The poorest excuse possible for continuing any program is to say, 'Oh, we've always done it like this before!'"

Mary K. Simkhovitch gives us a strong philosophical
statement which encourages social workers, musicians, artists,
teachers and neighbors to live, work, perform and create
with mutual respect for each individual when she says: "If
I, too, have learned anything throughout these many years,
it is surely this, that it is our common life that matters, and
that to stay apart from it is the death of art, of politics and
of religion."[61]

3

THE COMMUNITY MUSIC SCHOOL:
An American First

One cannot envision, plan, or construct any organization
without first knowing and expressing the philosophy which
should clearly state the organization's reason for being.
Much thought and consideration should of necessity be given
to the philosophical statement, and each operational or structural procedure should reflect the goals of the instituiton.

Oftentimes operational problems can be solved by techniques which are not in compliance with the stated organizational raison d'etre. This should never happen. All responsible members of the school's structure--members of the
board of directors, administrators, faculty members and clerical staff should keep this in mind constantly.

In her book Music, Youth and Opportunity, Janet D.
Schenck stated the following information:

> A Music School Settlement aims to put the highest
> musical education within the reach of serious students
> whose circumstances do not allow them to pay profes-
> sional rates. The student is taught by a thoroughly
> qualified teacher for a sum which does not force both
> parent and child to cheat the body in order to nourish
> the mind. The difference between the fee paid by
> the pupil and the cost of the lesson is made up by
> the School.[1]

In the doctoral thesis "The History of the Music School
of the Henry Street Settlement," the author identifies some
of the qualities of a community music school.

> Community Music School is used to indicate an insti-
> tution which offers musical instruction at a nominal

> cost, and which is non-profit, non-sectarian and is
> situated in the United States or Canada. This term
> is sometimes interchangeable with Music School Settle-
> ment.[2]

In these two statements it is important to note the
reference to the lower or reasonable fees to be paid by the
student and his family. It is also wise to note the use of
the words highest, serious or qualified. Each is a favorably
descriptive adjective indicating that such schools offer studies
and programs of the finest quality. No mention is made of the
student's need to have great talent, though such a pupil can
find a person under whose tutelage he will be well trained
and taught in a community music school. Quality and standards are observed in the educational process. The school's
responsibility is to offer the student the training he needs
at the moment, after he has been carefully evaluated and
placed.

There must be serious purpose and effort on the part
of the student. He should be responsible for reasonable
progress commensurate with his musical ability, his physical
adaptability to the instrument of his choice and his own intellectual capacity or intelligence.

In the 1957-1958 academic season the National Guild of
Community Music Schools produced a MANUAL--A Guide for
the Establishment and Administration of a Community Music
School. The National Guild stated this philosophy:

> The philosophy of a Community Music School embraces
> a multitude of concepts which arise from the aesthetic,
> social, psychological and economic requirements and
> conditions of people. The schools recognize Man's
> search for beauty and see in music an expression and
> gratification of this quest. Instituted at the request
> of people who wished to express themselves in a tonal
> medium, the Community Music School is dedicated to
> the realization and development of the innate musical-
> ity of the individual. The philosophy further contends
> that music is not the isolated experience of an indi-
> vidual, but also a group activity involving the entire
> imagination of composers, performers and listeners
> alike; that music is not simply the business of mu-
> sicians or the intellectually minded, but an expression

of the emotional fibre of mankind.

The Community Music School believes that music can be used as a tool to aid in one's social development by serving as a beautiful and significant unifying factor in family life. By bringing together people from different ethnic, economic and intellectual groups to share a common experience, music can promote an understanding and appreciation for the spiritual values of all people, as it is practiced in these schools. Through the cultivation of this medium of expression, people who would otherwise be inarticulate are able to reach out and communicate meaningfully with their fellow men. By actively participating in a field of interest as well as submitting to the mental discipline required in the study of music, the individual is better equipped to meet the obligations and needs of society as an active citizen, a responsible adult and a directed human being.

It is this respect for the intrinsic nobility of the individual, coupled with a consideration of his specific musical endowments, which permeates the fabric of Community Music Schools. Music instruction is not dogmatic, but flexibly geared to the potentialities and needs of the student. He is encouraged to make music an integral part of his life, and to this end the finest available facilities are harnessed. Well-qualified and inspired teachers, understanding of music, guidance through interviews and placement auditions, the opportunity to exercise discrimination and to develop musical taste by exposure to the finest of music, and the experience of working in an atmosphere devoted to the pursuit of beauty are all placed at his disposal.

Community Music Schools recognize few of the restrictions imposed by other institutions. Instruction is not confined to any one age group, nor is it limited by the student's financial circumstances. Through the granting of full or partial scholarships, the use of a sliding scale of fees, and by offering reasonable rates for all, the financial barrier, which so often stifles spiritual growth, is removed. A broad curriculum, presenting diversified instrumental, vocal and theoretical instruction, provides a greater choice of medium and creates a richer musical community.

In addition to these concepts, there is the responsibility of the Community Music School to function

in its community in a spirit of cooperation with social
service agencies, public and parochial schools and
other teaching and cultural organizations. It absorbs
the cultural birthright and creative aspirations of the
community, and returns this heritage and hope ful-
filled.[3]

[With a sincere attempt to maintain accuracy, the
above statement is quoted exactly as it was presented
in 1958. Since the National Guild broadened its base
to accept the other art forms and as of 1974 changed
its title to include the other arts, it is a simple matter
to substitute "the arts" for "music" and correct the
verb forms to reflect the title, the National Guild of
Community Schools of the Arts.]

Many of the National Guild's member schools reflect the
Guild's philosophy in their various publications--catalogues,
brochures and fliers using brief, succinct announcements. A
few short samples follow:

Cleveland Music School Settlement

When the Cleveland Music School Settlement was
founded, it was intended that no one be denied professional musical instruction because of his inability
to pay for it. Although the School has grown and
changed in many ways, the original ideal has remained
with fees set according to a sliding scale based on
the individual's ability to pay.

Catalogue, 1973-74

Neighborhood Music School, New Haven

The Neighborhood Music School is a private, nonprofit
institution incorporated for the following purposes:
1) to give individuals an opportunity to study, practice
and perform good music; 2) to bring into the home
the influence of the best in music; 3) to provide a
broad social service through this medium; 4) to furnish
musical instruction at fees as low as possible; 5) to
maintain a staff of capable teachers.

Brochure, 1978-79

USC Community School of Performing Arts, Los Angeles

To provide quality instruction and experience in music, dance and drama to the student who desired cultural enrichment as well as an intensive work for a career.

The introduction was so successful and popular with the children that parents requested year-around instruction.

In 1973 the name of the school was changed in order to reflect the subjects as a change in philosophy-- that all people who wished to study were welcome, not just children interested in becoming musicians.

Information flier, undated

Settlement Music School, Philadelphia

The SETTLEMENT MUSIC SCHOOL was founded in 1908 to give children the finest music education regardless of sex, race religion, physical disability ... Many of the children cannot pay the full fee and for those we do everything in our power. Aid is based on talent or proven need.

Catalogue, Seventy-first Season, 1978-79

National Guild of Community Schools of the Arts

The Guild's primary mission is to provide serious and meaningful arts instruction and exposure to all who seek it, regardless of age, ability or financial circumstances. Thus, while committed to the training and development of the individual, the Guild is also dedicated to the cultivation of an informed and discerning audience which understands and appreciates the arts and can support the preservation of its own cultural heritage.

National Guild of Community Schools of the Arts Brochure, 1985

Music and other art forms--dance, drama, pottery, painting and visual arts--contribute to the development of creativity
and artistic imagination. They bring personal satisfaction,
pride, a sense of accomplishment and contentment to the American
people, pre-schoolers, children, teen-agers, adults and senior
citizens. These modes of expression are found in all American
communities, urban, suburban and rural.

While Americans' appreciation for the arts may not have
been developing in so sophisticated a manner or in such depth
as it should have been in this richly endowed country, much
thought and interest is now developing throughout the land.
This is true for many reasons, one of which certainly is the
spread of community schools of the arts from coast to coast,
and the pattern of beginning to teach toddlers the fundamen-
tals or rudiments of music training such as done in the Suzuki Talent Education program.

It has taken us many years to recognize, evaluate and
ultimately to appreciate the talents that exist within our own
countrymen. Talents that have lain dormant for many years--
years when arduous labor occupied the time of most adults,
and when children at very early ages began to assist the
family to survive by performing tasks necessary to sustain
life. Little time was left for exploration within the arts!!!

Lying dormant in the souls of Americans does not indicate that there was a lack of interest in the arts. Rather,
as history shows, the flames of artistic creativity developed
and functioned best in the major cities such as Chicago, New
York City, Boston and Philadelphia where the very heaviest
populations forced people to live in congested, crowded, air-
less, hot and humid quarters in dank and dark apartment
dwellings where many family members shared few and small
rooms in the apartments. As described by Lillian D. Wald
in her book <u>The House on Henry Street</u>, "the family of seven
shared their two rooms with boarders--who were literally boarders, since a piece of timber was placed over the floor for them
to sleep on."[4]

One can imagine the anguish and compassion that Miss
Wald and her companion, Mary Brewster, felt as Miss Wald
continues with a further explanation:

...Any pride in the sacrifice of material comfort which

might have risen within us was effectually inhibited
by the constant reminder that we two young persons
occupied exactly the same space as the large families
on every floor below us, and to one of our basement
friends at least we were luxurious beyond the dream
of ordinary folk.

The little lad from the basement was our first invited guest. The simple but appetizing dinner my
comrade prepared, while I set the table and placed
the flowers. The boy's mother came up later in the
evening to find out what we had given him, for Tom-
mie had rushed down with eyes bulging and had reported that "them ladies live like the Queen of England
and eat off solid gold plates."[5]

This book is designed to present the advent and history
of community schools of the arts in this country. The schools
chosen for special study and consideration are member schools
of the National Guild of Community Schools of the Arts, which
celebrated its fiftieth anniversary in the Fall of 1987.

As stated earlier the community school of the arts had
its origin in the Settlement House Movement in this country.
The initial term which explained such an organization was
Music School Settlement or Settlement Music School. Many of
the early schools had the term settlement in their titles, (e.g.
Cleveland Music School Settlement, Cleveland, Ohio; Settle-
ment Music School in Philadelphia, Pennsylvania; Third Street
Music School Settlement, New York, New York; and The
University Settlement Music School, Toronto, Ontario, Canada).
All of these continue to use their original titles.

Using the term "community" in titles seems to have been
preferred by many organizations, for one frequently sees
Community Music Center, or Community Music School, Community School of the Arts, Community School of Music and
Arts, Community School of Performing Arts, etc.

In 1940 the organization (then known as The National
Guild of Community Music Schools) began a publication called
The Quarterly. In its first issue, Volume I, Number 1,
May 1940, the following article appeared:

OUR MOVEMENT IN RETROSPECT

History

In order to understand the real purpose of the Community Music Schools' approach to music it is necessary
to know its roots. The Movement started at Hull
House [sic], Chicago, in 1892 [sic], as a result of
observing the talents and possibilities for cultural
development among the children of the immigrants who
came to this country forty years ago. The effort
met with an immediate response, and lessons were made
available to those who could not afford the higher fees
charged for music instruction. In recent years certain schools have separated from the Music School
Movement and have become Community Music Schools.[6]

Schools of the arts came into being in a variety of ways.
There is no set pattern that must be followed in order to establish a successful organization. There is one element that
cannot be excluded, however, and that is the interest of the
members of the community. The setting may be urban, suburban or rural, but the genuine interest of the community is
essential to develop a school of the arts.

A brief review of the various approaches reveals some
interesting facts. The Hull-House Music School was evolved
in 1893 as part of the larger organization which was meeting
other needs of the community--urban and congested. It was
through the observations of the administrators that the need
for a music school was identified. Fortunately the settlement
house had a wonderful freedom of choice as to what should
be included in its program. There were no regulations or
licenses needed to start the school. The personal backgrounds
of both Jane Addams and Ellen Starr were full of excellent
exposure to the arts with enough experience for them to recognize and appreciate a good, well-established arts program within the structure of the settlement house. Hull-House was
also fortunate to have a musician of the calibre of Miss Eleanor
Smith available and qualified to establish and administer the
Music School when the opportunity presented itself.

Emilie Wagner, freshly graduated from Goucher College
in Baltimore, a college for women founded 1885, came at her
task to establish the Third Street Music School Settlement

in a different but idealistic manner.   She related her experience
to Janet Schenck in this way:

> "The inspiration of the school," she writes, "came
> from a book I read while studying Sociology at College,
> entitled 'A Palace of Pleasure.' I've forgotten who
> wrote it.   That drove me to New York, in my mind
> the place most full of opportunities, and the inspiration
> took form upon my hearing a choir being trained at
> the Cold Mariners Temple in Chatham Square.
>
> The School was opened in that building and after
> a short time moved into a tenement room where it
> struggled along until a friend suggested that the Col-
> lege Settlement might be interested.   Dr. Jane E.
> Robbins, then in charge, gave me the use of the front
> basement, which she had used to receive patients,
> ...Thus the School became connected with settlement
> work.   We outgrew this room and rented the top floor
> of a house across from 95 Rivington Street.   Then a
> committee of women, mostly from colleges, was found
> to help us, for teachers had been added, and more
> pianos, and the pupils numbered about 100.   Shortly
> afterward, University Settlement asked me to superin-
> tend some classes, and I started a small school there.
> Later the two committees united and rented a house
> at 31 Rivington Street.   By the time the Third Street
> property was secured, the School numbered 150 pupils,
> had an orchestra, and classes in singing and theory.
> Finally, on account of ill health, I was ordered out of
> the city.   But the School was needed and it lived."[7]

A beautiful and simple tale to be told.   Thus Miss Wagner
started her School in a different fashion--she began giving
music lessons, and the School gradually grew into a much larger and more complicated organization.   Though she was required to leave the city for reasons of health, it was the same
Emilie Wagner who returned to the City, and in 1907 founded
the People's Three Art's School (Center) "to enable children
specially talented in music, art, and the drama to secure a
good education at the smallest financial expenditure."[8]

Again the Third Street Music School Settlement is recognized as the first community music school established as such
in the United States.

Also in 1894 one learns of still another approach to the
founding of a community music school as we recall Mary Garrettson Evans, a woman of true vision and self-confidence as she
turned her idea of a People's Music School into a reality by
establishing the Peabody graduate's Preparatory and High
School. So successful was her program that within four
years the administration of the famed Peabody Institute of the
Johns Hopkins University saw fit to annex this fledgling school
to the upper school, as the Peabody Preparatory. The response of the community members surrounding it showed that
the school was needed and wanted by them. The immediate
response and attendance confirmed their position. It is a
tribute to the faculty members and the administrators of the
Peabody Preparatory that the success of this school has continued through its more than ninety years of operation. The
City of Baltimore, Maryland can be justifiably proud.

Greenwich House (The Cooperative Social Society) as
the new, venturesome organization was called in 1901, began
with a goal that it would determine what the particular problems of the community were as the neighbors themselves saw
them to be, rather than to superimpose ideas of the organization itself upon the community members regardless of their
needs, thoughts and ideas.

An indicated need of the neighborhood was recognized
with the establishment of the Music School after successful
summer concerts began on the front steps of the Jones Street
Building in 1903. Subsequently private lessons were offered
to those who wished to take them. The social contact that
is realized with ensemble playing was found to be a necessity
for continued interest of the students, and the founding of the
Music School offered a way by which that necessity could
be met.

Much like the experience at Henry Street, the needs
for arts training appeared almost immediately within the structure of the Settlements' basic programs--thus each organization
moved to satisfy a genuine neighborhood need. This has
been true of the establishment of community music schools
throughout the country as the history of the National Guild
will display. It is now true, not only of music, but of all
the arts included in the curricula of community schools of the
arts.

The dawn of the twentieth century saw the growth of
a firmly planted era of creativity and artistic development which
was to flower throughout the nation.   The arts were blossoming
in the lives of more and more Americans!

People were learning and accepting the fact that their
own talents, tastes and abilities were just as important to be
recognized and encouraged as those of others whose gifts and
aptitudes may have been discovered early in their lives.   Because of their sheer brilliance in any artistic field, they had
been given the opportunity to receive genuinely good, directed,
arts training.   Now the community schools of the arts grew
to achieve their own philosophical goals as originally intended.
The arts were truly for all!

So successful were these schools (at this time most community music schools) that in 1937 a national organization was
founded which was designed to bring together such schools
to discuss common problems (i.e. quality and standards of
music training) and to strengthen their position on the national
level, and shortly thereafter to be recognized on the international level.   The most amazing part of this all is that the
United States of America was at that very time period in the
throes of a national depression--one of the most devastating,
debilitating financial situations that this country had ever
faced over a long period of time.   Yet the significance
of the arts was important enough to have them not only survive, but to reach more people than ever before.

At the turn of the twentieth century, it seemed to be
true that most of the serious cultural activities were established
on the Eastern seaboard, (with the exception of Chicago) in
such cities as Boston, New York and Philadelphia with some
artistic ventures in Charleston, but they were mostly in performance, not in teaching or education.   This may have been
true in earlier days, but in the nineteen hundreds with the
coming of more and more immigrants bringing with them skills
and talents, it was inevitable that some of them would move
to different geographical territories to be able to use their
abilities to good advantage.   Many of them whose skills were
not in the musical vein wanted their children to learn to play
musical instruments.

In the City of Minneapolis, Minnesota, in the year 1907,
William G. MacPhail founded the MacPhail School of Violin.

Mr. MacPhail served as founder, director and teacher of
violin. There was no board of directors and no other faculty
members at the beginning. By 1913 the School boasted seven
faculty members, five violin teachers (including MacPhail)
and two in harmony, history and pianoforte. In a six year
period the School had grown considerably and MacPhail continued as director of the School until 1952 when he relinquished
that position and became the Chairman of the Board of Directors, and remained to function as such until his death in 1962.
During the span of his directorship the School grew to become
a College of Music offering undergraduate and graduate degrees until 1967 when it became The MacPhail Center for the
Arts of the University of Minnesota. This was all made possible because the MacPhail family donated the School to the
University.

Today it is a community music school accepting all applicants to the MacPhail Center for the Arts of the Continuing
Education and Extension, the University of Minnesota at
Minneapolis. A valuable lesson can be learned with this example for all communities that wish to start a community school
of the arts but find it difficult to begin. The city of Minneapolis and the state of Minnesota have given an example which
can be emulated by any new or struggling group in an urban,
suburban or rural community in this country.

The year 1908 saw the opening of a community music
school which built an exceptionally fine organization from a
very simple beginning. It was, and still is, the Settlement
Music School in Philadelphia, PA.

As what seemed to be a usual beginning for an East
Coast Community Music School, the initial teaching began in
the College Settlement. Blanche Wolf (later to become Mrs.
Isadore Kohn) and Jeanette Selig (later to become Mrs. Edwin
Frank) were two young volunteers teaching gym classes at
the College Settlement located at 4th and Christian Streets in
Philadelphia. After class one day in 1908 Jeanette suggested
that they continue to volunteer at the Settlement, but to change
from teaching gym to giving piano lessons. (Each girl had
had considerable music training.)

The head worker at College Settlement was a Miss Davis
who seemed to be pessimistic about the idea, but she told
the young women that if they could attract students, she
would make space available for them to teach.

In their plans for the musical program, Blanche and
Jeanette agreed that if the students would have to pay something for the lessons, the new experience would seem more
valuable to them. (This idea has continued in many community
schools of the arts throughout the country. The thought is
that if some payment is made, the exchange of money, no
matter how small, puts into the minds of the students and their
families that the undertaking of the study of music in the
form of instrumental lessons indicates a measurable value inherent in the music study. It has been the experience of the
author that parents appreciate the opportunity to pay at least
something on a regular basis for the musical education of
their own children. Not to have that opportunity cheats the
parent of his own self-worth and dignity.)

The two women decided on a fee of 5¢ per lesson (exactly one-half the cost of the lessons given by Emilie Wagner
in New York City fourteen years earlier). If the pupils were
unable to afford the fee, they could earn the lessons by doing
odd jobs such as dusting, running errands, etc. Here one
also sees one of the first examples of a "neighborhood need"
or a "service" grant's being offered at a community music
school--the American First in operation.

The two young women were not only enthusiastic and
dedicated to the work they were doing, but they were equally
good at proselytizing others to join their worthy cause of
bringing fine musical training to immigrant and underprivileged
children. Two men from the Philadelphia Symphony Orchestra
were the first who volunteered their services. They were
Mr. Samuel Belov and Mr. Johan Grolle, each of whom had
intense enthusiasm for the concept that everyone with the
capability of performing modestly, regardless of his ability
to pay, should have the opportunity to enrich his life by the
study of music.

Within a year Johan Grolle became the School's first
director in 1909. He was a violinist with a strong musical
background having studied at the Amsterdam Conservatory
in Holland. He, too, was an immigrant which made him com-
passionate and understanding of the children in the area, and
although his Old World mannerisms and discipline were sometimes intimidating, he was highly respected as a musician,
teacher, and philanthropist.

By 1911 the enrollment showed 40 students studying piano, 17 studying the violin and 3 playing the mandolin. In the very next year, 1912, the enrollment doubled, and by 1914 (the year in which World War I began) the enrollment was 250 with a waiting list of 100. The School was literally bursting at the seams.

At this point Mr. Grolle, Mrs. Frank, and Mrs. Kohn started the task of raising money to continue the exciting and vital work of the School. Through his association with the Ethical Culture Society, Mr. Grolle met Mrs. Samuel Fels who became interested in the School and agreed to become the chairman of its newly formed Board of Directors. Mrs. Fels introduced Mrs. Edward Bok (later Mrs. Efrem Zimbalist) and encouraged her to join the first Board of Directors of the Settlement Music School.

Mrs. Bok became so enamored with the School, that her continued activity caused her to be known as one of the "founding mothers." When the School outgrew its Christian Street headquarters, Mrs. Bok's father provided the funds to build a new building. Settlement Music School's home was erected in 1917 (the year that the U.S.A. entered World War I) at 416 Queen Street, which still exists and is used at the time of this writing. The Queen Street building was dedicated to the memory of Mrs. Bok's mother, Louisa Knapp Curtis, and subsequently this branch of the School was named for Mrs. Mary Louise Curtis Bok Zimbalist.

Shortly after the new school was built, Mrs. Bok's father, Mr. Cyrus Curtis, owner of the Curtis Publishing Company, generously offered to create an endowment fund of $100,000 if the Board of Directors would match that amount. The School successfully raised $120,000 and an endowment fund amounting to $220,000 was established in the name of the Settlement Music School.

An important factor must always be remembered about the Settlement Music School in Philadelphia, which is that the School was never intended for talented students only. Any industrious, sincere child was eligible to take lessons and was encouraged to study. It was important to recognize the very gifted children, however, and to inspire them to pursue their education in music.

Over the years there were many talented students. A special conservatory section was established for them within the Settlement, and some very special artists were engaged as teachers for them. As an outgrowth of this project, the Curtis Institute of Music was founded in 1924.

Accomplishments of the Settlement Music School are numerous, but here it seems relevant to recognize the efforts of Johan Grolle, who was the first director of the Music School and continued in that position for forty years, retiring in 1949. He was also vigorously important in the establishment of the National Guild of Community Music Schools in 1937. Grolle was also the first director of the Curtis Institute of Music from 1924 to 1926.

In 1909 the Brooklyn Music School Settlement opened as a branch of the New York Music School Settlement (The Third Street Music School Settlement), and it immediately made plans to become an independent organization. Earliest records show that the School initially was housed in four rooms belonging to the United Neighborhood Houses Association. In 1911 a home on Vanderbuilt Avenue was rented for teaching purposes. The building at 525 Grand Avenue, which housed the "Bloody Tub Saloon," was purchased in 1912, and the School "established Bach, Beethoven, Mozart and the moderns where conviviality was want to reign." The Grand Avenue property was sold in 1919, and the three houses adjoining the Academy of Music were purchased at $1.00 each. The Playhouse-Concert Hall was built in 1927.

During this rather "moving" period of time, Mary T. McDermott, founder and first president of the Board of Directors of the Brooklyn Music School Settlement, was to comment on the buildings in which the School was housed: "Our pupils were drawn to us solely by the excellence of our teaching, and by our spirit and ideals, not lured by the dazzling splendor and luxury of our school rooms."[*]

---

[*]The aptly stated phraseology of Marty T. McDermott was undoubtedly similar to the thoughts of other board members, directors, teachers, parents and students of such schools as the Third Street Music School Settlement, Hull-House Music School, South End Music School, Boston Music School

The first director of the Brooklyn Music School Settlement was Helen Van Inge. She and all the subsequent directors which included Irene Golden, Edith Otis, Livio Mannuccio, Charles Ennis, Daniel Rice, and its present director, Donna R. Merris have been performers in music and have had backgrounds in education as well. All adopted the Settlement Music School philosophy.

Like many of its sister organizations, the Brooklyn Music School* raises funds every year to meet operational costs by offering an annual raffle drawing, a Rummage Sale, and a Theatre benefit. The School delights in the fact that the famous American dance couple, Vernon and Irene Castle, were involved in the starting of this School, and they gave the first benefit performance for the Brooklyn Music School Settlement in 1912. Another point of interest about the School is that the prominent singer, Tatiana Troyanos, was a scholarship piano student who studied with Eleanor Troemel, a piano teacher who retired recently after having taught for over 40 years at the Brooklyn Music School.

It would be unfair to say that the City of Boston was slow in establishing a community school of the arts. It would be more accurate to say "slower." In 1910 the City did become alive and active as it founded not one but two community music schools. Both the Boston Music School Settlement and

---

(cont. from p. 103) Settlement, Neighborhood Music School, and the Henry Street Settlement Music School. Most are now in far more suitable surroundings than in the days of their beginnings. It was the spirit and dedication of those involved that overcame difficulties that were perhaps undesireable. Rather than to lose the opportunity of receiving proper exposure to the musical arts, students, much to their credit, accepted the opportunities to study as they appeared. Also to the credit of board members, administrators, contributors, etc., the physical plants of the schools are vastly improved in most areas at the time of this writing.

*In December, 1946, the School changed its name to the Brooklyn Music School. Why this change was made is not clear nor is it explained. Its Charter from the New York State Board of Regents was granted on May 2, 1912 and is still in effect at the time of this writing.

the South End Music Centre began in that year.   They shall
be discussed in the order in which they began.

It was the South End Music Centre that first came into
being, and its method or procedure was different from any
previously discussed.

>Established June, 1910, and organized as an inde-
>pendent body by residents and associates of the South
>End House to continue and expand the musical instruc-
>tion formerly given at the settlement. Aims: to fos-
>ter the love of music among the people; to raise the
>standard of musical taste; to offer instruction at
>moderate prices; to save and develop the talent of
>working-class children; to develop social expression
>through music; to bring together the music lovers
>of the district for their mutual advantages; to create
>a center of musical life which shall unite the city and
>the time.[9]

Here is a different technique, indeed. The residents
and associates of the South End House banded together to
continue the music program by acting themselves as a Board
of Directors. It is also necessary to understand that the
South End Settlement House had no jurisdiction over the
Music Centre, though their names were similar, the location
generally the same, and at one time music was part of the
program of South End House.

The Boston Music School Settlement, located at 110
Salem Street, was begun perhaps in a more conventional way
by the efforts of one individual.

>Established November, 1910, by Daniel Bloomfield "to
>raise the standard of musical appreciation, to develop
>the neighborhood's musical resources and to give to
>children of limited means an opportunity to secure a
>musical education."[10]

One finds little or no difference in the philosophies of
the schools; it seemed that a step forward would happen if
the two Schools merged. It took 58 years, but that is exactly
what happened in 1968. The plan and all its excitement is
expressed in a newsletter from the South End Music Centre,
Vol. VIII, No. 1, dated September, 1963:

CENTRE FOR THE ARTS IN THE SOUTH END

Since our February report, the proposed Centre
for the Arts in the South End has taken a major step
towards realization. For the benefit of new readers
of the News Letter, we ought to explain that, spear-
headed by the South End Music Centre and the Children's Art Centre, a committee was formed last year
to explore the possibility of an Arts Centre in the
South End which would draw together in an organic
unit the arts of music, painting, drama, and dance
and eventually, perhaps others. As the idea has
gradually taken shape, it has found increasing enthusiasm and support from a wide variety of organizations
and individuals. Now, thanks to a grant from Boston's permanent Charity Fund, the Art Centre's Development Committee has been able to procure the services of Mr. and Mrs. Russell Jelliffe of Cleveland for
a feasibility study to be undertaken this fall.[11]

The successful completion of the merger of the two
Schools is told succinctly in The 1985 Membership Directory
of the National Guild of Community Schools of the Arts, Inc.
where it states the following:

CMC [Community Music Center of Boston] provides
music education and related services to diverse con-
stituencies throughout metropolitan Boston. The
Center is the product of a merger of two historic
settlement music schools--The South End Music Centre
and the Boston Music School [Settlement]--both of
which were organized in 1910. The Center currently
services almost 5,000 people, including 4,000 in the
Boston public school system. In addition it reaches
out with programs for the elderly and handicapped,
and maintains a lively instructional center in Boston's
South End.[12]

It would be a complete oversight not to identify those
who were fundamentally responsible for the establishment and
directing of these two schools. The founder of the South
End Music Centre was Annie Endicott Nourse. She had a very
close relationship with that music school, since she functioned
at various times in different categories, such as piano teacher,
board member and Chairman of the Executive Committee

of the Board when Arthur E. Foote, the American composer,
was the Board President.

Miss Sarah Sprague was the guiding hand for the operations of the school for a long time. If she was not officially
the director, she probably should have been, because she
worked diligently in various management and directorial capacities from the 1920's to the 1960's when she became a board
member. Those who knew her found her to be very warm,
outgoing and willing to do whatever it was that the school
needed to be done.

It is significant to note the calibre of individuals who
functioned as well as administrators and faculty members. It
was these stalwarts who insisted that the quality of teaching
be high.

Arthur E. Foote (1853-1937) was unique himself in several ways. As it is reported in the New Grove Dictionary of
Music and Musicians,

> ...Foote enrolled in the harmony class of Stephen A.
> Emery at the New England Conservatory. He entered
> Harvard University in 1870, studying there under
> John Knowles Paine...with no thought of becoming a
> professional musician but merely to put the time to
> use before preparing for law, he began piano and
> organ lessons that summer [1874] with B. J. Lange,
> who was so encouraging that Foote decided on a career
> in music. Returning to Harvard for another year's
> work with Paine, he received in 1875 the first master's
> degree in music given in the U.S.A. Thus his entire
> training in composition was American, unusual for the
> time.[13]

The fact that one composer had gone through his com-
plete formal training to become a fully recognized composer
in this country is significant in the development of a musical
America. It is also acknowledged that when he was in Paris,
France in 1883, Foote did have a few lessons with Stephen
Heller (1818-1888), on the playing of Heller's piano music.
In 1920 Arthur E. Foote began teaching piano at the New
England Conservatory of Music, where he had at one time been
a student. In honor of Foote's 80th birthday the Boston
Symphony Orchestra played his Night Piece. He was also

elected to the National Institute of Arts and Letters. It is
evident that musical knowledge and sophistication had become
obvious by the development of so gifted and talented a composer as Foote and gratifying to the National Guild of Community Schools of the Arts that he thought enough of the
Music School Settlement Movement in this country to serve as
Board President in one of the first community music schools
in Boston.

The name of John Knowles Paine with whom Foote studied
was mentioned in Chapter II of this book noting that Paine
had been appointed to a full professorship at Harvard University. This was the first chair of music in this country. Mr.
Paine had his early training in his home town, Portland, Maine.
His American training qualified him enough to study later at
the Hochschule für Musik in Berlin, Germany where he con-
centrated on the study of organ and composition for a period
of three years.

The year of 1911 brings three community music schools
to life. They show development of such schools in different
kinds of communities: (1) in a smaller community that might
have been described as a college community though it had some
industry and was on the Atlantic sea coast; (2) in a suburb
of one of the major seaports on the Atlantic Ocean; and (3)
in a borough of New York City. They are, of course, The
Neighborhood Music School in New Haven, CT, The All Newton
Music School in West Newton, MA and The Bronx House Music
School in the Bronx Borough of New York City.

The Neighborhood Music School brought musical training
to the poor children of that city as described by Marshall
Bartholomew in his foreword to They Who Speak in Music,
by Clarence A. Grimes, which is a history of that School
published in 1957:

> No neighborhood in New Haven could have provided
> a better example of the gradual metamorphosis of a
> community from wealth to poverty than Wooster Street.
> A hundred years ago the region south of Church Street
> and along the harbor had been a center of the town's
> most prosperous and respected families; by the turn
> of the century it had become the crowded refuge of
> a largely immigrant population, poorly paid and cul-
> turally underprivileged.[14]

The School actually began giving music lessons in St.
Paul's Neighborhood House where a few rooms were allocated
for music lessons, and St. Paul's boasted of having two pianos.
The equipment was minimal, and lessons had to be scheduled
around practice sessions since the pupils did not have pianos
in their homes. (This practice was followed again in 1963
by Dorothy Maynor when she founded the Harlem School of
the Arts.) The School often allowed lessons to be taught in
the homes or studios of their teachers in order to let more
students enroll.

A brief history of the Neighborhood Music School appears
in the brochure of the 1978-1979 season.

> ...The Neighborhood Music School has its roots in the
> settlement house movement of the early twentieth cen-
> tury. It began as an arm of a larger organization
> based in the parish of St. Paul's Church in the Woos-
> ter Square area of New Haven. The original settlement
> was founded in 1911 and was called St. Paul's Neigh-
> borhood House. The function of the House was to
> address the social, educational, and medical needs of
> the immigrant population that was settled around the
> industry in that area.
> As the population became acclimated to the new
> surroundings and the professionals in the community
> assumed responsibility for social and medical services,
> the settlement house turned toward recreational pro-
> grams. The Music School, however, continued to
> attract students and retained its original purpose of
> providing high quality instruction in serious music
> to youngsters who could not otherwise afford to study
> privately.[15]

Once again one sees a reaffirmation of the earliest aims
and goals of social services in settlement houses in America,
patterned after the plans and purposes of Toynbee Hall.
The needs that were evident in the community and desired
by the neighbors were reflected in the program of St. Paul's
Neighborhood House. Their statement continues:

> A major change in operation occurred in 1957 when
> the Board of Directors decided to respond to a growing
> need in the community by admitting a limited number
> of full fee paying students. The student body

numbered between two and three hundred during this
period.

The program was carried on in an old town house
on lower Chapel Street, a few doors from St. Paul's
Church.[16]

Thus one sees the intention of the Board of Directors
embarking on an era, where students who were not necessarily
indigent and/or immigrant were allowed to participate in the
School's program. Many community music schools have wrestled
with this philosophical interpretation. This marks a solid step
forward to encourage students of other or different financial
circumstances to join with the less fortunate to share the
beauties of music and the other arts in an enriched, artistic,
communal experience at a community school of the arts.

At this point in its history the Neighborhood Music
School was required to cope with the problem of increasing
enrollment, partly due to the new policy, and as a result to
consider acquiring new space--not just more or additional
space--new space. This would entail a much larger financial
commitment than the School had ever undertaken previously.
An anonymous gift of $100,000 encouraged the Board of
Directors, the administrators, and the friends of the School
to work together to raise additional funds needed for the
construction of a new home for the Neighborhood Music
School.

It is undoubtedly an oversimplification to say that with
the initial donation and two fund-raising drives, each of which
raised another $250,000, that the mission was accomplished--
much to the credit of all parties concerned, that is exactly
what happened. Certainly the writing of that story will be
the task of one other than this author to tell the "fun" story
of the New Haven Music School Building project, other than
to mention that the new home has twenty teaching studios,
ten practice studios, four large classrooms, one Rehearsal/
Recital Hall, a Library, administrative offices, a Board Room,
a faculty lounge, a well planned coat room, and by serendi-
pity, perhaps, a "back lawn amphitheatre"--a physical plant
never even imagined previously.

Two personalities emerge from the history of this School
which deserve some special recognition. The first was Susan
Hart Dyer (1880-1922), who was considered the founder of

the School, and for one year its director during the 1915-
1916 season. Personal family problems required that she return to Winter Park, Florida where she was Director of the
Rollins College Conservatory in Winter Park, Florida. She
was a violinist, conductor, composer and poetess. She had
a great dedication to the Settlement Music School Movement
and was, indeed, affiliated with two community music schools,
the Neighborhood House Music School in New Haven, and
later in 1922 the Greenwich House Music School in New York
City. Her untimely death came immediately after her becoming
director there.

     She had attended the Peabody Conservatory of Music,
entering there in 1897 and receiving her Teacher's Certificate
in 1902. She earned a Bachelor's Degree from Yale University in 1914. Her great friend was Marion Rous who was her
assistant for the short time that Susan Dyer was the director
at the Greenwhich House Music School, and upon her death
replaced her as director of the Music School. Immediately
before her death Susan Hart Dyer wrote an annual announcement for the Music School. It was mailed just before her
final illness. These are in part her final words:

THE MUSIC SCHOOL SETTLEMENT

          ...What the public library and art museum mean to
     literature, science, painting and general culture, the
     Music Settlement School in a specialized way, means
     to the art of music, the art which at present is so
     ignored and neglected by the state. But it goes fur-
     ther in offering not only music itself, but the tech-
     nical training necessary to the fullest enjoyment and
     benefit to be derived from music. Because it is con-
     cerned with music, the most social and intimate form
     of artistic expression, the Settlement School can per-
     haps touch more closely the lives of those whom it
     serves than any other kindred agency, and offers in
     a way that is unique the emotional and intellectual
     outlets which are so necessary to a normal existence
     anywhere, but especially important to the youth reared
     in the artificial and overstimulating atmosphere of our
     congested cities.
          This form of expression, music, has of course al-
     ways been available to those who could pay for it,
     but it remained for the Settlement Music School to

bring it within reach of "the child in the street",
[sic] a service to society and to American culture
which can hardly be overestimated.[17]

To learn of Susan Hart Dyer's understanding and appreciation of the community music school's advent and development is gratifying, but the loss of her interest and dedication
cannot be measured. She seemed, indeed, to move in circles
which put her into direct contact with those involved with the
Settlement Music School Movement. Her early training in undergraduate days was at the Peabody Conservatory which itself has the Peabody Preparatory. That school was founded
on the same principles as the community music schools were,
and it is now a member of the National Guild of Community
Schools of the Arts.

She later attended the Music School of Yale, a University which has always been understanding of the work
done by the Neighborhood Music School, and it has helped
the School to find qualified teachers from among its graduate
students when the community music school needed additional
teachers. Robert Baisley, himself a Yale graduate, was the
director of the Neighborhood Music School at the time when
Clarence A. Grimes was assembling materials for and writing
They Who Speak in Music (a history of the Neighborhood
Music School). Mr. Baisley was asked to contribute the final
chapter of the book.

The second memorable individual affiliated with the
Neighborhood School who deserves special recognition is Jesse
Clarke Beecher (1868-1958), who taught piano at the School
for a period of thirty-five years from 1912 to 1947 and was its
director for twenty-eight years from 1918 to 1947, which is
one of the longest time spans for an individual at a Guild School.*

---

*Those with the longest tenure with a single Community Music
School are as follows: William G. MacPhail, founder, teacher,
first director and finally Chairman of the Board of Directors
of the MacPhail Center for the Arts, 55 years from 1907 to
1962; A. W. Binder, Director, 92nd Street YM/YWHA Music
School, 49 years from 1917 to 1966; Johan Grolle, Director,
Settlement Music School, Philadelphia, 40 years from 1909
to 1949; Sarah Sprague, dedicated to South End Music School
for an undeterminable amount of years, but certainly over 40

Miss Beecher also attended Yale University's School of Music
over a period of ten years from 1895 to 1905. This is accounted for by the fact that personal finances did not permit
her to continue unbroken attendance at the University. She
received her degree from Yale in 1905, a great tribute to her
perseverance. Undoubtedly it is true that the long time
span had really helped to cement the relationship of the Neighborhood Music School and Yale University.

Miss Beecher also believed in the Settlement Music School
as well as the Settlement Movement itself. In 1926 the Second
International Conference of Settlements was held in Paris,
France from June 30 to July 5. It was here, having attended
as a representative from the "Wooster Street Settlement" in
New Haven, that Miss Beecher met Jane Addams personally.
She was tremendously impressed with the sincerity and dynamic
expression of the pioneer of the American settlement houses,
and as a result of this meeting, two years later she visited
Jane Addams in the expanded Hull-House in Chicago.

Janet D. Schenck refers to these international conferences first in the preface of her book Music Schools and
Settlement Music Departments, and to the value of the American
music education program and its contribution to the international scene:

> In July, 1922, the first international conference of
> settlements was held in London. America stood out
> among the eight nations represented as having de-
> veloped a unique form of education, namely, settlement
> music schools and music departments.[18]

Schenck also comments on the lack of information available to the general public about these schools at that time:

> So quietly and unostentatiously has this new form of
> educational enterprise been developed that even those
> most interested, directors, teachers and board mem-
> bers, have found it hard to secure details about the

(cont. from p. 112) years; Eleanor Troemel, piano teacher,
Brooklyn Music School Settlement, 40 years; Howard Whittaker,
Director, Cleveland Music School Settlement, 37 years from
1947 to 1984; and Jesse Clark Beecher.

development of sister institutions...investigation
brought to light an annual report of the Music School
Settlement in New York; an item in Grove's Dictionary,
1920, stating that music school settlements were no-
tably successful in New York, Boston, Philadelphia,
and several cities in the West; and a note that the
South End Music School and the Boston Music School
Settlement were organized in 1910.[19]

The All Newton Music School, established in 1911 and
operated as an independent organization, brought forth a
solution to the problem of space in a manner which did not
necessarily please Mrs. Schenck and/or the other directors
of neighborhood or settlement music schools. The founder and
first director of the School was Miss Elizabeth Fyffe. The
School's name originally appeared in the listings of schools in
Janet Schenck's book, Music Schools and Settlement Music
Departments, as the West Newton Music School,* Pierce School,
raised a bit of commentary from the author. She footnotes the
following statement:

> One school, that is West Newton, Mass., carries on
> its work in a public school. Miss Elizabeth Fyffe,
> the director, reports that they have found it feasible;
> in fact financially it would have been impossible to
> have the school otherwise.[20]

Janet Schenck's feathers were a bit ruffled apparently,
as she continues in an additional paragraph of the footnotes:

> It is, however, impossible to create a really artistic
> atmosphere, and it would be a great pity if the ne-
> cessity for seeking cheap rent should delay the es-
> tablishment of music schools organized according to
> their own laws of being. In so far as increased use
> of public school buildings is an excuse for doing
> cheaply and badly something that ought to be done
> well and beautifully such use of public property is
> a drag upon programs. The ordinary public school
> is not the place for a music school.[21]

---

*It is understood that the name was changed to the All Newton
Music School to reflect more correctly the neighborhood and
community it served.

Mrs. Schenck must have been startled to see an article by Paul Rolland who was then the President of the American String Teachers Association appear in the November-December, 1965 issue of the Music Educators Journal. Its title was "Public MUSIC Schools: A new pattern of American Music Education." Dr. Rolland proposed that music lessons could be given in the after school hours in public schools and perhaps on Saturdays and Sundays. He dared to include the following statement in his article:

> My proposal is to channel the available teaching talent and public funds into a new type of music school, a Public Music School ...Let us get away from the outdated, archaic-sounding Settlement Music Schools, but let's channel the available teaching talent into a new, up-to-date Public Music School...[22]

The author was asked to respond to this article at the Spring National Music Council meeting at the Plaza Hotel in New York City on May 11, 1966. It was a simple task to point out that Dr. Rolland did not really understand what Settlement Music Schools really were. In response to the inadequacy of a public school for teaching individual lessons the following statement was made:

> ...Can you imagine the delight of taking a music lesson in the kindergarten, particularly if you are 15 years old and 6 feet, 2 inches tall? Can you envision the sound of a respectable violinist attempting to tune his violin to a typical piano in a public school--if, indeed, there is any at all?[23]

And then on the positive side:

> ...Our present organizations [Settlement Music Schools] enjoy complete autonomy, devoid of requirements to meet city or state regulations in relation to high school credits or college degrees. We are free to experiment, to teach what we wish and as we wish. We are able to require standards of our students and our faculties. We enjoy the interest and cooperation of the communities in which we exist. We enjoy the privilege of meeting the needs of those in our communities as the requirements for the communities are recognized.[24]

For the establishment and development of the All Newton
Music School, it was a wise decision of Miss Fyffe and her
Board of Directors to move ahead with the founding of the
School and to use the space that was then available to them
in the community where they were to operate.

In the beginning of this School's history, strong finan-
cial support came from Mrs. William Lloyd Garrison and Mr.
William Lester Bates. The original Board of Directors included
Miss Fyffe, president; Elsie S. Kimberly, clerk; Harry L.
Burrows, treasurer; Marguerite E. Barrage, Julia S. Day,
Richard B. Carter, Mabel T, Eager, Marlan L. Haskell, Pauline
S. Howard, Lucinda W. Prince, Margaret Hatfield, Harriet L.
Baker, Helen H. Pusifer, and Marion Chidsey.

The action of the Board of Directors of the West Newton
(now the All Newton School of Music) established a Board
of Directors, so in essence it was ready to take formal actions.
But it took a step which raises a philosophical, controversial
yet practical question. It is one that must be addressed by
all incorporated organizations. The question is this: Should
the director, headworker, or whatever the title is for the
chief administrative officer, actually be a member of the Board
of Directors? Notable examples of where the headworker was
a Board member include Jane Addams at Hull-House in Chicago;
Lillian D. Wald at the Henry Street Settlement on the Lower
East Side of New York City; and Mary K. Simkhovitch at
Greenwich House in Greenwich Village of New York City.

The question is still open for public debate.

Also in 1911 the Bronx House Music School was estab-
lished. Its founder was Mrs. Henry Morganthau, Sr., and its
first director at 1637 Washington Avenue in the Bronx was
Edgar Stowell. The current director is Amory Williams. Af-
ter many successful years and locations, the Bronx House
Music School moved to its present home at 990 Pelham Parkway
South in the Bronx. The School is a recipient of an annual
grant from LADO, Inc., the Ladies' Auxiliary of the Doctor's
Orchestra, which is used for scholarships for talented students.
Bronx House is also responsible for the development of the
USDAN Center, a summer music program held on Long Island.
Their philosophy is stated as follows:

> The aim of the school is to develop along with per-
> forming skills, understanding and appreciation of

music by both the child and adult student. A high
standard of instruction is maintained to provide the
student with a cultural growth and experience that
will be rewarding throughout his life.[25]

In 1917 Abraham Wolf Binder, who was a composer,
conductor, teacher and lecturer, envisioned a plan to found
a music school within the environs of a large community center.
His idea was to add a cultural dimension to the program of
the Young Men's/Young Women's Hebrew Association at Lexington Avenue and 92nd Street in New York City. The scholarly,
young musician was a man of fine intellect and great determination. It was he who encouraged the 92nd Street Y to
begin the program of the music school. Though the School
is an integral part of the total program, it is relatively independent in the running of its own program. Dr. Binder
was its director from 1917 to 1966--an enviable record! When
the music school began there was no separate Board of Directors nor a music school committee; some of the early records
are, therefore, not available.

The second director of the music school was Ilana Ruben-
feld who had been a choral director at the school for about
five years. The current director is Hadassah Binder Markson, who is the founder's daughter, and who also had been
a member of the piano faculty for twenty years prior to her
becoming director.

Two former students of the School who have since earned
national acclaim for themselves are Judith Raskin, soprano,
and Burl Ives, composer/singer. Over the years the faculty
of the School has included Stephan Wolpe, composer, Julius
Baker, flautist, Judith Raskin, soprano, Joanna Simon, mezzo-
soprano, and Shlomo Mintz, violinist.

Up to this point the institutions which have been established between 1886 and 1912 have been identified and described with the exception of two, the Lighthouse Music School
and the Cleveland Music School Settlement, the former in New
York City and the latter in Cleveland, Ohio. These are set
for the next section of this document, because they will help
to show the uniqueness and flexibility of the National Guild
of Community Schools of the Arts. Two other unusual and
significant schools will be included with the Lighthouse Music
School and the Cleveland School. They are the Harlem School

of the Arts and the School for Strings, both in New York
City and both founded after 1960.

SCHOOLS OF SPECIAL INTEREST

The schools will be identified separately. None of them
were the first or early established (from 1893 to 1908) of
the Guild Schools, but each has a unique or different quality
in addition to being a community music school.

The Lighthouse Music School

Around the turn of the century, music departments
were to be found in all of the residential schools for
young blind people in the United States. Three braille
printing houses offered catalogues of music for sale.
Then in 1905, Winifred and Edith Holt, founders of
The Lighthouse, introduced their first service to
blind people by making available to them free tickets
to opera. Thus did The New York Association for
the Blind come into being. Today, it provides 29
free services to more than 6,000 people.[26]

The brochure continues to give pertinent information
about the School itself with the following material:

A Music School Program Unfolds

The Music School is located in the 24-story Lighthouse
No. 1 building at 111 East 59th street, in the midst
of busy Manhattan, where it is accessible to the greatest number of people. There is also an extension
division in Westchester County which was opened in
1962. In the Manhattan school there are ten rooms
used as teaching studios and practice rooms. There
are, in addition, a library, a reception room, and a
recital hall which seats 75 people. The staff is made
up of blind and sighted teachers who give instructions
to approximately 200 students each week. The school
year extends from September through June.
Students vary in age from Nursery School children
to the occasional octogenarian. This wide range in
age is matched by an equally broad scale of musical

abilities. Entrance into the school is not competitive,
so that students are accepted purely on the basis of
their desire to study music, in addition to the requirement that they must be legally blind. Tuition
is free to all students. The school is part of the 20
services offered by the Lighthouse, which is a local
voluntary agency, supported by the public.[27]

A statement continues in this publication about the goals
and aims of teaching blind students.

Objectives

Essentially, our attitude toward the musical education
of blind people is that it does not differ greatly from
that of sighted persons. The same precision in performance may be exacted, and the same thorough grasp
of the intellectual qualities of music may be required.
The great diversity among our students requires that
we be guided by a flexible approach in the matter of
teaching--one which meets the needs of many people.[28]

The obvious advantage that a sighted music student
would have is to be able to see the musical score in order
to learn a composition. Since this is not possible for the
blind student, he must learn to read Braille notation:

Braille music is the most obvious departure from the
ordinary method of study. The system, like that of
literary braille, was developed by Louis Braille in the
1830's. Both systems are based on the 63 symbols
possible with the six-dot cell. This means, therefore,
that a braille symbol has one meaning in literary
braille and another in music; the reader knows how to
interpret it because of the given context... Reading
from a braille score is a tedious process in the early
stages of study, often for some of the brightest students. After a student has gained in experience, he
can read with considerable fluency. All music must,
of course, be committed to memory. In memorizing a
piano score, the blind person reads one part with one
hand while playing with the other. The process is
then reversed, and then the two parts are played
together.[29]

The Lighthouse of the New York Association for the Blind was itself established and incorporated in 1905. Informal music lessons were offered from 1913, and the Lighthouse Music School developed from these humble beginnings to a fully developed music curriculum in 1929. At the time of this writing instruction is being given in piano, voice, strings, winds and percussion. It also offers a comprehensive music theory curriculum, ensemble groups including a mixed chorus, a jazz workshop, and, proudly, the only opera workshop in existence in which blind and visually impaired singers participate.

An unusual and important aspect of the Lighthouse Music School program is the training of sighted music teachers to work with blind students, and workshops are periodically scheduled for the development and expansion of this part of the program. This phase of the School's program, in addition to the fact that all lessons are free for qualified and legally blind students, makes this School another first for the National Guild of Community Schools of the Arts. The dedicated and thoroughly trained teachers and administrators are a unique group of individuals.

There seems to have been no founder, per se, of the Lighthouse Music School (unless one recalls Winifred and Edith Holt, founders of the Lighthouse itself and the way in which they began by giving away tickets to the opera). The first director of the Music School is known to have been Marjorie Harding. Its second director was Dr. Charles J. Beetz who was the first totally blind director of the School. It is interesting to note that Dr. Beetz was a graduate of the National Conservatory of Music in America in New York City, which was founded in 1885. (See p. 77.) Beetz received his degree in the first decade of the twentieth century.

At the time of this writing the director of the Lighthouse Music School is George G. Bennette, who is himself a concert pianist. He has been blind since the age of four, and Bennette is a graduate of Oberlin College and the Juilliard School of Music.

The Lighthouse Music School continues to grow in enrollment. During the 1984-85 season the School had a student body of nearly 300. The continued increase in enrollment may

be partially caused by the fact that the School has added
Theatre to its list of course offerings. This is also answering
a need, since the School now has an opera workshop and additional theatre offerings should be very helpful to the young
singers as well as to others who may want to specialize in
theatre arts.

A special feature of the School is that musical scores
and materials are available to students in two media, Braille
and in large print. The latter is used by about 25% of the
students, those with sufficient residual vision to read it.
Thus the library consists of standard repertoire for various
instruments and voice, and theory texts and sight singing
books are also available.

A service to the country-at-large comes, from time to
time, when this School conducts workshops for training teachers from other areas to give instruction to blind students.
Three Guild Schools, those in Philadelphia, Newark, and
Buffalo, have developed programs for visually impaired persons of their communities as a consequence of sending faculty
to participate in those workshops. In addition the director
of the School and various other staff members are frequently
called upon to advise musicians throughout the United States
on the matter of instructing this special population.

The Cleveland Music School Settlement

The Cleveland Music School Settlement is one of the
most outstanding community music schools in the country. It
serves its community admirably by the use of its Main School
in various parts of its community. The entire Cuyahoga
County is its community in the North Central part of Ohio
and on the shores of Lake Erie.

The School has served as a model for other schools in
the United States and Canada. Under the skillful leadership
of Howard Whittaker for a period of 36 years (1948-1984) the
Cleveland Music School Settlement has grown to proportions
never envisioned in the earlier days. It has an excellent relationship with the Cleveland Symphony Orchestra, the Cleveland Museum of Art, Case-Western Reserve University, the
Cleveland School of Art and the Cleveland Institute of Music.
A unique geographical fact is that all of the above mentioned

organizations are literally within walking distance of each other
in a cultural pocket known as the University Circle. Students
who attend the Main School come in contact with performing
musicians at the city's famous Severance Hall, the home of
the Cleveland Orchestra. Recitals, concerts and special performances of all kinds are available to the students and to
residents of the entire county. As if at the hub of an enormous wheel sits the Cleveland Music School Settlement. Its
historical background is fascinating.

> In October, 1912, The Cleveland Music School Settle-
> ment opened its doors for the first time in Goodrich
> House. Fifty registered pupils paid 25¢ for individual
> lessons and 10¢ for class lessons. The School was the
> dream of Almeda Adams. Although blind since birth,
> she had mastered and taught music in Cleveland for
> many years. Having been told by her father of a
> school in New York that served people of limited
> means, she set about establishing one in her own com-
> munity. With the help of Adella Prentiss Hughes Miss
> Adams persuaded the Forthnightly Musical Club to
> donate $1,000, which was the first of many contri-
> butions from leading Cleveland families and organiza-
> tions.
> A year later, registration had more than tripled
> and by 1918 the Settlement had to move to larger
> quarters in the old Corning residence at Euclid Avenue
> and East 71st Street. In just seven years, The Cleve-
> land Music School Settlement had made its mark--two
> former students had become members of The Cleveland
> Orchestra.
> In 1923, the Settlement moved again, this time to
> a residence on East 93rd Street presented to the
> School through the generosity of Mr. and Mrs. Francis
> Drury. Fifteen years later, it moved to the present
> home, a 42-room mansion, with the help of the owners,
> Mr. and Mrs. Edmund S. Burke, Jr. Through the
> great interest of Mr. and Mrs. Elroy J. Kulas, the
> large stable was converted to a library in 1948, and
> the adjoining house, the former Charles Brooks resi-
> dence, was purchased in 1965.[30]

The growth of the School seemed to be continuous. New
building space seemed to generate bigger programs until it
now enrolls more than 5,000 students. The size and shape

of the School is described in its Catalogue for the 1984-1985 season:

> Today, the Cleveland Music School Settlement has more than 5,000 students enrolled at the Main School, Harvard East branch and affiliates (Koch School of Music and Rainey Institute) and in Extension Department programs at over 45 social agencies throughout the community.[31]

The records maintained at the Cleveland Music School Settlement are excellent. In response to the query regarding individuals who were uniquely associated with the beginning of the School, the answer was as follows:

> First Dean/Violin Teacher: Walter Logan, was on the faculty of Northwestern University, played with the Chicago Symphony, composed, was member of Cleveland Orchestra after its founding. Founded Young People's Symphony at CMSS.
>
> Adella Prentis Hughes: Almeda Adams approached Mrs. Hughes to establish the Settlement. Mrs. Hughes and the Fortnightly Musical Club members then began the planning with the Organizing and Incorporating Committee in Feb. 1912. The Founders were: Fortnightly Musical Club, Mrs. Dudley Blossom, M/M Francis E. Drury, Mrs. James E. Ferris, Samuel Mather, Mrs. M. Otis and Mrs. Lyon H. Treadway.[32]

Since Howard Whittaker retired at the end of the 1983-1984 season it was decided that a Self-Study should be undertaken to evaluate the program the School now had and to plan for a secure and imaginative future. Dr. Malcom J. Tait was appointed as director in August, 1984.* It became his task to initiate the steps of the Self-Study. Board of Trustees,

---

*Dr. Malcom J. Tait, Executive Director, Ed.D., M.A., B.A., Associate of the Royal College of Music, London, England. Formerly Director of Music Education and Kulas Professor of Music, Case Western Reserve University (1978-1984); Chairman of Music Education, University of Hawaii (1971-1977); Head of the Music Department, Waikato University and Hamilton Teachers College (1965-1969) and Chipping Norton Grammar School, Oxford, England (1959-1961).

faculty members, administrators and staff members were all
to participate and have input to the Self-Study.

Under the section on Purpose and Objectives the following Mission Statement evolved:

> To provide the finest training in music to children,
> young people, and adults with consideration of their
> ability to pay. To maintain a musical home where in
> addition to studying, there is an opportunity for listen-
> ing to performances of good music and where enrolled
> students will feel free to come for advice and guidance
> with personal problems. To provide services where
> the need arises in music therapy, music programs and
> classes in Settlements and other social agencies, and
> to establish branches.[33]

It is revealing to the interested observer that the philosophy of the Cleveland Music School Settlement has not varied
appreciably from the original concept of a community music
school's philosophy. (See pp. 89-92.)   While the
phraseology may be a bit more elegant and sophisticated, its
content expresses clearly the meaning intended.

One must note, however, that with changing times have
come slightly altered statements.   Janet D. Schenck's words
seem to indicate that the training at community music schools
was intended primarily, if not solely, for children, and that
since most of the children at that time were poor, all had to
be subsidized.   No mention was made of the adult student.

In the contemporary statement, approved by the Cleveland School's Board of Trustees, it is indicated that music
training is for "children, young people, and adults," and that
the fee to be charged will take into consideration the "student's ability to pay."   It is reassuring to know that such
training is available at any stage in life; particularly today the
community school of the arts agrees to address itself to the
problems of those who may be reaching their geriatric years
existing on fixed incomes, and who really desire and need
good artistic training.   Parts of the previous statement seem
to indicate a pattern that many schools have followed without
brazenly saying the words: All are welcome at the Community
School of the Arts!   This declaration includes the affluent,
the impoverished, and the bourgeousie, if you will--no one is

excluded! Yet each does his share to defray the cost of lessons, be they in music, art, dance, drama, etc. Thus in this magnificent movement, developed and encouraged in the United States of America, we all share--philosophically, financially, artistically, spiritually, and humanistically.

As the author perused and understood the response to the questions asked in the questionnaires which were returned from member schools of the Guild, it was enormously refreshing and exhilarating to comprehend that similar philosophies, aims and goals, and procedures are being adopted throughout the country in Community Schools of the Arts.

The Cleveland Music School Settlement has attracted artist teachers from around the world. At various times the School's faculty has included such artists as Severin Eisenberger, Leonard Shure, Theodore Letvin, and Clive Lithgoe, pianists; Joseph Gingold and Daniel Majeske, violinists; and Herbert Elwell, the American composer. Students who have gone on to achieve great distinction are Jaime Laredo, violinist; Seth McCoy, tenor, and Daisy Newman, soprano.

It is remarkable that the School has expanded its horizons to produce a Pre-School program which includes much more than musical training, though that is, of course, included. A flier describing this venture states the following:

> The primary purpose of the Pre School is to foster development of the education capabilities of each child, through a flexible program adjusted to the needs for social, emotional and intellectual growth. Pre School programs include experiences in the arts, science, nature, and literature. Perceptual skills and math and reading readiness are a part of the school's curricula, and all such activities to stimulate cognitive intellectual growth are related to the individual abilities of each child.[34]

The flier continues to explain the musical aspects of the Pre School:

> In particular, music experiences are many and varied. The children participate in music readiness classes even at the $2\frac{1}{2}$ year level; Dalcroze and Orff classes are part of the curricula for older pre-schoolers.

There are also numerous opportunities for youngsters
to explore and play simple rhythm instruments, and
they are exposed to an appropriate repertoire of songs,
classical music, and see a variety of cultural performances, including opera and ballet.[35]

The Pre School classes also include the parents by
having them demonstrate special skills which they may have.

Parents are encouraged to bring their expertise to
the Pre School by sharing their special talents--baking
bread, using a sewing machine, exhibiting the contents of a doctor's bag, showing the functions of a
microscope--all are exciting learning experiences for
young minds. Arrangements for such participation
can be made with the child's teacher. In addition,
there are parent-teacher meetings, and individual
parent conferences are scheduled to report on the
progress of each child.[36]

The teenagers have a special program for them which
allows them to use skills they have already mastered, as well
as to teach younger children to play musical instruments.
The program is called Teen in Training. The flier announcing
the program states the following:

Who Are We?
Cleveland teens today are "accentuating the positive"
through their work with the Neighborhood Centers
Teens-in-Training Program sponsored by the Cleveland
Music School Settlement Extension Department.
The T-'n-T Program offers teens with an interest
in music or dance an opportunity to become student
teachers in their special area of the arts. The teens
develop skills and confidence through teaching and
attending career-building workshops. They work
closely with professional teachers and Neighborhood
Centers Coordinators in all aspects of the program...
In Teens-in-Training everyone wins! The Neighborhood Centers are able to reach a greater number of
students because of the extra classes taught by student teachers. The teens gain experience and good
references to further their own career development.
The younger students get to know teens from their
own neighborhoods as role models for success. Both

the T-'n-T's and their students learn to channel their
extra energy in an enjoyable and creative way. Many
former T-'n-T's have gone on to college or to rewarding careers in music and other fields.[37]

The Cleveland Music School Settlement also supports
an extensive Music Therapy program. It produces a small
sheet explaining what music therapy is stating: "Music therapy provides the opportunity for personal and social growth.
Music experiences and activities are designed by the therapist
to encourage changes in behavior. Music is useful for therapy
because it interests people of all ages."[38]

The fact that a community music school attempts to support and run a Music Therapy program may raise questions
in the eyes of many. The Cleveland program reaches deeply
into the community at various social settlement houses and into
colleges and universities in the surrounding territory. The
brochure partially explains the goals of the Settlement Music
Therapy Program:

1) to encourage behavior that is appropriate and to
   control behavior that interferes with development.

2) to help children and adults deal more effectively
   with their surroundings.

3) to find new approaches to allow those with disabilities to learn musical skills.[39]

A staff of fully qualified personnel is an absolute requirement for a program of this size to be run effectively.
The program requires enough certified therapists to be available. In the 1984-85 Self-Study the program was well defined
in this manner:

The Music Therapy Department services children and
adults who have learning disabilities, physical and
mental handicaps, visual and hearing impairments or
behavioral disorders. The main goals of the Department are:

a. to modify specific behavioral patterns which inter-
    fere with individual development;

b. to help individuals react more effectively within
    their surroundings;

c. to develop ways to enable the handicapped to use
    music as an expressive art form (leisure time per-
    formance skill).[40]

The Self-Study continues:

> In 1984-85, nine registered Music Therapists are
> employed to work with health care and social service
> professionals, as well as family members to develop
> an individualized program for each student seen in
> individual/or group settings. An interview and eval-
> uation is granted anyone on request.[41]

The Music School also has added an additional step that
is unusual for Guild Schools, and that is to contract their
Music Therapy services outside the Music School itself. The
flier explains the procedure this way:

> Music Therapy programs are designed and staffed
> in educational, treatment and special service agencies
> throughout greater Cleveland by purchase-for-service
> contracts. Each program is tailored to the needs of
> the agency and can be contracted on an hourly, part-
> time or full-time basis.[42]

It is also necessary to state that the Department is approved by the National Association for Music Therapy as an
internship training facility (the first in the country to be established in a community arts program).

The establishment and development of the Cleveland
Music School Settlement presents a story that is to be admired
and emulated. Its growth in its community has spread through
many facets of Cuyahoga County's social service areas as well
as through its artistic and educational facilities. It is almost
on a humorous note that a report is made in the Self-Study
that refers to space, both in quantity and use.

Physical Plant

Reference has already been made to the long-range
planning report and the more effective utilization of

the physical space that is available. The Early Childhood Program and the Dance Program desperately need
re-location. The Music Therapy Program is very
cramped both for teaching purposes and office space.
Studio accommodation is, on the whole, quite excellent
although with more flexible student grouping some
areas of larger space may have to be found.[43]

It is with compassion that one views the problem of
space that dogs this highly successful institution. Undoubtedly the director and the Board of Trustees will find a satisfactory solution to the space problem.

The Harlem School of the Arts

The existence of the Harlem School of the Arts is a remarkable example of the creativity and imagination of one
brilliant, dedicated woman and the generosity of a church in
the community. Dr. Shelby Rooks, pastor of St. James Presbyterian Church and the husband of Dorothy Maynor, suggested and recommended that the Church allow their community
center space to be used to house the Harlem School of the
Arts. While it would be a temporary home for the time being,
this move would allow the School to start to operate. At first
the space was given at no cost to the School, until such time
as it became more firmly established. The reason for his
action was to add a new dimension to the lives of those living
in the area. Because other facilities were available to house
basketball, volleyball, games and other social activities, he
questioned why the Church should duplicate such programs,
thereby running competition with the local public schools,
YMCA, etc.

The elders of the Church approved the idea enthusiasti-
cally, particularly since the School was to be a community
music school in its truest sense. Two of the elders were
immediately appointed to the board of directors of the School
and served in that capacity for many years. It was an example of true community spirit, action and cooperation, one
of the finest in this country.

In the Parent/Student Handbook of 1984-85, the origin
of the school is explained in this manner:

The magnificient home of the Harlem School of the
Arts, fronting on St. Nicholas Avenue at 141st Street
in Manhattan, is the dream and creation of its founder
and first director, world-famous soprano, Dorothy
Maynor. Together with her husband, the Rev. Shelby
Rooks, she opened the School in the parish house of
her husband's St. James' Presbyterian Church in 1964.
    The School moved into its beautiful new home in
1977 after a long drive for the $3,600,000, raised by
the indomitable Miss Maynor. Described by her as
"an oasis of hope in a sea of despair," the School
was dedicated to the concept that a disciplined training in the arts offers Harlem's youth not only a chance
for professional careers in the arts but also a new
sense of self-worth and a joyful relief from the chaos
of their environment. [44]

The architect who designed the Harlem School of the
Arts building is Ulrich Franzen, and the following statement
appeared in the Architectural Record in May 1979:

When New York's City Club announced the 1978 winners of the coveted Bard Awards for local architectural
and urban-designed excellence, the jury noted the
predominance of projects that serve programs of social
significance. And none of the winners conformed
better to that description than architect Ulrich
Franzen's building...[the Harlem School of the Arts].
    Today the school strives to produce cultural ac-
complishment for between 700 and 800 local children
with a faculty of 44--while offering some facilities
for adults as well. And as a tribute to Maynor's concept, the building that houses her programs is as
fresh and well respected as it was when it opened
nearly a year ago, after a long seven-year collaboration
between architect and client. [45]

In the Parent/Student Handbook, 1984-85 an updated
account of the activities of the School is given which explains
further the scope of the School:

THE HARLEM SCHOOL OF THE ARTS--TODAY

HSA serves many people today, including a Senior
Citizens' program in creative writing, music, art and

--yeah-- dance. Children come from all over New
York City, Westchester, New Jersey and Connecticut;
they come in all colors, shapes and sizes to learn
Suzuki violin, or piano or oboe or drums or dance.
...Current enrollment numbers over 1,000 students
in the after-school and Saturday programs, plus more
than 360 public school children who come for arts
instruction during the school day.[46]

In 1979 the Harlem School of the Arts was most fortunate
to engage Betty Allen as the Executive-Director after the retirement of Miss Maynor. Betty Allen has dedicated herself
to enhancing the reputation of the School by arranging special
programs and concerts for the children to hear at their own
School and by encouraging the growth and development of
public school programs which bring public school students
to the Harlem School during regular school schedules. She
has also started special classes for senior citizens in many
of the art forms. Her interest in the professional performance
aspect of musical training helps those with true performance
abilities to gain the training needed to move into professional
circles. Though the majority of the students will probably
not attempt a performance career, the School under Betty
Allen's supervision stands ready to guide, train and assist
potentional public performers.

Betty Allen has worked to strengthen the Advisory
Committee by attracting significant and prominent musicians to
join the ranks of the School. The Committee includes such
names as Martina Arroyo, Louise Behrend, Winifred Cecil,
Justin Diaz, Leonard De Paur, Zubin Mehta, Arthur Mitchell,
Leontyne Price, Sherill Milnes, Beverly Sills, Isaac Stern,
Billy Taylor, Shirley Verrett, and André Watts. Betty Allen
has also been one of the Guild directors who worked ar-
duously for the fiftieth anniversary celebration of the National
Guild.

The School for Strings

Louise Behrend, founder and director of the School for
Strings, has first of all proved herself to be a performer of
great distinction. Her Town Hall debut on March 29, 1949
received exceptionally fine reviews, one of which carried the
following statements:

> The city of Washington may pat itself proudly on the
> back for having produced the fine young violinist,
> Louise Behrend, who gave her first Town Hall recital
> last evening. Few, indeed, are there local debuts
> as interesting musically as hers was, ...It seemed to
> this writer that Miss Behrend might well be called a
> female Szigeti. For her work is everywhere reminis-
> cent of his in the perceptive quality of her playing,
> its clean, stylistic authority, its imagination and
> sensitiveness. [47]

Miss Behrend was not only performing extremely well,
but she also proved to be an excellent teacher at the Music
School of the Henry Street Settlement where she joined the
staff in 1943. Her serious approach to teaching made her one
of the outstanding violin faculty members. It was she who
worked closely with the director to encourage after-school
music lessons for students in the public schools of the Fourth
District of Manhattan, a district in which Henry Street was
located. Her work produced excellent results. She also performed as a recitalist at the Playhouse of the Henry Street
Settlement which was always an inspiration to the students of
the School.

It was she who became most intrigued by the success
of the work of Shinichi Suzuki in Japan. So much so, that
she made plans to concertize in Japan and to spend time there
watching Suzuki in his work at Matsumoto. In a paper she
wrote called "No Shortage of String Teachers in Japan," she
explains relating her plans to the director of the Henry Street
Music School who was also the president of the National Guild
of Community Music Schools.

> Two seasons ago, Shinichi Suzuki visited this country,
> bringing with him ten of his Talent Education students.
> ...In my 25 years of teaching the violin, I don't be-
> lieve that anything has moved or excited me more
> than this performance. I decided then and there
> to go to Japan to observe and study Suzuki's teaching
> approach. ...I made my definite plans for the trip
> for the summer of 1965. When I told Robert Egan of
> Henry Street Music School about these plans, he asked
> me to represent the [National] Guild of Community
> Music Schools and to report back on this very exciting
> work. [48]

Indeed, Miss Behrend did go to Japan and came back
so thrilled that she planned with Egan to start a Suzuki program (the first in New York City) at the Henry Street Settlement Music School during the 1966-67 season.* As a result
of the success of this program, Miss Behrend began her own
School for Strings in 1970. The program at that school is
designed to teach string students of all ages and to train
teachers to use the Suzuki approach successfully. The new
location of the School for Strings is 419 West 54 Street,
New York City.

The National Guild of Community Schools of the Arts,
Inc. Membership Directory 1986 gives a clear statement about
this school:**

> This Suzuki-oriented school is designed to provide a
> comprehensive musical education in violin, cello, and
> piano. Children are accepted from the age of 3 on
> up. There are no entrance requirements or auditions,
> but admission is dependent on the parents' attendance
> at an orientation meeting, as the parents role is cru-
> cial for success in the Suzuki approach. Throughout
> the children's study, the School's deep commitment to
> ensemble playing is expressed; first through group-
> playing classes, and later through participation in
> the School's orchestras and chamber music groups.
> At the heart of the School lies its two year Teacher-
> Training Program where professional violinists, cellists,
> and pianists receive training in the Suzuki approach
> and techniques, and do supervised practice teaching
> in the School's community service division, its Special
> Programs for disadvantaged youngsters.[49]

Obviously Louise Behrend has continued her deep

---

*A complete account of this is found in the doctoral disserta-
tion, by Robert F. Egan, "The History of the Music School of
the Henry Street." New York University, 1967, pp. 247-261.
**One of the violin teachers selected to join the staff of the
School for Strings was Ruth Kemper, who had been the direct-
or of the Turtle Bay Music School in New York City and a past
president of the National Guild of Community Music Schools.
(More about Ruth Kemper's work is found in a later chapter.)

dedication to fine teaching and has not lost her understanding
of the needs of the disadvantaged, which she accepted early
in her teaching and professional career. This school, dedicated to fine string playing, should make a most important
and significant contribution to music education. Throughout
the growth and development of this School, Sheila Keats has
worked continuously in the administration of the School and was
its first piano teacher to use the Suzuki approach in piano
teaching at the School. Miss Keats, a graduate of the Juilliard
School of Music, also has a gift for prose writing which is
much in evidence in the materials released by the School for
Strings. Miss Keats is the associate director of the School.

Louise Behrend has also been responsible for the writing
of several articles on the Suzuki approach such as, "No
Shortage of String Players in Japan," "Rosin in the Left
Hand," "Listen and Watch the Exposure Team," and "Suzuki
Training Is Parent Training."

When the National Guild of Community Music Schools
changed its name to the National Guild of Community Schools
of the Arts (in 1974), it opened new channels for Guild membership. While initially the name change was suggested to
state more accurately what was happening in arts education in
such schools, the change also made it possible for schools
which taught different artistic disciplines to seek Guild membership. These disciplines could be in the areas of visual arts--
painting, pottery, photography, sculpture, or dance, drama,
theatre arts, etc. It was even possible that these schools
taught no music at all, a new concept altogether. Thus a new
membership category was established. (Naturally by-laws were
amended appropriately.)

The Baum School of Art

The school that first sought membership in the National Guild
under the new category was the Baum School of Art in Allentown, Pennsylvania. This School was founded in 1926 by
Walter Emerson Baum, a painter and member of the National
Academy, art critic for the Philadelphia Bulletin, and a teacher
of art.

It is fascinating to read the names of those who initially
assisted in the establishment of the School. They include the
following:

Walter Emerson Baum--founder and first director of the School

Flora Baum--wife of the founder-director who functioned as registrar, bookkeeper and secretary

Blanche Lucas--art teacher who organized the first class for 22 elementary school teachers in the summer of 1926

O. D. Havard--a local businessman who helped to equip and organize the business of the school

Percy Ruhe--editor of the Local newspaper who helped with publicity and donations

William Gibson--member of the Allentown School Board who provided housing for the School in the public school for the first 30 years

Charles Kline--created the first scholarship program for needy students

Max Hess--businessman and patron of the arts who donated the first property to the School (1956)

Dorothy Leonard--student, board member, teacher and director

Mary Barnett--registrar, secretary and bookkeeper

Mel Stark--student, teacher, outstanding painter and director.[50]

This represents a large cross-section of the local population, each of whom served in a capacity or capacities where he best fit. Community interest obviously led to community action in making the School become a reality. It is a tribute to these early founders that the records were kept in such fashion that they could be presented quickly and readily.

The current director is Dr. Rudy Ackerman, and like the founder's wife had done, Mrs. Rosemarie Ackerman functions on the administrative staff as the assistant director. In the brochure for the Spring, 1984 term, Dr. Ackerman made the following statement:

> Many times I have been asked, Why do individuals
> attend the Baum School? My answer is very simple.
> First, they have an interest in the visual arts.
> Second, they enjoy creating in an open and supportive
> atmosphere, and third, they feel a sense of fulfillment
> and pleasure in what they are doing. Of course, there
> are many other reasons, but the three in my answer
> usually provide a foundation on which the successful
> student builds.[51]

Dr. Ackerman further gives information about the School
in the next statement which includes the kind of recognition
of the fact that the Baum School of Art is truly a community
school of the arts:

> All of the classes are based on individualized instruction
> and provide a foundation if you are a beginner or a
> challenge if you are advanced. Previous training and
> experience are not prerequisites and no person has
> ever been refused admission because of his or her
> race, creed or financial status.[52]

The brochure tells of a wide variety of courses to be
offered to young and old, from small children to teenagers and
adults, such as Introduction to Media, Drawing and Painting
I, Drawing and Painting II, Ceramics: Creating with Clay,
Water Color or Landscape Painting, Understanding Photography,
The Art of Illustration, Drawing and Painting the Portrait,
and many other exciting and creative classes.

By reading the booklet The Baum School of Art Fiftieth
Anniversary 1926-1976, one learns much about the history of
the School, its staunch and loyal Board members, the many
problems of location and space it has encountered over the
years, its dedicated alumni, and about the distinguished accomplishments throughout its existence. Perhaps the most
significant achievement is that it is currently housed in the
Allentown Art Museum. The booklet states quietly:

> The new and beautiful Baum School at the Art Museum
> is the culmination of the collective efforts of many and
> the realization of Dr. Baum's 30-year dream.[53]

The founder and director of the Baum School of Art,
Dr. Walter Emerson Baum, deserves his appelation, "the father
of art in the Lehigh Valley."[54]

More and more arts organizations are finding the need
for affiliation with the National Guild. One such organization
is the struggling Bene-Duque program in Pittsburgh, Pennsylvania. The name is derived from the fact that the program
is housed in St. Benedict the Moor elementary school sponsored
by the Duquesne University School of Music; hence the name,
Bene-Duque program. It is in the Hill District of Pittsburgh,
primarily a black community. Music lessons are taught during
the regular school schedule by teachers sent to the school
by Duquesne's School of Music.

While for the past ten years the program has been supported by a local foundation and private donations, the difficulty in raising funds substantially lies in the fact that the
elementary school is part of the Catholic Schools' Board of
Education, which cannot underwrite the program, and the
University, of course, has its own Board of Directors, Development Office, etc. There cannot be a conflict of interest
in requesting contributions. Nevertheless, lessons are taught
to the children in piano, winds, brass and percussion in both
private lessons and group lessons on a regular weekly basis.

The person responsible for the total program is a former
director of a Guild School, and the cooperation between the
elementary school and the University is a delight to observe
and to understand.

It seems wise to conclude this chapter with a statement
from a former director about a community music school she
headed for some twenty years. It expresses the way in which
a school may evolve, and shows the devotion given to community schools of the arts all over the country:

The Roosa School of Music

The Roosa School of Music of Brooklyn Heights was
founded in 1940 by John King Roosa, who had been
head of the string department at the Brooklyn Music
School Settlement for many years. The school was
organized as a parent-teacher cooperative, which became officially designated the Roosa Music School
Associates. It functioned cooperatively until 1960.
Initially the school occupied four rooms in a brown-
stone house and had a faculty of five. As it grew,
extra space was found in the Brooklyn Women's Club

and the First Presbyterian Church. Several members
of the Herbert Pratt family, because of their interest
in Mr. Roosa's work, his program, and ideas, provided very generous support during the school's first
twenty years, which made its continuous development
possible. Mr. Roosa retired in 1955 but continued
with fund raising for scholarships almost until his
death.

In 1960, the school was incorporated and became
part of the Alfred T. White Community Center, sharing
a former church and large community building with
a nursery school and a teacher group, which it still
does. The Roosa Music School Associates evolved
into the Board of Directors, and Emily Franz, a former
faculty member, became executive director.

During Miss Franz's tenure, with the help of city,
state and federal grants, the school began an extensive
outreach program. Instrumental classes (strings,
recorder, and guitar) were provided in two public
school districts and in the South Brooklyn Neighborhood Houses. In cooperation with the Low Memorial
Child Center, music therapy classes were given to
children with cerebral palsy. Orff classes were conducted in three other day care centers. The program
in one of the latter soon evolved into a "satellite"
school which later became the Lefferts Gardens Community Music School. A three-year grant from the
Noble Foundation helped to establish a school in Sunset Park. Jeanne Lowe of the Roosa Music School
faculty was in charge of development and administration. In three seasons, the Sunset Park School also
became independent and is now a member of the National Guild of Community Schools of the Arts. Anthony
Masiello is director.

Other "extensions" of the Roosa School were in two
private schools, the Brooklyn Friends and St. Ann's,
where Roosa School faculty members gave individual
instrumental instruction to students during regular
school hours.

After Emily Franz's retirement in 1980, Paul Fran
became director in 1981 and served for one year.
Jeanne Lowe was appointed director in 1981 and served
until 1986. During those five years, the community
programs were continued, with the addition of choral
work and some new courses in different public schools.

At the Roosa School, Miss Lowe also introduced voice instruction, jazz studies, music therapy for disturbed children, and special music reading classes for adult beginners.

Clive Lithgoe is the Roosa School's present director. He had been head of the piano department at the Cleveland Music School for ten years, and director of the main school for the past two seasons. He has already presented some long term plans to the board and faculty and taken initial steps to implement them.[55]*

---

*The author is deeply indebted to Miss Emily Franz, director of the Roosa School of Music from 1960-1980, for sending him the beautifully descriptive letter about the Roosa School of Music reprinted above.

4

TWO DECADES OF GROWTH: The 1920's and 1930's and the Formation of the National Guild of Community Music Schools

The time span of 1920 to 1940 was a period of development and growth for schools that were to become members of the National Guild of Community Schools of the Arts. Fourteen schools were in the Eastern United States, five in the Mid-West, none in the South, one in the Far West and two in Canada. Two-thirds of these new schools were found in the Eastern United States, a trend that was to continue for some time. The majority of the Schools taught music only, though in later years some did branch into other areas of art instruction. One, however, is unique in that it taught visual arts only and still does at this writing. It is the Baum School of Arts in Allentown, Pennsylvania. A listing of the schools in chronological order follows.

Founded in 1920

David Hochstein Memorial Music School, Rochester,
   New York
Founded by Mrs. James Sibley Watson
Present Administrative officer: Dr. Karl Atkins,
   President

Hartt School of Music, Community Division, Hartford,
   Connecticut
Founded by Julius Hartt and Moshe Paranov
Present director: Dr. Michael Richters (Acting Director)

Diller-Quaile School of Music, New York, New York
Founded by Angela Diller and Elizabeth Quaile
Present director: Marjory Duncalfe

Founded in 1921

Community Music Center, San Francisco, California
Founded by Gertrude Field
Present director: Dr. Stephen R. Shapiro

Founded in 1922

Anna Perlow Music School of the Jewish Community
    Center, Pittsburgh, Pennsylvania
Founded by Anna L. Perlow
Present director: Allen Sher

Sutphen School of Music, Cleveland, Ohio
Founded by and part of The Phyllis Wheatley Association
Present director: Lavert Stuart

Founded in 1924

Brookline Music School, Brookline, Massachusetts
Founded by:--Information not available
Present director: Larry Zukof

Community Music School of Buffalo, Buffalo, New York
    (Name changed in 1948)
Founded by The Chromatic Club of Buffalo
Present director: Linda L. Mabry

Detroit Community Music School, Detroit, Michigan
Founded by Mrs. Eleanor Clay Ford and Mrs. Marjorie
    Russell Dykema
Present Director: Steven J. Nelson

Wilmington Music School, Wilmington, Delaware
Founded by:--Information not available
Present directors: Stephen C. Gunzenhauser, Artistic
    Director; Martha Collins, Administrative Director

Founded in 1925

Turtle Bay Music School, New York, New York
Founded by Eleanor Stanley White
Present director: Dr. Catherine M. Campbell

Founded in 1926

Baum School of Art, Allentown, Pennsylvania
Founded by Walter Emerson Baum
Present director: Dr. Rudy S. Ackerman

Community Music School (St. Louis, Missouri)
Founded in 1926 and merged with the St. Louis Institute
   of Music in 1974 to form the St. Louis Conservatory
   and Schools for the Arts
Present director: Shirley Bartzen, Dean

Founded in 1927

Henry Street Settlement Music School, New York,
   New York
Founded by The Henry Street Settlement and Hedi Katz
Present director: Philip E. West

Founded in 1929

Westchester Conservatory of Music, White Plains, New
   York
Founded by Nicolai Mednikoff
Present director: Laura Calzolari

Founded in 1930

Music School of the St. Christopher House, Toronto,
   Ontario, Canada
Founded by:--Information not available
Present director: Mary P. Leggatt

Founded in 1931

Music Center of the North Shore, Winnetka, Illinois
Founded by--formerly the Dushkin School of Music
Present director: Kalman Novak

Founded in 1936

92nd Street Y Dance Center, New York, New York
Founded by Dr. William Kolodney, responsible for
   bringing modern dance to the Y and to the general
   public
Present director: Sharon Gersten

Founded in 1938

Dana School of Music, Wellesley, Massachusetts
Founded by:--Information not available
Present director: Telemak G. Gharibian

Founded in 1940

Pittsfield Community Music School, Pittsfield, Massa-
    chusetts
Founded by--Information not available
Present director: Marion Maby Wells

Founded in 1940*

Roosa School of Music, Brooklyn, New York
Founded by John King Roosa
Present director: Clive Lythgoe

At this period in history, schools were being established
making the need for a national clearing house of ideas even
more pressing. Where would the directors of community
music schools turn to discuss problems which faced them and
their schools? Where would these directors go to discuss
trends of the times in relation to their schools? Let us take
a look at the economic, social and historical problems facing
this nation and the world during these decades.

During this period of history, the American people lived
through some very trying times. World War I had begun in
1914, and Europe was in a very turbulent state. This made
many who were recent immigrants very concerned about rela-
tives and friends whom they might have left in the different
warring European countries.

The next event was even more tragic for them, when on
April 6, 1917 the United States of America entered the fracas.
A period of great rejoicing overtook this country when on

---

*The above information may be verified by the National
Guild of Community Schools of the Arts, Inc., Membership
Directory 1985, or are answers to the Questionnaires mailed
to all Guild Schools. (In the files of the National Guild
of Community Schools of the Arts, Englewood, New Jersey.)

November 11, 1918 the Armistice was declared. For a time, at least, the world seemed to be at peace. The emotional strain on the entire nation had been enormous.

The year 1919 had had much political ferment, and on January 16, 1920 the XVIII Amendment to the Constitution of the United States of America, the Prohibition Act, went into effect making it illegal to buy, sell or import alcoholic beverages within the U.S.A. This legislation was to be enforced until Franklin Delano Roosevelt, the 32nd president of this country, announced the ratification of the XXI Amendment to the Constitution by the 36th State, which was Utah, thus ending Prohibition on December 6, 1933. Prohibition had lasted for a period of nearly 14 years.

For those who were observing this nation's financial affairs, stock market and business arrangements throughout the Roaring Twenties, a feeling of uneasiness should have been felt, but sadly, these were not recognized as serious problems. On October 29, 1929, to become known as Black Tuesday, the Stock Market crashed, sending this country into a financial tailspin. This turn of events and its economic ramifications continued to worsen until the country fell into one of the deepest depressions in its history. The depression was to last until the beginning of World War II which helped to stabilize the economy of the country.

At the helm, Franklin D. Roosevelt, the President, displayed a magnetic personality, a creative imagination, and excellent speaking ability. His radio broadcasts, called his Fireside Chats, became a source of comfort to Americans, young and old. They reflected the confidence he expressed in his newly planned legislation, and in the American people themselves. For those who listened carefully, security and confidence were predicated with his most famous quotation, "We have nothing to fear, but fear itself." His Acceptance Speech delivered at the Democratic National Convention in Chicago on July 2, 1932 included the following words:

> I pledge you--I pledge myself to a new deal for the American people. Let us all here assembled constitute ourselves prophets of a new order of competence and of courage. This is more than a political campaign; it is a call to arms. Give me your help, not to win votes alone, but to win in this crusade to restore America to its own people.[1]

And, indeed, the restoration began as the new president had promised.

If one had had any doubts about the value of the arts in the communities around the country, they were assuaged now. Not one of the community music schools affiliated with the National Guild faltered or stopped during the years of the depression, which continued until nearly the beginning of the next decade. These schools were forced to examine carefully the spending of pennies, to learn to exist on minimal budgets, and were forced to raise additional funds through unending fundraising activities. Such schools found solace in the arts and existed, sometimes painfully, for those for whom the arts were a comfort and a way of life.

The sharing of thoughts and ideas was important to those who were responsible for the running of schools of the arts. Janet Schenck relates how some of the cities with large populations where several schools existed handled this problem:

> In cities where several schools exist, central associations, or federations, have grown up for the exchange of ideas and the education of public opinion. The New York City Association of Music School Settlements, for example, includes seven schools: three separtley [sic] incorporated and four departments of settlements, with a total enrollment of 2151 students, 200 teachers and combined budgets which approximate $135,000 (in toto). They number, on their Boards of Directors some 150 interested people of prominence and standing in the community, and enjoy the sympathetic encouragement of two score or more artists who serve on their Auxiliary Boards.[2]

She further states some procedural techniques that these city-wide organizations followed:

> The association holds monthly meetings which are attended by representatives of the Boards, the directors of the various schools, heads of departments, etc. There are occasional conferences on the work of the different departments. General teaching lists have been compiled, school credits have been studied and a thousand and one difficulties have been smoothed away. During the present winter, a series of talks

by prominent men have been given, and a joint concert of all the schools held in Aeolian Hall.[3]

Schenck then cites other cities which follow similar procedures:

> The Inter-Settlement Music Committee of the Boston
> Social Union embraces three incorporated music schools,
> one of them having three branches, and seven other
> departments of settlements. The Committee each year
> carries on four inter-settlement concerts and organizes
> one large meeting to which all people interested in
> music schools are invited. Reports of work done in
> each of the different schools are brought to the meet-
> ings for discussion.
> The Philadelphia Association includes some eleven
> houses. Its program includes four major activities:
> a clearing house for the distribution of talent and
> development of concerts; a department for encouraging
> choral and group singing in the settlements; meetings
> for teachers; intersettlement concerts.[4]

The statement above, "a department for encouraging
choral and group singing in the settlements," is one that
should be observed and understood completely. It foreshadows
problems that will exist in the 1930's, both prior to the establishment of the National Guild of Community Music Schools
and problems with the National Federation of Settlements that
encouraged community music schools throughout the country
to found yet another national organization--and this, in the
midst of a severe depression--and for Music!

The Settlement House Movement in this country had
long been a serious supporter of the arts within its member
organizations. The Community Music Schools have, since their
origin, recognized and publicly stated that they, in truth,
were an offshoot of the settlement houses. Though they
worked diligently together and the Settlement Music School
was identified at the first and second conferences of International Federation of Settlements as a uniquely American contribution, internally they were beginning to appear as strange
bedfellows. Philosophies were developing that seemed to pit
the arts (primarily music at this period) against the social
workers and their problems. In some instances the identifiable
differences seemed to be only a matter of semantics. But

the differences seemed to remain and arguments became public information and were openly discussed.

The idea of some sort of National Music Organization for community music schools also had continued to boil and ferment. Janet Schenck again speaks for the music school settlements and community music schools (at this point almost interchangeable terms). She relates:

> The decade and a half between 1893 and 1911 constituted the period of pioneering in settlement music instruction. By 1910 the idea had thoroughly proved its worth under the restricted conditions imposed upon it in the settlement house.[5]

The reader cannot help feeling the sting of some of Janet Schenck's comments. In the quotation above the underscoring is done by this author to give another example of Schenck's caustic remarks. While she had given credit to the Settlement House Movement in her writings, she also speaks for the musician alone at times, and she occasionally verbalizes somewhat irreverently about.the very organizations which initially made it possible for music schools to begin their programs. This kind of comment was certainly heard by settlement house administrators and may have helped to cause a rift between the two groups.

Schenck did understand the value of a national organization to speak for those working in community music schools, and she gave her strength and effort to try to make this come about. She tells of the experience this way:

> An important off-shoot of the establishment of a number of new schools in 1910 was the desire on the part of founders to meet and discuss problems having to do with organization and administration. The first national conference of music school representatives was held in New York in 1911. The meeting formed itself into the National Association of Music School Societies, which met again 1912. The reports of these two conferences were most helpful and stimulating.[6]

Whether these fledgeling schools and their administrators were not yet equipped to undertake the responsibilities of

membership in a national organization or did not yet see the
value of it, or whether some of the boards of these schools
were not willing to underwrite the expense of such an undertaking, is unknown at this time. Nonetheless the national
organization did not survive on its first try. In her genteel
way Janet Schenck explains:

> After 1913 the association languished, and in 1916
> became defunct. Despite loss of interest, there were
> a few men and women who believed that those working
> in the Music Schools had much to give and to receive
> from each other; and more important still, had much
> to give the community in stimulating and guiding its
> interest in music. They saw music as a great force
> for good in the lives of all people.[7]

Schenck continues her description of the situation and
further connects the National Federation of Settlements with
the emerging National Guild:

> ...Chief among these was John [sic] Grolle of the
> Settlement Music School, Philadelphia, who in 1917
> induced the National Federation of Settlements to ap-
> point a committee on art, and during the following
> four years served as its chairman. In 1921, a separ-
> ate music committee was appointed, which in 1922 be-
> came the Music Division. The division has its own
> officers and executive committee, the latter chosen
> partly by the music committee of the city federations
> of settlements, and partly at large.[8]

In his intense desire to bring good music and good musical instruction to those who wanted it, Johan Grolle demonstrated his willingness to assume additional responsibilities
by accepting the chairmanship of those committees or divisions
which would give him the opportunity to use his persuasive
powers to encourage the various factions to work together in
harmony. Naturally his interest was in music primarily, and
then the other arts. His social conscience was also strong,
as we remember that one of his sincere interests in becoming
part of the Settlement Music School in Philadelphia was that
its aim was to bring music to all regardless of their abilities
to pay for the lessons.

The crux of the entire matter seemed to be between a

concept of what a Settlement House is supposed to be and
what a Community Music School is supposed to be. At this
point the reader must realize that each requires money, and
though that ugly word may not appear in philosophical statements, it is the foundation of the operation of any institution,
for profit or not for profit! A complicating factor seemed to
be the structure and responsibilities of the National Federation
of Settlements. Much anger was expressed by those on either
side of the dispute. Seldom did either listen carefully and
understandingly to the other when he expressed his ideas or
goals. An impasse was reached! This became a minor tragedy
for the arts and for social programs, particularly distressing
because they had principally worked so well together, and at
this stage had reached a point of diminishing returns.

Since one must identify the concepts of those so closely
involved with the musical/social problems, it is necessary to
observe the intended goals of each. Janet Schenck selected
a statement for discussion in a section of her book Music,
Youth and Opportunity, which could be used to argue on
either side. Her chapter title is "Interaction of Music School
and Settlement." Her choice comes from The Settlement Horizon
by Woods and Kennedy, and it states the following: "The
settlement ... is not committed to any doctrinal scheme of
society, past, present, or future. It seeks only the general
good, the widest fulfillment of human faculty, the most creative
interplay of humans wills."[9] Schenck then continues with
her own commentary:

> ...This fine description of a social settlement makes
> clear the fundamental principle of that movement.
> It must touch the neighborhood at a thousand points,
> its program must be largely influenced by the ebb and
> flow of economic and racial tendencies, above all its
> flexibility must be maintained.[10]

She then begins to reveal the path which she believes
a successful music school or department should and must follow. The path, however, might be fraught with danger, and
it must be examined and evaluated carefully, otherwise it could
lead to disaster. She cleverly throws the responsibility to
the headworker when she states:

> ...The headresident of a settlement must survey his
> neighborhood from every angle and must develop a

round of activities calculated to touch it from every
side. He probably has under him a corps of workers
representing a dozen or more different aspects of the
plan and each one urging that his own department
be given special consideration. [11]

The headworker or headresident is now the one who
must take decisive action. He obviously can do this only after
careful cogitation. The weight of the program clearly rests
on his shoulders.

Let us for a moment, however, explore the background
and training of the headworker and question his preparation
and capabilities for decision making regarding a music program. A few thought-provoking questions:

1. Does the headworker have any music or arts study
   in his background?

2. Were these good experiences? Or were they poor
   experiences which may have given him a somewhat
   negative attitude toward the arts in general?

3. Has the headworker actually visited and observed
   the work of the music program/any arts program
   in action? Any return visits?

4. Are there members of an advisory committee or even
   a board member with whom the headworker can have
   an objective discussion about the program?

5. What is the relationship between the headworker
   and the director of the Music School or chairman of
   the music department?

6. N.B. Does the music school's director or chairman
   of the music department understand the goals and
   aims of the total Settlement program?

The questions proposed above should make each partner
in this marriage consider carefully his/her responsibilities in
creating such a union in the first place. If the social worker
has in his educational background something more than one
course in Music History and another in Art Appreciation, he
may at least be a partially prepared individual who at some

time in his career may be called upon to evaluate a music or
art program. If this be entirely lacking in his professional
training, how can he possibly be prepared to make value decisions about any music or art program under his jurisdiction?

If on the other hand the musician engaged to be the
director of a Music School shows no interest or understanding
of the social work program in which his institution is currently
engaged, the situation will be a hopeless muddle.

Too often musicians who accept positions as directors
of music schools prove themselves to be inordinately poor arts
administrators. They seem to want to have the title and distinction added to their names, but fail miserably in realizing
the responsibilities of arts administrators. It is virtually impossible for a professionally performing musician to continue
such a career and assume the awesome task of running a fully
functioning music school. Very few have been able to succeed
at both simultaneously.

One of two solutions is possible if the still-performing
musician is so engaged. One solution is to hire additional
administrative personnel who will be empowered to make those
decisions necessary to keep the school functioning smoothly
on a day to day basis. (More about this later in the chapter.)
The second solution is have the performer wait to accept such
responsibility until he/she has decided to end the performance
career almost completely.

An excellent example of this is in the action of Dorothy
Maynor, the American soprano whose recital career was legen-
dary. At a point in her life she decided to curtail the performance career and dedicate her life to the establishment of
a community music school in the Harlem section of New York
City. As was discussed in an earlier chapter, through the
efforts of Dorothy Maynor, the Harlem School of the Arts is
now housed in a new $3.6 million building. This was only
possible through her full-time dedication to the effort of
running of the School and of raising money for the building
of the new structure.

Many music schools in their beginning stages will not
be forced to have faculty prepared to undertake the training
of young people ready for a concert career. The majority of
the students of any music school of this kind will be at the

beginning to intermediate stages. The enrollment of such schools will form almost a pyramid shape when put on a scale showing the heaviest enrollment spread at the bottom and tapering off to the top with the fewest students.

The conclusions drawn by Janet Schenck show an attitude that would be difficult for a headworker to accept at face value, particularly when that person is in the process of trying to fit a large program into a small budget. Schenck's plans for the development of a strong music program with much enthusiasm is excellent for the growth of a music school, but eventually the School grows at such a rate that problems of space and finances appear with such imperative pressure that the situation must be addressed immediately. Schenck states:

> The music department of a social settlement gradually becomes entirely specialized. The longer it is in existence the more pronounced the specialization, for the students grow older and their work more advanced.
>   At once a perfectly normal result takes place. The head of the music department begins to make demands which are well nigh essential in the development and realization of his aim. The pianos must be kept in good condition and this is almost impossible when they are constantly used for social clubs. A music lesson will endeavor to go on while a game of basketball is crashing on the ceiling above. A thousand and one difficulties will arise which makes the work of the music department almost impossible. In equal justice the headworker [sic] often feels he cannot very well curtail activities participated in by large numbers for the benefit of a small group.[12]

The reader can easily see both sides, and for the social service program which is important to the Settlement, there is a real problem which is largely spatial. Unless the organization owns, or is willing to rent other building space to be occupied exclusively by the Music School, there is really no solution to the knotty problem.

An example of this problem of space occurred at the Henry Street Settlement Music School. Though music, musical performances, special programs, etc., had been in the program from the earliest days of its history, Henry Street did not

have its Music School formally established until 1927. The
reason was the one Janet Schenck mentions. Henry Street
did not have space to house a Music School until a building
that led into its Playhouse was acquired. In 1927 the acquisition of the building at 8 Pitt Street took place, the Settlement then allowed Hedi Katz to formalize the Music School.
Its official dedication was not until November of 1928. Yet
the arts had permeated the Henry Street program.

One of the most difficult situations in which a music
school or department of music that is part of a larger institution finds itself is that the parent organization frequently
requests musical performances at various functions in the program, such as installation of officers of a club group, birthday
parties, special dedication ceremonies, etc. While a good music
school is anxious to find places for its students who are prepared to perform publicly, it is difficult to explain that the
School is not a placement bureau nor a casting office, nor a
professional agent. Naturally the School wishes to present
those students who will make a fine impression. Frequently
the requests for performers select times which would take
children out of their regular school day to appear. This
hardly seems quite fair. Probably the most discouraging experience is for students to appear at a spot where the piano
is in deplorable condition and almost impossible to play.

Schenck demonstrates that this has been happening for
many years when she gives the following information:

> Because a settlement has a music department it is often
> expected to provide music for social occasions without
> consideration of the effect of complying upon the ideals
> which alone make the existence of the department
> worth while. A music director goes to considerable
> effort to inculcate in his students a devotion and rev-
> erence for the art they are studying. This is shown
> on the occasion of a concert by silence while music
> is being performed...The settlement staff often finds
> it hard to understand why the music director hesi-
> tates to ask pupils to play between the acts of a
> play. [13]

The acquisition of space also entails the problem of
finding the financial resources to make the purchase of a piece
of property possible. While this may involve a one-time

expenditure of funds, it generally will involve a rather large
amount of money. Hopefully it will not leave the organization
with a healthy mortgage to be paid over an extended period
of time. This is a matter that must be decided upon by the
board of directors of the settlement house or neighborhood
center. Again a matter of policy must be established.

The action that Schenck advocated is one that puts
a barrier between the music school or department and its parent
organization. The school is no longer "requesting monies" or
stating a need for additional funds, but it is putting itself
in the position of making demands that will force a decision in
its own favor. Such an action creates an adversary relationship between the school and the settlement which neither desires. Schenck states:

> But at this point comes the real issue and one which
> can only be solved by the future. Gradually the
> music department becomes so large that it crowds
> other activities. Shall it move into a separate building
> and have a home of its own? It must be acknowledged
> that it is the secret dream of nearly every music
> director with whom the writer has talked. And if
> the settlement also agrees that this is a good solution
> and it is done, what is the next step? Shall it con-
> tinue as part of the settlement or shall it incorporate
> separately and thus become a Music School (indepen-
> dent)? This is a question which is now causing fer-
> vent discussion.[14]

The group that chooses to remain part of the larger organization is willing to accept the conveniences of being a
department and having all of its bills paid by an office other
than its own, accepting the absorption of any deficit in its
operations by the parent organization, salary checks drawn
by the business office of the larger organization from which
all necessary deductions have been withheld and accounted
for, all such records kept in order and work with the auditing
firm arranged by the other office, etc. Many advantages
can be realized by being part of a larger organization.

Schenck claims not to be on one side or the other, or
at least she claims no preference.

The writer advocates neither plan to the exclusion of

the other. The one fact from which there is no escape is that the settlement and the music department
need each other. Whether they are under the same
roof or even under the same incorporated body seems
unimportant compared with the possibility of achievement by working together. [15]

Congeniality is, of course, the best ingredient. One
must be able to evaluate the situation carefully, and the
worth of each program must be considered with equal im-
partiality. The director of the settlement must be able to
look at the music program (music school or department) in the
light of its contribution to the total picture. The director of
the music school or music department must recognize how his
school or department fits into the overall plan of the settlement or community center with similar objectivity.

Unreasonable requirements on the part of either person
will never lead to a happy solution, particularly if an impasse
has been reached. Demands or threats will only cloud the
issues further. Each party must have a fairly decent idea
of what the philosophical goals of the other are. Then prac-
ticality will take over in view of the available financial resources. Compromises will be reached!

Both parties will agree that on the staff of the larger
organization there should be a "social music leader." This is
a person who has the knowledge of what can be done musically
with pre-schoolers, children, teenagers and with adult
groups. The leader should be one who can use informal instruments, e.g., drums, tambourines, castanets, gongs, tri-
angles, etc. Recorders, pianos, guitars, banjos, and, most
of all, singing should be at his command. His talents should
be flexible enough to move to the instrument or activity needed
most at a particular time with a specific group.

The abilities of someone trained as a music therapist
might fit well into the situation. He should be responsible
to the director of the music school or department, though
he may be called into conferences with other workers in the
settlement program. Understanding of the other person's
views is an imperative!

A musician with this kind of knowledge can help to make
music a more functional aspect of the settlement. They are
sometimes rare birds to locate!

Folk songs reflecting the backgrounds of the neighbors are valuable tools for social music programs. They can be learned by all. The social music leader can bridge the gap between the training program which produces fairly skilled performers (the music school or music department) and those with little or no previous training who can be encouraged to take part willingly in informal music. This may lead to more serious musical study and performance! That is why the organization has a music school or department.

As one cogitates on the materials already presented, he recognizes the formation of "battle zones being drawn," so to speak. The one group consists of those involved in so-called professional music programs (those teaching in the conservatory style, to train additional performing musicians). Here is the elitist group who see music as an art of performance with entrance permitted only to a limited number. These students are those whom a teacher especially enjoys teaching. Their numbers are not large. Musically they are more rewarding pupils to instruct. Unfortunately those who train these budding instrumentalists frequently do not understand or see any value to the use of social music. They look down on those who teach it or use it for any purpose. Theirs is an extremely narrow and dangerous path, if music is to continue to be as important an art as it now is.

The second group utilizes music to reach more and more people as yet untrained in the musical art. This group of students should learn the value of participation in music by the use of eurythmics, singing, dancing, the use of simple instruments, etc. It can be used in other group activities, such as drama and dance. Also there are two aspects which are of vital importance and which, unfortunately, are frequently overlooked. The first is that from this group are often found those who do possess the ability to study more seriously, possibly with performance in mind; secondly from this group will also emerge those who become receptive audience members in later years. Teachers for this classification are very scarce.

Many of these teachers unfortunately feel that their work is not understood nor appreciated by the faculty in the "professional area." Possibly, if not probably, they are right. Teachers from the professional music faculty would not, and probably could not, do the work of the social music teacher.

Yet whether for reasons of insecurity or ignorance on their
parts, they will liberally criticize the social music teacher
as not doing his job, or worse and more of it, not knowing
what he should be able to accomplish. Too many professionals
prefer to exist in a conservatory situation only, and this is
not the picture of the music school settlement nor the community music school.

Congeniality returns, and let each member of the total
faculty and staff look into the mirror and ask himself, "Do
I know what the person in a different category is doing and
why? How do I fit into the picture?" The vast majority of
faculty members do this regularly and prove themselves to
be professional teachers. This is, of course, the great need.

Let us restate a short picture of fairly recent events
in the history of settlement houses and community music
schools from 1917 on.

In 1917 the National Federation of Settlements formed
a committee on the arts at the urging of Johan Grolle of the
Settlement Music School in Philadelphia, and he was appointed
the chairman of that committee. Naturally the other arts were
included in the responsibilities of the Committee on the Arts.
After a period of time, since music was the flourishing art
in Settlements, the directors of those schools which were independently operated and some chairmen of music departments
began to feel that since their area was so successful, music
should have more weight and attention than the other art
forms which were at least small and, in some cases minimal.

In 1922 the National Federation of Settlements created
a Music Division in response to the musicians' requests for
better representation and recognition. Again, Johan Grolle
was made chairman of this new Music Division. He would continue in this capacity along with his directorship of the
Settlement Music School until 1924 when he became the director
of the newly formed Curtis Institute of Music. He obviously
was a man of great musical talent, strong initiative and
determination, as well as being an outstanding diplomat. His
willingness to assume enormous responsibility can be observed
throughout his life. He took positions, stood by them firmly,
and earned the respect of administrators and faculty members
of community music schools and music departments, who
followed his lead quite willingly.

Much to the delight of many in each of those categories
Johan Grolle returned to his first love, the Settlement Music
School, in 1926 where he remained as director until 1949.

The Curtis Institute of Music had the financial backing
of Mrs. Bok from the beginning of the new school's establishment. It really was formed in recognition of the success of
the Settlement Music School, by becoming the conservatory
for the training of the most gifted and talented musicians,
whose very existence and musical successes had proved the
need for such a school in the Untied States.

Today the Curtis Institute of Music is a conservatory
of great distinction in this country. It is dedicated to the
development of excellent performers, and all students who are
accepted and attend the school are granted full scholarships.
Curtis continues brilliantly under the leadership of Rudolph
Serkin at the time of this writing.

It is fascinating to note the close relationship that this
School has had to the Settlement Music School Movement.
In addition to its recognized ties to the Settlement Music
School in Philadelphia, at its outset Grace Spofford (who later
was to become the director of the Henry Street Settlement
Music School in New York City) served as the Dean of the
Curtis Institute of Music from 1924 to 1931. Prior to either
of these appointments Grace Spofford had served in the ad-
ministration of the Peabody Conservatory of Music in Baltimore,
Maryland, for a period of seven years.

Emily McCallip Adler also served in the administration of
the Curtis Institute of Music at the same time as Grace Spofford did. Later Mrs. Adler was to become the director of
the Cleveland Music School Settlement from 1933 to 1945 and
subsequently as the director of the Neighborhood Music School
in New Haven, Connecticut, from 1947 to 1953.

The newly created Music Division of the National Federation of Settlements began in earnest to accomplish many of
its goals. Since Johan Grolle had accepted the position at
the Curtis Institute of Music, the Music Division needed to
find a replacement. As might have been expected, Mrs. Janet
D. Schenck was selected to take the chairmanship. In 1926
the Music Division planned and completed a request for funds
from the Carnegie Corporation in New York City. This was

one of the biggest projects ever submitted by them and it
was aimed at the development of social music in all settlements
in the country. The Division requested $80,000 to be spread
over a period of four years, or $20,000 annually for four
years.* The proposal itemized several steps to be followed
in completing the proposed program. There would be an experiment in social music at one settlement; there would be
a special training program for musical directors in conjunction
with the New York School of Social Work; there would be a
program to aid in the growth and development of new music
schools and music departments in settlements, and to help
in developing social music programs where they did not exist;
and finally there would be the organization of a library and
service programs for all settlements. This would, of course,
all emanate from the new New York office which the grant
would also support.

Attached to the grant request was a letter of support
and recommendation for the project signed by some of the most
distinguished musicians of that time. The list included Harold
Bauer, Albert Spalding, Leopold Auer, Serge Rachmaninoff,
Richard Aldrich, Ernest Schelling, Walter Damrosch, Ossip
Gabrilowitsch, Marcella Sembrich, Ernest Hutcheson, Pablo
Casals, Olga Samaroff, Felix Salmond, and Daniel Gregory
Mason. An impressive list, indeed, which included outstanding
performers of the day and important music educators.

In the National Federation office there was a flurry of
activity regarding the proposal, and underneath it all, it
seems, a feeling of impending success, particularly with the
support of the list of distinguished musicians, and in the
structure of the Federation itself such people as Frances
McFarland and Janet Schenck, and in the implied support of
the social workers such as Jane Addams, Lillian D. Wald and
Mary K. Simkhovitch.

When the affirmative answer of the grant was sent to

---

*An excellent description of the Carnegie Corporation Project
is found in great detail in the scholarly doctoral dissertation
by Nicholas John Cords entitled "Music in Social Settlement
and Community Music Schools, 1893-1939: A Democratic-Esthetic
Approach to Music Culture." Doctoral dissertation, University
of Minnesota at Minneapolis, 1970.

the Music Division on May 27, 1926, it was in the amount of
$25,000 (total) spread over four years, and with the proviso
that the National Federation of Settlements, or more accurately
its Music Division, raise an additional $25,000--or in other
words, it was to be a matching grant, a term so frequently
heard today.

With a letter of gracious acceptance from Janet Schenck
came a request that the National Federation of Settlements
be allowed a one year extension of time to raise their matching
funds. With that approval having been given, Mrs. Schenck
using her feminine charm wrote yet another letter, this time
requesting fervently that the Music Division be allowed to
begin the program without their having raised their required
funds. The Carnegie Corporation graciously agreed and said
that the Corporation would send the stipulated amounts of
money each year for four years. The program was started
in 1927.

Having just achieved this coup d'état at this time in
its history, the Music Division of the National Federation of
Settlements was the largest and most recognized section of
the National Federation, and since the members had literally
raised their own operating funds, it was almost a situation of
the tail's wagging the dog.

It was fortunate that the grant had come when it did,
because within a relatively short period of time the calamitous
Stock Market Crash came, on October 29, 1929--Black Tuesday.
Steadily thereafter the economy slipped into one of the worst
depressions this country had ever known. The early days
of the 1930's were some of the bleakest in our history. New
funds were almost impossible to raise at this time.

Because of its firm situation the Music Division continued
its normal operations and proceeded with the new project,
though at this point the entire National Federation organization was instructed to tighten belts and, if necessary, to cut
programs and budgets. After the last draft from the Carnegie
Corporation had been received, no amount of pleading by
Frances McFarland, who had assumed the directorship of the
project, raised any further funds from the Corporation.

This fact may have come as a rather sudden shock to
some of the people in the Music Division. Though they

admitted that they had had to work diligently to get the initial grant, to some it may have seemed that the Corporation should want to follow the program further.

But with all the financial difficulties and living with a declining economy, much to the credit of Settlement House personnel, both administrators and faculty, the staff and faculty members of community music schools, the very concerned and dedicated Board Members of each classification, and generous contributors, etc., the programs did continue in the geographical areas where they were established and located.

In thinking carefully about the difficult times through which Americans were existing, it seems incredible that in the New York City area alone, two new music schools came into existence and are still thriving at the time of this writing. The Arts prevailed and continued strongly even in financially difficult times. One of these schools is an independent, nonprofit organization, and the second school is a department of a larger institution. Only one of these schools was affiliated with the National Federation of Settlements.

The first school to be cited is the Turtle Bay Music School which is an incorporated, independent music school founded by Eleanor Stanley White in 1925. It is and always has been located on the East Side of Manhattan. A description of it appears in the 1985 Membership Directory of the National Guild of Community Schools of the Arts, Inc. which states:

> Located in the center of New York's residential East Side as well as in the heart of a growing corporate community, the School offers lessons, courses and recital programs to over 600 serious amateurs and beginners. Instruction for adults comprises over 70% of the School's offerings, and a newly formed primary division (children aged $2\frac{1}{2}$-10 years) has grown from 38 to over 200.[16]

By this very description one can see that the School has been functioning truly as a community music school by considering the needs of its neighborhood residents. They are serious young people who are becoming the concert-goers and those who see value in supporting the arts. From its beginning the Turtle Bay Music School has stood for the independence and autonomy of schools.

When the Henry Street Settlement considered establishing
its Music School in 1927, Lillian D. Wald solicited reactions
to the plan for the Music School submitted by Hedi Katz, the
School's first director. She contacted several important and
significant persons to respond to the plan. They included
Melzar Chaffee, director of the Third Street Music School
Settlement, Janet D. Schenck, director of the Neighborhood
Music School (which later became what is now the Manhattan
School of Music), Aaron Copland, the American composer, and
Walter Damrosch, the American conductor who had been born in
Germany. Miss Wald chose wisely and well when requesting sup-
port for the establishment of the Music School, before she recom-
mended the plan to the Board of Directors of the Henry Street
Settlement. This would naturally mean an increase in the over-
all budget of the Settlement.

The following were the responses from the four to Miss
Wald.

Melzar Chaffee replied:

> Having read the outline for the organization of a music
> school at the Henry Street Settlement by Hedi Katz,
> it gives me great pleasure to say that I thoroughly
> endorse this plan and am sure that Mrs. Katz will
> make a great success of such a school.

Janet D. Schenck answered:

> I have read over very carefully the plan for a music
> department as presented by Mrs. Katz.
> It seems an excellent one and I am only too glad
> to give it my endorsement. I am sure she will make a
> success of it and I shall be eager to see how it de-
> velops.

Walter Damrosch wrote:

> Your musical venture deserves every encouragement
> possible. There are thousands of musical talents in
> our city, especially among the poorer classes who need
> the best instruction and to whom efficiency as musical
> performers opens up a goldmine [sic] of artistic en-
> joyment and happiness.

Aaron Copland responded with an offer:

> I have seen the project for a Music School at the
> Henry Street Settlement as formulated by Mrs. Hedi
> Katz and can assure you of my warmest endorsement
> of the plan as drawn up by her.
>   I should be glad to serve on a committee for the
> successful carrying out of this project.[17]

And so it was that the Music School of the Henry Street
Settlement came into being. (At the time of this writing the
Music School is housed in the new Henry Street Settlement
Louis Abrons Arts for Living Center.)

Shortly the reader will see that Aaron Copland was to
play a much more important role at the Henry Street Settlement
Music School by making an outstanding contribution to the
contemporary music literature.

Hedi Katz was most anxious to make the Music School
well known by its distinctive performances. She realized that
this School was starting late when compared to the Hull-House
Music School, the Third Street Music School Settlement, the
Settlement Music School in Philadelphia, the Brooklyn Music
School Settlement, and the Greenwich House Music School,
etc. She wanted the School to be outstanding, and as a result
she planned a program that included the children's cantata
We Built a City by Paul Hindemith, coupled with Kurt Weill's
opera Der Jasager. "The History of the Music School of the
Henry Street Settlement" describes this episode in the life
of the School as follows:

> True to her determination to succeed and to assemble
> the most qualified people available Mrs. Katz enlisted
> the services of Lehman Engel, conductor, and Sanford
> Meisner, stage director, to present the new work by
> Kurt Weill on the stage of the Playhouse [of the Henry
> Street Settlement]. The case was composed of stu-
> dents of the Music School.[18]

On April 23, 1933, the New York Times thought enough
of the performance to give it a rather lengthy review with
many comments.

> The opera was preceeded by Hindemith's charming
> little "We Built a City," which the younger children
> of the school, directed by Rose Maria Tetralia, sang

with great spirit, and without notes--a striking tribute to their training, for even simple Hindemith is
far from easy.

The Music School of the Henry Street Settlement,
under the direction of Mrs. Hedi Katz, presented last
night the American premiere of "Der Jasager," a
short two-act opera by Kurt Weill, at the Grand Street
Playhouse...Weill's score abounds in vigorous rhythms,
fine contrapuntal writing and melodious felicity--the
last especially noteworthy in the beautiful air of the
Mother. The instrumentation is concise and very effective... The central fatalism of the little piece
brings it very close to the abstract quality of early
Greek drama. This element Mrs. Katz and Sanford
Meisner, who staged the production, wisely chose
to emphasize. The chorus formed the motionless
decorative groups each side of the stage [sic]. The
simple sets by R. A. Jones were moderately stylized;
eminently effective without being freakish. Action was
reduced to the necessary minimum. [19]

It is important to note that this community music school
was presenting such a contemporary venture during bleak
depression days. Creativity was not stifled by a lack of funds,
rather creativity was challenged to produce.

During gloomy depression years, the federal government
formed the Works Progress Administration (WPA). Harry L.
Hopkins was its Administrator, and in 1939 he was to become
the Secretary of Commerce in the Cabinet of Franklin D.
Roosevelt. The WPA formed the Federal Music Project:

Federal Arts Projects, four projects begun in the
United States in 1935 by the Works Progress Administration as a relief measure for artists. Federal support for the arts on the scale of these projects was
unprecedented in U.S. History...
The Federal Music Project (1935-1943) operated
symphony orchestras in cities across the nation.
Dance orchestras, bands, and choruses were also organized. In their first year, WPA orchestras performed more than 1,500 compositions by 540 American
composers. Music instruction was arranged chiefly
for public schools where it had not been regularly
provided, and music therapy experiments were conducted in a number of mental hospitals.

...After the WPA was terminated in 1943, no major
step toward federal support for the arts was taken
in the United States until 1965 when the National
Foundation on the Arts and humanities was established.
This program has made grants to artists, to theater
groups, and to music and opera societies. Funds
have been provided to help artists utilize new technology, to promote liaison between museums staffs and
community leaders, to expand art programs for the
under-privileged, and to assist the Associated Councils
of the Arts.[20]

When the WPA formed the Federal Music Project, Dr.
Nikolai Sokoloff, who had been the conductor of the Cleveland
Symphony Orchestra, was appointed its director. In a report
of the first nine months of the Project Dr. Sokoloff gives a
picture of the progress made from October 1935 to June 1936:

The Federal Music Project is nationwide, functioning
in a forty-two States and the District of Columbia.
From the standpoint of organizations, educational and
performing units have been set up and now, under
supervision, they have passed out of the stage of adolescence and have reached maturity.
    More than thirty-two million persons have heard
"in the flesh" concerts and performances by units of
the Federal Music Project since October, 1935. There
have been approximately thirty-six thousand performances in the period between January 1 and July 31.
    Music has no social value unless it is heard. These
figures show that it has not only been heard but that
it has reached a greater number of our people than in
any period in the history of the United States.[21]

The Federal Music Project boasted of a National Advisory
Board which included the following (just to name a few):

Dr. Walter Damrosch--Conductor and Composer, Olin
Downes--Music Critic, New York Times, William Ear-
hart--Supervisor of Public School Music, Pittsburgh,
Rudolph Ganz--President of Chicago Musical College,
Mr. Howard Hanson--Director of Eastman School of
Music, Composer, Edward Johnson--Director General,
Metropolitan Opera Company, Madame Olga Samaroff-
Stokowski--Concert Pianist, member of faculty of

Juilliard School of Music, Carleton Sprague Smith--
Director of the Music Division, New York Public
Library, etc.[22]

There were many other names of great distinction in the worlds
of music performance, composition, and education.

A further explanation of the scope and activities in the
first nine months of the program caused considerable concern
on the part of the National Federation of Settlements and the
individual community music schools. As the report continues
it states:

On June 30 these 15,000 musicians were enrolled in
the following units:

141 symphony and concert orchestras, absorbing
5,669. 77 symphonies, military and concert bands
with 2,793. 15 chamber music ensembles. 38 choruses,
quartets, and vocal ensembles. 141 teaching projects.[23]

One hundred forty-one teaching projects!!! That was
the figure causing great consternation. What was the Federal
Project attempting to do? Will they replace settlement music
departments and community music schools? Since all the government programs were free, many parents might switch their
children and themselves to the new project and save what little
money they were now spending for music lessons and classes.
These thoughts at first gave some directors and department
chairmen cold shivers. And what would be the quality of the
program under these circumstances?

Fears were somewhat calmed when the Federal Music
Project released its report with two statements in particular
giving figures and statistics about the first nine months of
the Project. The section on teachers stated this:

The program created by the Federal Music Project
for the rehabilitation and retraining of approximately
1600 teachers of music now on its rolls has disclosed
a vast and unexpected hunger for music among large
groups of our people. The classes over which these
WPA teachers preside enroll today literally hundreds
of thousands of persons divided about equally between adults and children.

These teachers are leading and directing classes
for group instruction, both vocal and instrumental;
they are presiding at community gatherings for talks
and demonstrations on music appreciation, history and
theory, and they are serving as conductors, instructors and coaches of choruses, bands and orchestras.[24]

These words created a picture of vast numbers of children and adults who were almost completely untrained and who
were receiving musical instruction in much larger numbers than
were ever considered at community music schools or settlement
music departments. Here again one sees the situation of large
groups representing "quantity of people in music education,"
as opposed to the smaller groups or individual instruction as
given in the community music schools and settlement music
departments, which would indicate "quality in music education."

If these words were not strong enough to placate those
who saw danger to "quality" music training in the government's
plans, subsequent statements assured the observer that teachers involved in the Federal Music Project were not intended to
replace or to assume positions of those already employed to
teach music programs in community music schools or settlement
music departments. The report continues in this way:

It is a principle of the Federal Project that the instructor may not enter into competition with a teacher
who is self-sustaining, and therefore the WPA teacher's
work has been largely with persons on relief, and with
WPA workers and their families, and the underprivileged. The response of these people has been amazing
and heartening, particularly in areas that have been
regarded as musically barren.[25]

In the New York City area there were some people who
were affiliated with a community music school or the National
Federation of Settlements, or both, and who played important
roles with the Federal Music Project. This was happening
right around the time of the formation of the National Guild
of Community Music Schools (now the National Guild of Community Schools of the Arts). Two such persons were Frances
McFarland and Ruth Kemper.

On July 22, 1937, Ashley Pettis who was the Unit

Manager, Music Education Division of the Federal Music Project
of the WPA, wrote the following memo to "All Supervisors and
Head Teachers of New York City":

SUBJECT: PERSONNEL CHANGES

On authorization given me by Mrs. Frances McFarland,
Assistant New York City Director of the Federal Music
Project, Miss Ruth Kemper is hereby appointed Director
of Music Education upon the resignation of Dr. Hannas
September 1st. Miss Elizabeth Rice will succeed Miss
Kemper as Head Teacher of Midtown Community Music
Center, 93 Park Avenue.[26]

Two days earlier Ruth Kemper had received a letter from
Mr. Pettis:

Dear Miss Kemper:

We have just had word that your appointment to Dr.
Hannas' position has been approved by Mr. Clifton.
    Will you please arrange to come in for a conference
with Mrs. McFarland at about 10:30 Thursday morning
[sic].[27]

On the day that the inter-departmental memo was sent,
Mr. Pettis also wrote a note to Ruth Kemper:

Dear Miss Kemper:

I am enclosing a notice which has gone out to all
Head Teachers and Supervisors this morning. I have
written to Miss Rice asking her to arrange her schedule so that she may study the work at Midtown under
your tutelage part time. I should advise that you
confer with Dr. Hannas as soon as possible and spend
a great portion of your assignments here in the office
in order to study the work first hand.
    I am very grateful to you for taking over this
very important work. I feel that you are the only
one qualified to do it and I know that your loyalty,
both to the project and Mrs. McFarland, will make you
a tower of strength.[28]

Ruth Kemper, who succeeded Eleanor Stanley White as

director of the Turtle Bay Music School and remained in that
position until her retirement in 1969, was obviously well respected in the community. Her knowledge of orchestral literature and violin solo materials was excellent. This is also verified by the fact she was invited to Boston to conduct the
Commonwealth (Massachusetts) Women's Orchestra on June 30,
1937. She received a letter of thanks for her efforts from
William Haddon, State Director of the Federal Music Project
in Boston:

> Dear Miss Kemper:
>
> May I take this opportunity to thank you most heartily
> for the service you rendered our project.
>   Everyone enjoyed your work and hoped that a
> woman conductor would eventually take charge of this
> unit.
>   I am enclosing a little memento of your visit. With
> best personal regards, I remain
>
>   Very sincerely yours, [29]
>   [Signed] William Haddon

The musical art so far as the serious professional musician is concerned involves itself with musical performance
and composition. The artist is concerned with highest performance standards. The composer strives to find new ways
to express himself in innovative and creative channels while
being responsible for maintaining good techniques in musical
form, harmony, counterpoint as well as current compositional
trends and skills.

Social workers, both case workers and group workers,
view music as a tool to be used during their professional
activities and are not so concerned with the intrinsic value
of music itself. They are apt to consider music in the same
category as a useful tool or game valuable at a given moment
in a group session.

Music is the primary factor to the professional musician,
but it is secondary in the mind of the professional social
worker. Here, perhaps, is the crux of the matter that caused
a rift between the Music Division of the National Federation
of Settlements and the independent community music schools.

It is also possible that neither side was listening to the other, or the separation might never have been. But looking back nearly fifty years makes it easier, perhaps, to see more clearly where the problem actually lay. One must also take into consideration the individual personalities of the people involved. Temperamental, irascible, argumentative, difficult, are all adjectives frequently applied to musicians, but in this case it was, perhaps, both parties to whom the unpleasant terms could be applied. At any rate, quietly but firmly a new national organization was born.

5

BIRTH OF THE NATIONAL GUILD OF COMMUNITY MUSIC SCHOOLS, 1937

Nineteen thirty-seven proved to be a year of much creative imagination even though this country was still officially in the Great Depression. There was a bustle of activity in all fields of endeavor throughout the land.

During the year, around the world, sadness was felt when France lost two of its most prominent composers, Albert Roussel (1865-1937) and Maurice Ravel (1898-1937). Ravel was particularly well known for his Sonatine for piano, Gaspard de la Nuit, also for piano, and his orchestral work Pavane pour une infante défunte. Probably his most familiar composition is his Bolero for orchestra with its continuous, repetitive, pulsating rhythm which persists throughout the entire work while gaining in volume and intensity.

And the United States of America recorded with sorrow the death of George Gershwin (1898-1937) at the age of thirty-nine. This talented composer had many of his musical plays appear on the Broadway stage. His more serious musical contributions included his very popular Rhapsody in Blue, first performed on February 12, 1924, in the Aeolian Concert Hall on West 43rd Street, New York City. The program on Lincoln's birthday was conducted by Paul Whiteman with his Palais Royal Orchestra with Gershwin as the piano soloist. It was an immediate success. Gershwin also served as the piano soloist at the premier performance of his Concerto in F for piano and orchestra on December 3, 1925. The Concerto was featured on the program of the New York Symphony Orchestra conducted by Walter Damrosch, who had actually commissioned the Concerto for that orchestra.

Later, George Gershwin was a member of the Music School Committee at the Henry Street Settlement Music School,

and it was he who first arranged a fund-raising benefit program for the School in 1930 at the New York Junior League
Building.

In 1935, George Gershwin completed his only venture
into the operatic world with his Porgy and Bess, which has
just recently been included in the repertoire of the Metropolitan Opera Company in New York City. His all-too-brief
career has made an enormous impact on the music of this country.

Three spectacular events showed the ingenuity and creativity of American engineers and construction workers when,
in 1937 on the East Coast, the Lincoln Tunnel, connecting
New York and New Jersey, burrowed under the Hudson River,
to make the second such linkage. On the West Coast, the
Golden Gate Bridge in San Francisco was opened to traffic
for the first time, and in the Pacific Northwest, Franklin D.
Roosevelt dedicated the Bonneville Dam on the Columbia River
in the State of Oregon. All of these events occurred when the
country was still in the throes of a depression.

Nineteen thirty-seven brought its share of bad news to the
country. Amelia Earhart, the American woman pilot, was lost on
a flight over the South Pacific and was never heard from again.
In the same year, two American business tycoons and philanthro-
pists died, each having been well-known for his generosity
to his country; Andrew Mellon (1855-1937) and John D. Rockefeller (1839-1937) were two financiers who died that year.

Upon his abdication from the throne of England, the
Duke of Windsor married Mrs. Wallis Simpson. Subsequently,
his brother was crowned King George VI of England. The
ceremonies were heard on a world-wide radio broadcast, the
first of its kind to be heard in the United States.

The literary and theatrical world produced a surprising
amount of material such as U.S.A. by John Dos Passos; To
Have and Have Not by Ernest Hemingway; John P. Marquand's
The Late George Apley, the Pulitzer prize novel for 1938;
Hamilton Fish, Pulitzer prize winner for biography by Allan
Nevins; Clifford Odets' Golden Boy; John Steinbeck's Of Mice
and Men; Kenneth Roberts' Northwest Passage; and A. J.
Cronin's The Citadel.

Americans (perhaps with tongue in cheek) were singing and whistling such popular songs as Whistle While You Work, It's Nice Work If You Can Get It, The Dipsey Doodle, I've Got My Love to Keep Me Warm and Bei Mir Bist Du Schön.

While the rest of the nation seemed occupied with other problems and their solutions, the directors of several community music schools throughout the country were becoming more and more concerned and cautious regarding the relationship between the National Federation of Settlements, particularly its Music Division, and community music schools which were independent and not affiliated with larger social-work-oriented institutions. Their fears, and perhaps justifiably so, were that others who were non-music-oriented might become strongly influential in determining the programs which were designed and followed in community music schools. As has been shown throughout this document, one of the main concerns among board members and administrators as well as teachers, has been the quality of the programs in community music schools.

In 1937, very quietly, twelve independent community music schools (even though some of their schools still had the term settlement in their names) met to form the National Guild of Community Music Schools with the full intent of keeping settlement-affiliated schools out of the new national organization. These twelve schools and their directors were as follows:

ALL NEWTON MUSIC SCHOOL, Elizabeth Fyffe, Director

BOSTON MUSIC SCHOOL SETTLEMENT, Linwood D. Scriven, Director

BROOKLYN MUSIC SCHOOL SETTLEMENT, Karp P. Mikhalenkoff, Director

THE CLEVELAND MUSIC SCHOOL SETTLEMENT, Emily McCallip, Director

COMMUNITY MUSIC SCHOOLS FOUNDATION, Edna B. Lieber, Exec. Director

FIRST SETTLEMENT MUSIC SCHOOL (Buffalo), Dorothy Hebb, Director

MUSIC SCHOOL SETTLEMENT (NYC), Melzar Chaffee, Director

NEIGHBORHOOD MUSIC SCHOOL (NYC), Janet D. Schenck, Director

THE SETTLEMENT MUSIC
   SCHOOL (Phila.), Johan
   Grolle, Director

TURTLE BAY MUSIC SCHOOL,
   Eleanor Stanley White,
   Director

SOUTH END MUSIC SCHOOL,
   George Faulkner, Director

WILMINGTON MUSIC SCHOOL,
   Winifred M. Jacobson,
   Director

In addition to the above information, the National Guild of Community Music Schools' early materials reveal that the National Guild fully acknowledged the fact that its schools were a definite outgrowth of the Settlement Music School Movement, and indeed, from the American Settlement House Movement itself.

The Guild wished then to refer to its own development and growth as the Community Music School Movement. Those who engineered the formation of the new organization were very careful to state their plans and procedures. In an outline of information and procedures, the following appears:

THE COMMUNITY MUSIC SCHOOL MOVEMENT

Origin: Community Music Schools are an outgrowth of the music settlement idea which had its origin in the eighties [sic] at Hull House [sic], Chicago, followed in 1894 by the founding of the Music School Settlement in New York City.[1]

Then follows a clear description of what a community music school is:

Design: These schools of music are separately incorporated organizations not affiliated with any social settlement, and offer instruction of the highest standard at rates placed within the reach of all economic groups. Through the schools, opportunity for musical growth and development is made available to thousands of students regardless of race, creed or color. The schools are non-profit making organizations, and are supported by membership dues, contributions, tuition fees, and grants from community chests.[2]

Then follows a simple statement of purpose:

> Purpose: The purpose of the Community Music School
> is to promote national culture through music based
> upon democratic principles. Such schools are unique
> in that they combine a high grade of music teaching
> with the fundamental principle that music is a vital
> part of living and is an essential element in the en-
> richment of the human spirit.[3]

And so, the die was cast! In order to prevent the
possibility of one anticipated evil, an even greater monster
may have been created. Let us look at the picture objectively.

Of the original twelve schools to form the National Guild,
the following schools were permitted to join even though the
word Settlement was in their names: The Boston Music School
Settlement, The Brooklyn Music School Settlement, The Cleveland Music School Settlement, The First Settlement Music School
in Buffalo, The Music School Settlement in New York City,
and The Settlement Music School in Philadelphia. They were
all independently incorporated.

In looking at the National Guild's list of member schools,
of those who were established and operating by 1937, the
following would have been ineligible to join (to name only a
few): The Peabody Preparatory, Greenwich House Music
School, the MacPhail Center for the Arts, University of Minnesota, the Bronx House Music School, the two schools in
Toronto, the Music School of the St. Christopher House and
University Settlement, the Lighthouse School of Music, the
Ninety-Second Street YM/YWHA, and the Henry Street Settlement Music School.

One of the National Guild's original goals was to issue
a publication that was to be informative, educational, and to
allow information about Guild schools to be released and shared.
The publication was to be called The Quarterly of the National
Guild of Community Music Schools. With all the organizational
problems, the Guild did not produce its first issue until May
of 1940. In its first issue is an article by Winifred M. Jacobson who was the Guild's Secretary-Treasurer and the director
of the Wilmington (Delaware) Music School. The article was
to explain to the public what the National Guild actually was.
It read as follows:

The Aim of the Guild

The National Guild of Community Music Schools unites thirteen music schools which represent a unique development in music education. It was formed to meet the need of concerted action in focusing attention on the nature and purpose of community music schools.

Before defining the aims of the Guild, it should be stated that the primary purpose of Community Music Schools is that of enriching the lives of individuals, less privileged financially, through participation in the performance, understanding and appreciation of music. An opportunity for music study with outstanding teachers is extended to students unable to afford the private fees charged by such teachers.

Representing the schools which preserve the highest traditions of music making, the Guild is endeavoring to achieve recognition of their standards through public school credits and college entrance requirements. A curriculum has been fully prepared which includes courses of study for piano, string instruments and voice used by all member schools. Individual students have in many cases received college credit for work done at Community Music Schools. It is the purpose of the Guild to have this accomplishment recognized and accepted for all students who are graduates of Community Music Schools.

The Guild purposes to study changing trends and policies of the music development of the country, such as government music projects, and the relation of our schools to the current movements.

The Guild is actively engaged in stimulating the development of leadership to meet the changing demands; in making our music centers available as work shops and laboratories in which new and important technics and ideas may develop.

The Guild hopes to consolidate our contribution to the musical and social life of our respective communities and to further the endeavor of our schools to assume their place as a community resource.[4]

It is interesting to note that the records indicate that there were twelve schools that banded together to form the new organization, The National Guild of Community Music Schools. Yet in the first edition of The Quarterly, Vol. I,

No. 1, May, 1940, Winifred M. Jacobson, the Secretary-Treasurer of the Guild, states in her article "The Aim of the Guild",
thirteen schools are indicated. In the article "The Work Units
of the Guild," the original twelve are correctly listed, with
one additional school, listed as follows:

> Community School of Music
> 9 Thomas Street, Providence, R.I.
> Incorporated 1933
> (Rents building well equipped for teaching.)
> President ... Mrs. Houghton P. Metcalf
> Secretary ..... Mrs. Niles Westcott
> Director .. Mme. Avis Bliven Charbonnel
> Yearly Budget .... $3,500.00[5]

This is the first and only reference made to this school.
It can only be assumed that this school is no longer in existence.

Thus the goals and aims of the new National Guild of
Community Music Schools are expressed and prove to be highly
commendable. The undertaking of having high school and
college credits transferable is an admirable aim which would
certainly take the time and efforts of many people, valuable
as it may be.

In the same issue of The Quarterly, the following information appeared:

> Musicians and Educators Who Endorse Our Movement
>
> Our movement has the endorsement of many of the
> leading musicians of this country who either through
> teaching, or through practical advice have helped us
> solve many of the problems which have been encoun-
> tered.
>
> The following musicians and educators are serving
> individual schools in the capacity of Advisory Council
> members:
>
> | John Barbirolli | Jose Iturbi |
> |---|---|
> | Pablo Casals | Fritz Kreisler |
> | Peter Dykema | Leopold Mannes |
> | Albert Einstein | Artur Rodzinski |
> | Myra Hess | Olga Samaroff Stokowski[6] |
>
> [Only a partial list of the 82 mentioned in the article.]

It is obvious in viewing the list of dignitaries, both in performance and in education, that the leaders of the newly
formed Guild were serious about the movement they were
building. To assemble so distinguished a list took time, effort and convincing on the part of those who founded the
Guild.

      The purpose for publishing The Quarterly is explained
in the same issue:

The Purpose of The Quarterly

       In submitting the first issue of The Quarterly to the
       membership of the National Guild of Community Music
       Schools, the Program Committee had had in mind to
       present the movement in its working details.
       The importance of the Guild becomes clear when
       one familiarizes himself with the scope and details of
       a movement which is bound to continue to develop
       the standards by which mass culture can be benefited.
       Music, as well as the other arts, is bound to influence
       the new movements which are more and more becoming
       of a collective nature. Because of the magnitude and
       rapid growth of such movements, the need of develop-
       ment of standards and the training of leadership is
       evident.
       In order that our membership may become still
       better acquainted with our work, the Program Com-
       mittee submits the first issue of The Quarterly of the
       National Guild of Community Music Schools, in the
       form of a statistical report. Later issues will inform
       our readers regarding the policies, research, and the
       social and individual contacts of our movement.
                                        PROGRAM COMMITTEE[7]

      The year 1937 was also the year in which great tribute
was paid to one of America's most famous and beloved composers, Stephen Collins Foster (1826-1864). His continuously
simple but melodically elegant style is recognized around the
world today. His unique ability to compose away from the
piano or any instrument reminds one of the fluent ability of
Franz Schubert, though Schubert used a table cloth occasionally, Foster tore up brown paper bags and used them for
composing a new song. A strange manuscript surface in either
case!

The University of Pittsburgh deserves great credit for supplying the site and maintenance of the Stephen Collins Foster Memorial, dedicated June 2, 1937. Just a word as to why the University made such a gesture:

> Stephen Collins Foster was born in Lawrenceville, Pennsylvania, now a part of the city of Pittsburgh, on July 4, 1826. His birthplace, the Foster family's beloved White Cottage, is no longer in existence. It was torn down in 1865, but the exact place where it once stood is known. A brick house located at what is now 3600 Penn Avenue, Pittsburgh, stands on the exact site of the White Cottage. For many years, this brick house was maintained by the City of Pittsburgh as The Stephen C. Foster Memorial Home. It is now in private hands.[8]

Foster's early successes were numerous, copious, and came from him at a young age:

> ...He was ambitious; he worked hard; his efforts were crowned with immediate and spectacular success. The six years from early 1850 through 1855 were the most successful of his entire life. Songs, compositions, arrangements and translations--more than one hundred and sixty works in all--poured from his pen during these years. Many of these works were of only passing interest; they enjoyed a brief period of popularity and then were forgotten, just as now most of the popular songs of the present are soon forgotten. But his genius was now at its height.[9]

At the dedication ceremony in 1937, the following statement was made:

> Pittsburgh's tribute to her gifted son, Stephen C. Foster, has been completed. A structure of stone and steel has been erected and dedicated to the memory of the modest, unassuming composer who wrote songs which have become the heritage, not only of his native America, but of the world...The idea of a Memorial to Stephen Foster was born in the mind of Mrs. Will Earhart in 1927, when she was president of the Tuesday Musical Club of Pittsburgh. ...The University of Pittsburgh soon entered into the project.

Through the cooperation of Chancellor John G. Bowman,
the University offered a site for the Memorial on the
campus and agreed to maintain and operate the building
after its completion...Ten years of conception, planning, financing, and construction are represented in
the Stephen Collins Foster Memorial of the University
of Pittsburgh.[10]

This is an example of Community Arts in action. Many
facets of the community were activated to bring the construction of the Foster Memorial into being. It began from the
individual who conceived an idea, a musical organization which
recognized the value of such a project, a major university
which saw the role it should play in the project, and the pride
of a city of one of its own citizens who deserved special recognition. It is probably true that any one part of the "team"
could not have accomplished such a difficult task alone. With
the combined efforts of all, the city of Pittsburgh and its
people stood to gain from the community action.

Another major university paid tribute to Stephen Collins
Foster when New York University inducted him into its Hall
of Fame for Great Americans in 1940, so that he was the first
American composer/musician to be so honored. It was more
than twenty years later before Edward MacDowell was so
honored. New York University has had a long and close relationship to Settlement Music with its particular association
with the Greenwich House Settlement and its Music School.
It is New York University that will house the archives of the
Greenwich House, and it was that University which encouraged
and accepted the doctoral thesis, The History of the Music
School of the Henry Street Settlement, by Robert F. Egan in
1967.

Contemporary American music was featured in 1937
at one of the most distinguished Settlement House Music
Schools, the Music School of the Henry Street Settlement
whose director was Grace H. Spofford from 1935 to 1954. The
performance, given in New York City, was the premiere of
Aaron Copland's play-opera, The Second Hurricane. It attracted considerable interest from New York City to as far
away as Tucson, Arizona.

The genius and creative imagination of Grace Spofford
coupled with her undeniably persuasive powers, brought

together the compositional talent of Aaron Copland, the directorial strength of Orson Welles, the unique ability of Edwin
Denby to write for the theatre, and the excellent orchestral
conducting technique of Lehman Engel, and she had created
an outstanding team with which to present an enjoyable and
entertaining performance. She added to this group the acting
abilities of Joseph Cotten and Charles Pettinger, the students
from the Professional Children's School, singers from the Henry
Street Settlement Music School chorus, the Seward Park High
School choral group, as well as those from the High School
of Music and Art. She had constructed a true community
production, drawing from the very mixed resources that existed in the surrounding area.

The charm of the Henry Street Settlement Playhouse at
466 Grand Street (today it is part of the Henry Street Settlement Louis Abrons Arts for Living Center complex) created
a pleasant atmosphere for the production.

Francis D. Perkins from the New York Herald-Tribune
had this to say about the performance:

> "The Second Hurricane" blew publicly for the first
> time last night at the Playhouse (once the Neighbor-
> hood Playhouse) at 466 Grand Street, where a nearly
> capacity audience witnessed this interesting experiment
> of Aaron Copland and Edwin Denby in writing a musical
> stage work designed for performance by young people
> ranging in age from eight to nineteen years. The
> children who formed the majority among the performers
> are pupils in the Henry Street Settlement Music School,
> which is sponsoring this production, the Seward Park
> High School and the Professional Children's School.
> The idea of such a "play-opera for school perform-
> ers" to use Mr. Denby's designation, was first sug-
> gested to Mr. Copland by Miss Grace Spofford, new
> director of the Henry Street Music Schools [sic].[11]

Pitts Sanborn reviewed the performance for the New
York World-Telegram and commented on the unpleasant weather
that accompanied the performance outside the theatre:

> While a hurricane raged in Grand St., "The Second
> Hurricane" enjoyed a "world premiere" last evening
> within the hospitable shelter of the Neighborhood

Playhouse. ...What fascinates the observer is the
unaffected naturalness of all that goes on...The difficult task of matching this text with music and achieving
a score simple enough to be readily available for high
school use the country over has been accomplished
by Mr. Copland with conspicuous skill and sympathy.[12]

The Cleveland Plain Dealer had this to say:

The children took to the music like ducks to water,
apparently unaware that it carried the stigma of
modernity so odious to certain grown-ups. ...The
youthful performers showed an enthusiasm for, and
understanding of this new idiom seldom found among
our routine-driven professionals, whose reverence for
the classics often blinds them to the values in contemporary expression.[13]

This must have been a busy year for the administrators
of the Music School of the Henry Street Settlement, since
immediately before the presentation of The Second Hurricane,
an unusual event occurred in a fund-raising benefit for the
Music School of the Henry Street Settlement. The Curtis
Institute of Music in Philadelphia, where we should remember
that Grace Spofford had been Dean of that School for seven
years, performed the music of Gian-Carlo Mennoti, his Amelia
al Ballo (Amelia Goes to the Ball), coupled with Darius Mih-
haud's opera Le Pauvre Matelot (The Poor Sailor). Fritz
Reiner conducted the performance at the New Amsterdam
Theatre on April 11, 1937. This was a fund-raising event
for the Music School of the Henry Street Settlement in honor
of Lillian D. Wald's birthday.

It is interesting to note that in 1937 this very active
and contemporary American Settlement Music School was not
eligible to join the National Guild of Community Music Schools.
Yet its work gained national and international recognition.

The next issue of The Quarterly appeared in March,
1941, as Vol. I, No. 3. It announced the coming of the
second annual conference of the National Guild to be held
Tuesday and Wednesday, March 18th and 19th, 1941. The
general topic was to be The Community Music School in American Life. At the opening session on Tuesday morning, the
guest speakers were to be the following: Hon. Newbold

Morris, president of the Council, City of New York; William
H. Kilpatrick, Emeritus Professor of Education, Teachers Col-
lege, Columbia University; and Stanley Chapple, Conductor,
Lecturer and Author.[14]

In just the selection of the guest speakers, there seemed
to be, perhaps, an element of confusion in the minds of the
administrators of the National Guild as to what their function
really was. After all, it was no secret that Newbold Morris
was for many years a part of the Fiorello LaGuardia mayoral
team, and he was a member of the board of directors of the
Henry Street Settlement. Surely the Guild did not intend to
re-educate him but rather to seek information from him. William H. Kilpatrick was a well recognized educator, and Stanley
Chapple, conductor, lecturer and author might be on either
side of the argument.

During the Wednesday morning sessions, the speakers
were all affiliated with member schools of the Guild, each of
whom was to address a topic of interest; Eleanor Stanley
White, director of the Turtle Bay School of Music, was to
preside, and the speakers and their topics were as follows:
Johan Grolle, director of the Settlement Music School in Philadelphia, "Music as a Need in the Development of Modern
Youth"; Emily McCallip, director of the Cleveland Music School
Settlement, "Leadership"; Wellington Sloane, director of the
Brooklyn Music Settlement, "The Adult and the Amateur";
and Melzar Chaffee, director of the Music School Settlement
in New York City, "The Contribution of the Community Music
School to American Life."[15]

Action began on the attempt to have studies at Community Music Schools transfer to colleges or universities. In
the same issue of The Quarterly, the following report came
from The Cleveland Music School Settlement:

> During the season, we were approached by the School
> of Education of Western Reserve University, with re-
> gard to a proposition whereby students who were
> enrolled at the School of Education, who could not
> afford to pay the fees required of them for their re-
> quired course at the Cleveland Institute of Music,
> might secure a similar course which includes two
> lessons a week, with the tuition at $50.00 per semester
> for the course. The University makes the decision

as to which students shall enroll.

Students receive credit at the University for this
study in our settlement, as also for their work in the
Theory Department here. This is dependent upon
matriculation at the University and upon passing an
examination satisfactorily.

The plan is working out very well. Mid-term exams
were taken at Western Reserve University, one member
of our faculty sitting on the Examining Committee.[16]

Another school that made inroads in this area sends
its report as follows:

Community Music Schools Foundation (of St. Louis)

We are cooperating with the High Schools in the credit
system which they use for outside music study.
These credits are recognized at Missouri University.[17]

And so, true to its promise, action had been taken successfully for the idea of transfer of credits from community
music schools to high schools and colleges that are willing to
cooperate. This much success so early must have given the
Guild members a great sense of satisfaction. Recognition was
being given to The National Guild of Community Music Schools
and its member schools.

The uphill struggle for acceptance and recognition had
already begun for the National Guild, but the enrollment of
member schools had stubbornly remained at twelve organizations. For some time this situation would remain with fewer
than desired organizations applying for and achieving membership status. In 1944 it must have been truly disheartening
to write for inclusion in The Quarterly, Vol. IV, No. 1, June
1944, "With deep regret we record the end of membership in
the Guild of the Manhattan School of Music. Our best wishes
are with the School in its new status."[18]

In her own recording in her books, Janet D. Schenck
noted that the Neighborhood Music School at 238 East 105
Street in Manhattan was founded in 1913 and incorporated in
1920. When the National Guild was formed in 1937, the name
of the school was still the Neighborhood Music School, but
in 1938, it was changed to the Manhattan School of Music
and retains that title today. In 1943 the Manhattan School

of Music began to offer music training on the college level.
It awarded its first baccalaureate degree in 1944 and was no
longer a community music school per se. Thus it had to come
to the parting of the ways with the Guild and to relinquishing
its membership in that organization. Such is the story of
success.

One must question in his own mind how dedicated Johan
Grolle really was toward the concept of a community music
school when he reads a paragraph which Grolle wrote to Eleanor
Stanley White at the Turtle Bay Music School on March 5, 1944
ostensibly to comment on the curricular structures in Guild
Schools, and then comments:

> The Manhattan School has done the right thing, It
> has worked itself up from a neighborhood school to a
> recognized school, leaving the door open for all the
> constructive community work Mrs. Schenck will do.
> ...We have passed the old period of doing good to
> children from the neighborhood. ...Somehow I am
> convinced that the life of the Guild, especially under
> postwar conditions is at stake. ...The general touch-
> ing-of-everything as practiced by the settlements has
> no place in our movement. We are specialists with a
> social point of view.[19]

Whatever his ulterior motives may have been, Johan
Grolle accepted fully the responsibilities of being the President
of the National Guild and worked diligently so that his duties
of office were effectively treated. He and Janet D. Schenck,
who preceded Johan Grolle as President (1939-1941), shared
the heavy duties of the chief executive officers and neither
received compensation for their labors. This continues to be
true throughout the Guild's history. In later years an executive-secretary was hired, and subsequently executive directors
have been engaged to handle the operational business of the
Guild's national office. Previously, the majority of the work-
load landed in the office of the President, who was also a
full-time director of a community music school. The secretary-
treasurer was in a similar situation with all the collection of
dues, banking and bill paying of the Guild to handle. The
officers of the National Guild, during its earliest days until
about 1967, deserve special credit and admiration for the monu-
mental tasks that they undertook for the survival of the
National Guild of Community Music Schools.

The officers of the Guild saw to it that the organization
was professionally handled, and that proper procedures were
instituted to guarantee that the professionalism would be continued.   An example of such procedures is reflected in a letter
from Winifred M. Jacobson, secretary and treasurer written
to Eleanor S. White, director of the Turtle Bay Music School,
dated June 12, 1941:

> You may recall that at the March meeting it was de-
> cided to evaluate the work of schools already in the
> Guild before setting up requirements for schools who
> wish to join the Guild.   ...The enclosed questionnaire
> was drawn up by the committee and approved at the
> May meeting.
>
> The purpose of the questionnaire is to secure in-
> formation on the present plan, procedure and accom-
> plishment which is being carried out in each school.
> The committee does not intend that the questionnaire
> be a measure of comparison with an ideal state of
> affairs which each school might hope for.   Its aim is
> fact-finding; to evaluate the standard of our schools
> in terms of the objectives which each school sets for
> itself and the actual accomplishment of these object-
> ives.[20]

And so it was that the National Guild wished to examine
its own household, so to speak, before setting requirements
for new members that would be unrealistic.   Johan Grolle also
wanted the directors or their designated representatives of
member schools to assume the responsibility for Guild actions,
not just leaving all the work to the executive officers.   He
chose to organize the structure of the Guild in a democratic
fashion with the representatives of the schools playing active
parts in Guild work.   He expressed this in a letter to Eleanor
Stanley White on February 3, 1944:

> ...As it has been my intention to have the develop-
> ment of the activities of the Guild as much as
> possible upon a cooperative basis, I feel that a cata-
> logue expressing the Guild should be based upon sug-
> gestions from member schools regarding text matters;
> purpose of our movement; our conception of teaching;
> our contribution to individuals and the community;
> the development of qualified leadership, teachers,
> players and community leaders.[21]

The intention of the Guild members to remain effective,
imaginative and contemporary, would be reflected in the thinking of the chairmen or members of various committees. Such
an example comes from the All Newton School's executive
director, Mabel B. Worth, in a letter to Eleanor S. White:

> Mr. Grolle has written to ask if I would serve with
> you on the nominating committee [for officers] of the
> Guild. I have just written him to say that I would
> be glad to do what I could.
>   In thinking over the matter of Guild organization,
> does it not seem wise to begin now to develop a more
> or less fixed policy in regard to tenure of office?
> In most organizations, rotation in office when definitely
> planned for, is felt to be a benefitial [sic] procedure.
> Perhaps it would be well now to start the idea of
> developing such a plan for the Guild. A term of three
> years with privelege [sic] of reelection is fairly flexi-
> ble and might be considered.
>   However, right now in the case of the president,
> conditions being what they are with no certainty as
> to what they may be in days to come, it seems not
> only wise but essential to prevail upon Mr. Grolle to
> keep the office for another year at least.[22]

Johan Grolle had been president since 1942, so that if
the rotation plan were to be adopted, he would still have one
more term. Since there was nothing in the by-laws outlining
such action, the nominating committee would have to present
the plan to the membership at the next meeting before such
a procedure could be adopted. (With a simple review of the
records it is obvious that some satisfactory arrangements were
made since Johan Grolle remained president of the National
Guild until 1949.)

There must have been a gnawing sensation in the
anatomy of Johan Grolle concerning the action taken by the
Guild by writing its by-laws in such a way that many of the
larger and most successful schools were not welcome. His
reasons may have been noble in the cause of music, and his
desire to keep the social work faction at bay was not new.
David Mannes had wrestled with the same problem when he
proffered his reason for resigning from the directorship of
the Music School Settlement on Third Street.

George Martin cited the reason in <u>The Damrosch Dynasty</u> (1983) when he explained the following:

> In April 1915 David [Mannes] resigned as director at the Third Street School. He had been thinking of doing so for more than a year. Mrs. Howard Mansfield, with whom he had built up the school two years earlier had moved from president to chairman of the board, a less active post, and Mrs. Frank Rowell now was president. Under the latter's leadership David privately felt that progress had "finally come to a halt, and where progress was impossible it seemed immoral for me to stay."
> Though he never publicly discussed his reasons for resigning, it seems likely that he was distressed by the school's turn to programs that were more social than musical. The conflict was in the name, Music School Settlement, and it was the same conflict that Frank Damrosch had faced in starting the People's Singing Classes and that always arises when an art is used for social purposes.[23]

Perhaps the problem is most clearly defined when Martin goes on to clarify the situation and asks a question that is not easily answered:

> ...Will artistic standards or social purposes prevail? For Frank, the issue had arisen at the start of a project of which he was founder and director; for David, after fifteen years in a project that, ultimately, others controlled. To reporters, of course, he said nothing against the school's new leadership and stressed that he wanted to give more time to the Music School Settlement for Colored People.[24]

Thus is clarified the problem that any music (or art) school faces, to define its purpose and goals, to state the population it intends to serve, to recognize realistically the kind of space, instruments and materials that are needed to operate effectively.

It is vitally important to recognize specific guidelines and to observe them in any plans the school may wish to undertake. It is commendable to dream, so to speak, and to envision excellent plans for production and expansion, but the real world, in terms of dollars and cents, will undoubtedly present itself at once. The real genius is the one who is able to achieve the desired results while also remaining within the confines of an annual approved budget. There are not too many who are capable of doing this, which is part of the reason why it is so difficult to find excellent or even adequate arts administrators.

An unlimited amount of money is not always the solution to a difficult problem. Careful cogitation and realistic projections are essential to successful programs. This is not to say that imagination should not be applied to planning of programs, particularly at budget planning sessions. Budget planning is generally the most difficult (and sometimes distasteful) task an arts administrator undertakes. It is, however, unavoidable.

While Johan Grolle had successfully directed the Settlement Music School in Philadelphia for over thirty years and had also served as director of the Curtis Institute of Music for two years, he had not served as the chief executive officer of a national organization. In all fairness, neither had Janet D. Schenck until she was selected in 1939 to serve as the first president of the National Guild of Community Music Schools. Each of them had served as chairman of the Music Division of the National Federation of Settlements, and Grolle had previously been the chairman on the Federation's committee on Art. Neither had been the president of the organization.

Now, as president of the National Guild, Grolle was facing the awesome task of running the Guild within rather severe monetary restrictions, where budgets ranged in the low hundreds of dollars annually. At the moment it seemed apparent that the only way additional funds could be raised was by recruiting and enrolling new member schools in the Community Music School Movement, as he chose to call it.

But where were the Schools?

The urgency of the matter is reflected in a letter which Grolle sent to the members of the Executive Committee of the Guild, dated May 25, 1944:

> ...The Executive Committee of seven members consists
> of Mrs. William C. Worth, Miss Edith Otis, Miss Emily
> McCallip, Miss Edith Lieber, Miss Eleanor Stanley
> White, Mrs. Winifred M. Jacobson and myself.   [With
> the exception of Grolle himself, all the members were
> women and at that moment the members of the execu-
> tive committee represented more than half of the total
> Guild membership.]
>
> I hope you will accept the nomination to be a
> member of the Executive Committee and that you will
> head a Committee of your own selection within your
> area to help with one of the most important steps--
> to enlarge upon the enrollment of the National Guild
> of Community Music Schools.   Last season you re-
> ceived a copy of the requirements for admission.
>
> ...Another important matter to be brought to the
> attention of the Guild membership is that the organiza-
> tion needs more funds.   There are various ways of
> adding to the Guild receipts: Board of Directors'
> contributions, individually and as a group...Parents'
> Auxiliaries...The time will come when we can approach
> Foundations for subsidies to extend our work.[25]

There is a humorous side to this.   When one reads the
letter Grolle sent to the members of his executive committee,
one realizes that apparently none of them knew previously
that she was a member of the executive committee.   He was
a martinet of the first order who expected no one to refuse.

His influence was strong among Guild members, and he
let his true philosophies be known clearly, especially by those
who seemed to follow his lead.   On May 10, 1944, he wrote to
Edna B. Lieber, director of the school in St. Louis, and
stated after commenting on the need for standardized curricula
in Guild schools:

> Our weak spot is that we have started a policy of
> everything to meet the demand.   We have as directors
> or patrons the amateur group [sic].   Now we must
> stand out as experts and as understanding leadership.
> A little less third person and a little more of the first
> person, is in order.   We are artists.   We have a far
> deeper insight into music and humanity than most pro-
> fessionals.   We have experimented.   We have made
> mistakes and realized them.   But out of it all has

come to us the competition of the cosmic value of art
and its influence upon people; professionalism and
commercialism have separated people from the art which
is within them. Showmanship, ego, charlatanism and
pressure of doing the other fellow out of a job are
not the best elements from which art can come. Art
is a personal ambition and it must be one of the highest
we are capable of.

I believe this is the basic philosophy of our work,
and so far as I am concerned, will never change within
me. We must be willing to pay the price. ...If we
do not work, we soon will all be dead because the
mass movements as started by the public schools, certification in order to get a job, and much nonsense
are seriously interfering with the real function of
laws underlying art. Our schools have a decided
message. Quality in quantity.[26] [It is interesting
that he sent a copy of this letter to Eleanor Stanley
White, the director at the Turtle Bay Music School.]

Johan Grolle expresses clearly his value of the arts and
also somewhat of a criticism of Settlements by his statement,
"We have started a policy of anything to meet the demand."
His ability to work arduously is undeniable and credit must
be given to his dedication to musical art.

The Music Division of the National Federation of Settlements sent out its report in June, 1943, Vol. III. In it
Jeannine Cossitt, chairman, started the publication with an
article entitled "Music and Leisure." Her words set the pattern
for future reports and for educational guidelines:

The educator's job for future generations concerns
complete cultural as well as physical enjoyment of
leisure. Leisure time activities, hobbies, like all
other tendencies, grow and are intensified with
exercise. Not having anything to do also grows with
exercise. Soon something must be done about this,
for one of the forces which makes for delinquency is
unoccupied leisure time. ...Program for leisure is
more than keeping children off the street by means of
wholesome occupation. ...Often we tend to treat too
casually the development of a skill connected with
leisure. ...Persistence, regularity of application to
a task, are qualifications which do not necessarily

exist of themselves. One is not born with them. But they can be acquired if environmental conditions permit and encourage their development.[27]

All of the above statement is applicable to the study of music and musical training. Johan Grolle would have accepted it easily. The implications for the teacher of any art form are vast and must be continued with additional enforcement and greater expansion. It is true, however, that this statement would be accepted both by the National Federation of Settlements and the National Guild of Community Music Schools (currently Schools of the Arts). There is great commonality between the two national organizations. Perhaps neither group was able to see the forest because of all the trees.

Included in the report is a statement by Edna Lieber, Director of the Community Music Schools Foundation in St. Louis. She states:

> ...Seven faculties are simultaneously at work in the satisfactory performance of a musical composition: hearing of the keenest quality; the quickest and most accurate sight; tremendous digital skill, which is most rare; a mathematical sensitivity; tonal memory; emotional balance; and general physical and mental coordination of the highest order.[28]

Miss Lieber wisely continues to enlighten the reader with the following statement:

> Instead of this perfectionist attitude, adult music education, as well as children's, should aim first for a general knowledge which fosters interest and second a modest attainment in performance to have sufficient skill for easy and pleasurable playing of worth while [sic] musical literature, that is all that is required of people who enjoy reading or athletics, or nature study or what not. Then why so much more of the most difficult of all?[29]

Since the Settlement Music School in Philadelphia was a member of the National Federation of Settlements at the time of that bulletin, Johan Grolle, as all other directors and department heads, was asked to make his contribution to the publication. As might have been expected, he chose to write in a vein that explained the importance for Music Schools to stress the quality of the music taught under their jurisdiction when he said:

> We are trying to uphold quality in adapting our work to the social and personal situations we are meeting all the time. The purpose of our work makes the focus upon the cultural values of music primarily, but we are not neglecting the social qualities....
> Where the general settlement should use music as a social contact, the specialized house must build the cultural centers where specialized work of quality and standard can be secured...The specialized house also offers environment that can absorb him. As an economic necessity, however, the specialized house must focus upon the avoidance of the turnover that is a characteristic of the more social and informal approach. [He signed his statement] Johan Grolle, President, National Guild of Community Music Schools, Philadelphia.[30]

All the other contributors identified themselves with the name of the agency by which they were employed.

One of the purposes of The Quarterly was to share information, problems, trends, etc. with other Guild schools to evaluate conditions as they seemed to be at that date, to offer suggestions or aid to member schools, and as early as June, 1942, the issue began to inquire of the member schools how World War II was affecting the operations of the individual schools. The questions asked in the informal survey were of a practical nature primarily concerning the basic operations of each individual school. The Quarterly reported the following information:

HOW WAR CONDITIONS ARE AFFECTING OUR SCHOOLS

I. Enrollment of Older Students:
    Schools report little or no change; Four find enrollment dropping noticeably; two note pupils dropping out because of defense work. Two report a slight increase--in the case of Turtle Bay, "chiefly young women in business or the professions". All Newton reports most of the older students will work on farms or in industry this summer.

II.   Readjustment of Schedules:
Four report no readjustment to date, two an
increase of work for children and premilitary-
age students. Cleveland reports more daytime
teaching; St. Louis, more night instruction because of teachers in defense work. The All
Newton schedule has been affected somewhat
by the fact of its using a Public School building.
Brooklyn has felt in some degree the change
in Public School schedules. Buffalo has had
to make concessions for absence and tardiness
in the case of defense workers. Philadelphia
and Manhattan School of Music have readjusted
schedules as a result of faculty losses to the
armed services.

III. Loss of Faculty:
Six Schools report a total loss of fifteen to date;
four expect further loss in the Fall. Four
schools have not been affected yet. One faculty
member from Wilmington is in the Navy; one from
Manhattan School of Music is in charge of music
for convalescent soldiers in a large Army hospital;
one from Philadelphia is in the Navy Band, and
another in charge of the music program at an
Army Camp in the South, etc.[31]

The Quarterly also carried in this issue an extract of
an article by the Russian composer Dmitri Shostakovich published April 1942.

MUSIC IN WAR-TIME RUSSIA

The upsurge of patriotic feeling which has seized the
peoples of the Soviet Union, defending their free life,
has created a splendid foundation for the growth of
new artistic achievement in time of war. Our theatres
are working intensively, staging new plays, creating
new characters, awaking noble and heroic sentiments
in the people. Along with their new productions they
present the world's great dramas of past epochs.
Our symphony orchestras are presenting their
usual concerts with great success. Our musicians, as
always, delight composers with their profound understanding of the compositions they perform. But

critical Soviet listeners follow the concerts keenly.

These facts are highly important to us and terrible
to Hitler and Goebbels. In those days of bloody battles unceasing thunder of guns, we may tell the world:
Music does not cease in besieged Leningrad. Art,
which in any other country would be relegated to the
background at such a time, which would take shelter
far from the battle lines, has become a weapon striking
at the enemies of our country. From the inspired
sounds of symphonies, songs, marches and oratorios,
the Soviet people draws [sic] strength for the struggle.[32]

If careful perusal is given to the various issues of The
Quarterly, one finds the expression of the depths and serious
dedication of the National Guild's leaders. Their approaches
to the art of their choice, and to the teaching of that art,
are explained in the most edifying, uplifting terms, so much
so that it is almost a spiritual encounter for those of us who
have had the joy and emotional experiences gained through
personal performances. But even more so, from the exhilara-
tion and satisfaction of teaching those who desire so much to
express themselves musically and artistically.

The selection of articles to appear in The Quarterly is
excellent, and each author comes from the ranks of those
who are knowledgeable in the field about which he writes.
The two chosen to appear in the February, 1943 issue of The
Quarterly, Volume V, Number 1 are Serge Koussevitsky, conductor for so many years of the Boston Symphony Orchestra,
and Edwin Hughes, who was then the Executive Secretary
of the National Music Council and prominent piano teacher and
musical editor.

The first is by Serge Koussevitsky in his address to
students at the Berkshire Music Centre during the summer of
1942.

The tide of war has reached us. The old world is
shaken. The fundamental principles of civilization
have received a severe blow. Not only culture and
art, but life itself has been put to question.

Yet, in our own world there is hope, and if there
ever was a time to speak of music it is now, in America. It is during the troubled periods in history that
those who believe in the values and inheritance of

culture stand in the front rank, battling to help an
endangered humanity...

Today we have a glowing evidence that music is
regaining possession of the real cultural place that
belonged to it in the past, before inconceivable growth
of a mechanistic civilization lowered the cultural values
of musical art...

The blessed sign that music is recovering its spiritual and deeply humanitarian meaning comes to us from
the scorched plains of Russia. It comes as a mounting
protest against human suffering, brutality and op-
pression. The spirit of a young, vigorous, heroic
nation finds its expression in the powerful medium of
music with which the Russian people are so richly endowed...

This music finds a resounding echo in the heart
of the American people who, as an equally young and
spirited nation, realize the importance of art in the
intense materialism imposed by war, and who keep an
unfailing sense for truth, sound judgment and freedom...

I recall words said to me by a naval officer: "We
go to protect America, our people and our civilization;
and we expect those who remain in the rear to protect
the cultural values of our nation. We are willing to
die to conquer peace for the future; but what will
peace and future be, if our culture is not preserved?
...we must all fight to save real values." ...Remember
that America has a great responsibility towards the
agonized European world. She holds her traditions
and culture from the old world and has now been given
the flaming torch of all the suffering and oppressed
peoples to carry, to keep burning until the time of
peace. And then America will be able to restore the
cultural wealth which was entrusted to her, and which
she alone can save from destruction. [Reprinted with
permission of Dr. Koussevitsky.][33]

Dr. Koussevitsky was Russian born himself. Thus he
knows much about what he speaks when he talks of Russian
people and their artistic values. And, of course, Russia
was an ally of this country during that altercation known as
World War II.

In that period the war was constantly on the minds of

every man, woman and child, whether in service or not.
Patriotism was fervently high, and it had become standard
procedure to perform the National Anthem before any public
performance. It was difficult to find a pleasant topic for discussion then.

Edwin Hughes was responsible for the highly successful
piano series The Master Series for the Young. It included
works of Bach, Mozart, Chopin, Schubert, etc., with each
composer's work in a separate volume edited by Mr. Hughes.
At that time he was also the Executive-Secretary of the National Music Council, which is the only federally chartered music
organization in the country. Hughes had a very heavy responsibility which he shouldered very successfully, that of select-
ing topics for the agenda of the Council's meetings usually
held in New York City. At such a meeting early in 1943,
his address or report to the Council members was entitled,
"Music in Wartime and Post-War America," excerpts of which
are presented here:

> Reports from various parts of the country indicate
> a substantial increase in the classes of private music
> teachers, and not a few educational institutions have
> had larger enrollments than usual this year in their
> freshman classes. The sale of printed music, popular
> and serious, is booming. Not in fifteen years has it
> reached such dimensions as in 1942. The sales of
> albums of piano music and songs in particular have
> increased greatly, indicating that more persons are
> making music in the home. This kind of musical ac-
> tivity, will doubtless increase as joy-riding diminishes
> still further. ...Concerts in the two principal halls
> in New York during November just equalled the num-
> ber given in the same month a year ago. ...Carnegie
> Hall reports the largest aggregate attendance since
> 1918 at its musical events this season. ...The urgent
> task in civilian musical activities at present is to keep
> alive and active, to the greatest extent possible, the
> institutions, organizations, enthusiasms, movements,
> that have brought our music life to its present grati-
> fying level. ...Our art music will certainly suffer
> after the war if it is allowed to languish now. Let
> us strive, then, to keep the musical blood flowing,
> even at a diminished speed, in every worthy musical
> effort. ...The reconstruction will be that much easier

if the instruments of reconstruction are still in existence, and we do not have to begin much of our work
again from the ground up.[34]

Thus we find Edwin Hughes bolstering the spirits of
those Americans involved in the music industries, and those
in higher education, as well as the ones in the private teaching sector. Interest in the arts was increasing steadily, and
it must be remembered that during these war years, the
economy of the nation had risen to a decent and respectable
level. People who had not previously been able to afford
desired music instruction, were now financially able to do so.
It is a pity to realize that it took a world war to make it
possible, but at least the trend turned in the right direction.
America was becoming more alive musically and artistically.

At the end of the war, the G. I. Bill made it possible
for veterans, both men and women, to continue their musical
and artistic educations subsidized by the Government. This
fact followed by the baby-boom kept the numbers asking
for musical and artistic training rising, both for children and
adults. Community music schools and schools of the arts have
developed in many sections of the country where they did not
previously exist.

Though the National Guild of Community Music Schools
was founded initially by those who no longer desired to be
affiliated in any way with the settlement houses throughout
the country for fear of lessening the quality of the musical
instruction being given in community music schools, many of
its directors and teachers still felt a strong sense of social
consciousness. So much so that The Quarterly reflected the
thinking of those whose social leanings and acceptance of
social responsibilities caused them to consider non-musical
problems. An issue of The Quarterly devoted considerable
space to those current writers' social considerations which
were facing America at that time. Since there was no name
attached to the lead article called, "A Note for the Times",
one can only assume that it was written by Johan Grolle himself, or if not, that the article certainly had his distinct approval. In the issue of December, 1944, Volume IV, Number
2, The Quarterly article states:

A recent Guild survey covering problems raised by the
war situation deals with juvenile delinquency and

> teen-age problems as they affect students attending
> the Schools of our movement. The Schools report
> that they have no problem of this nature--which brings
> us at once to the question whether the contacts of
> young people with art are not one of the strongest
> influences in directing the natural desire for self-
> expression, which, undirected, may be considered the
> underlying cause of most teen-age problems. [35]

The idea of musicians and artists having strong senses
of social responsibility, particularly those associated with community music schools, has been a long established truism.
The author, however, knows of no serious investigation which
has proved that a study of the arts has in truth prevented a
child from becoming a delinquent, nor an adult from becoming
a criminal. It is true that the percentage of those who have
seriously studied one of the arts and who also had been involved in some non-socially-approved activity, is low. Any
further question about this issue must be answered by thorough investigation by those who are qualified to prepare and
pursue such an inquiry.

The next paragraph in the article is almost impossible
to take seriously.

> Walking in crowds, observing young girls approaching
> men in uniform, observing also the need for compan-
> ionship of young men in the service who have been
> taken away from their normal home environment, hear-
> ing the conversation, we cannot help wondering what
> would be the result if a greater number of these grop-
> ing young people were led from the street corner to
> the music school. [36]

It would certainly seem that the writer of the above statement
is placing an exorbitant amount of preventive or curative
powers to the study of music, or any art for that matter.
It is doubtful that all the social pressures brought upon young
people, in war time or not, can be assuaged by musical or
artistic endeavors.

In the same issue come the words of Edith Otis who was
then the supervisor of music at the Brooklyn Music School
Settlement, which would almost seem as if the National Guild
of Community Music Schools should revert to its more

"settlement house orientation". (The confusion is evident in
the minds of many of the leaders of schools that are Guild
members. The social responsibility has not disappeared from
their consideration, nor has their realization of the need for
musical integrity as far as quality and standards go. By
this time a reconciliation between the arguing forces seems to
be approaching within the forseeable future.)

The article by Edith Otis is entitled, "The Music School
and the Social Agency," and it states its own case as follows:

Educational institutions have a tremendous responsibility both now and in the post-war period of adjustment in that the thoughts of our future generations
are molded, to a great extent, within their walls.
Necessarily problems will be many, yet never has
there been greater opportunity for the liberal arts
to prove their value than today, and surely there
has never been a moment when the work of the Community Music Schools can be of such far reaching
importance.
Although we as music schools come in contact with
a large number of people who are primarily interested
in this branch of the arts and who come to us for
specialized work, there are also a great many people
and institutions we do not contact to the extent we
should. Foremost among these are our social agencies
who, for lack of funds and the discontinuance of W.P.A.
assistance, have been unable to include music in their
recreational programs. These institutions are coping
with some of the most vital problems concerning and
confronting the youth of today. They are striving to
iron out racial disturbances and to promote greater
cooperation and understanding. Although they deal
largely with a class of individuals not found in our
music schools, what would be of greater value at this
time than for us to extend the scope of our work to
include a well organized program for such community
centers?[37]

And now we hear the plea of the performing musician
asking for permission to find a way for community schools
of the arts to bring their valuable assistance to other social
service agencies unable to bring the arts to those who need
them, but who are those who may not achieve the level of

professional performers in their use of the arts. The compassion shown by those who started the settlement music
school movement, such as Emilie Wagner, Blanche Wolf Kohn,
Jeanette Selig Frank, Johan Grolle, Samuel Belov, Mary T.
McDermott, Almeda Adams, A. W. Binder who were later joined
by Dorothy Maynor, Louise Behrend and Ann Hirsch, has not
died in the hearts of serious minded musical performers and
teachers. Edith Otis concludes her article with the following
paragraph:

> Though on the one hand we must continually strive
> to raise our standards to meet the demands of those
> students seriously interested in furthering their musi-
> cal studies with us, on the other hand let us realize
> that we have a rare opportunity just because of our
> non-professional community spirit to be of real assist-
> ance to a large majority of young people who would
> otherwise not come in personal contact with good music
> at all.[38]

It is imperative that all who are engaged in the arts
realize the full value of the arts--how far they extend to reach
people of all ages and sizes, colors and nationalities. We
battle vigorously against prejudice in race and religion, color
and national origins, yet highly skilled, talented artists can,
and do, become prejudicial toward other phases of the art
form they profess to call their own.

While quality and standards are the magic words that
fit into any community music school's program and curricula,
it has always been assumed that each student was treated
separately and within his own limitations or strengths. As
the Settlement Music School in Philadelphia and the Music School
Settlement of Third Street in New York City insisted that
each child is acceptable if he expresses the desire to study
music, and he is judged or rated according to his own natural
abilities. Neither organization has dropped the term, settlement, from its name and each has extended into the community
wherever it was needed and wanted. This includes, on many
occasions, work they had done in their local public schools.

Yet each of these two schools can point to many students
who have gone on to professional performance careers such as
Leon Bates, Clamma Dale, Mario Lanza, Jaime Laredo, and
Jerome Lowenthal from the Settlement Music School in Philadelphia, and Marion Feldman, Joseph Gingold, Sidney Harth,

and Jeanette Scovotti from the Third Street Music School
Settlement in New York City. These represent successful performers who are former students of only two schools of the
National Guild's list of member schools, which at the time of
this writing number to more than 160 schools. It is evident
that the quality and standards are significantly high in community music schools.

Johan Grolle was determined to produce a brochure for
the Guild that would tell the story of community music schools
and to this end he worked diligently. On May 17, 1945, he
sent yet another message to the members of the Executive
Committee expressing his concerns and urging them to take
action. In part his letter read as follows:

> In putting things together mentally, I feel I would
> like very much to mention in the "Forward" [sic] and
> as a first draft under the heading of "History" [sic],
> the beginnings of each school; when they were begun;
> the evolution from the charity idea, low fees, to
> higher standards than dilettantes and volunteers can
> develop. I think this is one of the roots of our move-
> ment and would give us an opportunity to point out
> the natural evolution of quality, constant improve-
> ment, and development of standards.
> I also want to point out one of the roots of the
> Guild, from the Third Street first initiative to the
> music division of the National Federation of Settlements;
> and finally the National Guild of Community Music
> Schools. ...We are not dealing with what I or some-
> body else thinks best, but with what is the true reality
> involved, and that must be put into such form that
> it differs from the trite economic and at the same
> time is not too dilettantish or sentimental.[39]

At this point, Mr. Grolle seemed to be making his points
too strongly and was not nearly so effective as he had been
in earlier years. At any rate, in 1946 he saw his dream
realized in the form of a booklet handsomely designed and
very dignified in appearance, in a light grey color with maroon
printing. Its foreword stated very simply:

> In submitting this Handbook, the National Guild of
> Community Music Schools aims to inform the general
> public, the music profession, and public school and

college music departments concerning its history, its
philosophy and the curricular standards maintained
by the membership of the organization.[40]

The committee members who worked with him in the
preparation of the booklet did achieve many of his goals, for
the booklet did contain things in addition to the simple foreword, a directory of Guild schools, the listing of officers, a
statement about the Community Music School movement, admission requirements, standard curricula of Guild schools, etc.
And so, after nine years of struggle which included establishing the Guild itself, surviving a national depression, and the
onslaught and conclusion of World War II, the National Guild
of Community Music Schools was formally announced by the
publication of its informative brochure.

Probably the most significant contribution in the booklet
was the listing of requirements for admission to the National
Guild of Community Music Schools. This section of the booklet
is shown below:

The enlarging of the Guild through the extension of
its membership holds an important place in future
plans of the organization. In order to maintain the
standards of the Guild, the following Requirements
for Admission have been adopted by the membership:

I. Schools applying for membership must have been
in existence for not less than five years in order to
be eligible.

Schools applying for associate membership must
have been in existence a minimum of three years.
Election to membership is based upon a majority vote
of Guild members.

II. The functioning of the school: The schools must
function through a Board of responsible trustees, a
staff, a suitable executive and a musical director or
Council of heads of departments.

III. Finances: Suitable budget must have been maintained for the five-year period for full membership,
or three-year period for associate membership; and
must meet with the approval of a Finance Committee
appointed by the Guild.

IV.   Tuition Rates: Tuition rates must guarantee
that the school is a non-profit-making organization.

V.   Number of pupils: Minimum of one hundred.

VI.   Curriculum: The plan of the curriculum and the
functioning of the same must be approved by a committee appointed by the Guild.

VII.   Survey: A survey of the school must be made
by an individual or a committee appointed by the
Guild.   Such matters as equipment, etc., must be
approved at this time.

VIII. Revoking of Membership: Member schools which
fail to maintain required standards may have their
membership revoked or temporarily suspended upon the
recommendation of a Committee on Standards appointed
by the Guild. [41]

It is important to note here on page 10 of the National
Guild's booklet, a statement is included under "Organization":

The constitution and By-Laws of the Guild provide
for:

4. Memberships: (a) Independently incorporated
Schools of Music operating according to the principles
of Community Music Schools, giving evidence of permanence and stability, possessing a suitable faculty
and equipment and showing satisfactory proof of the
maintenance of standards prescribed by the Guild,
may be admitted to Guild membership upon the vote
of two-thirds of the Guild members.   Associate membership is open to any school whose standards meet
the Associate Membership requirements of the Guild. [42]

It is also amusing to note that membership dues for full
institutional members were $15.00.   At that time the Guild was
already a member of the National Music Council. [43]

At least in its first catalogue or bulletin, the National
Guild of Community Music Schools did not include the damning
statement that appears in some of its earlier typewritten
materials which state the applying schools must "not be

affiliated with any social settlement." It did say, however,
"independently incorporated schools."

And in 1947 Johan Grolle began his final two-year term
as president of his beloved National Guild of Community Music
Schools. He was coming near retirement age, and at this
point, he and the members of the Guild were casting around
to determine who would be available to shoulder the responsibility in 1949. The Guild was at a serious point in its history
since it was not growing in numbers, and many were trying
to examine their past and to rectify any mistakes that might
have been made.

This year, 1947, proved to be one of great activity
throughout the world. Maria Callas, the famous Metropolitan
Opera soprano, made her debut in Verona, Italy, in Ponchielli's opera La Gioconda. Benjamin Britten's opera Albert
Herring had its first performance in Glyndebourne, and Gian-
Carlo Menotti composed his operas The Medium and The Telephone, which were later to have a long run on Broadway and
which are performed frequently today. Pablo Casals, the
internationally known 'cellist, vowed never to play again in
Spain as long as Franco was in power.

Jackie Robinson was the first black man to sign a major
league baseball contract in 1947, and it was also a year that
brought New York City to a halt with a heavy blizzard of
nearly 28 inches in late December. Three Americans died in
1947, each very prominent in his own field: Willa Cather
(1873-1947), the American authoress; Al Capone (1899-1947),
probably the best-known American gangster in his time; and
the colorful Fiorello H. LaGuardia, famous mayor of New York
City, who read the comics on Sundays to the children of New
York City over radio station WNYC during a newspaper strike
in that city. The theatre world was captivated by Tennessee Williams' play A Streetcar Named Desire, which was
to win the Pulitzer prize for drama in 1948.

A young man who had received his Bachelor's degree
from the Cleveland Institute of Music and his Master's degree
from the Oberlin College Conservatory arrived on the scene
in Cleveland, Ohio. He became the sixth director of the
Cleveland Music School Settlement. His reign was to last
thirty-six years. His contribution to the success of that
school is enormous. It was he who arrived at the right time

to be of great assistance to the development and growth of
the National Guild of Community Music Schools when he became
its third president in 1949. For both organizations he was
a tireless worker who also had much creative imagination.
His name is Howard Whittaker, and he is also recognized as
an American composer.

Mr. Whittaker had barely had two year's experience
running his own school in Cleveland, when he was called upon
to assume the responsibilities of the presidency of the National
Guild. Obviously one of the most important tasks to tackle
was to increase the membership of the National Guild. Neither
Janet D. Schenck nor Johan Grolle had been able to accomplish
this assignment.

There were many angry people in the ranks of the
National Federation of Settlements, angry at the way in which
the Guild had been formed to the exclusion of many of their
organizations. Some felt very deeply hurt that their programs
were not considered "good enough." But they were even
angrier still when they learned that some schools were considered good enough to join both the national organizations.
As mentioned earlier, a number of the schools who were among
the giants in the field were not allowed to join the Guild because of their settlement affiliations. They would not let
the National Guild forget the damage that had been done
to the pride of their organizations. They identified themselves
as schools in the community; therefore, to them community
music school, settlement music school and music school settlement were synonymous and would stay that way!

The National Guild could not avoid some feelings of
guilt, particularly because of the way in which the Guild
was secretly and very quietly formed in 1937. It is also
noteworthy that the Guild did not even elect officers for
a period of two years when Janet D. Schenck was chosen as
the first president of the Guild. (She, who at one time
was chairman of the National Federation of Settlements' Music
Committee!) Little action could they take to recruit new
member schools when their national organization was not very
firmly structured itself. And if growth were to come, from
where could it come except from settlement music schools?
It was a most unfortunate situation for all parties concerned,
and a unique problem for a new, young president.

6

THE LABORED GROWTH OF THE NATIONAL GUILD OF COMMUNITY MUSIC SCHOOLS/SCHOOLS OF THE ARTS, 1949-1966

It was evident in the minds of all concerned that the National Guild of Community Music Schools needed additional member schools if its voice was to be significant in the world of music and music education. It had for its base a firm group of schools known for their success and seriousness of purpose. It had become abundantly clear that growth in membership could not be achieved so long as the Guild retained its restrictive membership requirements, that of independent incorporation of each school, and the element that was worse and more of it, no affiliation with any social settlement house.

The director of each school had clearly in mind that the Guild had been formed to protect musical excellence in each of the schools. Affiliation with settlement houses suggested the lowering of standards in musical performance. Without looking for any further solutions or patterns to follow, the splinter group who formed the Guild decided that it would be prudent of them simply to prevent the objectional element from joining its organization. Only it was becoming more and more evident that the plan did not work. With the loss of the Neighborhood Music School (now the Manhattan School of Music) from its ranks, the original twelve members were down to eleven.

The membership was decreasing, not increasing. The new, young president saw the task before him and plunged into the murky waters striving for progress. It seems best to follow a chronological path for the next few years citing the highlights and pitfalls of progress.

It had been recognized over the twelve years of the Guild's lifespan that if there were some project or undertaking

of musical significance for the Guild to sponsor, the message
of its own existence and offerings would become better known.
The National Guild should be the sponsor, not an individual
Guild school itself.   Greater recognition of the Guild as an
important national organization could be achieved.   Up to now
no such project had been suggested.

At this particular moment a young choral director and
radio announcer in New York City who also lectured on music
at New York University had been doing a musical series of
programs over the City's community radio station, WNYC,
called Music for the Connoisseur.   His name was David Randolph.   He used carefully selected recorded music which
featured recordings of excellent musical quality but which
were not heard on a regular basis.   Such works as familiar
Haydn and Mozart compositions, or the well-known symphonies
of Beethoven and Brahms were not heard on Music for the Connoisseur.   In the September 1946 issue of Musical America
the following description of Randolph's program appeared in
the section called "Radio for Record Programs--A Sounder
Pattern":

Music Off the Beaten Path

The basic idea of his Music for the Connoisseur is
simple.   Its material consists of "music off the beaten
path"--never such items as the Fifth Symphony and
1812 Overture which are played to death everywhere.
Program commentary is free to the point of sounding
ad lib.   Randolph daily sharpens his personal axe
for the types of commentary which are dry and technical in the usual program note style--the kind which
constantly belittles or else talks over the listener's
intelligence.   Likewise he campaigns against the gushy
variety which is loaded with the aesthetics and super-
natural qualities of music.
Although the music he includes in the programs
is assuredly of a superior level, he presents it in human, interesting and seemingly easy to understand
even to a person of relatively limited musical background.   To Randolph the stiff shirt and white tie
approach must go if audiences are to be brought
closer to a sincere enjoyment of music.[1]

Since David Randolph had previously had no contact
with the National Guild of Community Music Schools, here is
further corroboration of why Mr. Randolph and his unique
program were chosen for Guild sponsorship. This article
appeared in New York City in the Daily Worker, written by
Bob Lauter in his column "Around the Dial" on May 26, 1949:

Music for the Connoisseur

It's time that someone threw bouquets at David Randolph, and I'm going to try to do it.

For years David Randolph, a musicologist and
lecturer at New York University, has offered a program, Music for the Connoisseur, over the city station, WNYC, at 8:00 P.M. on Tuesdays. At 1:00
P.M. on Sundays the station offers a transcribed re-
peat performance of one of his earlier programs.

You might call Randolph a classical disc jockey because he plays records and comment [sic] on them,
but such a description does not do him justice. What
he says is always as important as what he plays. He
has been doing his job for years, and maintaining a
surprisingly high standard of excellence for each
program.

Some of his programs may have only a museum interest, such as the one in which he presented unusual
recording boners. One of these was an oratorio in
which the record caught the conductor's voice as he
sang along in loud and off-key ecstasy. Another was
a recording of a Bach choral work in which the mike
picked up the sound of an auto horn outside the studio. The frank aspect of this was that the timing and
pitch of the auto horn was so perfect that it had to
be pointed out before it was recognized.

Randolph had committed mayhem on some recordings.
Once he played presto violin passages at very slow
tempo to point out how many inaccuracies there are
in such passages, even when played by master violinists, and how the human ear does the kindly job
of hearing what it ought to hear under such circumstances. Whenever Randolph has resorted to a dis-
tortion of a recording for such purposes, he has always been considerate enough to omit the name of the
recording artist.

The most important aspect of his program, however,

are [sic] his discussions and illustrations of musical
theories and problems. He has contributed to an
historical appreciation of music and composers. While
many people insist that no one can talk an audience
into enjoying music as such, Randolph has talked people into enjoying music they have never enjoyed before....WNYC pioneered in broadcasting symphony
orchestra rehearsals, an idea that was picked up by
a network. The network program received an award.

David Randolph's program deserves a large[r]
audience than WNYC can give him. The title, Music
for the Connoisseur, is a little misleading, if not for-
bidding. It is not music for the connoisseur, but
simply music for people who like music.[2]

And so the idea for a project was conceived. It was
to present the David Randolph series of twenty-six programs
over a radio station in each city where a Guild School existed,
and the National Guild of Community Music Schools was to be
the sponsor of the program, with the local radio stations do-
nating the time as a community service. The concept for this
community action seems to have been Howard Whittaker's with
a strong assist from Ruth Kemper. Whittaker sent a letter
giving a progress report on his recent actions. The letter
was dated June 29, 1949:

Dear Miss Kemper:

I finally managed to reach a program chairman of one
of the local radio stations to see about the possibility
of using Randolph's transcriptions. The situation
seems to be this: First, I must clear with the local
office of the union: second, with their approval I
can then clear with Petrillo (both steps are necessary
due to the fact that we would be using recorded music
on transcription); third, acquire at least one record
of Randolph's program to play for the station who
would be granting us the time gratis in view of it
being a public service; four, approach the New York
Community Trust and see if they would be willing
to finance the project.

I would suppose that each member school would
have to clear with their local union if they once had
word that I had cleared with the national office for
all schools. The third step would also be necessary

Top: Jane Addams, founder of Hull-House, Chicago. Bottom: Hull-House Music School, c. 1893. (Photos courtesy of the University of Illinois at Chicago, The University Library, Jane Addams Memorial Collection.)

Top: Lillian D. Wald, founder of the Henry Street Settlement, New York. (Photo courtesy of the Henry Street Settlement.) Bottom: Henry Street Settlement Louis Abrons Arts for Living Center today. (Photo courtesy of Prentice, Chan, & Ohlhausen, Architects, and of the Henry Street Settlement.)

Top: Emilie Wagner, founder of Third Street Music School Settlement, New York. Bottom: Third Street Music School Settlement, c. turn of the century. (Photos courtesy of the Third Street Music School Settlement.)

Top: Mary Garrettson Evans, founder of Peabody Preparatory, Baltimore. Bottom: Peabody Preparatory in earlier days. (Photos courtesy of Dean Eileen Cline of the Peabody Conservatory of Johns Hopkins University and the Peabody Preparatory.)

Janet D. Schenck, founder of Neighborhood Music School, New York, now the Manhattan School of Music. (Photo courtesy of Mrs. Josephine Whitford and the Manhattan School of Music.)

Top: Johan Grolle, first director of the Settlement Music School, Philadelphia. Bottom: Main branch of the Settlement Music School, Mary Louise Curtis Bok Zimbalist Building, Philadelphia.

Top: Germantown branch of the Settlement Music School.
Bottom: Kardon Institute of Music for the Handicapped,
Settlement Music School, Philadelphia.

<u>Top</u>: Howard Whittaker, director of the Cleveland Music School Settlement, 1948–84. <u>Bottom</u>: Cleveland Music School Settlement, main building. (Photos courtesy of the Cleveland Music School Settlement.)

Three additional buildings of the Cleveland Music School Settlement. <u>Top</u>: Kulas House. <u>Middle</u>: Griffiths House. <u>Bottom</u>: Gries House. (Photos courtesy of the Cleveland Music School Settlement.)

Top: Dorothy Maynor, founder and first director of the Harlem School of the Arts. Bottom: Harlem School of the Arts, recital area. (Photo courtesy of Ulrich Franzen & Associates, Architects.)

Community Music Center of Boston.

Top: Louise Behrend, founder and director of the School for Strings (New York), with string ensemble. Bottom: School for Strings, front entrance of new home.

Top: Dr. Herbert Zipper, first executive director of the National Guild. Bottom: Monroe Levin, president of the National Guild, 1983-87. (Photos courtesy of the National Guild of Community Schools of the Arts.)

Top: Lolita Mayadas, executive director of the National Guild of Community Schools of the Arts, 1981 to present. Bottom: Aaron Copland, American composer who wrote The Second Hurricane for the Henry Street Settlement Music School in 1937.

THE SECOND HURRICANE

A PLAY OPERA IN TWO ACTS

Libretto by
EDWIN DENBY
Music by
AARON COPLAND

C. C. BIRCHARD & CO., BOSTON

Cover of the original vocal score of Copland's <u>Second Hurricane</u>.

FROM THE ORIGINAL PROGRAM
WORLD PREMIERE
APRIL 21, 22, 24, 1937

THE SECOND HURRICANE

A PLAY OPERA FOR HIGH SCHOOL CHILDREN

MUSIC AARON COPLAND *LIBRETTO* EDWIN DENBY
CONDUCTOR LEHMAN ENGEL *DIRECTOR* ORSON WELLES
LIGHTING BY FEDER *ASSISTANT DIRECTOR* HIRAM SHERMAN

AT THE PLAYHOUSE 466 GRAND STREET NEW YORK

UNDER THE AUSPICES OF THE MUSIC SCHOOL OF THE HENRY
STREET SETTLEMENT — GRACE SPOFFORD, DIRECTOR

CAST OF CHARACTERS

QUEENIE	VIVIENNE BLOCK
GWEN	ESTELLE LEVY
GIP	ARTHUR ANDERSON
LOWRIE	BUDDY MANGAN
BUTCH	JOHN DOEPPER
FAT	HARRY OLIVE
JEFF	CARL CRAWFORD
THE TEACHER	CLIFFORD MACK
MR. MacLANAHAN	JOE COTTON
RADIO OPERATOR	CHARLES PETTINGER

With an Orchestra of 20.

First two scenes are laid in a high school and a radio station; the
rest on a rise of ground in a waste country near a great river.

Time — the present.

MUSIC SCHOOL OF THE HENRY STREET SETTLEMENT
Adult Chorus — Lehman Engel, Director

MUSIC SCHOOL OF THE HENRY STREET SETTLEMENT
Little Children's Chorus, Josephine De Nigris, Director

Chorus of High School Children from Seward Park High School
Gertrude Berliner, Head of Department of Music
Isabel Meade, Director of Chorus

IV

Cast list from the original publication of The Second Hurricane.

for all schools since we would have to be sure of the
radio time (26 weeks) if I go ahead with the fourth
step and approach the Trust. I thought it might be
nice if you would convey this information to Mr. Randolph and tell him that I will let you know as soon
as possible whether or not we can go through with
the project....You might also tell him that the station
here in town seemed quite interested and that I think
it would be very successful if we can get it through.[3]

Whittaker's next action was to write to James C. Petrillo
of the American Federation of Musicians. His letter, dated
July 5, 1949, had two enclosures, one the brochure of the
National Guild, and two, the brochure of the Cleveland Music
School Settlement. In part the letter read:

Dear Mr. Petrillo:

...At our last executive committee meeting in New
York we discussed the problem of community-wide
adult education in music. It was felt at this meeting,
as it was a few days earlier at the National Music
Council meeting that the educational institutions in this
country could do much more in the field of real adult
music education to the betterment of the musician and
the organization in which he taught and played.
    In this regard I had a conversation with Mr. David
Randolph who, I had been told, was giving an excellent series of broadcasts in a local New York station
called "Music for the Connoisseur." This program was
offered as public service with Mr. Randolph volunteer-
ing his time, and grew out of a lecture course which
he had been offering at New York University. The
project the National Guild has in mind is to purchase
from Mr. Randolph enough recordings to supply all
of the Guild schools. The Guild schools will then clear
time with their local stations to play these recordings.
It will be introduced as a public service offered by the
National Guild of which their organization is a member....When I returned to Cleveland I consulted Mr.
Repp, president of our Local, as well as one of our
radio stations, and they immediately recommended that
I clear with you for 26 such programs. The point
which I wish to make quite clear as a Union musician
myself and as president of the Guild, is that these

recordings would include dialogue and previously
recorded music.

I trust you will give this careful consideration and
will let me have as early a reply as possible since I
will have considerable work to do in arriving at a
budget for Foundation support as well as clearing the
broadcasting time.

Thank you for your trouble.

Yours truly,

[Signed] Howard Whittaker[4]

Mr. Petrillo replied succinctly on July 8, 1949:

Dear Mr. Whittaker:

This will acknowledge receipt of your letter of July
5th, concerning the broadcast which the National
Guild of Community Music Schools wishes to sponsor.

Since this is both an educational and public service
program, the American Federation of Musicians will
have no objection to the use of the recordings described in your letter.

It is understood that these broadcasts will carry
no commercial announcements.

Yours very truly,

[Signed] James C. Petrillo
President[5]

The months of July and August continued to show a
flurry of activity on the parts of Ruth Kemper, Howard Whittaker and David Randolph to promote the Guild project for
the coming season, though undoubtedly time and tempers
must have been running short. Miss Kemper wrote to Julius
Rudel, the director at the Third Street Music School Settlement, on July 20, 1949, to ask his assistance in contacting
officials at the local CBS station and stated the following:

As it stands now, there seems to be a definite possibility of financing, through a Foundation or private
funds, the cost of the records, and we are waiting to

learn from Mr. Randolph how much that would be.
The next step seems to be for the Guild schools to
clear with local stations for a series of 26 half-hour
broadcasts, offering them the use of the records as
a public service. Mr. Whittaker has evidently done
this in Cleveland. I am sure the networks would not
be interested in such a program, but one of the bid
stations might as a local feature at a less popular
hour. I wondered if CBS would consider it for the
11:30-12 midnight spot, simultaneously with the WOR
Deems Taylor Concert. Mr. Randolph told me he does
not think it wise for him to enter into the discussion
with the station at this early stage, and suggested
the Guild make the initial contact.

Mr. Whittaker wants to submit the plan with the
request for financial support to a Foundation in September, so there is no time to lose. As you know
Mr. Fassett personally it would be helpful if you would
write to him, as you suggested, describe the plan,
and tell him I will call to ask for an appointment to
discuss it with him. I shall wait to hear from you
before doing so, and will keep you informed as to
developments.[6]

Much responsibility rested on the shoulders of David
Randolph to present the actual cost figures for the transcriptions, but with all his other activities he was not able
to produce the budget figures quickly. It was not until
August 25, 1949, that he wrote to Howard Whittaker the following letter:

Dear Mr. Whittaker,

I've finally managed to find the figures, on the production of the transcriptions, and am frankly rather
surprised to discover that they're so low.

Fifteen copies of each half-hour broadcast can
be made for $122.50.

The breakdown of the figures is as follows:

studio recording time $25.00 per hour
processing of masters   30.00 per master
16" Vinylite pressings
    (10 to 26 pressings)   2.50 per pressing
(These can be double or single face, standard groove,
at 33 1/3 RPM.)

In all likelihood, the figure of $122.50 per broad-
cast will be more than the actual cost. I have allowed
one full hour of studio recording time for each half-
hour broadcast. This is much more than I'll actually
require, so that the cost will be less. Moreover, in
order to achieve the most efficient use of the time,
I would plan to record at least two broadcasts at each
session.

The above figures apply only to the cost of production. They do not include my own services. Since
you are in touch with the budget situation, I thought
I'd wait for a suggestion from you as to what might
be allotted for the purpose.[7]

Before Miss Kemper left New York for a vacation, she
wrote the following letter to Mr. Whittaker:

This is a short report on what I was able to find out
at CBS. Mr. Rudel did not write to Mr. Fassett,...
so I took matters into my own hands just before I left
N.Y. and after talking to the network dept. finally
got through to Mr. Worden of the Public Service
Dept. of CBS, the local station. The network could
not consider our programs, but Mr. Worden said he
might be able to put some on as spot programs. He
was certain they would not be considered in a consecutive series, but seemed interested in the type of
program as a public service, and said he would take
it up with the program dept. I saw him the day I
left, and gave him the Guild booklet, also sent him a
Turtle Bay leaflet as an example of the type of school
the Guild represented. He seemed particularly interested in the fact that we were non-profit institutions,
and wanted to be reassured of the fact that we did
not plan to use the programs for propaganda other
than the name of the Guild as co-sponsor.[8]

It is amazing that these two people spent so much time,
and gratis, to bring about the project. Since there was no
central Guild office at this time, there was no other way this
business could have been handled. The situation points up
the desperate need for a national office for the Guild and an
employed staff to assume responsibility for administrative
problems of the Guild. It was to be many years before such
an office was to be realized.

Mr. Whittaker wrote to David Randolph on August 30 giving him the following information:

> Miss Kemper mentioned a total cost of $3,000.00 for 15 pressings of the 26 programs, excluding your fee. I would suggest a fee of $50.00 per record, or a total of $1300.00 for the 26 recordings. This then would result in a total figure of $4300.00 which it would be necessary for me to find.
>
> This total seems to me appropriate for the public service rendered; however, I must admit that I might find foundation support difficult at such a price. In the event that I do, perhaps the wisest course will be to pursue a 13 program series.
>
> In any event, will you please let me know if you consider my proposal fair to yourself as I want to contact the New York...Fund as soon as possible. [9]

On the same day that this letter was written, Miss Kemper's efforts were rewarded since she received a letter from Clarence Worden, the Director of Special Features and Public Service at WCBS in New York City which read in part:

> Dear Miss Kemper:
>
> ...At the moment, we are hopeful of being able to clear the time for presenting the series on a weekly basis but there are one or two kinks to be straightened out at the end. meanwhile, [sic] will you please get to me as soon as possible a recording by Mr. Randolph of a typical program. I think it would be to your great advantage not to delay in this matter.
>
> Cordially yours,
>
> [Signed] Clarence Worden

September 7--a handwritten note at the bottom of the above letter:

> Mr. Randolph has been away, and I talked to him only last night. He has promised to bring me the record today or tomorrow. Evidently does not have them at home. This much more hopeful! Note and check just came from Mrs. Worth. Many thanks! [10]

For the moment let us return to the membership problem.
Early in September of 1949 Julius Rudel, who was the director
of the Third Street Music School Settlement, upon the request
of Howard Whittaker, wrote to Maxwell Powers, who was the
director of the Greenwich House Music School. The message
in his letter was an invitation for the Greenwich House Music
School to join the National Guild of Community Music Schools
as an associate member. This was obviously a method of contacting Mr. Powers to sound him out about the Guild. Mr.
Powers' letter of response to Mr. Rudel, dated September
21, 1949 read in part:

> I have reviewed with great interest your brochure
> regarding membership to the National Guild of Com-
> munity Music Schools. There are many categories
> which are commendable and if I may be so bold, there
> are many that I seriously question. I fail to see why
> a Music School that meets the necessary requirements
> for membership should be penalized to an "associate"
> position because they are affiliated with a Settlement
> House. A school such as ours which is now starting
> its 44th season, which completed last years [sic]
> registration with 1,124 students, certainly could not
> accept a secondary roll [sic] in an organization that
> dealt with Settlement Music problems.
>
> I think that the purpose and fundamental ideals
> of your organization are sound and healthy and I
> further feel such idealism should be shared on a [sic]
> equal basis instead of reducing its reception to a
> lesser degree. If the problems concerning Settlement
> Music School finds a common denominator then we
> would wish to feel that our contribution towards the
> solution of such problems would be received on an
> equal basis. I am afraid we could not enter into
> the true spirit of your organization unless such a
> condition were brought about. [11]

And so Maxwell Powers stated his case clearly. Since
his school was offered an associate membership, which did
not include voting privileges on issues brought to the Guild
for solution, he made it clear he was not willing to consider
joining. He indicated his School's distinguished history and
enrollment, and said he was not willing to play a lesser role
in the national organization.

Mr. Rudel read Mr. Powers' letter at the next Guild meeting and gave it to Howard Whittaker. The ball was now in Whittaker's court and he knew what to do with it. His letter to Mr. Powers, dated November 28, 1949, is quoted in part:

> At the Executive Committee Meeting of the National Guild of Community Music Schools held last week in New York we reviewed the possibility of changing our by-laws in order to accept music schools with settlement affiliations....In order to expedite this matter, Mr. Rudel agreed to contact you with the idea that we offer an associate membership to those organizations which were not autonomous. At the meeting Mr. Rudel presented your letter which I now have and if you will refer to it as of November 21, I believe this is the essence of what you said. You are interested in possible membership in the Guild and do agree with the purposes, however you feel that an organization such as yours must have full voting privileges in order to be equally represented. If my analysis is true then I think it would be well for us to clarify the extent to which your voting privileges would represent an autonomous music school point of view and in what way your decisions might be limited from the standpoint of the Board of Trustees of the entire settlement....In closing, please let me reiterate that the National Guild is not thinking in terms of a "closed corporation" but is very much interested in growth and public interpretation.[12]

On the very next day, November 29, 1949, Mr. Whittaker sent a similar letter to Grace Spofford, the director of the Music School of the Henry Street Settlement, giving her all the basic information and to her letter he added the following information:

> I am very sorry that I have not had the opportunity of meeting you and seeing your school the few times that I get to New York, however, I did get a very fine picture of the work you are doing from Miss Helen Hall when I saw her in Cleveland and I also received a rather complete set of brochures and publicity items which Mr. Robert Egan gave to me when he first came back to our city.

It has appeared to me more and more necessary for
organizations such as ours to get together and plan
programs and policies which not only strengthen our
point of view but also extend our ideas to the general
music public.[13]

Howard Whittaker played a very diplomatic role when
he tried to improve on a most unfortunate situation that was
not of his own doing. He must have been very much aware
that the problem had gotten considerably out of hand. As
often happens in such occurrences objectivity disappears and
personalities become the issues rather than carefully considered
observations of the problems as they really are.

On December 21, 1949, Grace Spofford responded with
a brief note but goes no further than to express interest,
when she says:

We are very interested to know that at the Executive
Committee meeting of the National Guild of Community
Music Schools held recently in New York, the question
was brought up about changing the by-laws in regard
to the admission of Music Schools with Settlement affiliations.
We are members of several groups and, while we
do appreciate the advantage of being associated with
organizations of similar purposes, we question whether
at the present time we ought to consider membership
in the National Guild of Community Music Schools.
Our Music School has complete freedom in all its
artistic purposes, and we feel that its Settlement
setting is of extraordinary advantage to us.
I feel sure that the National Guild will develop
interestingly and creatively under your leadership,
and we appreciate this overture on your part.
Miss Hall and I both join in best wishes for your
success.[14]

Thus Miss Spofford made those who had left her school
outside the newly formed National Guild work just a bit harder
to entice her and her school into the Guild, and it will be seen
that she was very firm in her request for information and
definite, guaranteed answers. (Helen Hall was undoubtedly
disturbed by the argumentation between the National Guild of
Community Music Schools and the National Federation of

Settlements. She herself had been the president of the
National Federation for several years, and no such discussions
had taken place earlier. Helen Hall was also staunchly behind
the inclusion of the arts in settlement programs.)

While very much involved in the recruiting of new member schools, one must remember that Whittaker was also very
concerned about the David Randolph radio programs sponsored
by the National Guild. In the fall of this year on September
8, 1949 to be exact Kemper again wrote to Whittaker with the
following information:

> The CBS ball seems to be rolling along at a good
> speed, in fact may need a little restraining until the
> question of funds for the records is settled. Mr.
> Randolph took the records to Clarence Worden today,
> and was given definite encouragement about a weekly
> series, possibly 9:45 to 10:15 on Sunday mornings, or
> late evening on a week-day. They want to be assured
> of 26 weeks, however. It seems that Worden, who
> is not too musical himself, has consulted Gordon Gra-
> ham, assistant director of the program department,
> and others in the office who are regular listeners to
> the Randolph programs, and received an enthusiastic
> report. Clifton Fadiman is also a "fan" who had written
> Randolph about the broadcasts, so the ground work
> of interest of is there. [15]

On September 15, 1949, Ruth Kemper sent another message to Howard Whittaker:

> David Randolph had a long conference the other day
> with Gordon Graham and Don Ball, in which they said
> they wanted a sample complete recording including
> announcer, to be made by the station for presentation
> to the "higher-ups". Evidently considered it settled
> as far as they were concerned, and felt, confident
> it would meet with approval. D.R. is preparing that
> recording now. The matters they were most concerned
> with aside from the actual programs were 1) that there
> would be no cost whatever to the station; 2) that all
> mail would be handled by the Guild, the address to
> be given over the air; 3) that there be no commercial
> aspect. [16]

The talks had progressed to a very exciting point,
largely because of the excellence of the Randolph programs,
and the fact that the programs would be of public service and
not commercial. The time slot for the program kept getting
to be more and more desirable. Also a telegram from Kemper
to Whittaker was sent on September 15, 1949, which read:

> CBS negotiations on basis of Sundays 1:30 to 2:00
> beginning October second reached point where deci-
> sion regarding financing vital stop Randolph willing
> to start series with personal broadcasts on own respon-
> sibility stop Is investigating wire recordings as
> possible cheaper please advise me immediately
>
> Ruth Kemper[17]

Whittaker responded on the same day:

> Advise Randolph to start with personal series. Am
> interested in cost of wire recordings
>
> Howard Whittaker[18]

It seems wise now to relate the entire David Randolph
broadcast story. The author has tried in the previous pages
to show the complicated responsibilities that arose for the
attention of officers of the National Guild. Distance to other
Guild schools proved to be a severe problem, requiring that
fair amounts of time be spent which involved the U.S. Mail
Service, Western Union and a small amount of the Telephone
Company. Finances made it imperative for these people to
operate as economically as possible. Yet the pressure of time
made daily procedures difficult to supervise in their own
schools and to continue the work of a national organization.
The need of a national office was becoming more and more
necessary.

Voluminous correspondence regarding the radio project
was a necessity. Even when many of the principal people
were in New York City, it was no simple task for Ruth Kemper
to keep Howard Whittaker well informed regarding all the
Guild's activities and responsibilities that arose from the project itself. Courtesy required that all parties be informed,
and yet decisions had to be made quickly. The amount of
activities and important human beings regarding the radio

series sounds almost like a radio script with its own cast of characters, and so it shall be treated as the tale is told:

The Musical Notebook: <u>A Radio Series</u>

<u>Cast of Characters</u>:

<u>Howard Whittaker</u>, director of Cleveland Music School Settlement and president of the National Guild of Community Music Schools

<u>Ruth Kemper</u>, violin teacher and assistant director, Turtle Bay Music School and chief Guild contact person in New York City

<u>David Randolph</u>, musicologist and lecturer, New York University, and host and announcer, Station WNYC, New York's Community Radio Station

<u>G. Richard Swift</u>, General Manager, radio station WCBS, New York City

<u>Miss Edna Lieber</u>, director Community Music School, St. Louis, MO

<u>C. B. Hunter</u>, program director, radio station WCBS, New York City

<u>Clarence Worden</u>, director, special events and public service, WCBS, Columbia's Key Station in New York

<u>Donald Ball</u>, program director, radio station, WCBS, New York City

<u>John Marshall</u>, assistant director, Rockefeller Foundation, Humanities Division, New York City

<u>Eric Strong</u>, Joseph I. Richman Associates, Public Relation firm New York City

<u>John O. Foster</u>, Ferris, Harsch & Foster, Public Relations firm, Buffalo, NY

<u>William R. Rich</u>, assistant program director, WBEN (NBC), Buffalo, NY

Harvey C. Smith, program director, radio station, WDEL,
     Wilmington, DE

J. Phillip Plank, Wilmington Music School, Wilmington, DE

Letter: Kemper to Whittaker, October 3, 1949

> I have just come from an interview with Clarence
> Worden of CBS. David Randolph will make the two
> sample recordings some time this week, at which time
> I hope to be present. In the meantime, Mr. Worden
> ras [sic--has] requested that a letter from you be
> sent at once to G. Richard Swift, General Manager,
> Station WCBS, 485 Madison Avenue, stating that "you
> have been advised by me that WCBS is interested in
> presenting, through joint effort with the National
> Guild of Community Music Schools, a new series of
> half-hour programs by David Randolph as a public
> service" [quoting Mr. Worden]. Also, stating that
> there will be no cost to them other than the usual
> for the actual broadcasting of the program.[19]

Letter: Whittaker to Kemper, October 5, 1949

> I am quite pleased that this has moved so well in New
> York. However, it is impossible for me to make any
> commitment at this time regarding the financing of
> these programs by the National Guild since I must
> clear with all Guild schools for air time before I can
> even approach a foundation for financial support.
> I know full well that no individual or foundation
> would make any commitment unless I could guarantee
> that the money spent would be used in the public
> service for all the Guild schools. I am afraid that
> this matter for the Guild is going to have to wait
> at least through this season until we get the sample
> records from Randolph to send and clear with all the
> schools.
> If, however, Mr. Randolph wants to provide the
> recordings for WCBS for this season then I see no
> reason why he shouldn't do so on his own.[20]

Letter: Kemper to Whittaker, October 18, 1949

> ...If I had had any idea whatsoever that you had not

received the records I could have checked with Mr.
Randolph and seen to it that they were sent. He
admits he was remiss in not doing what he assured
both of us he would, and tells me he sent them at
once after learning of your letter. Whether it is too
late now to follow through with the schools only you
can determine....This is the way things stand now.
CBS likes the sample half-hour record and wants to
put the program on Sundays at 1:30-2 P.M. David
Randolph, in order not to let us down completely at
this stage, states that he is willing to do the whole
series without fee as a live program, including the
Guild as co-sponsor with CBS as originally outlined.
CBS agrees to this, providing they have a statement
from us to the effect that there will be no cost to them
other than the usual studio maintenance...While the
benefit to the Guild would be local, it is after all a
large and important locality, and we could not ask for
better publicity. This series could also serve as a
trial balloon as to subject matter and approach....The
matter now lies wholly in your hands as President of
the Guild. I have taken great pains to keep you fully
informed about proceedings here, and Mr. Randolph
and I have prepared the ground so the Guild can
have first-class publicity without cost to us except
that incidental to the handling of mail, etc. It is
necessary for them to make their definite plans for
this hour in the immediate future, and are waiting to
hear from the Guild....

P.S. November 19th [she must mean October 19th]

As this letter was on the point of being sent, David
Randolph phoned. He says CBS wants to start the
series on November 6th. He had already discussed
the possible change of his program with WNYC and it
is necessary for both stations to settle the matter at
once. The CBS program would be at the same hour
as his present WNYC, and his large following at this
hour would follow him to the new station. He would
retain his Tuesday evening program on WNYC, but
whether they would be willing to change the Sunday
to a later hour is in question. CBS has no objection
to this, providing it is at least three hours later.
The subject would not be duplicated, of course.
    Please let us hear from you immediately.[21]

And so November 6, 1949 was to become the starting
date of the radio broadcast featuring David Randolph sponsored by the National Guild of Community Music Schools.

Letter: Kemper to Whittaker, October 19, 1949

> In my conversation with Mr. Worden yesterday I
> suggested to him that the generally uncertain financial
> situation of the moment was probably affecting the
> chances of financing the record project at the moment.
> I see no point in informing him of the details of the
> arrangements between Mr. Randolph and the Guild,
> and think you will agree as to the wisdom of this.
> By the way, have you heard Sigmund Spaeth's
> new program Saturday 10-10:30 A.M. on WBAC? He
> has the backing of the Nat'l Federation of Music Clubs
> and says he receives quite a mail response. It is
> a straw in the wind, and shows that a network is not
> adverse to a music program of this type if they can
> count on an audience.[22]

Letter: Randolph to Whittaker, October 19, 1949

> Radio station WCBS, in New York City, has agreed
> to broadcast my series of programs on Sunday after-
> noons, from 1:30 to 2:00 o'clock, beginning Nov. 6,
> 1949.
> In view of the importance of this series of broad-
> casts to the furtherance of the Guild's plans, and
> since the funds for the "transcription" project have
> not yet been obtained by the Guild, I am willing to
> undertake these WCBS programs on my own responsi-
> bility.
> I am doing so because of my belief, and my hope,
> that the prestige to be gained from having the pro-
> grams heard over WCBS (the key Station of the Colum-
> bia Broadcasting System) will aid substantially in the
> efforts to secure approval and support for the "trans-
> cription" project. The programs will be presented
> as a public service, jointly by WCBS and the Guild.
> Therefore, the National Guild of Community Music
> Schools will not be obligated to me financially, for this
> WCBS series.

Very truly yours,
[signed] David Randolph[23]

The above letter was the more formal or business-like communication that Randolph sent to Whittaker. A more personal letter was included in the mailing which stated some things that were rather confidential to Whittaker:

> ...Originally, the Officials of Station WCBS...heard the transcription of my previous WNYC broadcasts, and they liked them enough to want to schedule them on Sunday mornings, at 9:45 o'clock. Then, they asked me to make one that they might play for the officials of the Network. If the Network officials liked the program, there was a possibility of their putting it on at the choice hour of 1:30 on Sunday afternoon. This meant that the Network people would have to be sufficiently convinced of the value of the series, to warrant their taking off the air whatever program has been on at that time up to now, and giving that time to my programs, instead....The accompanying letter will release the Guild from any financial responsibility to me for this WCBS series. In short, I shall undertake it "on a gamble" so to speak, in the hope that, eventually the "transcription" program will become a reality....Here, may I make one urgent request. In order to obtain CBS's acceptance of the program, I will have to discontinue my Sunday broadcasts on WNYC, which, as you can realize, are extremely important to me. WNYC already knows about this. I should be very chagrinned, now, if for some reason, WCBS does NOT put the programs on the air, because of any lack of authorization from the Guild. In that case, I shall find myself with neither program.[24]

One can readily understand how these arrangements could be mutually beneficial to both parties when CBS carried the program. For the National Guild it was a prestigious event for them to sponsor such a distinguished broadcast, and highly advantageous for Mr. Randolph to have his remarkable series presented by the New York CBS station. It is no wonder that Mr. Randolph was willing to present the broadcast on his own responsibility at no cost to the Guild. All parties stood to gain including WCBS.

In his letter to Ruth Kemper written on October 20, 1949, Howard Whittaker quietly expressed his appreciation for all of Ruth Kemper's efforts on behalf of the Guild:

Your part in handling this matter for the Guild is greatly appreciated by me as I know it will be by all member schools and I am sure that the publicity of this series prior to what we hope will be done throughout the country will be beneficial for us all....Thank you again for all your trouble.

Sincerely yours,

[signed] Howard Whittaker, President
National Guild of Community
Music Schools[25]

It seems quite humorous (and could only happen in a Community Music School at that time) that Howard Whittaker attached a postscript to his letter which read, "P.S. I just received your violin curriculum. Thanks. HW." Through all the efforts and struggles that these two stalwart Guild leaders had seen, the basic work required at their schools continued despite the many distractions and responsibilities caused them by their Guild activities.

Letter: Whittaker to Swift, dated October 20, 1949

I should like to express my thanks for your interest in providing a series of programs by David Randolph as a public service co-sponsored by the National Guild of Community Music Schools with Station WCBS.
It is understood that this series will be provided without cost to WCBS other than the usual maintenance. Mr. Randolph will act as his own announcer and should he ever find it impossible to be present will make a recording which can be used.
I thought you would like to know that the National Guild is in hopes of providing a similar series of programs by Mr. Randolph in all of our local communities. I think that such a series will be very significant in the adult educational field of music and naturally follows in accordance with the plans of the National Guild of Community Music Schools.[26]

Letter: Whittaker to Randolph, dated October 21, 1949

I received the good news...that your programs had been accepted by WCBS...This is very exciting news

and I think it very generous on your part regardless
of the personal prestige involved for you to offer your
services so that we may be able to share in this
program as well as to get the project under way on
a national scope...I am sorry that I cannot guarantee
you anything at this time but with this proposed series at WCBS I think it will certainly help in acquiring
the money to make this project possible on a nationwide basis.[27]

As the day of the first broadcast approached Ruth
Kemper kept Howard Whittaker well informed as to the progress being made in New York City. New York City Guild
schools were all working towards a successful broadcast and
a generous audience to hear and respond!

Letter: Kemper to Whittaker, November 4, 1949

I suppose you have had a reply from CBS and know
that all is going well. If you have a powerful enough
set you might be able to pick it up, but Mr. Randolph
will save you a copy of the script anyway. The station has been most cooperative. They have even
broken down to the extent of allowing him to include
in the script the suggestion that they write to CBS
directly, or rather to him in care of the station, or
to 244 East 52 St. for information about the Guild.
One notice has already appeared in the Times, and
more will undoubtedly come out this Sunday in other
papers. He tells me that he has been told that spot
announcements have been heard over the station already.
    The enclosed card has been sent by the three
schools to nine hundred individuals and organizations.
Third Street is mimeographing small flyers to give out
to students as their list is so large they could not
afford to send to all their students.[28]

The auspicious day, Sunday, November 6, 1949, came,
and all the advance preparation seemed to have succeeded in
building a respectable radio audience. The broadcast was
very successful, and all those involved were delighted at the
results.

Letter: Randolph to Whittaker, dated November 10, 1949

Here is the script of the first broadcast, as it was actually given, on Nov. 6th.

A few very interesting and extremely gratifying results have already taken place.

First; the mail response was very good. As of Wednesday afternoon, 32 letters and cards had been received at the station. This an excellent response, for a first broadcast, of a serious music program. ("Invitation to Music", in five years of Nationwide broadcasts on CBS, received a total of only three letters!)

Second; "Variety", the bible of the entertainment world, gave the program a very fine review, which I've enclosed.

Third, and most important; the time of the broadcasts has been changed. Starting this Sunday, Nov. 13th, the program will be heard for the half-hour immediately preceding the N.Y. Philharmonic-Symphony broadcast! We could not have hoped for a better spot. (2:30 to 3:00 PM EST)

One disadvantage goes along with that time change, however. On every fourth Sunday, the program will not be broadcast, in order that CBS might put on the program "You are There" [sic], which, I understand, is a fine series. Hoverer [sic], the disadvantage is very slight, since we'll be on for three out of every four Sundays.

We seem to be off to a good start.

Most cordially,

[signed] David Randolph[29]

The script itself was simple but effective, and while it certainly mentions the National Guild, it has no hard-sell material. Mr. Randolph was also the announcer. The script was as follows:

CBS 1 (duplicate complete):
Sunday, November 6, 1949 (opening broadcast)
1:30 - 2:00 P.M.

Randolph (cold): Good afternoon. This is David Randolph speaking. Today I'd like to open my Musical Notebook to a page called Humor in Music. This is the

first of a new series of Sunday afternoon broadcasts,
presented as a public service by Station WCBS, in
cooperation with the National Guild of Community Music
Schools.

And I plan to take a rather informal approach. I
don't think we have to listen to music with a worried
look on our faces, and with our heads in our hands.
After all, composers are human beings, and I think
that our enjoyment of their music is increased, as we
become more aware of the human person behind the
music.

We also find composers...even the very greatest
of them...sometimes quite relaxed in their music...just
writing music for fun.[30]

The music played during the program included:

Sextette in F (Musical Joke)	W. A. Mozart
Divertissement (Wedding March)	Jacques Ibert
Carnival of the Animals ("Dance of the Sylphs" and "Pianists")	C. C. Saint-Saëns
Façade ("Yodelling Song" and Popular Song: "Tap Dance")	William Walton
Patience ("Am I Alone?")	Gilbert and Sullivan
God's Bottles	Randall Thompson
Hary Janos Suite ("Napoleon")	Zoltan Kodaly
Divertissement ("Grand Finale")	Jacques Ibert

Only a portion of each of the works was played demonstrating the example described by Mr. Randolph in his intro-
ductory comments, which were short and to the point. One
brief section of the composition was repeated to help the
listener identify the way in which the humor was expressed
in music.

Randolph (anyway): There we've seen a few of the
ways in which composers achieve humor in their music.

Of course, they're not the only examples, by any
means. In the course of these broadcasts, I'd like
to look into many other aspects of music with you.
For example, there's the way in which Jazz has influenced symphonic music. We'll also look into the
manner in which composers express different emotions
in their music. And next Sunday, I'd like you to
see how a number of folk songs became the basis of
some large orchestral works.

And by the way...Let's make this a "two-way" af-
fair. If YOU have any comments about this program,
or any requests, why not jot them down on a post
card and send them along to me.

This program has been presented as a public service, by Station WCBS, in cooperation with the National Guild of Community Music Schools...a group of non-
profit schools, of which there are three in New York
City. If you'd like any information about the work
of these schools, or, if you'd like to send me your
comments, I suggest you write to me...David Randolph,
at Station WCBS...or to the National Guild of Community Music Schools at 244 East 52nd St., New York
22.

I'm glad you were able to join me today, and I
hope you'll be with me again next Sunday afternoon.
This is David Randolph saying..."See you next
week."[31]

The radio series was launched, and quite successfully
so. The materials selected by Mr. Randolph were musically
excellent, and his ability to tie the various compositions into
a cohesive whole was remarkable to say the least. It was now
the responsibility of the officers of the National Guild to raise
the funds to continue the series indefinitely. This was a
large task, indeed!

The program envisioned and planned by David Randolph
received much critical acclaim. Many well-informed people
wrote to him in admiration. To give a few:

I hope you will put me down as one of the admirers
of "Music for Connoisseur"...It is certainly the best
program of its sort on the air.

Clifton Fadiman

I especially liked your running commentary, which
was both informed and instructive. You get my vote
as my favorite Master of Musical Ceremonies.

Louis Untermeyer

I want to tell you how much I enjoy your programs,
and that whenever my concert schedule permits me
to be at home I never fail to hear them.

Alec Templeton

Although the music he includes in the programs is
assuredly of a superior level, he presents it in such
a way to make it human, interesting and seemingly
easy to understand even to a person of relatively
limited musical background.

Musical America[32]

Many listeners who resided in the surrounding area
within reach of WCBS wrote every week. As many as thirty-
five to forty letters were received after each broadcast.
Some expressed genuine satisfaction, and they came from New
York City, Long Island, Connecticut, and New Jersey:

This is the first time I have written to a radio program, but I was impelled to by the sheer enjoyment
I derived from listening today to your program on
WCBS. Both my wife and I are looking forward to
many pleasant Sunday hours listening to you.

Dr. and Mrs. G. B.
New York City

We listen to you without fail every week. By 'We' I
mean my neighbors in this building, and my friends
elsewhere. You are an institution with us. Now that
you are on CBS I feel more hopeful about the four
big networks. Perhaps, a change is coming--maybe
they are going to turn over a new musical leaf--for
99% of their musical programs are a disgrace to the
U.S. ...I mean embarassing [sic]. Here's wishing
you every success with your CBS program! I just

hope the new outfit appreciates you as much as we
do.

> Mrs. D. B.
> New York City

...[your programs] are worth-while as an intelligent
musical discussion that is not too technical for the
average person to understand.

> A.S.
> Morristown, N.J.

...and don't often get to hear live lectures. But
your's are more than alive, they set one to explore
and think...

> A.G.
> Flushing, L.I., N.Y.

We, and all our friends to whom we have recommended
your "Musical Notebook" as being one of the most
worth-while programs on the air, feel that it gives
us one of the pleasantest half-hours in radio, if not
the pleasantest.

> E.G.G.
> Westport, Conn.

...I have never been too fond of classical music or
attended any concerts--however, your "musical critics"
program today has certainly inspired me...

> D.G.
> Harrison, N.J.[33]

Even though rather elaborate preparations were made
to present requests to two New York City based foundations,
the results brought no monies to continue The Musical Notebook on CBS stations.

On August 4, 1950, the New York Community Trust
sent the following brief letter to Mr. Whittaker:

Even though we are not in position to expand our

operations to include a participation in the financing
of the particular project described in your recent
letter, we appreciate your writing as you did and
thank you for the material relayed to us.

                              Very truly yours,

                    [signed] Ralph Hays[34]

On November 15, 1950, the Rockefeller Foundation sent
the following message to Mr. Whittaker:

I have your letter of November 8 about the possibility
of some assistance from the Foundation to utilize in
its member schools records made by Mr. David Randolph.
      Actually, the Foundation at present is not active
in the field of music, so that it is a little difficult to
see how the Foundation could be of assistance. But
I do personally share the high regard in which Mr.
Randolph's work is held, and if Miss Kemper wishes
to talk to me about this possibility, I shall be glad
to do so.

                              Yours sincerely,

                    [signed]   John Marshall[35]

An example of how an irritating situation can be carried
to unexpected levels is shown when one learns of the episode
created when John McDowell, Executive Director of the National
Federation of Settlements wrote to Howard Whittaker on March
19, 1951 stating:

I have been called by the executive of a settlement
which has a music school not affiliated with the National Guild of Community Music Schools.*   There was

_____

*The caller's identity can hardly be concealed though Mr.
McDowell did not reveal a name, it was undoubtedly Maxwell
Powers. There were not very many settlement houses with
a music school not affiliated with the Guild, and his anger
at being stepped over is understandable, though the act may
well have been an innocent one.

some resentment of the second paragraph of the note
concerning the Guild in the <u>Bulletin</u> of the National
Music Council of January, 1951. I was asked whether
the Federation Board had ever requested the Guild
to serve, in an advisory capacity, on music in settlements and neighborhood houses. I had to say that
no such action had been taken although you had kindly
offered your services to the Federation and that you
had personally been used by some settlements in that
capacity.

I am not asking for any action on your part in
relation to the note in the <u>National Music Council
Bulletin</u>, but this protest we have received does point
up the need for exploration at the earliest possible
opportunity of desirable relationships between the
Guild and the Federation as well as between local
community music schools and settlements in the same
community.

The settlement or music school executives who are
affiliated with the Federation and not with Guild [sic]
for whatever reason, can be forgiven for being somewhat resentful if the Federation goes to another for
advice on its musical program in settlements rather
than to our own member agency.

This comment perhaps reveals some of the task
ahead in relationships for the Guild as well as for the
Federation.[36]

Now the implied problem or injury has involved three
national organizations, the National Music Council, the National
Guild of Community Music Schools and the National Federation
of Settlements. The implication is that the National Guild had
tried to usurp authority by offering advice to agencies belonging to another national organization. This was certainly not
the intent of Mr. Whittaker, and it must be remembered that
Mr. Powers was not only the director of the Greenwich House
Music School, but of the entire Greenwich House Settlement.
Thus he had considerable authority within his own organization,
more so than almost any other music school director in a
settlement program.

It must also be remembered that Mr. Whittaker was the
director of the Cleveland Music School Settlement, and many
settlement houses may well have turned to him, since the

term "settlement" was in the name of his school.   Innocent
errors all around!

Naturally, a response was expected by Mr. McDowell,
and on March 29, 1951 Mr. Whittaker replied with the following:

> I have your letter of March 24 regarding the call you
> received by an executive of a settlement who was con-
> cerned with the statement in the National Music Coun-
> cil Bulletin regarding the Guild acting in an advisory
> capacity to the National Federation.
> I am not in a position to know who edits the material
> that we send to the Music Council, however, I think
> it might help to clarify this one matter if you were
> to contact the person who called and explain that the
> only action the Guild had taken was to offer its ser-
> vices if the Federation should so desire; and that this
> was the information that we had submitted for publica-
> tion.   It is unfortunate that the statement that was
> printed in the Bulletin was misleading and I am sorry
> if this has caused any resentment.
> I believe I mentioned...the fact there was some
> feeling on the part of people outside the Guild as
> well as those in the Guild regarding the relationship
> of a community music school to the settlement field
> and vice versa, and I concur with you entirely that
> there will have to be a considerable amount of explora-
> tion done to clarify an issue which, I think, has been
> caused not so much by the organization of the Guild
> (since some of us are members of both) but rather a
> matter of personal ill will brought about through cir-
> cumstances long since past.
> I hope you feel as I do that the important thing
> is how we can improve the social concept as exemplified
> by the settlement in the Guild schools as well as im-
> prove the caliber of work being done in the music
> departments of settlements; and I can well appreciate
> that this is going to have to be handled in a most
> tactful fashion so that no one will feel threatened but
> rather that a real spirit of cooperation will be
> achieved.[37]

These two gentlemen seemed to want to ameliorate the
situation and to be sensible in future dealings.   Let us look
now at other events in relation to National Guild membership.

The entire situation was very unfortunate. Most of the people in the correspondence had been long-time acquaintances if they were not considered personal friends of each other. Ruth Kemper, Grace Spofford, Frances McFarland, and Helen Hall had all worked in the musical and social service areas for at least fifteen to twenty years. They were on a first-name basis among themselves. At this time it seems unbelievable that the entire situation had been allowed to degenerate to the condition in which it found itself in the early 1950s.

On June 27, 1951, Whittaker again wrote to Grace Spofford inquiring whether Henry Street might now be interested in Guild membership. Here briefly is a selection of statements in that letter:

> I received a letter from Ruth Kemper in which she
> said that you and Frances McFarland [and she] had
> all had lunch together and discussed some of the ideas
> which had been brought out at our meeting with
> Lillie Peck and Jean Maxwell [both of the National
> Federation of Settlements]...I think I mentioned in
> the course of our meeting that the Guild had finally
> taken action at our annual conference in February
> [1951] on the matter of revised membership require-
> ments in the Guild. These requirements now fall into
> three categories, i.e., full, associate, and auxiliary
> membership. The clause on full membership is as
> follows:
>   Incorporated schools of music operating according
> to the principles of Community Music Schools, giving
> evidence of permanence and stability, and possessing
> a suitable faculty and equipment and showing satis-
> factory proof of the maintenance and standards pre-
> scribed by the Guild. Such schools have full voting
> privileges."[38]

Finally information was being made public about the action the Guild had taken in careful revision of the Guild's by-laws, preventing it from being so restrictive. Contrary to earlier procedures, schools which were part of a settlement were now eligible for membership in the National Guild of Community Music Schools.

Howard Whittaker continued his letter by asking Grace Spofford a direct question to which he did not receive an

affirmative answer until early Fall. He placed his question
this way and with a short explanation:

> Having reviewed our correspondence of a year ago,
> I wonder, in the light of this change in our By-laws,
> whether you and your Board might now be interested
> in Guild membership. ...I am in hopes that you feel
> as I do that there is much to be done in the general
> picture of Music School Settlements and Music Depart-
> ments in Settlements, which can certainly be better
> implemented if we use the Guild for the purpose for
> which I think it was intended.[39]

Mr. Whittaker sent a similar letter to Maxwell Powers
to which he was not to receive an answer until December 26
of that year.

Spofford had spent the summer in Europe and did
not return to her desk until September and was then in the
throes of the School's registration period for the 1951-52
season. She did take the time to dictate one more letter clar-
ifying two points.

> I have just returned to my desk and just now con-
> sidered your letter of June 27th.
> There is just one matter on which I would ask you
> to clarify the situation. In any listing of the member
> schools, would the Music School of the Henry Street
> Settlement be listed as a full member or would it fall
> into another kind of membership? The clause on full
> membership could be interpreted as including us since
> Henry Street Settlement is incorporated, but I would
> want to be very sure of this point before we could
> consider joining.
> It is with no sense of false pride or any arrogance
> that I would have to insist on this point, merely that
> the reputation of our Music School might be injured
> by our being considered an auxiliary or associate
> member of such an association.
> This will sound a bit abrupt, but we are in the
> midst of registration which may pardon any rudeness.
> Best of luck.[40]

Finally the Music School of the Henry Street Settlement
was at least considering becoming a member school of the

National Guild of Community Music Schools, just twenty-four years after its own establishment in 1927.

Whittaker was so anxious to conclude the arrangement with Grace Spofford and the Henry Street Settlement that on September 17, 1951, at 12:28 p.m. he sent a telegram:

> Grace Spofford, Director of Music School Henry Street Settlement:
>
> Regarding letter of Sep 13 Stop Henry Street would be accepted as full member and so listed in the Guild.
>
> Howard Whittaker Pres, National Guild of Community Music Schools[41]

On September 25, 1951, Miss Spofford sent a formal letter accepting full membership:

> We have decided to apply for membership in the National Guild. Your telegram clarified the entire matter and we understand that we are accepted as a full member and so listed in the Guild.
>   Ruth Kemper suggests that we send our check for $50 to Miss Andrews of the Music School Settlement.
>   Best wishes in this crowded and interesting moment in our registration which, I trust, is about the same in your esteemed part of the world.
>
>   Cordially,
>   [signed]   Grace Spofford[42]

Howard Whittaker politely responded:

> I was very pleased to receive your letter stating you had decided to apply for membership in the National Guild. I have a rather complete folder on your organization but if there is any new material--brochures, etc., that you would like me to present at the Executive Council Meeting, then I would suggest that you send them on to me.
>   After the presentation of this material, we shall, of course, take formal action on your membership.
>   In the meantime, I feel that the decision on your

part will prove most significant and we can look forward to a pleasant collaboration.

Sincerely yours,

[signed]   Howard Whittaker
President[43]

A considerable amount of time had passed since Mr.
Whittaker had written to Maxwell Powers offering the Greenwich House Music School full membership in the National Guild.
That letter had been written in June of 1951.   More than six
months had elapsed before a return letter came.   Dated December 26, 1951, the following letter was written to Howard
Whittaker which must have been an unexpected surprise:

Dear Mr. Whittaker:

I wish to apologize for not having answered your
letter sooner.   However, it was not through negligence
that you did not hear from me.   I found it necessary
to wait until such time as the National Federation of
Settlements clarified in my mind exactly what it is
they want me to do as Chairman of their committee
on music.   Since speaking with Mr. John McDowell
and one of his associates, it is now clear what this
committee's function will be.
In light of this the Greenwich House Music School
will be very happy to be considered for membership
in the Guild and if you will send us the necessary
application forms we shall fill them out promptly.
Thanking you very kindly for extending this invitation to us, and I sincerely hope our affiliation
will be of mutual benefit.

Very sincerely yours,

[signed]   Maxwell Powers
Director[44]

As requested, Mr. Whittaker included the list of questions
which all applicants or prospective schools were to answer
before admission to the National Guild.   He further stated
that he had a folder and file about the Greenwich House Music
School.   The answers to the itemized questions and a current

catalog would be all that were needed. The formal presentation of the application for membership to the Guild would be presented to the Executive Committee of the Guild's Board of Directors for approval on Friday, February 1, 1952.

What a coup for the young president! Whittaker had accomplished in just three years what none of the venerable, old guard leaders with all their sagacity had not been able to achieve in twelve years. Now both the Music School of the Henry Street Settlement and the Greenwich House Music School, two of the giants in the country, so to speak, were both full members of the National Guild of Community Music Schools!

For the reader to refresh his memory, let us recall a few facts stated in previous sections of this book. There have been other efforts by the National Federation of Settlements to create an alliance with music educators around the country. The first strong evidence is that in 1917 the National Federation invited the National Association of Music School Societies to affiliate with the National Federation of Settlements and to meet with them at Valencia, Pennsylvania at its national conference on June 3-6, 1917, as reported by Nicholas John Cords in his doctoral dissertation, "Music in Social Settlements and Community Music Schools".[45] The Association agreed and did attend the conference.

As we also know, the National Federation did in truth form an Arts Committee in 1917, and Johan Grolle was appointed chairman. Music dominated the concerns of the Committee on the Arts, as might have been expected. None of the other arts seemed to have a champion, and as a result very little consideration was given to them. By 1921 a separate Music Committee was structured in the National Federation, and once again Johan Grolle was appointed chairman. Further we know that Janet D. Schenck also served as the chair of the Music Committee at a later date. When the Carnegie Grant was not renewed, the two Committees eventually ceased to function, though the Committee on the Arts was the first to become inactive.

On January 17, 1952, Mr. Whittaker received a letter from Maxwell Powers which stated an attempt on the part of the National Federation to involve Howard Whittaker much more

closely in their organization. One can only believe that there
were those in the Federation who were arts oriented and who
wanted a viable, monitored arts program emanating from the
national office, and since Mr. Whittaker seemed to be one
with creative imagination and good administrative abilities, he
should be on their Arts Committee with Maxwell Powers as the
chairman of the committee. The letter read as follows:

> For some time many of us have felt that the absence
> of an art program in the National Federation of Settle-
> ments was a very serious omission in the work of
> settlement houses throughout the United States. We
> have felt that this omission did not represent those
> of us who have created large art programs within
> our organizations. There is an ever-existing need
> for the transmission of ideas of programs and thought
> with other centers. It is quite logical that the Nation-
> al Federation of Settlements should be the representa-
> tive organization to coordinate this art program.
>   With this in mind the executive committee of the
> National Federation of Settlements have voted to es-
> tablish an Arts Committee. We hope to present a mean-
> ingful program of the work done in the arts at the
> annual conference in Milwaukee. I am writing to ask
> if you would be willing to serve on this committee.
> I know that your long interest in the arts and the
> work you are doing in this field will be of immeasur-
> able help in stimulating such a committee.[46]

Mr. Powers further involved Whittaker by asking him
to present a speech at the Federation's annual conference in
Milwaukee in May, 1952. This is verified by the fact that
the opening line of his address was "I have been asked by
the Chairman of the Arts Committee to discuss the function
of the National Guild of Community Music Schools, how its
members integrate themselves into social and cultural work of
a community and how others may follow the patterns of work
which have been established by the Guild Schools in giving
to the various communities a vital and socially significant
music program."[47]

Whittaker obviously took the task very seriously and
prepared an excellent, informative and brief address which
gave the listeners a clear picture of the National Guild
and what its functions were. Since this period in Guild

history is most significant, for the growth spurt was to begin
slowly at this time, it seems valuable to present his exact
words in part:

> Perhaps I should begin by defining a community music
> school, or music school settlement as they are referred
> to, and also outlining a brief picture of our growth
> and development. The first such organizations [sic]
> was founded in 1894; it represented a pioneer develop-
> ment on the part of settlement people and socially
> minded musicians to place music within the reach of
> us all, particularly those in the more crowded neigh-
> borhoods in large cities. The guiding ideal was to
> combine a high grade of music teaching with the fun-
> damental principle that music is a vital part of living,
> and an essential element in the enrichment of the hu-
> man spirit. ...It is interesting to note that many of
> the Guild schools began as music departments in settle-
> ments, that most are now separate incorporated organ-
> izations while others have continued in their affiliation
> with settlements but with the same high proficiency
> and development as their separate neighbors. ...It
> is also to be noted that some community music schools
> ...changed and became professional conservatories
> of music. This is evidenced by the outgrowth of the
> Curtis Institute in Philadelphia, and the Manhattan
> and Mannes Schools in New York...several years ago
> the National Guild was approached by the National
> Association of Schools of Music to join their ranks.
> This proposal was based solely on their recognition
> of the high musical standards maintained in Guild
> Schools, but did not take cognizance of the social im-
> plications involved in our work. It was mainly for
> this reason that we declined their invitation which I
> felt was significant, and served to dispel the dichotomy
> of music versus social services and to rejuvenate us
> in our avowed purpose as musical, social service
> organization.[48]

(It seems relative to state that the author was sent as chairman of an examining team from the National Association of
Schools of Music in 1981 to survey the Neighborhood Music
School in New Haven upon that School's request for membership in the NASM in their non-degree-granting division.)

Mr. Whittaker's address to the National Federation continues:

> ...Our membership now totals 16 member schools;
> five in greater New York City, three in Boston, and
> one in Philadelphia, New Haven, Wilmington, Buffalo,
> Cleveland, St. Louis, Los Angeles and San Francis-
> co. ...While each school is well equipped to develop
> the potentialities of the individual to the professional
> level, the importance of understanding and participa-
> tion in music for the non-professional is stressed. It
> is also interesting to note that in a recent survey of
> our composite student body which numbers approxi-
> mately 10,000, we found that in many schools our
> adult enrollment ran as high as 25%; many of these
> people are taking part in some form of music study
> for the first time.
>
> There is a Guild [sic] curricula provided each
> school and each school is autonomous in its applica-
> tion. Comprehensive courses for preparatory (kinder-
> garten age) through advanced (or college level age)
> are offered, and a diploma or certificate of accomplish-
> ment is given by the school to those who elect to
> complete the work through the advanced departments.
> Further flexibility is provided in that in general no
> specific time is required in our curricula for the
> completion of a course. ...With regard to the higher
> echelons of national and international musical and
> social enterprise, the Guild is a member of the National
> Music Council where we have taken an active part in
> the framing of resolutions, reporting our activities,
> promoting Guild concepts, and making special reports
> such as a recent one on Adult Music Education. We
> have been equally active in UNESCO, where we have
> been represented since the first national conference
> in Philadelphia to the second in Cleveland where we
> reported on our activities to the third in New York
> last February where the President of the Guild was
> invited to serve as a discussion leader at the meetings
> of the Group Work on Music.[49]

The reports of the work of the National Guild were being
disseminated to many sectors, thanks to the efforts of the
Guild's officers, particularly the president. The same information was released to the National Music Council, the National

Federation of Settlements, and to such individuals or groups
who might have requested it. There could have been little
doubt about the intentions, goals and actions of the Guild.
Its willingness to cooperate, help or assist whenever possible,
could not be misunderstood.

But it was this very idea which was misunderstood by
Mr. McDowell when he contacted Whittaker about the information in the National Music Council Bulletin, stating that he
had had a telephone call from a settlement director, etc.
Certainly the National Guild was making every effort to ameliorate any misunderstanding, hoping for improvement in relationships with any other national organization.

With its extended activities, there was the increasing
recognition of a necessity for a national office or headquarters
with an executive officer to do the ordinary business of the
Guild, to release information about the Guild, and to keep the
affairs of the Guild in order. This would include, of course,
the financial affairs, which in turn would require that the officer be much involved in the fund-raising efforts of the
Guild. This would also include any foundation appeals, etc.
Obviously the position would be a full-time job which would
require understanding and dedication to the Guild.

The next communique which came from the National
Federation of Settlements was in the form of a letter from Maxwell Powers who wrote to Howard Whittaker on May 26, 1952
to make a specific request:

Dear Mr. Whittaker:

Pursuant to our conversation in Milwaukee, I am taking
the liberty of writing to request that you make the
following proposal on my behalf to the next executive
committee meeting of the National Guild of Community
Music Schools. Unfortunately, other plans will prevent
me from presenting this proposal in person.
I would like to suggest that the Guild consider
membership in the National Federation of Settlements.
If the Guild were accepted to membership, they would
become members as a Federation, thereby giving them
Board Representation in the Federation, plus two delegates at large. I wish to point out that this form of
membership would in no way impair the sovereignty

of Guild membership. The Guild would, of course, continue to enjoy the autonomy and freedom it now has, but would further strengthen our relationship with those Settlements throughout the country that need our assistance and guidance. I think you will agree that this was brought into even greater focus at our Arts Workshop in Milwaukee. Settlements throughout the country are operating music and art programs that are open to serious criticism as to quality and content.

In the spirit of Guild Philosophy, are we not duty bound to come to the support and lend our experience to those organizations that need it so desperately? Our membership to Federation would have the further stabilizing effect of developing an Art Program which could easily be incorporated into Guild concepts.

I wish to further point out that several current Guild members represent organizations whose program goes beyond a music school and includes departments in the theatre, dance, ceramics, visual and graphic arts. Those of us who have such broad art programs do not have an opportunity to present our problems to Guild membership as currently operated.

Once again, Federation Membership would allow a free interchange of thoughts on programs that would broaden the horizen [sic] for the Guild, as well as the over 300 organizations now affiliated with the National Federation of Settlements.[50]

The invitation to join the Federation was received and almost immediately rejected by the executives of the member schools of the Guild. No amount of persuasion could change the thinking of the executives. Their experiences with agency executives of the National Federation had disillusioned them to a point where they felt that such an affiliation would lower the standards of music and musical performance. Their attitudes were not turned in favor of settlement workers nor executives.

Howard Whittaker was very unhappy about this turn of events. He had thought that the two warring factions would come to agreement as he told Maxwell Powers in a letter of June 19, 1952:

Dear Mr. Powers:

As you may have already heard from Grace Spofford
or Ruth Kemper the Executive Committee of the Guild
did not vote for our becoming a member of the National
Federation of Settlements. I am, of course, sorry
about this development because I felt that your letter
pointed out most clearly that membership in the
National Federation would in no way impair the autonomy of the Guild and I further pointed out that following my conversation with Mr. Kennedy in New York
that this represented an opportunity for us to come
to the support of Music Departments in Settlements
throughout the country. There appeared several
reasons why the various members of the committee did
not feel that we should join. Paramount among these
seemed to be the lack of understanding on the part
of settlement people for music and cultural programs
of high standing by agency executives and to some
degree the National Federation itself. This point of
view is understandable but my personal opinion is
that each group is apparently waiting for the other
to make some move which will spell off doubt and
rectify the most difficult situation. If Guild members
have the idea that settlements should become pseudo-
cultural centers and settlement people feel that cultural
programs should be relegated to nothing more than a
minor activity then certainly no programs will be
made.[51]

It is a difficult task for a young musician to be assigned
to teach in a straight settlement house situation. If there
be a music school in the program, some children will naturally
gravitate toward it. Others will not. Perhaps these children
have not had the opportunity to receive good musical exposure
yet in their lives. But if his case worker or group worker
also sees no value in the arts, the situation becomes intolerable.
In some schools of social work there is little or no training
in the arts--music or any other art form. How can the young,
inexperienced case worker or group worker know how to use
the arts as tools to aid and encourage a child? How can he
make a referral to any art form if he has so little information
himself? How can a headworker know how to evaluate a program in any of the arts when deciding on the success or
failure of an arts program? Too frequently the background

of the settlement leader is so sketchy in the arts, that he
can hardly be blamed for not knowing what can be expected
in any art program.

But on the other side of the argument, not every musician is musically, artistically, or psychologically capable of
being the music person in a settlement program. Using a
similar observation as above for comparison, the thoroughly
trained performer, graduate of a proper conservatory would
have little or no training in sociology, history (beyond music
history), child behavior, psychology, or the humanities.
Neither side is the innocent lamb. Seldom have they really
sat down to discuss common aims and problems. One cannot
learn everything in staff meetings.

Each person, social worker and musician, should determine in his own mind first what his real capabilities are.
The unsuccessful and disgruntled musician should not attempt
to expose his limited talents to work with children in a social
service situation. Teaching under these circumstances must
be something he really wants to do, and if so, has prepared
himself to undertake the challenge. It is an art in itself to
be able to reach children through the arts, particularly in
an informal setting.

The social work supervisor should not expect to have
a band ready to perform after one year's preparation. It
may very well be a long time for a genuine musical experience,
enjoyable and gratifying, to emanate from the music sessions.
Would it not be better for each party to come to an agreeable
discussion of how to solve a pressing problem--musical or
social, rather than to have each party ridicule the other?
Peace! Pax! Shalom! Friede! Pace! Whatever!

Mr. Whittaker concluded his letter as follows:

> It is perhaps due to the find [sic--fine] cooperation
> I have received from Settlement executives here in
> Cleveland and in return what I hope has been my
> sincere cooperation with them that I have an optimistic
> point of view. However, I can appreciate that your
> job as Chairman of the Arts Committee will be no sim-
> ple matter regardless of the excellent start you made
> in Milwaukee. I am sure the Guild executives are
> waiting and watching to see what you will be able to

accomplish; and in this I am sure you know that you
can count on my assistance and I hope on theirs as
well.[52]

For the 1952 - 53 season and part of the next year,
peace and quiet seemed to be present, at least between the
two gentlemen in question, and it appears that Mr. Powers
did not attend many, or for that matter any, of the Guild's
meetings. But on October 20, 1954, another letter of severe
tone was sent to Howard Whittaker from Maxwell Powers which
read:

Dear Mr. Whittaker:

For the past several meetings of the Greenwich House
Music School, we have discussed in great detail our
organization's membership in the National Guild. In
the process of discussion there were many things
which were brought to light that were very favorable
towards Guild affiliation and, I must unfortunately
add, there were many facets of discussion which were
not so favorable.

Our Music School Committee was essentially concerned with the future of the Guild. We cannot see
at this time that our continued membership will offer
our Music School enough of an incentive to continue
our relationship. We had hoped that the Guild would
spearhead the thinking for community music schools
all over the country. We had also hoped that there
would be meaningful projects as a result of Guild affiliation which would give the members an opportunity
to serve these people who are least able to afford
the high cost of professional music training, and who
could benefit immeasurably by the experience and
musical concepts embodied in a community music school
atmosphere. Unfortunately there has been no evidence
of this fond hope.

Added to the above, we received a bill which more
than trebled our previous year's membership. Since
the exorbitant membership fee is not included in our
current operating budget, we are unable to meet this
cost.

Upon motion duly made and seconded at our Music
School Committee meeting on October 20, 1954, it was
resolved that we "submit our resignation to the National

Guild of Community Music Schools".
    This letter will serve notice that we are hereby
resigning effective immediately.[53]

    The National Guild of Community Music Schools had taken
major steps to open its doors for new and qualified community
music schools to become members of the Guild, and it had
turned its attention to at least one project in which the name
of the Guild was to be familiarized throughout many parts of
the country.   The organization's goals were admirable and
achieved.   The Randolph radio broadcasts formed an important
vehicle to bring all the member schools together working
toward a common project.   Each member school was to contact
the major radio stations in its community on behalf of the
National Guild, of which it was a member.   The purpose of
the contact was to encourage the stations to air Randolph's
Musical Notebook, which was an excellent musical presentation,
to its broadcasting areas as a community service with the
sponsorship of the National Guild of Community Music Schools.

    Even if the contact did not result in actual broadcasting,
the names of the school and of the National Guild of Community
Music Schools were brought to the attention of stations which
may not have known anything about the work of the Guild
and its member schools.   Strong leadership on the part of
the president of the Guild had made the member schools realize
his determination to make the Guild a nationally recognized
organization.   His seriousness of purpose and enthusiasm
coupled with the indefatigable Ruth Kemper and her continued
efforts on the Guild's behalf, made it possible for the Guild
to stand tall and move forward with strength and vigor.

    After five years of dedicated work for the Guild, Mr.
Whittaker decided to follow procedures established by the
Guild's by-laws and to step down as president, to allow him
to engage in work related to his own school and to cultural
projects in the Cleveland area.   Before he was to leave office,
however, he prepared and presented a five-year plan showing
how he envisioned the continuation of the National Guild of
Community Music Schools.   His plan in part appears below:

A PLAN FOR THE FUTURE

Howard Whittaker, President

...From this experience [the presidency] I have
found that our members differ in the following respects:

1)   Their geographical location effects [sic] the
     procurement of teachers.

2)   The size of budgets range from several thousand
     dollars per year to over one hundred thousand
     dollars per year.

3)   Financial support is derived from Community
     Chests, special gifts, endowments, drives,
     fees - but for the most part in differing
     amounts, percentages, and/or combinations of
     support.

4)   There are some differences in administrative
     structure.

5)   There are differences in the manner of setting
     fees.

6)   The schools have varying backgrounds and
     history, but not in the extreme.

From the same experience I believe that the following
represents a sameness or parallel in our schools:

1)   We all appear to have a similar motivation
     or concept or philosophy regarding our work.

2)   Our teaching practices, procedures, and
     curricula are basically of the same stock.

3)   Our personnel practices (including teachers
     salaries) in the broad sense are basically simi-
     lar.

4)   Most important, we serve the same type of
     students - age groups, economic groups, cross-
     section groups.

If I were to try to balance our similarities against
our differences in order to determine whether or not
we needed a Guild (better yet whether it was worth
the time, effort and money) my answer would probably
be qualified because of the variations in our budgets
and financial support; in this day and age one doesn't

have to look far to see that the most potent national
organizations are those with strong financial ties and
uniform financial backing.

However, my last paragraph is an oversimplification
for several reasons. The most important of which is
the none too subtle yearning on the part of people
in our field over the last thirty years at least (quite
a period before the Guild was organized) to establish
the Community Music School idea on a recognized
national basis with adequate financial support and
proper growth and development. "Here lies the rub."
We are living in an age of organization at every conceivable level and for every conceivable (sometimes
unbelievable) reason or purpose. The Community
Music School people have been on the side lines
watching the tremendous growth and organization over
the past thirty years of the professional schools of
music in conservatories and universities, the upsurge
or organized private music teachers, the expansion
of public school music, and the stabilization and
recognition of social workers in all of their specialized
fields. Have we ever had a Guild conference when
this frustration, or better, "reaffirmation of faith"
did not spring up spontaneously in lucid times from
the floor and from practically every one present?

...To be perfectly candid I can see no real future
for Community Music Schools without a strong National
Guild. And to be equally candid I think the time is
ripe for us to expand our thinking, broaden our base,
and establish our movement for all to see.[54]

In some ways he was castigating the directors of the
schools and leaders of the Guild for not keeping abreast with
the times and the needs of the organization. He then presented his ten-step plan in brief outlined form and suggested
which members of the Guild were to assume what responsibility:

I.   The need for a Guild Executive-Secretary
         (Mrs. Adler appointed for the 1953-54 season)

II. Future Financial Needs
         (responsibility of the Ways and Means Commit-
         tee, Miss White, Chairman)

III. National Guild Schools and Public School Co-operation
> (responsibility of the Executive Committee and Conference Program Committee)

IV. National Guild Training Programs, Meetings and Seminars
> (responsibility of the Executive Committee to determine what steps should be taken)

V. Secondary Instrumental Instruction in National Guild Schools
> (responsibility of the special committee appointed last year with Mr. Ward as Chairman)

VI. Extension Programs to Settlements and other Social Agencies
> (responsibility of the Executive-Secretary and social committee appointed last year to study affiliation with the National Federation of Settlements)

VII. Development of a Strong Inter-School Student Youth Program
> (responsibility of a special committee to be appointed)

VIII. National Guild Summer Camp
> "prayers"

IX. Continued Active Part in National and International Musical Affairs
> (responsibility of Guild officers)

X. National Guild Service Statistics
> (responsibility of special committee to be appointed)[55]

And so Howard Whittaker, president, whose term of office was now completed, left his plan for the future of the National Guild of Community Music Schools. Though he no longer was president, Whittaker still functioned fully in Guild activities and directed his School until his retirement at the end of the 1983-84 academic season.

The directive and push from the five-year plan of Mr.
Whittaker's and the discussions that followed in meetings and
conferences were an effort to operate as a national organization, not just as individual schools. Many of the schools'
directors and their boards of directors were faced with pressing problems in their own locales, and had become Guild
members in order to learn how to solve their basic problems.
Now they were being asked to think in larger terms on the
national level, and in some cases to become leaders in special
areas.

With the possible exception of one or two schools, the
annual worries concerning the balancing of the budget were
ever present. They had difficulties staying solvent. Of
course, most of them were able to balance their budgets,
with very little, if any, monies left over. Now the member
schools were being asked to find ways for supporting the
National Guild. Though their interest was keen, they also
realized that there was no money at home which they could
draw upon to give to the Guild no matter how great the emer-
gency. Many of them agreed with the plan outlined by Mr.
Whittaker until they reached the subject of money. Then they
were completely nonplussed as to what to do.

Yet all of this simply pointed up the need for a national
office of the Guild to tackle some of these problems--but that
too cost more money, or it would have been done long ago.
The National Guild is certainly not the only non-profit organization in this country to face the problem. No easy
answers were to be found, and many began to look to Washington
to begin to fund some cultural organizations. But that was a
dream.

Five of the points that Whittaker outlined which were
readily acceptable to Guild members were: (1) that there was
a definite need for a national office with a proper staff to
run it; (2) that better inter-school (community music schools
and neighborhood public and parochial schools) cooperation
should be earnestly pursued; (3) the setting up of a Guild
training program which would be helpful to members who might
be looking for administrators and to supply administrators to
newly organized schools; (4) that emphasis on extension programs with settlement houses and social agencies should take
a priority, (today we refer to the outreach programs--another
name for the same thing); and (5) that the Guild should

broaden its horizons both nationally and internationally to play
a greater role in national and international musical affairs and
events.

And on each recommendation hung a considerable number
of dollar signs! But the words had to be spoken, and bit
by bit the Guild undertook its responsibilities and cautiously
moved forward.

It was this situation and dilemma which faced Ruth
Kemper who was to become the fourth president of the National
Guild from 1955 to 1957. The pressures of being the assistant
director of the Turtle Bay Music School and a violin teacher
on its faculty with the additional burdens of being the president of the Guild, caused her not to accept a second nomina-
tion for the presidency.

At this point, Dr. Herbert Zipper, who was then the
director of the Music Center of the North Shore in Winnetka,
Illinois (formerly the Dushkin School of Music), who was an
excellent conductor and musician, and who had come to America via the Philippines at the time of the holocaust in the Nazi
occupied areas of Europe, appeared on the Guild's horizon.
He is a man of great charm and personality, and one who ac-
cepts responsibility graciously and clings tenaciously to solve
what at first seems to be an insurmountable obstacle. In addition to his outstanding musical talents he possessed strong
administrative abilities. He has been a strong advocate of the
National Guild for the past thirty years, and still remains
dedicated to the National Guild, active and enthusiastic,
though at the time of this writing he is in his eighties. He
still makes fairly regular trips to the Republic of China to
help with the growth and improvement of symphony orchestras
in that country.

Herbert Zipper brought Grace Nash to the faculty of the
Music Center of the North Shore and thereby introduced her
to the National Guild. She remained at the School in Winnetka
for many years before moving on to other activities and institutions. She is well-known today for her outstanding contributions to early childhood music education, both by her books
and her lectures and demonstrations.

Zipper was also responsible for raising funds for the
Guild's Philippines Project and the Arts for All Program about

which more will be said later. He further raised funds to
establish the Guild's national office.

During this period of the Guild's history, its member
schools began to receive inquiries from many parts of the
country asking for information about establishing or starting
a community music school, or how to handle specific problems
which might face such schools. There was no information
piece published by the Guild to send in response.

The National Guild's conference in 1956-57 was held in
Winnetka, Illinois. During an executive committee meeting in
the previous season Dr. Zipper had encouraged Robert Egan
to assume the responsibility of preparing a manual or booklet
to answer the need felt by the organization to have material
ready for mailing when inquiries came. The first step was
to prepare a questionnaire which each school would answer
to prepare a pool of information that did present a true picture
of the overall formation of a community music school. Thus
was formed the beginnings of another National Guild project,
since each Guild member school was to contribute fundamental
information about its own basic structure. Contrary to the
experience of other researchers, all member schools of the
National Guild responded to Egan's questionnaire making it as
accurate and complete as possible.

The assembling of materials and their collation were done
by the staff of the Music School of the Henry Street Settlement. The results and their duplication were completed in
time for the Guild's conference in February, 1958 in Pittsfield,
Massachusetts, with the Pittsfield Community Music School
acting as the host school. Its co-directors were Marjorie and
Jan Stocklinski who supplied an enormous room with ample
table surface space for the assembling of the first complete
copies of the Manual: A Guide for the Establishment and
Administration of a Community Music School, compiled 1957-
1958. One of the sessions of the conference (which otherwise
might have been a relaxing free period) was designated to be
an assembling session for the Manual. The completed pages
and previously labeled covers were driven up to Pittsfield from
New York City by the people who attended the conference
from the Henry Street Settlement Music School.

In a relatively short session the attendees in single
file circled the large tables which had the individual piles of

pages carefully placed in order by the staff from Henry Street
and assembled the first two hundred copies of the Manual.
A representative of each member school was given one copy
gratis for his school. The balance of the copies were to be
returned to Henry Street. Additional copies could be ordered
at the cost of $2.00 plus postage per copy. The mimeograph
stencils were to be stored and saved at Henry Street to complete additional copies when they were needed.

There was a charm to the scene when Guild members
who were directors of schools, faculty and staff members,
worked closely and amicably together at this simple task. It
reflected a coming together of many from far distant places to
work at one common assignment. Conviviality and Gemütlich-
keit permeated the atmosphere, which only needed to be or-
chestrated to appear as a scene from a beautiful, musical
presentation.

Before leaving the discussion of the Manual it is sensible
to quote the Foreword statement, which in its own way reflects
the same philosophy which Howard Whittaker espoused in his
statement to the National Federation of Settlements, offering
the services of the Guild to any who needed it.

> This MANUAL is dedicated to the new and struggling
> organizations that bear the distinctly American name,
> Community Music School. Our firm belief in this move-
> ment has been the spark that has encouraged us to
> prepare this booklet.
>   As one peruses this manual, the myriad problems
> that beset a school of this type will become evident,
> and their vastness may well prove discouraging to
> those who are first entering the field. But the
> National Guild of Community Music Schools wishes to
> offer assistance to any who feel that their obstacles
> are insurmountable. Ours is a dedicated area, and
> one which we believe to be extremely valuable to our
> nation as a whole.[56]

During the following years of Herbert Zipper's presidency, there was a decided growth spurt in the size of the
National Guild. He also set an excellent example to the member
schools and to the communities at large in his work in Winnetka. His work with the public schools in that area had
their music programs improved enormously by his imagination

and selection of personnel to produce the desired results. He
further enriched his community by establishing an orchestra
which toured in the schools and various community centers
really in the greater Chicago territory. While involved in
these activities, he continuously kept his examining eye on
events in Washington for the opportunity to request monies
to support Guild activities. Several foundations were steadily
informed about Guild activities. More will be said later about
this unusual and admirable gentleman.

In 1961 the Guild urged Robert F. Egan, the director
of the Music School of the Henry Street Settlement in New
York City, to assume the responsibility of the Guild's presidency. Zipper extended strong support to the candidacy
of Egan, and he accepted the honor and the fully expected
hard work from 1961 to 1965.

Several projects were undertaken in this period, some
clearly answering the charges in Whittaker's Five Year Plan,
and others following trends which seemed to be advisable at
that time. At the urging of many directors, there was a plan
developed to allow the Guild to hire an executive-secretary,
if only on a part-time basis. This enormous task made it
difficult to find a person with the necessary qualifications
who would accept the job. A recommendation from Dr. Paul
Freeman, director of the Hochstein Memorial Music School in
Rochester, New York stated that a young, enthusiastic woman
of his faculty, and herself a graduate of the Eastman School
of Music, would be a person he strongly recommended. She
came down to New York City for an interview with the Guild's
president. Her vivacious personality and her interest in the
Guild, coupled with her willingness to accept a part-time
position, and Dr. Freeman's willingness to give her office
space to function from the Hochstein School at no cost to the
Guild, seemed to answer the Guild's needs for the moment.
Miss Alice Conway, a harpist, and teacher at the Hochstein
School was engaged as the executive-secretary.

Alice Conway took her job most seriously. She began
immediately to suggest ways in which she could make the Guild
more evident in the United States and Europe. She saw very
quickly that the Guild had made its last publication of its
The Quarterly--The National Guild of Community Music Schools
in March, 1947, Volume VI, Number 1. Her first goal was to
prepare a publication with perhaps a new name, but with

seriousness of purpose. Subsequent goals were to continue
the publication on a regular basis perhaps including articles
from other journals and publications that would be of interest
to Guild members. The plan was similar to that of The Quarterly.

Miss Conway, at the urging of Dr. Freeman, suggested
that there be a performance contest for students of Guild
schools throughout the country to compete for awards to summer music camps, scholarships, etc. This had never been
done previously but at this time in Guild history it was to be
tried, so long as no cost rested on Guild shoulders. With
much enthusiasm the contest was proposed and accepted by
the Guild membership to be offered in the 1964-1965 season.

Combining the two projects, Alice Conway brought about
the first contest of the National Guild students from around
the country, coupled with the first publication of a Guild
magazine or booklet. It is needless to say that hers was a
position far greater than part time, yet she moved ahead.

The new Guild publication was to be called Guild Notes,
and in its first issue the Guild president described the contest
supported by the National Guild. The president's letter read
as follows:

> The National Guild of Community Music Schools has
> reached a landmark in its history by presenting a
> national contest open to students who are enrolled
> in Guild Schools from the east coast to the west coast.
> This was the first attempt at such a venture and it
> was decidedly encouraging to see the number of appli-
> cants.
> The contest was divided into five categories as
> follows: Senior Piano Division, Junior Piano Division,
> Senior Instrumental Division, Junior Instrumental
> Division, and Vocal Division. Each school was limited
> to sending only two participants to any one category.
> An impressive number of students were entered in the
> national finals after preliminary eliminations in the
> local schools. Contestants came from New York City,
> Boston, Cleveland, Rochester, (N.Y.), Buffalo, Phila-
> delphia, (Pa.), New Haven, (Conn.), and Wilmington,
> (Del.).
> Such a response points the way for future activity

of the National Guild. An interest in national competitions and affairs is clearly indicated. Members of
the Guild and interested parties should turn careful
thought to what further activities can be undertaken
on a national level that would be of similar interest
to member schools.

Since our entire nation has turned active interest
to the Cultural advancement of all people, the National
Guild of Community Music Schools shares, along with
other organizations of this kind, the deep responsibility to assume a role of leadership for the presentation of musical opportunities for all. As part of the
President's Great Society, we should feel honored to
have the privilege to participate on both local and
national levels.[57]

It is fascinating to read in the same issue of Guild
Notes a report on the conference of the National Federation
of Settlements held in March, 1965 in the City of Philadelphia.
Most significant of all are the words of Francis Bosworth, of
the Friends Neighborhood Guild of Philadelphia:

On March 18-20 [1965] the National Federation of
Settlements and Neighborhood Centers sponsored a
conference on "Utilizing the Arts for Youth Develop-
ment" in Philadelphia. Among those attending from
the National Guild of Community Music Schools were
Robert Egan, Guild president and director of the Music
School of the Henry Street Settlement, Alice Conway,
Guild executive secretary, representing the Hochstein
Memorial Music School, Richard Kauffman, acting
director of the Cleveland Music School Settlement, and
Mrs. Marjorie Lentz, a teacher at the Cleveland School.
Mrs. Henry Hosmer and Miss Helen Morton, both board
members of the United South End Settlements in Boston
were also present along with other teachers and
directors from around the country.

The basis for the discussions was this statement
drawn up by the 1962 Conference with Francis Bosworth, Executive Director of the Friends Neighborhood
Guild in Philadelphia as chairman:

"Bringing people together of different backgrounds,
the arts provide a stairway of social mobility. They
have proven themselves to be equally valuable for
every cultural level, and can become the bridge for

communication between all segments of society. They
are also a powerful social weapon on the side of beauty,
for building individual standards of taste, home and
in city planning. Through art the individual can gain
great satisfaction and find a medium for his natural
creativity; he becomes self-disciplined as well as
'group-disciplined.' He learns limits--of his own
abilities, of materials and of time itself. He becomes
sensitized to beauty and to his fellow man. Through
art the deprived child can acquire the cultural background essential to successful schooling in his early
years and to enriched living in the years of maturity."

It was emphasized that "the ends and goals of the
art program should be shared and accepted by the
entire settlement and interpreted with sensitivity to
the entire community. This program should meet
the highest artistic standards possible and, in order
to attract and retain qualified personnel, the arts
must have equal status with all other departments
of the settlements. The teacher of the arts is a spe-
cialist as is the professional social worker, clinical
psychologist or other persons of professional discipline,
and all must work together for the common good. The
arts staff are the apostles of the settlements' purpose
to help each individual find significance in life."

Continuing from this point in Philadelphia, Mr.
Bosworth urged the need of carrying on in the settlements strong arts programs and stated that settlements
could take advantage of the supplementary services
provisions of the Federal Education Bill which will
provide funds for art programs. "Education is our
job. The arts better than any other segment of education can be our instrument."[58]

The words expressed by Francis Bosworth at the conclusion of his address to the conference of settlement house
workers from across the country could easily have been stated
by one of the officers of the National Guild of Community
Music Schools. The message would have been the same. It
would seem to have been the ideal statement for consideration
at meetings of the National Guild as well as the National Federation of Settlements.

At this time in its history the National Guild was striving
desperately to achieve realistic goals which would be possible

for it to accomplish successfully. It wanted to have an un-
biased evaluation of its structure and program to be done by
someone who was a recognized, scholarly individual whose
own work in the field of the arts in social situations was well
known and accepted widely. The Guild's choice for this project was Dr. Max Kaplan, musician and sociologist, whose
work was considered exceptional, particularly for his thorough
studies on leisure. Dr. Kaplan was shortly to begin working
with Dr. Robert Choate on the famous Tanglewood Symposium
which was to be held from July 23 through August 2, 1967.
That symposium was to cause a considerable stir in music
education and sociology classes. The Guild commissioned Max
Kaplan to do a survey of Guild schools and programs and to
submit his report, which Kaplan was to entitle "National Guild
of Community Music Schools Observations and Recommendations."
It was completed and sent to the National Guild on May 1, 1966,
and was the Guild's attempt to have an outside observer evaluate the Guild to help it clarify or identify new directions for
it to follow.

Dr. Kaplan paid careful attention to the Five-Year Plan
done by Howard Whittaker when he stepped down as president.
There were many similarities in thought, but obviously some
new areas for cogitation were explored. Kaplan visited eight
cities and fifteen schools, which displayed a real cross-section
of the National Guild schools. He commented about each
school he visited, giving a verbal description of neighborhoods,
schools themselves, and made observations of the differences
in communities.

In his detailed report Max Kaplan made ten recommendations in each of two categories, National and Internal. Much
discussion was included, but only the recommendations themselves are to be listed in this document. They were as follows:

A.   Recommendations: National

1.   It is recommended that the Guild develop a
positive, bold, and constructive program to
relate itself to a variety of national and
international, state, and local agencies and
institutions and movements.

2.   It is recommended that the Guild revitalize

its National Advisory Committee, or create a
new one if necessary as a sounding board for
large policies.

3.   It is recommended that a permanent headquarters
be established by the Guild, with a fulltime
staff, organized records, and all other requisites
of a central office.

4.   It is recommended that a public relations firm
be engaged to advise in all matters relating to
program and organization, as a basis for a
constructive campaign of public education and
fund raising.

5.   It is recommended that a national drive for
funds be planned with professional advice, to
reach into private, foundation, governmental,
or all other potential sources.

6.   It is recommended that the Guild plan and pursue
a membership campaign.

7.   It is recommended that a plan be developed for
the creation of new community music schools.

8.   It is recommended that the name of the organization be reconsidered, to conform more accurately
to its present membership.

9.   It is recommended that the Guild immediately ap-
ply for a "planning grant" of $7,500 under
Title IV of the Elementary and Secondary School
Act.

10.   It is recommended that private foundations be
approached only after the Guild has developed
a coordinated plan for moving on these or other
programs and recommendations.[59]

Dr. Kaplan has a strong sense for organization and
careful planning as is seen in both of his lists of recommenda-
tions--national and internal. He also has great sensitivity
for other human beings and what their needs are.

B.   Recommendations: Internal

1.   It is recommended that the functions of the
     proposed Executive Secretary be specified
     in respect to his relationships to member
     schools as well as to the general Guild struc-
     ture.

2.   It is recommended that the Guild conceive
     and organize a training program for adminis-
     trators.

3.   It is recommended that constructive thought
     be given by the Guild to a redefinition of
     its membership.

4.   It is recommended that fresh thought be
     given to the purpose and structure of meet-
     ings of the Guild.

5.   It is recommended that a regular, ...onthly
     mimeographed bulletin be established for
     distribution to directors, other staff mem-
     bers, board members, and faculty.

6.   It is recommended that special communications
     be prepared to assist in developing clear
     identity with the Guild and understanding of
     it.

7.   It is recommended that the Guild, as well
     as individual schools, examine sources of
     funds created for welfare purposes that are
     conceivably or overtly related to the arts.

8.   It is recommended that the Guild look with
     sympathy toward a larger proportion of adult
     activity.

9.   It is recommended that a Guild proposal be
     drafted for foundation examination to move
     schools toward a nucleus of salaried faculty.

10. It is recommended that the present report
     be considered more as a plan for a plan than
     as a definitive set of recommendations.[60]

And now the National Guild of Community Music Schools
had a set of guidelines to follow in its effort to expand and
be recognized on the national musical horizon.   Certainly the
work of Max Kaplan, whose interest in the Guild is undying,
had made a noble effort to observe the Guild's structure,
membership and possible areas for growth.

To bring further attention to the Guild, Dr. Zipper had
evolved a plan that would demonstrate the use of community
music training in a manner never before shown clearly.   The
community music school idea was, as we know, a completely
American original.   Now came a plan which was to develop a
symphony orchestra and a music training center for the Filipino population, particularly in the city of Manila.   It is best
here to present the full report made by Herbert Zipper at
the annual conference of the National Guild held in Toronto,
Canada on November 12, 13 and 14, 1967.   The program report covered the time period from June of 1966 when the
operations actually began, to November 1, 1967, just before
the annual conference.   It was stated as follows:

> The Philippine Fellowship Project, undertaken jointly
> by the Manila Symphony Society and the National
> Guild of Community Music Schools through an enabling
> grant of the JDR 3rd Fund, is in the second year of its
> function in Manila.   At this time it seems appropriate
> to draw conclusions as to the impact of the project
> on the musical scene in Manila and the promise it
> holds for the future.   For the sake of clarity I should
> like to recapitulate the main objectives of our program.
>   (1)   To get acceptable standards in the heretofore
> neglected instruments, i.e., cello, doublebass, the
> woodwind and brass instruments;
>   (2)   To enhance the status of these instruments
> in the minds of students, music educators and the
> public;
>   (3)   To establish modern methodologies for these
> instruments in music schools, music departments of
> universities and among private teachers;
>   (4)   To assemble a basic library of modern study
> materials and to assure that Filipino teachers will be
> able to continue the work after termination of our
> project;
>   (5)   To teach the care and maintenance of instru-
> ments and, in the case of reed instruments, the art
> of reed making;

(6)   To teach and to propagate chamber music
playing and acquaint professionals, students and the
public with the heretofore neglected literature;

(7)   To contribute to the improvement in the performance quality of the Manila Symphony Orchestra
and other ensembles in Manila and provincial cities;

(8)   To increase the activities of the Manila Symphony Orchestra to a level that will enable the Manila
Symphony Society to offer to its musicians yearly contracts not later than by 1970.

The following comments are listed in the same
order as the stated goals to which they relate.

(1)   Instruction in doublebass, begun in June,
of 1966, was concluded on June 15, 1967.   The results
are best summed up by the Times, as follows: "New
York for Doublebass - The playing of the doublebass
here will be never the same again.   The difference
in its handling between then and now was Gary Hickling."   Similar results are being achieved by the
other teachers, and I am confident that after termination of their tour of duty, new standards will have
been established.

(2)   The many appearances of the fellowship teachers in solo recitals and chamber music concerts, their
lectures and demonstration classes in universities,
music schools and at the Jefferson Library of the USIS
are designed to raise the status of these instruments.
The steadily increasing demand for appearances of
our fellowship teachers and their best students as
solo performers is an indication that we are reaching
our objective.

(3)   A basic methodology on all instruments taught
is available to all institutions and local teachers.
This practice will be continued in the future and beyond
the duration of the project.

(4)   Study materials for all five instruments and
standard chamber music works featuring these instruments have been acquired through funds contributed
by the friends of the Manila Symphony Orchestra in
the United States and in the Philippines and by a contribution in kind by the West German government.
The training of Filipino teachers for the purpose of
continuing the work after the conclusion of the project
has been given priority from the beginning.   Gary
Hickling, for instance, worked with five mature

musicians intensively toward that end and they are
now successfully continuing his work. Teachers on
the other instruments are now teaching beginners
under the supervision and guidance of our fellows.
While it is too early to assess fully how competent
these teachers will be, there is no doubt that funda-
mentals are now properly approached and there is a
vast improvement in basic methodology.

(5) The two string teachers, in cooperation with
a local string instrument maker, have been able to
refurbish practically all of the local basses and cellos.
Not only have they been properly adjusted but by
giving the correct standards Filipino craftsmen are
now capable of keeping these instruments in good
condition. In the case of wind instruments, both professionals and students are being taught the essentials
of maintenance and minor repairs, and craftsmen are
being advised. Thomas Woodhams was able to rebuild
five of our old bassoons while some of his students
worked with him as apprentices. A new reed gouging
machine has been ordered from the United States and
accessories and tools have been purchased from funds
raised in the Philippines and the United States. Both
last year and this, I have bought in the United States
and imported to the Philippines duty free, instruments
for teaching purposes at a valuation in excess of
$6,000.00 which amount I have raised personally in the
U.S. and in the Philippines.

(6) Chamber music concerts in all kinds of different combinations have been given in the past and are
scheduled for the future. Ensemble classes for enrolled students and outsiders also, with no tuition
charged, are regularly held under the guidance of
our teachers. This, in fact, is one of our most successful functions at the present time.

(7) The improvement in the performance quality
of the Manila Symphony Orchestra is already very
noticeable, not only to the professional ear but also
to the public at large. This is the result not only of
formal instruction but also of the example given by
our teachers to their fellow musicians. The generally
improved professional attitude stems also from a newly
gained pride in artistic achievement.

As a result of our project it is more likely that
exceptional talents will be detected and receive special

attention. The Music Promotion Foundation of the
Philippines, a government-funded institution, may
now extend these scholarship grants to students on
the heretofore neglected instruments. I just received
such a grant from this foundation for a highly gifted
music teacher from Iloilo which will enable this man
to attend a second year of study in Manila. A directive by Education Secretary Carlos P. Romulo, allowing provincial public school teachers to study with
our teachers in Manila on official time, is helping to
improve standards in provincial communities as well.
All this is bound to affect beneficially the future
growth of instrumental music in the Philippines.

(8) In addition to the direct artistic benefits
derived from our project, the fact alone that the
Manila Symphony Society received financial assistance
from an American foundation and technical assistance
from a national organization in the United States,
has awakened renewed local interest in the Society,
and a more widespread feeling of responsibility for
the growth and maintenance of its orchestra.

The Woman's [sic] Board, an auxiliary entity of
the MSS, which I was able to organize last year, has
become a vital committee, assisting financially as well
as in all facets of public relations. Three new projects have been organized this year. Thus, by more
than tripling the activities of the Orchestra and by
institutionalizing the new projects, the MSS will be
in a position in the not too distant future to offer its
musicians of the orchestra annual contracts. This will
not only stabilize the economic situation of the orchestra members but will also result in far-reaching artistic improvements.... I also wish to report that as a
permanent base for teaching, the research center of
the University of the East has made studio space
available, not only for their own students but for any
outside students who may wish to receive instruction.
In addition, our boys are teaching one day at the
University of the Philippines and in some other institutions as well. In this fashion, attendance records
of both teachers and students are kept in orderly
fashion and through the offices of these institutions
we are assured of regularity and discipline.

Of course, I am well aware that only a continued
struggle for higher achievement can be a safeguard

against the deterioration of standards. I am well
aware that in a newly developing country like the
Philippines where the climate is not conducive to mental
and physical exertion, the improvement and maintenance of standards is more difficult than in countries
where tradition furnishes built-in safeguards. In
newly developing countries we must offer patient assistance in planting the seeds out of which tradition
may grow. The gratifying improvement in other areas
which I have witnessed during the past 28 years, made
possible through improved communications and the
availability of foreign specialists, make me confident
that we are planting in fertile ground.

This is an example of a global community, so to speak,
concentrating on the cultural lacks of a community located in
the Philippines, including a national organization from the
United States, an American foundation, the dedication of a
serious and talented conductor and teacher, and those factions
in Manila (Orchestra Board, Women's Committee, Universities,
department of education, etc.) working closely together to
bring about the development and strengthening of a cultural
organization in the form of a symphony orchestra, and the
development of a good music education in the Philippines
Island.

So successful was the first year of operations that the
director of the JDR 3rd Fund contacted Herbert Zipper to
assure him that an additional grant was being sent to the
treasurer of the National Guild of Community Music Schools
for the continuation of the project in Manila. His letter read
as follows:

Dear Dr. Zipper:

I am pleased to confirm our telephone conversation
in which I informed you of the action of the Trustees
of the JDR 3rd Fund in approving a grant of $35,000
to the National Guild of Community Music Schools to
continue the teaching project for the Manila Symphony
Society for an additional year.
    I am enclosing a copy of our grant notification
letter to Mr. Egan.
    The Trustees noted in particular the great import-
ance of your personal participation to the success of

the project in the past two years and wished to express its appreciation for your many and varied services on behalf of the Manila Symphony Society.
With best wishes.

Sincerely,

[Signed] Porter McCray
Director[61]

The project continued over a highly successful three-year
period.

This example of international communities in action
proved to be exciting for the National Guild, and much praise
was given to the American organization which agreed to cooperate. It did sometimes, however, cause some grief in the
total operation with the mail service failing at times to deliver
the paychecks to the men in the program. This further
complicated bank accounts and records kept by the Guild in
New York City. Eventually all the problems were successfully
solved, making the entire project seem to be most satisfactory.

A program very similar to the Philippine Fellowship
Project was undertaken by the National Guild in 1970 in which
Herbert Zipper was once again to be the Executive Director.
This one was to be known as The Seoul-Taipei Music Fellowship
Project of the JDR 3rd Fund, in co-operation with the National
Guild of Community Music Schools.

A memorandum from Herbert Zipper describes a meeting
that took place on August 17, 1970, at the Hotel New Korea
in Seoul which states the following information:

> Those present were: Dr. LEE, HYE-KU, Dean, Col-
> lege of Music, Seoul National University; LIM WONSIK,
> Music Director, National Symphony Orchestra and
> Director, Seoul High School of Music and Art; Mdm.
> CHAE TUCK SHIN of the School of Music of Ewha
> Women's University; DOO SUN KIM, Chairman, Col-
> lege of Music of Hanyang University; KIM, CHANG-
> WHAN, Concertmaster, Seoul Philharmonic Orchestra;
> DR. HERBERT ZIPPER, Executive Director, National
> Guild of Community Music Schools. (The representa-
> tives of Yonsei University and Kyong-Hi University
> being ill were represented by Mr. Lim.)

THE PROJECT, as discussed during the meeting.
A grant made by The JDR 3rd Fund authorizes the
National Guild of Community Music Schools to engage
one oboist and one bassoonist for service as fellowship teacher-performers in Seoul and Taipei for the
period of one year, beginning in October, 1970, with
a second year, subject to approval by The JDR 3rd
Fund during the month of May, 1971. The two Fellows
will be assigned alternately to each of the two cities
in such a way that while one works in Seoul the other
will work in Taipei, exchanging places approximately
every four months.

Their assignment will be to teach students of the
participating institutions, to assist professional teachers and performers, to introduce modern methodolo-
gies and the Literature of their respective instruments,
to coach chamber music groups and solo players and
to perform with local music groups. Time permitting,
they also may accept private students. While the
fellows will be paid for their services by the National
Guild, including all of their travelling expenses, the
participating institutions will make available adequate
teaching facilities and will also provide adequate living
quarters for the Fellows. Since they will work alternately, only one housing facility in each city needs
to be provided.[62]

The cooperating and participating institution were de-
clared to be the Seoul National University, the National Sym-
phony Orchestra, Hanyang University, the Seoul Philharmonic
Orchestra, Ewha Women's University, Kyong-Hi University,
Yousei University, and the Seoul High School of Music and
Art. The Co-Chairmen of the Project Committee are Dr. Lee,
Hye-Ku and Mr. Lim Wonsik.[63]

The striking similarities of the two projects spoke highly
of the success of the first one in the Philippines. The project in Seoul and Taipei was equally successful, and the reputation of the National Guild of Community Music Schools once
again proved to be of the highest calibre in these foreign
lands. Again an example of the global community was in action.

7

"ARTS FOR ALL" AND
THE NATIONAL OFFICE OPENS

One of the biggest and most exciting projects that the National
Guild has ever undertaken was inspired by the federal government's establishing of the Title I Elementary and Secondary
Education Act of 1965. It is the most outstanding example
of community action that can be found anywhere. The community includes the federal government, the state of Arkansas,
three counties, Ashley, Draw, and Chicot, and six school
districts, with the National Guild of Community Music Schools
acting as consulting and cooperating agency with Dr. Herbert
Zipper, the Project Director. Funds provided by Title I of
ESEA 1965 made it possible to begin the program in 1969.
The project's title was a Mobile Academy of the Performing
Arts for Children of Rural South East Arkansas, Arts for All.

A booklet published by the National Guild describes the
program as follows:

> The purpose of the Mobile Academy is to make avail-
> able for children in rural communities a superior edu-
> cation in the performing arts. An effective education
> in the arts is not only an end in itself but also en-
> hances the general learning ability of children, es-
> pecially the non-verbal arts, when used as preparatory
> disciplines in the initial stages of formal education.
> Beyond that, the Mobile Academy is designed to im-
> prove, in general, the quality of life in rural areas.[1]

The program offered not only music, but the theatre arts as
well.

The major thrust of the project was, of course, to bring
the arts to the people. It is obvious that children and adults who reside in rural areas do not have the opportunity to

involve themselves in the arts, because great distances make
it impossible to be at the spot where the musical or theatrical
experiences might be.   Thus the Mobile Academy served a
valuable purpose.

The booklet explains further why the project should
prove to be an effective tool used to expose those in rural
areas to the arts which they may never have experienced
before, and it explains that the program can be run economically with skillful teachers:

> The project is based on the premise that its objectives
> can be realized through the employment of a handful
> of highly skilled and dedicated artist-teachers.
> Specialists in their respective field, who under compe-
> tent leadership and in conjunction with public schools,
> can adapt their skills and can create pertinent materi-
> als appropriate for the cultural education of rural
> children.   Economical use of expert personnel and
> equipment through mobility and cooperation of conti-
> guous school districts should prove that effective
> cultural education in rural America is feasible.[2]

One of the criticisms of funding from national organizations, both private and governmental, is that once a program
has been developed and is successful, that the community
which may have received the grant must then undertake the
financial burden of continuing the program by itself.   It has
been said many times that if the locality had had the money
in the first place that it would not have had to ask for a
grant from a foundation or from some governmental program.
It is important to note that this had been considered before
the grant was given.   "The Arts for All" booklet explains
the thinking that went on in rural Arkansas and in Washington,
D. C., as well as in the minds of the officers of the National
Guild, and particularly in Herbert Zipper's.   The booklet
states the following:

> The final objective of the program is to work toward
> local recognition of its intrinsic values so that even-
> tually the communities involved will want the Mobile
> Academy to continue permanently.   Since its operational
> cost is less than four percent of the educational bud-
> get of the six participating school districts, the
> financial requirements are not out of proportion.[3]

Once again one envisions the genuine community cooperation that is so essential to support an arts program. If there were no other value than cooperation and planning with five other school districts, the venture would be educational and inspirational for those involved to learn what they might be able to bring to their own communities.

The booklet states the need for education in the performing arts when it stipulates:

> Education in the arts is essential. As man needs science to relate himself to outer reality, he needs art to become conscious of his inner life, ...Growing up with the arts holds the promise for a richer life and we owe it to the people of this nation that they are not deprived of it. In childhood they must learn, so that the sights and sounds of art can reach them in maturity.[4]

As the project was so carefully planned, it intended to eliminate what has become a most controversial issue in the attempt to encourage integration--that of busing children to other areas, as the booklet states:

> The scheduling of these services rendered by an expert faculty will be coordinated between the school communities in a manner to assure the most economical use of teacher time and to keep travel time at a minimum. It is an essential feature of the Mobile Academy that the services will be rendered where the children are, thus eliminating entirely the busing of children for both group and individual instruction.[5]

The final steps of the project will be the dissemination of the results of the experiment. This will be accomplished through the offices of the National Guild of Community Music Schools.

At the beginning of the project in 1969, an article appeared in the Arkansas Gazette on Sunday, July 27, describing the plans for this special project. The article was written by Janice Clark. Excerpts of it follow:

> His very name, Dr. Zipper, has a sort of Mary Poppins sound. And while he didn't come into Southeast

Arkansas borne on the winds by an unfurled umbrella,
he came with much the same general purpose as did
Mary Poppins when she floated in on people in the
movie bearing her name.

Dr. Zipper, a native of Austria, who for 39 years
has been director of the Manila Symphony Orchestra,
and is also director of the National Guild of Community
Music Schools, is devoting his life and a tremendous
amount of energy to spreading the gospel of music
and its consequent joys all over America.[6]

The article then described the staff who would work with
him, giving a brief resume about each that stated in part:

1) Michael M. Salzman, B.M., M.M.
   Supervisor and program coordinator
   Teacher of brass and percussion
   formerly Director of Music, District No. 29,
   Northfield, Illinois

2) Wilma McCool Salzman, B.M. and Teacher's Certificate from the Orff Institute of Salzburg, Austria
   In charge of pre-school and elementary music
   for children in primary grades

3) John Enis, pianist, B.M., M.M.
   In charge of group and individual piano instruction

4) Young Nam Kim, Korean violin virtuoso, B.M., M.M.
   formerly a member of the Seoul Symphony Orchestra, Won a national contest bringing him
   to USA to concertize.
   In charge of string program

5) Richard Bayer, B.M.
   In charge of group and individual woodwind
   instruction

6) Robert McHarry, B.M.
   Elementary education and piano

7) Virginia A. Bryan, B.F.A.
   In charge of instruction in the theatrical arts
   and dance

8) <u>Donald Swanson</u>, Guitarist. Professional training
   at Case-Western Reserve University and
   Cleveland Music School Settlement
   He teaches guitar.

9) <u>Daniel B. Prankratz</u>, B.M.
   Violincellist
   Teacher of 'Cello[7]

The article concluded with the following statement:

"This experiment is being watched by educators all
over the country. If we make this a success you may
help children all over the United States!" said Zipper.[8]

Herbert Zipper is a man of fine intellect and many
talents. He is one who should be known and recognized fully
by those who believe in the value of the arts for all people.
His continued devotion to the arts and arts education is not
equalled by many. A brief description of his background
reveals that he was born in Vienna, Austria, in 1904, and that
he became a naturalized citizen in this country in 1951. He
married Trudl Dubsky in 1939, who was a dancer who later
taught dance at the Music Center of the North Shore when
Herbert was its director. His educational resume shows that
he holds the Master's Diploma from the Vienna State Academy,
granted to him in 1926.

His professional career follows an impressive list of
achievements that include his being a conductor of the Vienna
Madrigal Association, professor at the Conservatory of Düssel-
dorf, Germany, and guest conductor in many and various
European cities in his early career. He is known for his
having composed the music for political satires in Paris, France
in 1926, and his having been the conductor of the Manila
Symphony Orchestra since 1941, as well as Head of the Academy of Music in Manila at the same period of time. After his
release from a Japanese prison camp in the Philippines during
World War II, he reorganized the Manila Symphony Orchestra
and gave some 130 concerts for members of the armed forces
and civilians during 1945 and 1946.

He arrived in the United States in 1946, and since that
time has been a lecturer on opera, symphony and composition
at the New School for Social Research in New York City; was

appointed musical director of the Brooklyn Symphony Orchestra in 1949 and was engaged each summer to return as conductor of the Manila Symphony Orchestra; he was also appointed conductor of the Chicago Businessmen's Orchestra in 1955.

He is best known to Guild members as the director of
the Music Center of the North Shore in Winnetka, Illinois from
1953 to 1967, was president of the National Guild of Community
Music Schools from 1957-1961, and was appointed its first
executive-director from 1967-1972 (for which he was largely
responsible for raising the funds). His most recent ventures
have taken him to the People's Republic of China where he
has conducted symphony concerts in Beijing, Tianjin and
Guangzhou.

After his diligent efforts to establish the Mobile Academy
in the Arts for All program, it must have been an immense
disappointment for him to have to deliver at least part of his
"Executive Office Report" at the 1969 annual Guild conference.
This report included the following information about the Mobile
Academy:

> By the middle of July telephone calls from Arkansas
> to Manila advised me that the anticipated funds for
> the continuation of the Mobile Academy beyond August
> had not been appropriated, and since Congress was
> adjourned there was no hope of getting funds from that
> source that would enable us to continue beyond Aug-
> ust.[9]

One can imagine Zipper's frustration with his being in
Manila and the forces which might make adjustments being in
Washington, D.C. and in Little Rock, Arkansas! As usual,
Zipper took action. His report continues as follows:

> SOS letters to the State Department of Education of
> Arkansas, to Dr. Arberg and others did not have any
> positive results. You will remember that I flew, at
> my own expense, from Manila to Little Rock on August
> 25 in order to meet the Governor and to save the
> situation, but I was not successful. The faculty of
> nine members was disbanded and the equipment now
> is stored at the Monticello High School. On October
> 21, I had a meeting at the State Department of Educa-
> tion of Arkansas in Little Rock with all State Officials

and Superintendents concerned, in order to explore all avenues for resuming operation of the Mobile Academy. The meeting did not yield any tangible results.[10]

It was further learned by Dr. Zipper that the funding of the Title I program had been passed by the House but not the Senate. It was further learned that even if the Senate appropriated the funds, such funds would not be available until early Spring, and the funds would have to be spent by June 30 of that year. Sadly it must be reported that the Mobile Academy Program was shelved.

For some pleasant news, the Manila Project received unexpected kudos from a member of Local 802, Arnold Fromme, who was unknown to Zipper. He wrote in the July 1969 issue of Allegro, the publication of Local 802 of the American Federation of Music in New York City:

> The Manila Symphony, with whom we performed under the very able direction of Oscar Yatco, has progressed from a near-amateur ensemble to a respectable professional organization with some excellent strings. One of the important factors responsible for this progress has been a program instituted by the John D. Rockefeller III Fund and the National Guild of Community Music Schools. It is one of the most effective and exciting examples of American musical foreign aid I have come across. Outstanding young American instrumentalists, conservatory graduates, are engaged for a period of at least a year to live in Manila performing in the orchestra and teaching advanced students, professionals and teachers. Due to the exceptional talent, industry and enthusiasm of all the participants, the results in this program have gone even beyond expectations.[11]

So while one Guild project was considered highly acceptable by knowledgeable outside observers, another had fallen on hard times. One who has not attempted fund-raising efforts cannot understand the extreme disappointment and frustration of having a program which was initially funded, suddenly curtailed for lack of approved funds.

It is important to note that the Title I project proposal

from the State of Arkansas had in truth included a statement
that the community itself would have sufficient funds in its
educational budgets (less than 4% of its total budgets) in the
future, but not immediately. Many communities had had projects rejected since they had not included such information in
their proposals.

The time element was the crippling component.   There
was no time for the State of Arkansas and the cooperating
counties, Ashley, Drew and Chicot, to adjust at such short
notice.   Three years hence, the program might well have been
absorbed by the local communities.   They would have had the
time to consider, plan and fund in their own budgets.

The Guild had many problems to solve and adjustments
to make.   After nearly thirty years of struggle and dedication,
the member schools of the National Guild of Community Schools
were able to see that many things were falling into place for
the Guild.   Grants were coming to its aid from both the private and public sectors.   For many years, the Guild had
remained too provincial, and it held very conservative views,
afraid naturally that otherwise it might be forced to give up
its artistic and educational independence.   Still it was unhappy
that no organization, public or private, or any one individual
seemed to come to its financial assistance on a regular basis.

Many directors of Guild schools were not sophisticated
fund raisers, so to speak, and had to realize that neither
private foundations nor public grantors were willing to underwrite on-going, existing programs.   Rather they preferred
to start new programs with some idea of how funded programs
could be continued by the community after a period of three,
or maximum of five years, of financial assistance by the private foundation or by a public program grant.

The plight of already existing musical organizations
seeking funds for their operations was singled out for special
note in The Arts Reporting Service, Number 7, November 20,
1970.   Its publisher was Charles C. Mark who was to succeed
Herbert Zipper as executive-director of the National Guild.
That issue states the following:

> Two national organizations exist in this country which
> year after year do their job quietly, contribute far
> more than their share to the musical betterment of

> the nation, and yet go comparatively unnoticed when
> the big money is passed around. Without them, we
> would be a poorer country indeed. ...they are
> National Guild of Community Music Schools and Young
> Audiences. The schools [public] continue to treat
> music as a subject too enjoyable to be part of the
> "hard" study areas, and as a result the general popu-
> lation continues to whistle in the dark ...[12]

Observations such as the above delight the hearts and
minds of those who work so diligently to raise funds for valid
programs, such as community music schools and schools of
the arts. While they cannot influence already decided opinions,
they can in fact alert those who are in positions to help in
the future distribution of monies for those independent organizations struggling to find the means to continue good programs.
Mr. Mark's astute comments were in reference to those schools
which are responsible for their continued programs.

In 1967 the National Guild of Community Music Schools
(as it was then known) did receive assistance which supported
a major move which was to establish more firmly the national
organization, per se. Through the continued efforts over the
years of Dr. Herbert Zipper, a breakthrough finally came.
The National Endowment for the Arts provided a major stimulus
to the community arts movement in this country when it began,
in 1967, to give a series of grants to the National Guild of
Community Music Schools. These grants enabled the Guild
to establish its national office. (The organization had been
incorporated in the state of New York in 1954.)[13]

This information is verified in The Arts Reporting Service in its December 17, 1972, issue (Volume II, Number 9),
which states:

> The National Guild of Community Music Schools has
> written to say that the National Endowment for the
> Arts does indeed support the good work of their mem-
> bers. The NEA has granted $17,500 to the Guild
> for the fifth consecutive year to support the services
> of the national office. These services include encour-
> aging the establishment of new community music schools,
> organizing cooperative programs with educational sys-
> tems, and assisting existing schools to expand their
> services and financial resources. ...The community

music schools need and deserve direct support from
the new Arts Expansion Program, if the intention of
this program is to affect the lives of disadvantaged
people most effectively.[14]

The new national office of the Guild was opened at 626
Grove Street in Evanston, Illinois. Its Executive Director was
Herbert Zipper, and he began his job with enthusiasm and
diligence. Since the executive directorship was a full-time
position, and he had no school of his own to operate, Zipper
could turn his attention to uniting the member schools in a
common bond to help them to speak as a unified body. The
schools could also take action in national issues if necessary.
But speaking as a national organization, their effect or clout,
if you will, became more powerful and forceful.

As an example of the kind of action that could be taken
is reflected in the action at the Annual Meeting of the National
Guild of Community Music Schools on November 11, 1969.

Dr. Zipper had contacted the Hull House Association
since he was now located in Evanston and was remarkably close
to their organization in Chicago, and his position allowed him
time to make necessary contacts to assist in establishing or
augmenting settlement arts programs, as well as encouraging
outside organizations to join the National Guild. He received
this reply which was read at the Guild's Conference in November, 1969 in New York City.

Dear Dr. Zipper:

Hull House is still alive, well and working hard in
Chicago but living beyond our means has caught up
with us. Faced with expenditures far beyond our income, with government grants shrinking and more
and more groups competing for the private dollars,
we have had to undergo serious program retrenchments.
These included all areas of programming and administration but since you are primarily interested in the
arts, I must report that we have closed our Art and
Music Camp, our central theatre, dance and music
programs and are doing everything we can to assist
our local satellite centers to develop community related, pay-as-you-go non-deficit arts programs.
There are still some music and dance classes, some

excellent high quality crafts, and we are heartened
by the plans for community drama directly related and
involving low income Blacks and Latins and Appala-
chians.

I am sorry that we will not be able to send someone
to your New York Conference.

[Signed] Robert T. Adams
Executive Director
Hull House[15]

Much discussion followed the reading of the letter. It
was clearly pointed out that the Hull House situation was in-
dicative of the present serious financial crisis faced by all
institutions which were dedicated and devoted to the arts.
The minutes of the meeting held on Saturday, November 8,
1969, at 8:00 p.m., reveal the following:

It was the sense of the meeting that the Guild should
take a positive position in this matter and that a
committee consisting of directors of Mid-Western schools
should prepare a resolution to be presented to the
Annual Meeting on November 11.[16]

The following resolution was prepared and sent to the
Hull House Association on November 11, 1969, from the
National Guild:

RESOLUTION RE HULL HOUSE ASSOCIATION

Adopted Unanimously at the Annual Meeting of the
National Guild of Community Music Schools
On November 11, 1969
Held at the Harlem School of the Arts, New York

WHEREAS, Hull House has been a pioneer in organizing the
central importance of music and related arts in improving
the quality of life for disadvantaged people, and
WHEREAS, Hull House has now felt it necessary to abandon
many of the music and related arts components of its programming, and
WHEREAS, the settlement movement in the U.S. as a whole
has traditionally looked to Hull House for leadership, and
now will undoubtedly be influenced by this action, and
WHEREAS, the National Guild of Community Music Schools,

representing the combined interests of some forty music
schools throughout the U.S. and Canada, stands willing
to assist Hull House in taking steps to find means to maintain this vitally important program, now

THEREFORE, be it resolved that the National Guild of Community Music Schools express their distress over this pre-
cipitous course of action, and urge that Hull House explore,
together with the Guild, represented by the Executive
Director, Dr. Herbert Zipper, all possible ways to maintain this vitally important program in the Chicago area.[17]

It seems appropriate to mention here that 1969 was the
year for the Society of the Third Street Music School Settlement to celebrate the 75th anniversary of its founding, the
first independent community music school in this country.
A bit of nostalgia is presented here as it appeared in the
anniversary booklet--the reminiscences of Harry Golden, the
American author and humorist:

> Music was one of the great joys among the poor im-
> migrant families of the Lower East Side of New York.
> If you walked along the street in the summer you
> heard music coming out of most of the open windows;
> that "one, two, three, four," of the little girls prac-
> ticing the piano; and the monotonous wail of the boys
> on the violin. More often, of course, the phonograph
> was going full blast; opera, Neapolitan folk songs,
> and cantorial chants, depending upon the neighborhood
> you were in.
>   And the people of each neighborhood left their
> deposits--some individual contributions, a uniqueness
> which helped to enrich America as she made way for
> new people.
>   For all these people of perhaps four or five differ-
> ent nationalities, music was not only the common lan-
> guage but also a common love.
>   Men made great sacrifices for music. In many
> homes, the purchase of a violin for the young son was
> included in the same budget along with the money for
> food, rent, and clothing. And thousands of little
> girls boasted, "I am taking piano lessons." In my
> own home, my mother had figured out a good system.
> She ordered me to hang around the house while my
> sister Matilda was getting her piano lessons, "and
> listen to everything the teacher says," my mother

warned. One day after my sister's lesson, the teacher
called me, "Come here, let me see what you could do."
My mother was embarrassed and offered both an apol-
ogy and that second fifty cents, but the teacher would
have none of it. She said that she had this two-for-
one experience in many homes, and she seemed happy
about the whole thing.

And in the midst of this hunger, along came the
Settlement House, which not only tried to give dignity
to the individual and help the newcomer to become a
citizen, but also offered free music lessons. Thousands of children learned to play and to love music.

And it did not matter that the talent was meager,
as in my case. What did matter was that we were
cultivating a taste for one of the basic values of our
existence as well as a considerable degree of self-
esteem and proof of individual worth.

Third Street Music School Settlement still stands
and its role is perhaps different from what it once
was. The neighborhood is different and so are the
people. But music has not changed. The love for it
is constant as always. Music lessons were perhaps
not America's greatest gift to the immigrant, but one
of the kindest and certainly the best intentioned.

Let us hope this gift can be bestowed along the
Lower East Side through many more succeeding generations at the Third Street Music School Settlement.[18]

These two organizations are the first and second community music schools in the United States. The Hull-House
Music School began in Chicago as a department of the larger
organization and accepting only those students who showed
special musical abilities. The Third Street Music School Settlement began on the Lower East Side of New York City teaching
music to those pupils who desired to study. As Mr. Golden
stated the amount of talent was not important, but the exposure to good music was.

Both organizations began in the 1890s, Hull-House Music
School in 1893 and the Third Street Music School Settlement
in 1894. Each grew over the years and included bit by bit
additional performance areas: dance and drama as well as
crafts and visual art work. Each attracted great attention
nationally and was admired enormously in its own community.
Each was supported largely by voluntary contributions; each

survived the shock of World War I followed by Prohibition and
the ravages of the Great Depression. Each remained in the
neighborhood in which it started, though each also spread into
satellite centers, as Mr. Robert T. Adams of Hull-House chose
to call them. Each held firm during the time of World War
II and the turbulent 1950s and 1960s. Each solved the problems of rising costs in the 1970s, though in different ways.
Hull-House chose to abolish the arts programs it had sponsored for so many years, although it encouraged its satellite
centers to continue the arts they had, so long as no additional
expenditures were incurred. Third Street on the other hand
preferred to remain in its community, work its program into
the neighborhood even more diligently by bringing its program
into the New York Public Schools in the after school hours.
Third Street went even further into a difficult period financially when a new building was purchased to expand its program and to put Third Street on East 11th Street in Manhattan.

One organization approached the economic problem by
supporting what might generally be considered the social
settlement house need, while the other supported the arts as
a tool in its community.

One unique aspect of this comparison is that neither
organization limited itself to teaching music only, though music
was without a doubt its heaviest concentration. Over the
years, the records show that each of them added drama, dance
and the visual arts. (This was also true of Henry Street,
Greenwich House, the 92nd Street Y, and many other schools
and departments.)

The involvement of the other arts in community music
schools became so common that in the early 1970s, member
schools began to request and to urge that the name of the
National Guild be changed to describe more accurately the
scope of the programs that the schools were undertaking.
Some of the directors were reluctant at first to change the
name, because the Guild had been successful at writing proposals and receiving grants from the private sector and the
federal, state and local agencies. It was thought that a change
of name might cause confusion when additional requests were
sent to various foundations, agencies and governmental offices. The topic was to be continued for some time yet.

As the executive director of the Guild, Herbert Zipper

wanted the member schools to express their own thoughts on
a given issue. He could be the spokesman, but only after he
knew their thinking. In a letter sent to all Guild members on
December 1, 1969, he stated the following:

> Mr. Howard Taubman of the New York Times who
> lately has assumed a policy-directing position on this
> newspaper, mentioned to me in Manila during the
> opening ceremonies of the cultural center, that he
> would be interested in learning more about my work
> in the Guild, and that I should see him whenever we
> both happened to be in New York.
>
> Last week on Wednesday, November 26 and on
> Friday, November 28, I had the opportunity to discuss
> with Mr. Taubman in great detail the present aims
> of the Guild and the workings of its member schools,
> the problems we face especially in regard to the rapid-
> ly changing cultural scene and the resulting financial
> difficulties.[19]

Howard Taubman stated that he would need to focus on
a special problem that was of importance to the Guild and of
interest to the New York Times. At a following meeting, the
two men discussed the topics that had been presented at the
National Guild's Annual Conference just recently held in New
York City. The topic agreed upon was the inclusion of the
contemporary popular forms within the curriculum of community
music schools. Zipper sent the above-mentioned letter to all
schools requesting answers to the following questions:

1. Do you offer presently courses in the popular arts
   and, if so, what kind?

2. If not, do you intend to offer such courses, and
   if so when?

3. If you don't have such intentions, what is your
   reason?

4. Do you find resistance among the members of your
   faculty, and if so, is it among a minority or a
   majority?

5. Do you find resistance among the members of your
   Board, and if so it is [sic] among a minority or a
   majority?

6. Do you feel that the inclusion of the popular arts
    does or would increase your student body substan-
    tially?

7. Does or would the inclusion of the popular arts
    add to your financial burden?

8. Does or would the inclusion of the popular arts
    affect the reputation of your school, and if so,
    which way?

9. Does finding of competent teachers pose a major
    problem?

10. What is your school's present total enrollment?[20]

Zipper wished to reflect the thinking of the member
schools, and he sent the questionnaire for definite and con-
clusive answers. His concluding comments stated:

> It is important, however, that I receive an answer
> from all schools, even if the majority of the questions
> cannot be answered, since for once I really need a
> 100 percent response, postmarked not later than
> December 12.[21]

The conscientious way in which Mr. Zipper approached
his work as executive director was to be admired and continued through the entire time he held the post.

On December 17, 1969, Zipper again wrote to the member
schools with information regarding governmental appropriations
for both the National Endowments of the Arts and the Humanities. He included the following information:

> Here is some news appropriate for a more cheerful
> Holiday Season. ...Total appropriation $15,790,000
> as compared with $11,500,000 for the past year. ...
> For "EDUCATION" Congress passed a total appro-
> priation bill based on a special resolution which in-
> creased the amount requested in the administration
> budget by one billion dollars. ...President Nixon,
> however, let it be known that he would not spend
> the additional money even if it was appropriated by
> Congress.

> Letters to the White House urging the Administration
> to authorize spending these additional funds, with
> special consideration for education in the arts, are
> now in order.[22]

He then expressed his concern for the appropriations
that would definitely affect the Guild, but he also displayed
some cautious optimism:

> To what extent all of this will affect the Guild will
> not be known before the end of January or the first
> half of February. However, I am in steady contact
> with the Deputy Chairman of the Arts Endowment,
> Mr. Michael Straight, and I entertain justified hope
> that eventually we will get the support requested for
> the current fiscal year. The same is true of the
> Rockefeller Foundation, since Norman Lloyd encouraged
> our request for renewal of grant support. Some of-
> ficials in the Office of Education are hopeful that
> public pressure will cause the President to release
> the additional funds which then would favorably af-
> fect our projects, especially those in cooperation
> with the Chicago and Arkansas public schools.
> In regard to our proposed national "Arts for All
> Fund", I have consulted numerous persons and in-
> stitutions, and in general their reactions have been
> very positive. Much will depend upon our ability to
> organize a strong Board of Trustees to head our
> "Fund". Your suggestions in regard to naming per-
> sons and possible contacts are welcomed and needed.
> Please give this your attention and let me have the
> benefit of your thoughts, and remember that this is
> of immediate importance to your own school.[23]

The Arts for All program had attracted such attention,
and Herbert Zipper saw the continuance of this program under
the leadership of the National Guild as one program which
would help to fund the national office and extend assistance
to those who wished to establish new schools. In a letter
dated March 2, 1970, Zipper sent the following information
to the member schools:

> You will recall, I am sure, that I was authorized at
> our Annual Conference 1969, New York City, to ex-
> plore the possibility of organizing an "Arts for All

Fund" of the Guild, designed to give financial aid to
our member schools, to assist in the organization of
new schools, and to assure permanence of our National
Guild Office.

A most important step toward realization of this
plan was finding a personality of unquestionable sta-
ture and prominence who would accept the chairmanship
of the "Fund". I am happy to be able to announce
that ARNOLD GINGRICH, publisher of "Esquire"
magazine, President of the Board of Trade, and well-
known author, has accepted the chairmanship of the
"Arts for All Fund". All who attended the last Annual Conference met Mr. Gingrich, and all who heard
him speak will agree that his acceptance constitutes
a big step forward toward attainment of our goals.
...The next step now is the formation of a Board
of Trustees of the "Fund". Mr. Gingrich feels that
this is our responsibility and although he wants to be
consulted on the final choice, we will have to propose
a list of nationally known personalities from various
parts of the United States and Canada. For the time
being all that is requested of you is the suggestion
of names from your own region. Will you kindly discuss this matter with your Board members and then
let me have your suggestions as promptly as possible.[24]

The efforts and energy put into the Arts for All Fund
proved to be worthwhile, and a most distinguished Board of
Governors was assembled and announced in a handsome booklet
reading as follows:

ARTS FOR ALL FUND

Board of Governors

Arnold Gingrich, Chairman & Publisher
   Esquire, Inc.
   New York, New York

Edward L. Bernays, President
   Bernays Foundation
   Cambridge, Massachusetts

Abe Fortas, Partner
   Fortas & Koven, Attorneys
   Washington, D. C.

<u>John H. MacFadyen</u>, President
    Associated Councils of the Arts
    New York, New York

<u>David C. Melnicoff</u>, Vice President
    The Federal Reserve Bank of
    Philadelphia, Pennsylvania

<u>Dr. Merle Montgomery</u>, Vice President
    Carl Fischer, Inc.
    New York, New York

<u>Col. Samuel R. Rosenbaum</u>, Trustee
    Music Performance Trust Funds, 1948-70
    Philadelphia, Pennsylvania

<u>Roger L. Stevens</u>, Chairman of the Board
    John F. Kennedy Center for the Performing Arts
    Washington, D. C.[25]

As chairman of the Arts for All Fund, Arnold Gingrich wrote an excellent message in the bulletin in which he expressed his ideas of what a Community Music School is, and it is reprinted here revealing the freshness he brought to the national organization:

> Community Music Schools are among the few institutions as much concerned with hand crafting an individual as with developing his talents. At member schools of the National Guild of Community Music Schools, a desire to learn is the only prerequisite to enrollment. Advice and guidance with personal problems is as much a part of the curriculum as exposure to artistic excellence.
> By whatever name they are known--Community Music Schools, Settlement Music Schools, or Community Music Centers--Guild Schools have performed a vital function in developing our nation's cultural heritage. Since their inception in the 1890's, Community Music Schools have fulfilled their basic purpose: to expose as many people as possible to the finest standards of the arts under the guidance of professional artists, persons who, but for these schools, would not find opportunity for such instruction.

The current state of unrest in our cities under-
scores an imperative need for improved communication
and re-dedication to active participation in the arts.
Community Music Schools, because of their philosophy
and history are in the forefront of meeting the cultural
and spiritual needs of all people. Through arts education, they have given literally untold numbers of
young and old the opportunity to broaden their vision
of humankind.

In recent years the National Guild of Community
Music Schools has undergone a remarkable growth in
its membership. Community Music Schools now are
found in many cities from the east to the west coasts.
At the Annual Guild Conference in 1970, delegates
announced the formation of a national Board of Governors for the new "Arts For All Fund". This fund will
enable the Guild to strengthen music school services
where they now exist and to establish them in communities where they are not currently available.

It is with the sincerest conviction that I have accepted the chairmanship of the "Arts For All Fund".
I am convinced that through financial participation of
corporations, foundations and individuals, it will provide the means for bringing people together productive-
ly. Under the umbrella of arts participation better
human understanding will be achieved.

[signed] Arnold Gingrich[26]

The realistic approach, that is that any one source of
funding will not last forever, was used in the thinking of those
who established The Arts For All Fund as shown in the bulletin under the sections entitled "Purpose" and "Meeting the
Needs--Now":

The "Arts For All Fund" will make possible greatly
expanded Community Music School services at a time
when community involvement in and understanding of
the arts can best make a meaningful contribution to
the fabric of our lives.

The Fund's Board of Governors is charged with
the responsibility of planning a ten-year development
program and detailing budgetary requirements for:

1. Assuring the permanence of the National Office
   of the Guild.
2. Rendering financial aid to member schools of
   the Guild throughout the United States.
3. Assisting in the initial financing of new schools
   to be organized in areas where Community Music
   School services are not now available.[27]

And continuing in the next section of the bulletin, the
practical side of the question is addressed quite clearly:

> The Office is partly supported by dues from its member
> schools. But its major support in recent years has
> come from the National Endowment for the Arts, a
> federal agency created by Act of Congress in 1965,
> and the Rockefeller Foundation. However, the Guild
> Office cannot continue to count on its two major sup-
> porters indefinitely since their funds are provided
> only to give impetus during the formative years. It
> must seek and find support from other sources on a
> much broader nationwide basis.[28]

Concluding statements in the Arts For All Fund bulletin
are as follows:

> Unlike conservatories, where the major thrust is the
> preparation for earning a livelihood in music, Commu-
> nity Music Schools treat music and other performing
> arts as an artistic and cultural experience that is an
> important part of one's life and a help to good citi-
> zenship. ...Some educators hold that music is a
> key to learning to read. Some physicians find music
> another tool in their armamentarium for the treatment
> of mental illness. Some psychologists believe that the
> interpersonal relationship inherent in the music les-
> sons, as given in a Community Music School is helpful
> in treating some of the ills of society.[29]

The Arts For All Fund was launched as planned at the
National Guild's annual meeting in Cleveland, Ohio, in November 1970.

One learns from the "Report on the Activities of the
Executive Office of the National Guild" (covering a time span
from October 1, 1969, to September 30, 1970) that the work

indicated to be done by Arts for All Fund was really already
in its formative stages when it states:

> The New Orleans Philharmonic Symphony Orchestra,
> aware of the lack of competent string instruction in
> New Orleans, especially on the elementary level, in-
> vestigated the possibility of offering such instruction
> to schools in New Orleans. For this purpose the
> Guild's consulting services were requested by the
> orchestra management. Since the concert and rehear-
> sal schedule of the orchestra members makes them un-
> available for a regular instruction schedule, a plan
> was adopted to offer Suzuki type string instruction
> by employing specialists for this purpose. In addition,
> the citywide organization of a training orchestra for
> elementary and secondary school children was en-
> visioned.
> A preliminary proposal and budget was written by
> the executive director of the Guild and subsequent
> negotiations with the Rockefeller Foundation led to an
> initial funding of the project of $18,500 by the Rocke-
> feller Foundation, in addition to some financial com-
> mitment by ten participating elementary schools. ...In
> January, 1971, the executive director of the Guild
> will spend some time in New Orleans in order to eval-
> uate the ongoing program and to plan for its expan-
> sion.[30]

One of the reasons for establishing the national office
was for just such a purpose, and this example presents an
early success. The Guild was not required to set up the
program, but the Guild's executive director was selected to
evaluate the program. This reflects the esteem in which the
Guild was held by important musical organizations and by public school administrative officers.

Another example of the continuous cooperation of the
Guild and its executive director is shown by efforts made
to expand and to suggest methods of financial support for the
Newark (NJ) Community Center of the Arts. It is related
in the same report.

> In consultation with the executive director of the
> Guild, a long range plan was developed for the sup-
> port of this institution, which had been established

in 1968 with the aid of the Guild. For this purpose
the executive director attended meetings at the school
and at the Prudential Insurance Company of America
in Newark. A proposal was submitted to the local
business community and to the Ford Foundation.
For a 4-year period the Ford Foundation subsequently
made a grant in the total amount of $200,000 to be
matched with an equal amount by the business community.[31]

The activities of the executive director kept him extremely busy and occupied when the report also shows other
consultation with various organizations:

The following institutions have contacted the Guild
for the purpose of planning projects that will offer
Community Music School services to their respective
communities:

University of Southern California
University of Minnesota
University of South Florida
Cincinnati Symphony Orchestra
Executive Committee of the Chicago Orchestral Asso-
    ciation
Cornish School of Allied Arts, Seattle, Washington
Washington State Council for the Arts
Wisconsin College Conservatory, Milwaukee

and various other community and civic associations
in various parts of the country.[32]

Zipper makes a personal observation:

It has been our experience that once a project has
proved its worth to a community and its benefits are
demonstrable, the establishment of a sound financial
basis becomes feasible. The funding of a new program
in its initial phases poses the greatest difficultiesm
[sic] and it is for this purpose that the Guild expects
the ARTS FOR ALL FUND to provide the necessary
means.[33]

In addition he indicated the services rendered to the
Guild's own member schools:

In addition to the regular communication between the
Executive Office and the Guild Schools, special consulting services were rendered and field trips were
made to schools in the following cities during the fiscal
year 1969-70:

Boston, Massachusetts
Newton, Massachusetts
Rochester, New York
Detroit, Michigan
St. Louis, Missouri
Portland, Oregon
San Francisco, California[34]

And according to the list and record of his consultations with
both those outside the Guild and the member schools within
the Guild, he recorded thirty-two consultations spread over
ninety-three days during the time period indicated in his report. The National Guild of Community Music Schools was,
indeed, realizing the benefit of having an executive director
who was capable and dedicated to the work of spreading
the word about the Guild. He was also a man of excellent
reputation and was recognized and accepted by the world of
musical organizations and musicians, as well as by educational
institutions and educators themselves.

It was a great shock to all the members of the National
Guild when on January 31, 1972, Herbert Zipper sent the
following letter to all the Guild member schools:

To use Harris Danziger's words: "A new era begins,"
for the Guild as well as for me. I have accepted the
position of Project Director that was offered to me by
the University of Southern California's School of the
Performing Arts.
...Consequently I will serve the Guild in my present
capacity until July 1, 1972, when this office will move
to Washington, D.C., and I will move to the Los Angeles area. My work there will start on September
1, 1972.[35]

The Guild president, Harris Danziger, sent a letter to
the directors of all the Guild schools stating that Zipper would
soon be leaving his post as executive director of the Guild
but with a few comforting words:

As we wish Herbert godspeed, good health and fortune,
and as we congratulate the USC on landing such an
individual, we must also realize that he leaves a situation full of tremendous possibilities for our futher
[sic] growth.

First Herbert is not leaving the Guild. His duties
at the USC will include the establishment of new community music and art centers. [36]

While this information of Herbert Zipper's resignation
and acceptance of his new position may have been sudden to
the majority of Guild directors, it was not so to the Board
of Directors and its Executive Committee. New and different
organizational plans had been going on for some time. This
is also explained in Danziger's letter to the Guild members.

...the Board of Directors and its Executive Committee,
which have been meeting regularly since the Annual
Conference, have set up a new structure for our work.
Briefly, the Guild's activities will be divided into three
geographical regions: East, Middle West and West.
(Incidently, the western region will be in charge of
Herbert.*) It is hoped that this structure will elicit
the creative energies of individual directors and keep
us in close contact with the Guild throughout the
year. [37]

This was the first step that the Guild had taken to
divide itself into regions or districts. The size of the organization had grown to such an extent that a more manageable
format was needed. All meetings could not continue to be of
national scope. Closer proximity to member schools and shorter distances to travel for meetings would save both time and
money for the member schools in the three regions, yet meaningful contacts could be made more easily, and more joint efforts could be undertaken by the member schools of their own
regions. It was so successful that later there were even more
sub-divisions, but until then the national scene was divided
into ten regional chapters:

I.   New York Metropolitan

---

*Mr. Danziger probably meant that Herbert would be in charge
of the western region, not the other way around.

Much enthusiasm has been generated about this sub-
dividing of the country into more efficient smaller groups.
Since the annual meetings are held once a year in the Fall,
the regional chapters may arrange for chapter meetings at
times most convenient for them.   The executive director is
frequently invited to regional meetings as a consultant.   All
of this has proved to be very acceptable to all parties involved.

There was, of course, much concern in the minds of
the directors of the schools as to who would be chosen to fill
the position of executive director.   In his usual competent
manner, Herbert Zipper answered this question in his letter
of January 31, 1972.   Much to the credit of the Board of
Directors of the Guild and the Executive Committee, arrangements had been completed for an easy transition.   The letter
read in part:

> During the past months the Guild's Executive Com-
> mittee and I have worked out most of the details for
> a smooth transfer of responsibilities of this office.
> Most important, we were able to engage Charles C.
> Mark to become the Guild's new Executive Director.
> Mark and I have become close friends during the past
> five years and it was he who was most sympathetic
> to our work during the initial years of "Endowment"
> support.
>   Charles C. Mark has a master's degree in social
> work.   He was the first Executive Director of the
> Winston-Salem Arts Council (1958-61); the Founding
> Director of the Arts and Education Council of St.
> Louis (1961-64); Arts Consultant to the White House
> (1964-65); Director of State and Community Operation
> and Director of Planning and Analysis of the National
> Endowment for the Arts (1965-69); President of the
> Performing Arts Council of the Los Angeles Music

Center (1969-70); and, since 1970, Publisher of the
Arts Reporting Service. There is no better man in
America for the Guild.[39]

Zipper sent his last communication to Guild members on
May 16, 1972, in which he communicated the new address for
the national office and indicated that future communications
should be sent to Charles C. Mark:

> During the next weeks I will be engaged in making
> all the preparations for a smooth transfer of respon-
> sibilities to my friend and successor, Charles C. Mark,
> including the moving of our National Office from here
> to the Washington, D.C. area.
> Please note that from July 1 on, the new address
> of the Guild office will be:
>
> National Guild of Community Music Schools
> 9214 Three Oaks Drive
> Silver Spring, Maryland...
>
> This will be most likely my last circular Guild
> letter that will be sent to you, and, to be candid,
> I confess I am doing this with mixed emotions. These
> have been five hectic but very enjoyable years, and
> although I had hoped for much greater progress I
> believe the Guild is in better shape now than it was
> five years ago. ...
> My best wishes go to you, your associates, your
> faculty, and the welfare of your institution.[40]

And so the "new era" for the National Guild of Community Music Schools began on July 1, 1972 with Charles C.
Mark as the new executive director of the organization. An
undated communication from him was received by the directors
of member schools in early September, 1972. It read as follows:

> It's difficult to know how to start communication with
> all of you since some of you I don't know at all and
> some I know only slightly. But let me begin by saying
> that I will be as open and informative about the ac-
> tivities of the Guild as is humanly possible, leaning
> perhaps toward the prudent to avoid raising hopes
> unnecessarily. I have spent a good deal of time in

the past few weeks pouring over the files and available material about each school, so I do feel I have
begun to understand some of the problems and accomplishments of all the schools. In addition to getting
acquainted at least on paper, here are some of the
highlights of the past month.

The Guild has been granted $17,500.00 by the
National Endowment for the Arts on a matching basis
toward the operation of the Guild offices. This grant
has become virtually an annual occurrence and testi-
fies to the confidence which the NEA has in our work.
Matching funds, over and above the usual important
income from dues, is [sic] now being sought. The
prognosis is good.

A second grant from the NEA is in the last stages
of approval. This $45,000.00 non-matching amount
will be used to provide direct fund raising and management counselling to member schools. The Carl W.
Shaver Co. has been tentatively engaged to continue
the work they have begun as our research and development counsel, becoming in effect our field staff.
...Fund raising services were the most requested assistance by the schools (almost unanimously). The
next question then is whether other recommendations
resulted from the study.

The answer is that a number of important recommendations have been made, and these have led to
some important new ideas and plans. All will be revealed in November in Philadelphia at the Annual Conference.

...I hope to spend considerable time during October
traveling to see as many schools as possible, mostly
in the East. I will call or write for appointments.
I hope to get to know all of you very soon. Meanwhile, if I can be helpful to you in any way, please
let me know. [41]

True to his word, Mr. Mark organized the conference
in the Fall of 1972 in Philadelphia. On May 10, 1973, he sent
the following memo to the Members of the National Guild:

At the annual conference in Philadelphia I made a
statement that I would bring Guild matters of importance to your attention whether these matters were
good news or bad news. As we are approaching our

annual Spring meeting, I am therefore bringing to
your attention matters which are both good and bad
news, but unfortunately mostly bad news.

1. After several conversations and exchanges of
enthusiasm, the Rockefeller Brothers Fund has elected
not to act favorably on our request for a grant which
would in part finance the ongoing programs of the
Guild and allow for modest expansion. As you know,
the Guild office is supported partly by a grant from
the National Endowment for the Arts and partly by
required matching funds. In the past these matching
funds have come from a private foundation which has
a policy of automatically terminating its grants after
a certain number of years. Therefore, the RBF re-
fusal has put us in a very bad financial situation.

2. Mrs. Pat Shipman, my assistant, found the in-
stability of the arts more than she bargained for, and
because of heavy personal obligations has found it
necessary to accept another job. ...The proposal
to the National Endowment for the next fiscal year
seems to be progressing favorably, but still must
pass several more hurdles this Spring. (I hope to
have some news when we meet on the 21st.)

I hope to see all of you on May 21 at the Lighthouse
Music School when we talk about these problems and
opportunities among others at our Spring meeting.
Until then, I send you all my best personal regards.[42]

As part of his duties and responsibilities, Charles Mark
wrote an annual report covering the activities of the National
Guild of Community Music Schools which was primarily intended
as a report for National Endowment for the Arts. It was to
show the progress made under the grants received from the
National Endowment for the period from September, 1972 to
July 1973.

The first part of the report indicated the change of
executive-directors in July, 1972 which also necessitated
the move of its national office to Washington, D. C. It further reported the arrangement the Guild had made with the
C. W. Shaver Company of New York City. Shaver's is a distinguished consulting and fund-raising firm. During the annual
meeting of the Guild from November 12th through the 15th,
1972, a task force was appointed by the president to develop
a detailed plan for the Guild to follow in strengthening the

Guild and its forces and to find new ways to expand the membership of the National Guild.

The task force met for two days in New York City and made recommendations which were unanimously supported by the Board of Directors on February 9, 1973. These recommendations were as follows:

1. That the name of the Guild be changed to "National Guild of Community Schools of Music and the Arts".

2. That the membership be opened to non-music arts schools without restrictions other than those of quality, and that the membership requirements be revised to reflect these changes.

3. That a committee be appointed to examine the question of standards for membership of music schools and those community schools which are not currently offering music training as part of their program.[43]

The above recommendations were later approved by the Guild at a meeting on May 21, 1973. Other matters about informational workshops which were to be held in four different locations for Guild members were explained. The report ended with the following paragraph:

> As the fiscal year draws to a close, two new schools are beginning to serve their cities, and 12 other communities are asking for help to organize music schools. Those agencies founded in the past ten years which are offering instruction in art forms other than music are inquiring about the program of the Guild and showing interest in joining in a national association of community [sic--organizations] serving arts schools. The C. W. Shaver Co. has completed its long range study and stands prepared to offer assistance for a national endowment campaign in the future, providing the national board is strengthened and expanded. If sufficient funds are found in the coming year to support the needs of the Guild, there is every reason to believe that the community school movement can begin to make substantial progress.[44]

Working with the Task Force and upon the request of the membership, the C. W. Shaver Company prepared a comprehensive guide for fund raising and financial administration. The Shaver Company would also have a member of the firm present at regional workshops to discuss financial and fund-raising problems with administrators and board members of the member schools and any other interested and invited guests. These workshops proved to be extremely helpful to members of Guild schools.

The workshops were scheduled in the eastern part of the country first. (Since the California area had had some consultation already by Guild representatives, it was decided not to go out there again so soon, but to wait until the Fall of the year to go west.) The first workshop was held in Buffalo, New York where 32 attendees were present from as far west as Cleveland, Ohio and as far east as New York City (not to leave out Rochester and Syracuse). The second such workshop was held in Winnetka, Illinois where 19 people assembled. The last two were held in Boston. At the first in Boston, 30 registered with 5 guests present, and the second had 43 registrations with six who did not appear.

Thus the four workshops attracted the attention of 118 concerned individuals, with interest shown by 129. Obviously, this was truly an important area to both administrators and board members. Several suggested that in the future administrators and board members could be placed in two separate groups meeting simultaneously.

Attached to the report was a covering letter dated August 24, 1973, from Charles Mark to the members of the Guild which contained the following information:

> The attached is the annual report of the activities of the Guild and the executive office. Primarily it is prepared for the National Endowment for the Arts as an evaluation of the progress made under the grants received from that agency. It does not cover the time from July 1, until the present.
> I wish that some good news could be reported at this time, but as the report states, no funds have been available for any activities since July 1, and my time has necessarily been spent pursuing other means of income. As a result of these efforts it has become

necessary for me to submit my resignation as of November 1, 1973.

...I remain devoted to the cause of the community music schools and intend to assist in every way possible short of assuming full time responsibility. Please consider me available and willing to help whenever you believe I can be helpful. Meanwhile, until after the conference I shall be here and working for you as time permits.

Sincerely,

[signed] Chuck Mark[45]
Charles C. Mark

The National Guild was now faced with one of the most severe situations it had ever experienced in its history. This was not an unknown happening, nor was it an exclusively Guild experience. Several organizations faced identical dilemmas. Since the initial days of government grants in the 1960s, institutions and organizations who had received such grants became dependent on them (erroneously!) as an annual and expected grant. Many had not made proper preparation for the time when such funds were no longer available to them. And valuable employees naturally depend on continuous earned income. Neither individuals nor organizations can continue to exist without a considerable amount of financial support to be used as a backlog on which to rely, or enough income from its own endowment funds to be able to continue operations until grant funds arrive to be used as requested. Some organizations report that it took nearly a year for them to receive monies allocated to them by grant letters of intent. This is not generally true of foundation grants.

To state the resolutions to this anguishing problem, it is best to say simply that the National Endowment for the Arts sent the following letter dated May 15, 1974, to the Guild president, Dorothy Maynor, who was also the founder and director of the Harlem School of the Arts in New York City:

Dear Miss Maynor:

It is a pleasure to inform you that Grant A 40-31-159 in the amount of $32,000 is awarded to the National

> Guild of Community Music Schools, Inc. Grant funds
> are for costs of maintaining your national office to
> improve inter-school communication, and to provide
> fund-raising/financial management and artistic/adminis-
> trative consultant service programs as outlined in
> your application (AO3382-73) dated December 27, 1972;
> revised April 5, 1974, and correspondence referred to
> below. The grant starting date is October 1, 1973 and
> the grant ending is December 30, 1974.[46]

And so the National Endowment for the Arts did recognize the efforts of the National Guild and saw fit to appropriate
funds to help implement the program as envisioned by the
Guild. This grant was appropriately mentioned in the National
Guild's report of its May 1974 meeting:

> It is the principal goal of the National Guild in 1974,
> with the support of our National Endowment grant, to
> offer programs aimed at: strengthening underdevel-
> oped member schools; building new schools of the arts;
> and inviting the membership of schools which are al-
> ready sensitively serving their communities' needs as
> well as placing an emphasis on high artistic and edu-
> cational standards.[47]

The 1973-74 season had been one of extreme difficulty
for the National Guild, and the problems had at times seemed
insurmountable. Finding a new executive-director for the
Guild who would be willing to join the staff of a national organization, particularly one which was facing such difficult
problems at the moment, and even more, that this person was
to be the chief executive officer responsible for the total
operation of the organization, made the selection much more
difficult.

Members of the Guild, particularly those in the New
York Metropolitan Regional Chapter, proved willing to help
in whatever ways they could. The Guild was fortunate to
find a woman with a strong music background who came recommended by a board member, and who had had experience in
running a state-supported arts agency in Michigan. By late
Fall or early Winter of that season, Dorothy Amarandos joined
the staff as executive-director of the organization.

Also in a spirit of assistance, the C. W. Shaver Company offered temporary office space at their Madison Avenue

offices at a very reasonable rate. By extremely careful use
of what limited funds were available, the Guild was able to
stay alive. One member school offered (with the approval of
its Board of Directors) an interest-free loan over a short
period of time to relieve the immediate cash flow problem experienced by the Guild. (It was very shortly repaid.)

The community schools of the arts which are members
of the National Guild are honorable, hard-working schools
which struggle daily to raise the funds to continue their normal operations. The experience of seeing the Guild in such
a temporary financial bind, brought fear and terror to their
minds. Many solutions were offered. The most devastating
of these included doing away with the position of executive-
director altogether, or worse, to close the national office
completely.

After having struggled for thirty years without a national office, those who remembered when there was none stood
firm on the premise that the establishment of the national office had been the greatest accomplishment of the National
Guild throughout its history. For those Guild members who
were younger or perhaps less experienced, it was understandable that the problems of maintaining and running the national
office had never been completely understood by them, since
they had generally operated in a local venture, not one on
the national scale. The operating costs of the Guild and the
keeping of qualified people to run the office could seem fright-
ening, indeed.

Many aspects of the establishment of the national office
were providential. A very large number of circumstances
came together at one time:

1. Seed money had become available on both the
   national and state levels allowing for arts education to be at least partially supported.

2. Educational trends had shown success in several
   new approaches to teach the young--even the very
   young, i.e. Operation Headstart for pre-school
   children.

3. The newly understood and emphasized teaching
   methods of Shinichi Suzuki in Japan; Zoltan Kodaly

in Hungary; re-evaluation and recognition of Emile
Jaques Dalcroze and his eurhythmic techniques.

4. The impact of the MENC and its state affiliated
   chapters actively bringing much information about
   music education to the public at large.

5. The national significance of the American Symphony
   Orchestra League and its effect on communities
   to support professional orchestras, community
   orchestras, college orchestras, etc.

6. The establishment of Arts Councils, state and
   local, which made available arts experiences to
   communities all over this country.

7. And, of course, the development of community
   music schools throughout the United States and
   Canada, and the establishment of the National
   Guild of Community Music Schools later to be called
   the National Guild of Community Schools of the
   Arts.

Each of these examples is a significant part of the cultural
development that has grown within our own country over the
last thirty years.

And at this same time period there was also Herbert
Zipper who stood ready to spring at the opportunity to bring
the arts to all. He was in a unique situation. His school
in Winnetka was operating smoothly so that a transition to a
new director or management was quite possible, he saw the
need for the national office and was the one with the background and experience to become the executive-director of the
Guild; he knew all the member schools and their directors.
He was also fired with the enthusiasm and spirit to work diligently toward bringing the Guild to its full capacity. He
had the same qualities of leadership as did Janet D. Schenck
and Johan Grolle. His personal life allowed him to do that
which he thought was necessary. Herbert Zipper took the
ball and ran with it!

The very thought of eliminating the national office would
have been tantamount to the complete destruction of the Guild
itself. Some of the member schools had looked forward or

expected the Guild to come to the financial assistance of its
member schools. Now it seemed that the schools should come
to the rescue of the Guild.

The former was, of course, partially realized when arrangements for the Music Performance Trust Funds to support
musical programs in the communities of the members seemed
one way for some financial realization to come through the
national office to member schools. It was, however, unrealistic
to hope that financial returns to member schools could become
a regular, secure source of income. The major organizations
do not supply financial aid to their constituents, including
the Music Educators National Conference (MENC), the National
Association of Schools of Music (NASM), the American Council
for the Arts (ACA), the United Neighborhood Houses (UNH),
and the National Federation of Settlements (NFS). The National
Guild of Community Schools of Music and the Arts (later shor-
tened to the National Guild of Community Schools of the Arts),
was in the same position exactly as the other national organizations.

Funds can frequently be raised by a national organization to undertake a special project or study with the cooperation of its institutional members, but national organizations
of this kind can seldom, if ever, raise funds for the basic
operations of individual member schools. The National office
can offer services to help struggling schools with administrative and structural problems and with fund-raising techniques,
advice, and suggestions. These were the very kinds of things
that the national office was attempting to accomplish.

Mrs. Amarandos walked into a hotbed when she accepted
the position of executive-director of the Guild. Her previous
experiences had been such that she felt she would be capable
of handling the National Guild's problems, if all worked
together.

There was also some confusion in the minds of some as
to what responsibilities were assigned to whom, especially to
the executive-director. That person is an employee of the
National Guild and takes his directions from the national board
of directors, and primarily from the elected president of the
Guild. Many members of the Guild seemed to feel that all the
administrative responsibilities were handled by the executive-
director. Such was never the case.

Since Herbert Zipper had functioned previously for four years as president of the Guild (1957-1961), and since he was now the executive-director of the Guild, and since it was recognized that he was a fine leader, it was thought by some that he was certainly the one to make all decisions. In reality, Dr. Zipper constantly consulted the president of the Guild, who was Harris Danziger, during Zipper's six years as the executive-director. Most Guild members listened to his good counsel and were generally pleased with his advice; thus they tacitly accepted the fact that he was in charge of the total operation.

It is readily understandable that such a mistake could be made. Directors of Schools of the Arts have their own internal problems to solve, and it is a comfortable feeling if someone in authority could and would make the necessary decisions correctly. This in turn would relieve the members of the burdensome responsibilities having to do with the proper directions for the Guild to take. Perusal of Guild minutes, directors' reports, publications, etc., will reveal that all major proposals or steps were properly presented and approved by the membership. The mechanical details were, indeed, the responsibility of the national office and its director, including the preparation of requests for grants from the public as well as the private sectors.

Once again member schools began to question the lengthy name of the organization, The National Guild of Community Schools of Music and the Arts. Dorothy Amarandos polled the membership for suggestions and ultimately for voting on a name change, if there was to be one. In the December 12, 1974, issue of the Guildletter, the report was as follows:

RESULTS OF THE VOTE FOR A SIMPLIFIED NAME

Out of a quorum vote of 28 members, 15 votes were cast for: "National Guild of Community Schools of the Arts".

3 votes were cast for: "National Guild of Schools of the Arts".

4 votes were cast for: "National Guild of Community Schools of Music and the Arts".

1 vote was cast for: "National Guild of Community Music Schools".

5 votes were cast with imaginative new name
suggestions (all different) ...Interestingly enough,
15 votes were cast for the addition of the subtitle:
"An Association of Community and College Preparatory
Schools of Music, Dance, Drama and the Visual Arts".
There you have it, folks, and unless we hear objections to the contrary, we will hereafter call ourselves "NATIONAL GUILD OF COMMUNITY SCHOOLS
OF THE ARTS" with subtitle when space permits.[48]

There were apparently no objections from the membership,
and the title was changed in all the appropriate places.

Despite the financial problems that existed and which
devoured much time at meetings, constructive activity continued for the development of projects and efforts that had been
in discussion for some time. One of the efforts was the revision of the by-laws of the organization, primarily to restruc-
ture them so that the terminology would encompass the larger
scope of the Guild which now included many arts forms, not
exclusively music.

Dorothy Amarandos worked very hard to produce a set
of regulations that would be acceptable to the member schools.
This project had been begun as early as the 1973-1974 season.
Up to now it had been put on the back burner, so to speak.
Until the problem of the replacement of the executive-director,
after the resignation of Charles Mark (announced in August,
1973) had been accomplished, nothing could be satisfactorily
completed. The document that was produced bore the title
"Code of Regulations," and it was approved by the membership
on November 9, 1976. Its preamble states in part:

<u>Preamble</u>

We, the representatives of Schools of the Arts and
individuals, believing that the perpetuation of the
arts is fundamental to our very existence and that
instruction and expert individual education in all art
disciplines is an increasingly important influence and
vital factor for the welfare of all persons of all ages
in all social, ethnic and economic groups as well as
communities, local, national and international, do as-

sociate ourselves as the National Guild of Community Schools of the Arts to make this education more universally available. [49]

In order to clarify its outlook and intentions it further states in part:

> The purposes for which the corporation has been formed are as follows:
> To provide a central organization through which the community, neighborhood, settlement or college preparatory schools of the arts, and other educational organizations may become members of or affiliated with the Corporation and may centralize their activities, coordinate their aims, and effectively cooperate with each other and with other social agencies or community, state, regional, national and international levels through the systemization of methods and teaching standards; ...to foster and promote a greater public appreciation and understanding of the ideals and importance of the community schools of the arts; to broaden and extend the general interest in said schools and the effective work thereof, and to aid in the establishment of music, dance, drama and the visual arts as permanent and vital influences in the society; ...in general, to promote and assist in the development and improvement of sound philosophies of arts education, their greater utilization, and in the public understanding and appreciation thereof; ...The statement of purposes contained in this Code of Regulations is intended to implement (but not to state purposes or authorize powers different from or in addition to) those purposes for which the National Guild of Community Music Schools was organized, as set forth in its Articles of Incorporation. [50]

The Code of Regulations of the National Guild of Community Schools of the Arts, Inc. re-affirmed the goals and ideals of the original organization, The National Guild of Community Music Schools. It further includes the following articles: I--Membership; II--Meetings of the Members; III--Trustees; IV--Officers; V--Committees; VI--Fiscal Year; VII--Corporate Seal; VIII--Amendments; IX--Order of Business;

X--Indemnification. After a period of three years, the Code
of Regulations was put into formal, printed form in 1979.

A most interesting undertaking was started by the
National Guild in the Fall of 1976 in the form of an Internship
Program designed to train administrative personnel who might
then find employment at one of the Guild schools. Frequently
a request came from one school to all the others to help in
finding a knowledgeable, reliable person for an administrative
position in the school. Nowhere was there a program to train
people to assume these vitally important positions.

The Guild presented a "Summary," a report of the project, in October of 1977, in which the following information
was given:

> Traditionally, there has been no formal program of
> study designed to prepare qualified candidates to
> manage these unique arts/education/service facilities.
> But it was not until the early '70's that such a need
> was felt. At that time, an increasing number of pub-
> lic schools were terminating or curtailing their music
> and art programs for budgetary reasons. Existing
> Guild schools were forced to expand their own of-
> ferings to take up the slack; and, to meet this chal-
> lenge, new schools were opened in previously unserved
> areas. These two occurrences created an unprecedent-
> ed demand for administrators familiar with the philo-
> sophy and management of non-profit, community-based
> schools of the arts.
> The National Guild began to meet that demand when
> it implemented its administrative Internship Program
> in September, 1976.[51]

It was carefully planned to select five host schools from
the ranks of successfully established and operating Guild
schools. The directors of the five schools and Dorothy Amarandos, Executive-Director, and Dr. Lester Glick, President
of the National Guild, were to function as the Internship Committee. Marcy Horwitz (who was later to serve in a very prominent position with the Guild) was engaged as the project
coordinator.

After establishing guidelines for the Internship Program,

the Committee began to solicit applications from qualified candidates for eight available Intern positions. Qualified candidates were those individuals who had already completed serious academic or pre-professional training in their chosen artistic discipline. There were approximately thirty-five applications received.

The time span of the project was to be three thirteen-week sessions, Fall, Winter, Spring. Stipends were to be $1,500 per each thirteen-week session. The program was jointly sponsored by the following: (1) The Cleveland Foundation; (2) The Abner D. Unger Foundation; (3) The National Endowment for the Arts.[52]

The Schools involved were:

Cleveland Music School Settlement
11125 Magnolia Drive
Cleveland, Ohio   44106
   Howard Whittaker, Executive Director

David Hochstein Memorial Music School*
50 North Plymouth Drive
Rochester, New York   14614
   Helen Tuntland, Director

Music Center of the North Shore
300 Green Bay Road
Winnetka, Illinois   60093
   Kalman Novak, Director

Neighborhood Music School
100 Audubon Street
New Haven, Connecticut   06511
   Kenneth Wendrich, Director

Settlement Music School
416 Queen Street
Philadelphia, Pennsylvania   19147
   Sol Schoenbach, Director[53]

---

*Hochstein's Intern, Juan Vasquez, was accepted for the Fall Session. However, personal commitments prevented Mr. Vasquez from participating at the last minute. Hochstein, therefore, did not participate in the actual running of the Internship Program as had been planned.

The candidates were all interviewed either in person or by telephone by members of the Internship Committee. The following applicants were accepted and assigned to one of the member schools:

Name	Artistic Interest	Assigned to
Sally Bauer	Music (pianist)	Music Center of the North Shore
Armand Belmonte	Music (pianist)	Neighborhood Music School (New Haven)
Bradford Boardman	Arts and Crafts	Cleveland Music School Settlement
Oliver Bright	Music (French hornist)	Cleveland Music School Settlement
Susan Gmeiner	Arts	Settlement Music School (Philadelphia)
Ardith Robandt	Music (pianist)	Music Center of the North Shore
Monica Sokolsky	Music (pianist)	Cleveland Music School Settlement
Maxine Stock	Sculpture, Art History	Cleveland Music School Settlement

Susan Lichten, the "Ninth Intern", trained at the Neighborhood Music School in New Haven, and she participated in the Program without compensation of any kind. [54]

The following evaluations provided the Guild with materials showing the worth of the Internship Program, both from the interns themselves and the directors who actually supervised the program in their own organizations. A questionnaire was sent to the host directors and the interns which revealed the following information:

...the majority--75%--of the host directors reported
their satisfaction with the Program on six separate
points. However, the following recommendations were
made in regard to future implementations of the Internship Program:

Future candidates for the Internship Program
should be more mature artistically.

The follow-up mechanism should be more tightly
defined. Most host school directors--and the interns
themselves--were confused as to the purpose and scope
of the following mechanism.

Interns should be trained in pairs, rather than as
single students.

A maximum of four interns per year should be
trained until needs can be thoroughly documented.

It was suggested that the Internship Program could
be coordinated with an academic program in arts administration. It was also suggested that the Program
might be restructured on a regional basis in order
to expedite the funding and recruitment. A third
recommendation was that the Internship Program be
coordinated with a new school development program
in order to guarantee a follow-up mechanism and/or
future employment of the graduate Interns.[55]

At the completion of the Internship Program, all nine
of the interns settled into positions related to some phase of
community arts activities. This is considered to be a mark of
genuine achievement by the National Guild of Community Schools
of the Arts. If funds were to become available, the program
could be reinstated as a part of the National Guild's regular
program relatively easily.*

A program such as this truly represents the interest

_____

*An interesting note appears in the Summary which states:
Although the Internship Program was run during the 1976-
1977 season on a pilot basis, it was apparently assumed, by
our own membership as well as the general public, that the
Guild would continue the Program during 1977-1978. Accordingly, we received over a dozen applications before formal word
was released in August of the termination of the pilot program.[56]

and action by the arts within communities. Training young
people (and not so young people) to understand the structure
and operations of community schools of the arts as well as the
philosophies and responsibilities of such organizations is very
much a duty of the National Guild. At the earliest possible
time, it is hoped that this program will be revitalized.

At this time in its history, Dorothy Amarandos left the
employment of the National Guild of Community Schools of the
Arts. Fortunately, there were two young women on the staff
who were able to assume the responsibilities for the national
office as explained in the Guildletter of January, 1977:

> President's Message
>
> The National Guild enters the New Year with some
> important changes in personnel, and with some ideas
> garnered from the Washington Conference that will
> be pursued during the year ahead.
>   We are fortunate to have Marcy Horwitz as Acting
> Director, with Sandie Kaplan as her assistant. These
> capable young women come from our own Guild family,
> and are steeped in the philosophy of the community
> school of the arts. Marcy has been an acting Guild
> school director, and Sandie, daughter of Annetta Kap-
> lan, director of the Metropolitan School for the Arts
> in Syracuse, has worked and performed in Guild
> Schools.
>   All national arts associations are having financial
> problems; we are no exception. We are taking steps
> to economize, and will submit a revised budget to the
> Board at its next meeting. Even so, we expect to
> maintain services to our members.
>   The word most often heard at the Washington Con-
> ference was "coalition". We are exploring various
> plans to work with other arts associations in the fields
> of funding, programming, and lobbying. This is time-
> consuming, but should prove productive.
>   ...I believe that the Guild has an important mission
> to fulfill; working together, we can achieve it. [57]

A bit of additional information was included in the January 1977 Guildletter under the heading "Who's Who at the
National Office":

Due to recent staffing changes, Marcy Horwitz has
been named Interim Director of the National Guild.
From student to teacher to administrator, Marcy has
participated in many facets of Guild School operations.
Assisting her is Sandie Kaplan who received an M.A.
in piano from SUNY at Stony Brook, where she had
a teaching assistantship. Both of them are ready and
willing to help you in whatever way they can.[58]

Assuming the responsibilities of running the office of
the National Guild was no easy undertaking. Marcy Horwitz
and Sandie Kaplan had both worked in the national office previously and were well acquainted with the needs of the organization. They proved to have creative imaginations, and produced some excellent materials and reports of the National
Guild's work.

This was especially true of their assembling and presenting summaries of National Guild conferences. Their ingenuity
produced a wealth of accurate information describing the
Guild's activities, as well as stating in writing significant issues about which the Guild had to be concerned.

The first report of the proceedings of a national conference was entitled "The Washington Connection." That conference was held in November of 1976, and as the title indicates,
held in Washington, D.C. At the outset of the conference,
Dr. Lester G. Glick, president of the Guild, began the event
with his opening address. It included a quotation from an
article by Hilton Kramer which had appeared two weeks earlier
in the New York Times:

The signs are pretty clear that neither a Carter nor
a Ford administration would attempt to reverse the
present trend towards larger subsidies for the arts.
If there can be said to be a single issue in this campaign beyond partisan dispute, it is this one--another
measure, of course, of the extent to which both the
arts and public support for them have established themselves in American life.[59]

This was a very apt quotation to use; it was presented
to the correct organization and in the proper city. It set
the tone of the conference which included such prominent
personages as Walter Anderson, Director of the Music Program
of the National Endowment for the Arts; Dr. Harold Arberg,

Director of the Arts and Humanities Program, U. S. Office
of Education; Darrell deChaby, Public Information Officer of
the National Endowment for the Humanities; Samuel Hope,
Executive Director of the National Association of Schools of
Music; Jack Kukuk, Assistant Director of the Alliance for Arts
Education; John Mahlmann, Executive Director of the National
Art Education Association; Charles Moody, Director of Develop-
ment for the Music Educators National Conference; Jack Morris-
on, Executive Director of the American Theatre Association;
Wendy Perks, Executive Director of the National Committee
for the Handicapped; Forbes Rogers, Executive Director of
the Alliance for Arts Education; and Jacqueline Sunderland,
Director of the Arts for Aging Program, to name only a few
of the resource speakers called upon to make presentations.[60]
The Guild had done its homework and taken advantage of its
Washington, D. C. location for its 1976 annual conference.

It was also at this conference that an event occurred
which passed entirely unnoticed. It was the first time that
the name, Lolita Mayadas, had appeared in registration for a
Guild Conference.[61] At that time, she was employed at the
David Hochstein Memorial Music School in Rochester, New York.
In just a few years hence her name was to take on much more
significance and recognition, for she was to become the executive-director of the National Guild of Community Schools
of the Arts.

The next conference was entitled "Explo! '77--Arts
Education and Human Development." It was held in San Francisco, California. At this conference a special event took
place that was to bestow an honor on one of the Guild's distinguished past school directors, past presidents, and past
executive-directors, all in one person!

In 1974 the National Guild established the Col. Samuel
Rosenbaum award which is named in honor of the National
Guild's long-time friend and supporter. The award is given
annually to some individual whose work exemplifies and pro-
motes the ideals to which the National Guild and its membership
are dedicated.

Dr. Lester G. Glick, president of the National Guild,
bestowed the Col. Samuel Rosenbaum Award upon Dr. Herbert
Zipper during the festivities on Monday evening, November
28, 1977. Dr. Zipper's tireless efforts throughout the many

years of his career as musician, educator, organizer, and mentor have been an inspiration to us all. To his many previous honors, the National Guild fondly added its own recognition and affection. [62]

Much discussion was encouraged when the attention of the conference was turned to the then newly published book, Coming to Our Senses, the Rockefeller panel report of which David Rockefeller, Jr., was chairman. This book had created a considerable reaction the moment that McGraw-Hill published it.

The panel discussion was arranged with Allen Sapp acting as the moderator. His opening statement included the following:

> We meet here today in a familial sense, understanding the assumption and understanding the aspirations and showing in the commitment of our lives our convictions about the substance of the Report. ...It's an important document; and making that fact known is, again, a primary function of all of us here on the Panel, and I think of all of you after this meeting. It's an historic document, and it has many positive, concrete suggestions--as well as some 95 or so individual attitudes on development. [63]

In addition to Dr. Sapp, the panel consisted of Lucille S. Abrahamson, San Francisco Board of Education; Grant Beglarian, School of Performing Arts, University of Southern California (more recently fulfilling his responsibilities in Washington, D.C.); Peter Coyote, California Arts Council; Lester G. Glick, Cleveland Area Arts Council; Clark Mitze, California Arts Council; and Frank Oppenheimer, The Exploratorium (San Francisco). The panel discussion proved to be a lively event to say the least--a most successful undertaking!

Other sessions were very enlightening, such as "Two Ways of Taking Art into the Schools," presented by The Alvarado Arts Workshop, and The Missing Link Theatre Company's "Arts Education, Arts Experience, and Personal Growth"[64] attracted many of the delegates. The two young women had proven themselves to be imaginative and creative.

In subsequent years the conference also had intriguing

titles such as Arts in a Troubled Society, which was presented
in Toronto, Ontario, Canada, from November 12th through the
15th, 1978.[65] Dr. George Tatham from McLaughlin College of
York University gave the keynote address which bore a title
similar to that of the conference. His speech bore the name
"Arts in Our Troubled Society," in which he reviewed the
historical development of settlements and community schools
of the arts. Other sessions of the National Guild conference
were: "The Role of the Arts in Mental Health"; "Teacher
Training Workshops at the Lighthouse Music School"; "The
Questionable Role of the Royal Conservatory of Music's Graded
System"; "Theory, Special Populations and the Suzuki Method";
"Ontario Arts Council and its Role in Funding Arts Education
Activities"; "The Role of the Arts/Arts Education Prevention
of Personal and Societal Problems"; "Arts Education as an Ef-
fective Tool in the Intervention of Personal and Societal
Problems"; and "Successful Programs Combining the Arts and
Social Services."[66]

One sees a return to topics which once again combine
the talents of artists and social workers, even as in the beginning days of The Third Street Music School Settlement,
Hull-House Music School, Henry Street Settlement and later
its Music School, the Settlement Music School in Philadelphia,
The Neighborhood Music School in New Haven, the Schools
in Boston, Cleveland, Buffalo, etc.

At this conference the Colonel Samuel Rosenbaum Memorial Award was given to the Keynote Speaker, Dr. George
Tatham, with the following statement:

> A geographer by profession, Dr. Tatham has pursued
> an active interest in music throughout his long and
> distinguished career; as a member and 15-year presi-
> dent of the University Settlement Music School's Board
> of Directors; as impromptu pianist at McMaster College
> festivities, and (we're told) occasional composer of
> original songs!
>   With affection and appreciation, we take pleasure
> in acknowledging Dr. George Tatham's contributions
> to the field with this presentation of the 1978 Colonel
> Samuel Rosenbaum Award.[67]

The Conference in 1979 was held in St. Louis, Missouri,
with the title: A B C: Arts--Basic to the Child.[68] This

particular title and topic were chosen since this was the year, 1979, which the United Nations had designated as the International Year of the Child. The National Guild of Community Schools of the Arts dedicated its 42nd annual conference to that theme. It was also an important conference for it was on October 30, 1979 that the membership of the Guild formally considered its Code of Regulations, amended it and adopted it in its final form.

Marcy Horwitz and Sandie Kaplan worked diligently to continue the work of the Guild, and their creative imaginations organized meaningful conference agendas and assembled significant members of the communities in which conferences were held, as well as those national figures who were prominent in the fields of the arts. Their final effort in this capacity was the 1980 conference which was held in Boston, Massachusetts from November 9th through 12th. The title of the Conference was Putting It All Together (so it works).[69] The title referred to the multiplicity of the arts taught in Guild Schools--music, theatre, dance and the visual arts. Taking advantage of being in Boston, the resource speakers included Philip K. Allen who had served in both the Massachusetts State Senate and House of Representatives and was also the president of the Board of Trustees of the Community Music Center of Boston and vice president of the Boston Symphony Orchestra; T. J. Anderson, composer, Fletcher Professor of Music at Tufts University and a member of the Massachusetts Council on the Arts and Humanities, and whose biography is listed in the new Grove Dictionary of Music and Musicians; Janet Baker-Carr, assistant director of the Harvard Institute in Arts Administration, a member of the Financial Assistance Advisory Panel of the Massachusetts Council on the Arts and Humanities, a trustee of the Cambridge School of Ballet and the Cambridge Society for Early Music; and Leo L. Beranek, vice president of the Boston Symphony Orchestra, trustee of the Opera Company of Boston and a member of the M.I.T. Council on the Arts.[70]

Allen Sapp, president of the National Guild bestowed the Rosenbaum Award upon Philip K. Allen with the following statement:

> Mr. Allen's career exemplifies, as does the history of the community music school of the arts movement, a dual commitment to issues of quality and of social

responsibility. As an educator and administrator, he
has worked with such schools as Phillips Academy
and Harvard University--and he serves as a Trustee
of Hurricane Island Outward Bound School. He has
served...as Executive Secretary of the Republican
State Committee--and he was Selectman of the Town of
Andover. He is a Vice President of the Boston Symphony Orchestra--and Chairman of the Board of Trustees of the Community Music Center of Boston.[71]

Many carefully selected topics were to be presented
during the 1980 conference which were meaningful and informative for the delegates present. They included the following:

Special Problems of Divisional Schools (divisional
schools are those which are part of a larger organization, not independently operated--this subject is
reminiscent of problems discussed which led to the
formation of the National Guild); Early Education in
the Arts--as the Guild's title expresses it, no longer
was just music education, but education for all art
forms; Hiring an Arts Administrator for your Organi-
zation--again referring to administrators for all kinds
of arts institutions; Long-Range Planning for Nonprofit
Organizations; Is there a Computer in Your Future?[72]

After such a successful conference, it was with regret
a few months later that each member of the Guild received the
following letter from Marcy Horwitz, dated February 13, 1981:

Dear Friends:

It's been nearly five years since I first came to work
for and with the National Guild. Then, as now, my
commitment to the community school movement was un-
wavering.
    Although my faith in our work remains steadfast,
I do feel that both the National Guild and myself need
a change of pace. I have therefore tendered my
resignation to the National Guild's Board of Trustees.
This decision reflects only my own need for a new
environment and new challenges; it in no way indicates
disagreement or disaffection with any of you.
    I would like my resignation to take effect on or
about 15 May 1981; I will, of course, continue to

devote full attention and energies to the job until I
am officially separated from the organization. I will
let you know of my plans for the future as they
develop.

I shall always remember our years together with
pride, a sense of accomplishment, respect and genuine
fondness. For giving me the chance to work with all
of you, for your encouragement and support, and for
your understanding, I thank you very, very much.

Cordially,

Marcy Horwitz, Executive Director[73]

Once again the National Guild was in search of an
executive-director. It was imperative to have one, and it
was a necessity to have the national office situated in a locality
which was reasonably permanent. Frequent changes of address
led only to confusion and not sensible stability. The national
office for five years was located at 626 Grove Street, Evanston,
Illinois; next, for one year only, it had the address of 9214
Three Oaks Drive in Silver Spring, Maryland; then for far
less than a year it was located at 654 Madison Avenue, New
York, New York; from September 1, 1974, the national office
was moved to 200 West 57 Street, New York, New York where
it remained until April 18, 1979 when it was moved to the
historic Flatiron Building at 175 Fifth Avenue, New York, New
York. The last move was made for reasons of economy. It
kept the national office in New York City but in a location not
so convenient as the one near Carnegie Hall. Marcy Horwitz
and Sandie Kaplan continued the Guild operations at the last
address until summer of 1981.

In the years 1967 to 1981, the National Guild had four
executive-directors: Herbert Zipper (1967-1972); Charles C.
Mark (1972-1973); Dorothy Amarandos (1973-1977); and Marcy
Horwitz (1977-1981). After the announcement of Miss Horwitz's
resignation, the Guild made a valiant effort to find the right
person to fill the position.

The organization was extremely fortunate to find Lolita
Mayadas who was available at that time and who came with unusually fine experience and a willingness to put forth great
energy and dedication. She was herself a fine pianist, having
studied at the Royal Schools of Music in London, England

where she studied piano and allied subjects. In 1956 she was
awarded the Licentiate of the Royal Schools of Music in performance.

In addition to her strong musical background in both
teaching and performance, Lolita Mayadas had been the executive director of the Calcutta School of Music, which was founded in 1915 and is the leading preparatory music school in India.
Her tenure there was from 1965 to 1975. From 1975 to 1979
she was Dean of Students and Registrar at the David Hochstein
Memorial Music School in Rochester, New York which gave her
considerable insights into the concepts of the Community
Schools of the Arts movement. In the 1979-1980 season she
was the Director of Administration of the Florida Philharmonic,
Inc. in Miami, and for the 1980-1981 season she was the Administrative Director of the Grove Dance Theatre, also in Miami.

Lolita Mayadas was engaged during the summer of 1981
as the executive director of the National Guild of Community
Schools of the Arts, a position she most successfully holds
at the time of this writing.

The new executive director wrote a report dated February 5, 1982, and presented it to the Board of Directors of
the National Guild. It contained the following information:

Office move

The Guild office was moved from New York to Teaneck,
New Jersey, to the home of the executive director with
effect from August 3, 1981. The total costs of the
move amounted to $592. All necessary legal require-
ments as a result of this move, such as insurance,
taxes, etc., have been completed.[74]

The national office now was located in nearby New Jersey
with all the advantages of proximity to New York City, the
cultural center of the country and home of many community
schools of the arts. One additional advantage of the New
Jersey location is a considerable reduction in office rent and
operations. This has proved to be a most satisfactory arrangement. One additional move made recently has changed
the Guild's address to 40 North Van Brunt Street, Englewood,
New Jersey, still, of course, with the same executive director.

The February 5th director's report also told of progress being made in the operation of the Guild including a Long Range Plan, a revised budget for FY 1981-1982 prepared and approved by the Board on 10/15/81. A Conference Committee and the executive director took in hand all arrangements for the Guild Conference which was held jointly with the College Music Society in Cincinnati, Ohio, from October 15-18, 1981. The Guildletter had been increased in size, scope and distribution, since the mailing list was increased from 300 to about 1500 names and organizations. The Guildletter was to be published six times each year beginning February, 1982. Applications for grants were being prepared, particularly to the National Endowment for the Arts for support of the Guildletter.

A special note was made of the efforts of Carl Shaver and Company to assist the National Guild by kindly agreeing to provide the following service to the Guild on a pro-bono basis:

> A regular article entitled "Money Talk" for the bi-monthly Guildletter
> A Staff Consultant for the Fund-Raising Committee (Halsy North has been named)
> Update the funding Guide issued by the Company in 1973 for Guild members.

In consultation with the President, Mr. Henry Bridges, the Advisory Council and other Committees of the Board were in the process of being established. Dr. Lester Glick had agreed to be the Chairman of the Advisory Council in order to assist the administration in contacting members for that body.

The spirit of the National Guild was strong and determined to continue the program of the organization and to become financially secure at the earliest possible time. The new executive director had affairs firmly in hand, a clear indication of what was to happen in the future years of her association with the Guild.

The Guild's hiring of Lolita was to prove to be a serendipitous event, for with her came her husband, Azim Mayadas, who was himself a pianist of distinction as well as a successful business executive in many different situations. He had been a member and Chairman of the Works Management Panel of the Calcutta Management Association; Convenor of the National

Seminar on Energy--An Indian Profile; a member of the Indian
Mining Association; Deputy Custodian General of the National-
ized Coking Coal Mines; Vice Chairman of the Calcutta Selected
Coal Association; he was also the Honorary Concert Manager
of the Calcutta School of Music. In this country he was the
Assistant General Manager of the Rochester Philharmonic Or-
chestra from 1975 to 1978, and the General Manager of the
Florida Philharmonic, Inc., in Miami from 1978 to 1981.

His musical training included piano performance studies
and music theory at The Trinity College of Music where he
received the Licentiate from the College. He had been a
prize winner of the Franz Liszt Festival in Budapest, and the
London Music Festivals, and he was also the music critic for
the Hindusthan Standard (a national English newspaper). For
many years he was the pianist and speaker for All India Radio
and a member of the AIR Audition Panel. He also functioned
as a volunteer for the Guild in various capacities and assumed
a position on the staff as the person responsible for the
preparation of requests to foundations. Azim was personally
responsible for the assembling and preparation of important
statistical information used in reports published by the National
Guild over the past several years.

In 1982 an important study of the National Guild of Com-
munity Schools of the Arts was made by the Center for Arts
Administration of the University of Wisconsin-Madison. The
Research Associate was Alfred D. Andreychuk, E. Arthur
Prieve was the Director, and Sharon Leslie the Program As-
sistant. The opening statement appears as follows:

> The National Guild of Community Schools of the Arts
> is an association of over 70 non-profit, non-degree
> granting schools, offering high quality instruction in
> music, dance, drama, and the visual arts. Its mem-
> bers include conservatories, preparatory departments,
> divisional schools, social service centers and community
> schools, many of which trace their roots to the settle-
> ment house movement of the late 1900's. These
> schools are now a potent force in non-degree arts
> education, serving an estimated 60,000 students in
> regular and in contractual programs.
>   Today, in response to the demand for their ser-
> vices, a majority of these schools have expanded
> into satellite operations, extension programs, and

projects in cooperation with public schools, museums, and other cultural organizations. They provide fully qualified professional faculties committed to artistic and educational excellence and offer their students a comprehensive curriculum designed to meet the needs of people of widely different ages, ability and economic background.

The primary purpose of these schools is to provide low-cost instruction to all who seek it, either for personal enrichment or for the development of a special talent. Many nationally known artists received their early training at these schools. Founded in 1937, and incorporated in 1954, the National Guild serves its members in several ways:

- It monitors quality by evaluating each school before election to membership and by approval of its Certificate programs.

- It provides a forum for the exchange of information through the publication of newsletters, bulletins, and employment openings.

- It organizes regular annual conferences thereby providing a common meeting ground for those in the community arts field to discuss current issues and specific administrative, pedagogic, and funding concerns.

- It arranges regular regional meetings within its chapters to encourage local participation by arts educators. Collaborative projects such as concerts and workshops are also arranged.

- It provides technical assistance as required, through the central office and through counseling by means of its network of arts administrators.

- It publishes regular surveys and research studies.

- It acts as an advocate for the community arts school movement.

- It provides access to scholarship funds.

The Guild is a member of the National Music Council and the Assembly of National Arts Education Organizations.[75]

This description of the Guild is an updated and clarified picture of the organization. One can recall the efforts of the early school directors who banded together to create the National Guild of Community Music Schools. Their goals, aims and directions were clearly stated as early as 1937 and can be found again in the above statement with a recognition of the Guild's expansion, reflected by the change in its name, and its strength and vision as it planned its 50th Anniversary celebration in 1987.

Topics in this report, copyrighted by the National Guild of Community Schools of the Arts, Inc. and the Center for Arts Administration, University of Wisconsin-Madison in 1982, include the following study results: student enrollments, student financial aid, Boards of Trustees, other school characteristics, budgets, both earned and contributed income, and administration and other expenses, tuition fee structure, administrative and support staff salaries, faculty salary structure, and fringe benefits. An introduction and statement of the methodology used are given at the beginning. The complete study is available at the national office.

Long after the Guild's initial struggle to increase the number of member schools from twelve (and briefly eleven) schools, the membership has increased astonishingly to 160 schools in 1986, which are scattered all over the United States and Canada. The figures below will trace the size of the membership from 1981 to 1986. All figures were tallied in the months of July to be consistent:

Year:	1981	1982	1983	1984	1985	1986
Total Number:	61	70	80	120	140	160

It is also significant to understand the mix of the curricula taught at the various member schools. The majority of the schools offer music only or music and other art forms. Relatively few schools offer dance only, or visual arts alone. The breakdown is as follows:

Year:	1981	1982	1983	1984	1985	1986
Music or music and other arts:	61	70	80	118	135	153
Dance only:	0	0	0	1	2	3
Visual arts only:	0	0	0	1	3	4

For years the National Guild Schools were found in only a few states throughout the country. Current data reveal that this has changed considerably. At the time of this writing, Guild Schools are found in 32 of the 50 states in the Union, plus the District of Columbia and four in Canada. (One of the states having a Guild School is Alaska.)

Year:	1981	1982	1983	1984	1985	1986
Number of states:	18	19	20	27	31	32

Still, however, the Northeastern part of the country has the greatest number of community schools of the arts. The current breakdown is as follows:

Year:	1981	1982	1983	1984	1985	1986
Northeast:	40	47	55	73	83	93
Midwest:	14	14	15	22	28	33
South:	2	5	6	14	17	21
West:	5	4	4	11	12	13

Careful perusal of the above data and cogitation about them show that despite the rapid growth in membership from 1981 to 1986, the National Guild at the time of this writing, in its 49th year, has 95.6% of the member schools offering music instruction, a fact that recalls the importance of music in the establishing of community music schools near the turn of the twentieth century. It is true also that roughly one-half of the member schools reflected in that figure do offer training in one or more of the other art forms.

Dance is now taught in 40% of Guild schools (64); theatre/drama is in the curriculum of 28% of Guild schools (45); and the visual arts are found in 25% (40).

Only seven of the current 160 member schools teach only dance or only visual arts. This small number is expected to grow gradually by the month of July, 1987.

Perhaps the biggest increase has been registered by schools which are part of larger organizations, or the so-called divisional schools. From a relatively small number in 1981, they are now 60 in number, or 37.5% of the entire membership of the National Guild, and they are part of settlement/neighborhood houses, community centers, conservatories, colleges or universities. The remaining 100, or 62.5%, are independently operated institutions. Though between the two factions, there has been turmoil and unrest over the years, the divisional schools and the independent schools have learned to work together.

Although separation seemed inevitable in 1937, much credit is due to both factions, divisionals and independents, who have finally learned that e pluribus unum, a truly American concept for a uniquely American institution, the National Guild of Community Schools of the Arts.

8

ADDENDA:
"Those Important Extras"

WHT SOME ARE SAYING ABOUT THE NATIONAL GUILD

OF COMMUNITY SCHOOLS OF THE ARTS

The Guild and its member schools deserve to be recognized
for the admirable contribution they have made to the artistic
education of all Americans.

> Frank Hodsell, Chairman
> National Endowment for the Arts

It is difficult to conceive of any successful musician who has
not been bred and nurtured by a community arts school.
After the family it was the place where the artistic seed found
fertile ground in which to grow, the first impressions of the
larger artistic world, and later one of the first steps in the
artistic profession, a profession which has always included
teaching.

> Robert Suderburg, President
> Cornish Institute
> Seattle, Washington

I need not dwell on the extraordinary vital service the Guild
provides to the arts education of all Americans through its
member institutions in virtually every section of the nation.

> Grant Beglarian, President
> National Foundation for
> Advancement in the Arts

I am struck once again by the great variety of these endeavors
that you are embarked upon and how well they represent the
diversity and variety of the arts themselves....What you are

doing gives special enrichment to the human spirit, and so
many wonderful opportunities to talented people.

> Hon. Livingston L. Biddle, Jr.
> Past Chairman of the National
> Endowment for the Arts

NATIONAL GROWTH AND REGIONAL CHAPTERS

As the National Guild experienced a growth spurt in
the late 1960s and the 1970s, it became necessary to divide
the country into regional chapters. This allowed for the
member schools to make closer contacts and relationships with
their neighboring sister schools, and also to have chapter
meetings two or three times a year as desired. It also encouraged the institutions to present combined school programs
and concerts, as well as to exchange faculty recitals. Reports of these events can often be given at the National
Guild's annual conference.

At the time of this writing the National Guild has
ten chapters spread over the United States and Canada.
They are identified as follows:

Chapter I   NEW YORK (CITY) METROPOLITAN

Chapter II   NORTHEAST (Connecticut, Maine, Massachusetts,
New Hampshire, Rhode Island, Vermont)

Chapter III EASTERN GREAT LAKES (New York State--ex-
clusive of New York Metropolitan--and Ontario, Canada)

Chapter IV MIDATLANTIC (Delaware, District of Columbia,
Maryland, New Jersey, Pennsylvania, Virginia)

Chapter V   CENTRAL GREAT LAKES (Indiana, Michigan,
Ohio)

Chapter VI WESTERN GREAT LAKES (Illinois, Iowa, Minnesota,
Missouri, Wisconsin)

Chapter VII WEST COAST (California, Nevada)

Chapter VIII CAROLINAS (in process--North Carolina, South
        Carolina)

Chapter IX   BLUE GRASS (proposed--Kentucky, Tennessee)

Chapter X   NORTHWEST (proposed--Alaska, British Colum-
        bia, Canada, Oregon, Washington).[1]

    Naturally as new schools are founded and added, they
will be placed in the regional chapter which best accommodates
their needs. Since additional schools appear frequently on
the horizon, it behooves the National Guild to reflect on the
growth of the organization and in which territories the growth
has occurred.

    Perusal of the "1984-85 Annual Report" of the National
Guild of Community Schools of the Arts shows where that
growth was between the 1983-84 and 1984-85 seasons:

Chapter	Geographical Region	'83-84	'84-85	Decrease or Increase (+ or -)
I	NY METROPOLITAN	33	35	+ 2
II	NORTHEAST	21	27	+ 6
III	EASTERN GREAT LAKES	7	7	None
IV	MIDATLANTIC	20	24	+ 4
V	CENTRAL GREAT LAKES	11	15	+ 4
VI	WESTERN GREAT LAKES	11	13	+ 2
VII	WEST COAST	9	8	- 1
VIII	CAROLINAS	3	4	+ 1
IX	BLUE GRASS	3	3	None
X	NORTHWEST	2	4	+ 2
		120	140	+20.[2]

The northeastern section of the United States still claims the largest number of Community Schools of the Arts, at least in the National Guild's membership. In the comparison of just two seasons, 1983-84 and 1984-85, an increase of twenty new member schools is found, spread throughout the country. In this comparison one finds that the largest increase of new member schools appears in Regional Chapter II, the <u>Northeast</u>, which fundamentally is comprised of the New England States. If Chapters I and II were to be combined, the increase would become eight schools, or 40% of the total national increase. Truly then, the most heavily populated area in the United States does have the greatest number of Community Schools of the Arts, and the Guild membership in this geographical territory seems to be growing continuously.

It is interesting noting that the most frequently requested area for study continues to be music, even though many current schools offer other art forms, dance, drama, theatre and the visual arts. This is contrary to the supposition by many that the Guild's opening its doors to other areas of concentration has caused the increased membership. Those schools which teach exclusively one art form, other than music, do not account for the continued rise in membership. Music still attracts the greatest number of students.

Additional analysis of the National Guild's records and materials reveals other enlightening facts about the National Guild itself. In the chart below one sees the dates when schools were recently founded. All of the indicated schools are currently members of the Guild, and all started between 1970 and 1985.

1970	6	1975	2	1980	5
1971	5	1976	5	1981	9
1972	2	1977	5	1982	4
1973	4	1978	4	1983	9
1974	3	1979	3	1984	1
	20		19		28	Subtotals

67   Grand Total[3]

When one remembers the early days of the National
Guild, he recalls that there was a total of 12 member schools.
Janet D. Schenck and Johan Grolle were most anxious to expand the membership, but there were not many schools to
invite for Guild membership. Yet the ideals and goals of
the Guild leaders did not alter or change. Quality and standards were words frequently used by them. It is rewarding
to realize the strides that the National Guild has made in its
fifty year history. By 1983-84 the membership had risen to
120; by 1984-85 it reached 140; by the conference in Washington, D. C., in 1986, the total membership was 160 schools.
The Guild hopes to have its membership rise to 200 schools
by the time it celebrates its fiftieth anniversary.

In the "1984-85 Annual Report" still another chart
reveals the population of the areas where Guild Schools are
being formed or finally recognized as Community Schools of
the Arts. The categories are classified by size of the population in that community. They are listed as A, B, C, D,
and E. The total membership of Guild Schools is determined
by adding the numbers shown in categories A, B, C, D, E
for each academic season from 1980-81 to 1984-85. The chart
is as follows:

	Population	'80-81	'81-82	'82-83	'83-84	'84-85
A	-20,000	17	21	21	30	35
B	20,000-100,000	12	14	17	28	34
C	100,000-500,000	10	9	10	24	26
D	500,000-1 million	9	12	13	14	17
E	1 million & over	13	14	19	24	28
A-E:	Total membership	61	70	80	120	140[4]

In the same annual report (1984) some additional facts were
presented under the title "As a Matter of Fact...."

The 140 schools of the National Guild of Community
Schools of the Arts

- have a combined annual budget of over $35 million,

or an average annual budget per school of $255,050;
- operate 200 separate facilities (including branches);
- have a total enrollment of over 120,000 students at their own facilities (by head count);
- serve some 150,000 people annually in outreach instructional programs, including approximately one-third of that number in public school programs.

In addition, based on a sample survey in October 1985:

- 1 out of every 3 students is a member of a minority group (36% of the total student enrollment), as listed below:

Black	20.7%
Hispanic	6.6%
Oriental	6.5%
Native (Indian)	0.1%
Other	2.1%

National Guild schools have raised almost 39% of their total budgets from contributed (or unearned) income as listed below:

Unearned (or contributed) Income (100%)

Private Funds	81%
(grants, contributions, and individual giving)	
Public Funds	19%
Federal 6.0%, State 8.5%	
Local/City 4.5%	

- 17 schools are agencies of United Way

- 11 schools have received Challenge and Advancement Grants from the National Endowment for the Arts[5]

MEMBER SCHOOLS OF THE NATIONAL GUILD OF COMMUNITY SCHOOLS OF THE ARTS

Alabama

CONSERVATORY OF FINE AND PERFORMING ARTS OF
  BIRMINGHAM - SOUTHERN COLLEGE
800 8th Avenue West
Birmingham, Alabama   35254
(205) 226-4960
Music
Thomas Gibbs, Director

MONTGOMERY SCHOOL OF FINE ARTS
1062 Woodley Road
Montgomery, Alabama   36106
(205) 262-3151
Margaret Johnson Roby, Director

Alaska

ALASKA CONSERVATORY OF MUSIC
c/o Alaska Pacific University
3500 University Drive
Anchorage, Alaska   99508
(907) 276-8181
Music

California

CLAREMONT COMMUNITY SCHOOL OF MUSIC
P.O. Box 53
Corner Mountain & Bonita Avenues
Claremont, California   91711
(714) 624-3012
Music
Joan Bernison, Interim, Acting Director

COMMUNITY MUSIC CENTER
544 Capp Street
San Francisco, California   94110
(415) 647-6015

Music
Dr. Stephen R. Shapiro, Director

COMMUNITY SCHOOL OF MUSIC AND ARTS
405 Ortega Avenue
Mountain View, California 94040
(415) 961-0342
Music, Visual Arts
Mary Bender, Executive Director

COMMUNITY SCHOOL OF PERFORMING ARTS
3131 South Figueroa Street
Los Angeles, California 90007
(213) 743-5252
Music, Dance, Drama
Toby Mayman, Executive Director
Joseph Thayer, Dean

EVERGREEN MUSIC CONSERVATORY
4521-A Van Nuys Boulevard #105
Sherman Oaks, California 91403
(818) 761-5560
Music
Gail A. Acosta, President

INLAND SUZUKI MUSIC SCHOOL
264 W. Etiwanda Avenue
Rialto, California 92376
(714) 875-4074
Music
Regina Jang, Director

PASADENA CONSERVATORY OF MUSIC
1815 Queensberry Road
P.O. Box 91533
Pasadena, California 91109-1533
(818) 798-9426
Music
Wynne Stone & Silke Sauppe, Directors

UNIVERSITY OF REDLANDS COMMUNITY MUSIC SCHOOL
Redlands, California 92374
(714) 793-2121
Music, Theatre
Dr. Robert Walters, Director

Connecticut

CAMERATA SCHOOL OF MUSIC & DANCE
411 Park Road
West Hartford, Connecticut 06119
(203) 236-2304
Music, Dance
Dr. Allen Gater, Director

CENTER MUSIC SCHOOL OF THE JEWISH COMMUNITY CENTER
P.O. Box 3326
Newfield Avenue at Vine Road
Stamford, Connecticut 06905
(203) 322-7900
Music
Adina Salmanssohn-Affelt, Director

HARTFORD CONSERVATORY OF MUSIC & DANCE
834/846 Asylum Avenue
Hartford, Connecticut 06105
(203) 246-2588
Music, Dance
Edwin DeGroat, Director

MUSIC FOUNDATION FOR THE HANDICAPPED OF
    CONNECTICUT
University of Bridgeport, Breul Hall
600 University Avenue
Bridgeport, Connecticut 06601
(203) 366-3300
Music, Dance, Visual Arts, Puppet Theatre
Patricia P. Hart, Executive Director

NEIGHBORHOOD MUSIC SCHOOL
100 Audubon Street
New Haven, Connecticut 06511
(203) 624-5189
Music, Dance
Peter Mansfield, Executive Director

UNIVERSITY OF CONNECTICUT COMMUNITY MUSIC SCHOOL
Department of Music, Department U/2
University of Connecticut
Storrs, Connecticut 06268

(203) 486-2484
Music
Andrea L. Graffam, Director

UNIVERSITY OF HARTFORD
Hartt School of Music, Community Division
200 Bloomfield Avenue
West Hartford, Connecticut   06117
(203) 243-4451
Music, Theatre
Michael Richters, Acting Director

Delaware

CHRISTINA CULTURAL ARTS CENTER
800 East Seventh Street
Wilmington, Delaware   19801-4496
(302) 652-0101
Music, Dance, Domestic Arts, Performing Arts, Visual Arts
Joseph Brumskill, Executive Director

DELAWARE MUSIC SCHOOL
P.O. Box 442
Milford, Delaware   19963
(302) 422-2043
Music
Frances Riddle, Executive Director

WILMINGTON MUSIC SCHOOL
4104 Washington Street
Wilmington, Delaware   19802
(302) 762-1132
Music
Stephen C. Gunzenhauser, Artistic Advisor
Martha Collins, Administrative Director

District of Columbia

D.C. MUSIC CENTER
16th & Harvard Street N.W.
Washington, D.C.   20009
(202) 265-8324
Music
Bernice Fleming, Director

THE LEVINE SCHOOL OF MUSIC
1690 36th Street N.W.
Washington, D.C. 20007
(202) 337-2227
Music
Joanne Hoover, Director

Illinois

THE CONSERVATORY OF CENTRAL ILLINOIS
312 West Green Street
Urbana, Illinois 61801
(217) 328-4445
Roger Brown, Executive Director

THE MERIT MUSIC PROGRAM
410 South Michigan Avenue (Suite 710)
Chicago, Illinois 60605
(312) 786-9428
Music
Alice S. Pfaelzer, Executive Director

MUSIC CENTER OF THE NORTH SHORE
300 Green Bay Road
Winnetka, Illinois 60093
(312) 446-3822
Music
Dance Institute for Therapy
Theatre through the Arts
Visual Arts
Kalman Novak, Director

MUSIC INSTITUTE OF THE LAKE FOREST SYMPHONY ASSN.
700 E. Westleigh Road
Lake Forest, Illinois 60045
(312) 295-2135
Music
Ellen Reid Eastman, Chairman

THE PEOPLE'S MUSIC SCHOOL
4750 North Sheridan Road
Chicago, Illinois 60640
(312) 784-7032
Music
Rita Simo, Director

ROCKFORD COLLEGE MUSIC ACADEMY
5050 E. State Street
Rockford, Illinois   61108-2393
(815) 226-4040
Music
Eleanor Stanlis, Director

SHERWOOD CONSERVATORY OF MUSIC: COMMUNITY MUSIC
    SCHOOL
1014 South Michigan Avenue
Chicago, Illinois   60604
(312) 427-6267
Music
David Boldgett, Executive Director

THE SUZUKI-ORFF SCHOOL FOR YOUNG MUSICIANS
300 West Hill Street
Chicago, Illinois   60610
(312) 337-4363
Music
Peggy Wise, Director

Indiana

INDIANAPOLIS PERFORMING ARTS ACADEMY
P.O. Box 80281
Indianapolis, Indiana   46280
(317) 255-1972
Music, Dance, Theatre
Jean Gurvitz, President

Iowa

PREUCIL SCHOOL OF MUSIC
524 North Johnson Street
Iowa City, Iowa   52240
(319) 337-4156
Music
Doris B. Preucil, Director
Karen H. Chappell, Managing Director

Kentucky

MOREHEAD STATE UNIVERSITY ACADEMY OF ARTS
P.O. Box 1368
Morehead, Kentucky   40351
(606) 783-2483
Music, Dance, Visual Arts, Media Arts, Creative Writing
Milford E. Kuhn, Jr., Director

Maryland

SHIRLEE B. BART MUSIC CENTER
3300 Old Court Road
Baltimore, Maryland   21215
(301) 486-1905
Music, Dance
Dr. Irene Grossman, Director

PEABODY INSTITUTE OF THE JOHNS HOPKINS UNIVERSITY,
     PREPARATORY DIVISION
21 East Mount Vernon Place
Baltimore, Maryland   21202
(301) 659-8127
Music, Dance, Theatre
Fran Zarubick, Director

Massachusetts

ALL NEWTON MUSIC SCHOOL
321 Chestnut Street
West Newton, Massachusetts   02165
(617) 527-4553
Music, Dance
Paulette Bowes, Director

BEECHWOOD COMMUNITY LIFE CENTER
225 Fenno Street
Quincy, Massachusetts   02170
(617) 471-5712
Music, Dance, Visual Arts, Theatre
Betty J. Southwick, Director

BELMONT MUSIC SCHOOL
582a Pleasant Street

Belmont, Massachusetts   02178
(617) 484-4696
Music
Ruth L. Scheer, Director

BROOKLINE MUSIC SCHOOL
P.O. Box 181
Brookline, Massachusetts   02146
(617) 277-4593
Music, Dance
Larry Zukof, Director

CAPE COD CONSERVATORY OF MUSIC & ARTS
Route 132
West Barnstable, Massachusetts   02668
(617) 362-2772
Music, Dance, Theatre, Visual Arts
Richard Casper, Director

CHILDREN'S ACADEMY OF PERFORMING ARTS
7 Merritt Street
Marblehead, Massachusetts   01945
(617) 631-8599
Barbara Eyges, Director

COMMUNITY MUSIC CENTER OF BOSTON
48 Warren Avenue
Boston, Massachusetts   02116
(617) 482-7494
Music
David Lapin, Executive Director

COMMUNITY MUSIC SCHOOL OF SPRINGFIELD
200 Birnie Avenue
Springfield, Massachusetts   01107
(413) 732-8428
Music
Eric Bachrach, Executive Director

DANA SCHOOL OF MUSIC
103 Grove Street
Wellesley, Massachusetts   02181
(617) 235-3010
Music
Telemak G. Gharibian, Director

GROTON CENTER FOR THE ARTS
P.O. Box 423
Groton, Massachusetts   01450
(617) 448-3001
Music, Dance, Theatre, Visual Arts
Irene Buck, Executive Director

INDIAN HILL ARTS
P.O. Box 1228
Littleton, Massachusetts   01460
(617) 486-9524
Music, Theatre, Visual Arts
Mary Ann Brandt, Director

THE MUSIC SCHOOL AT RIVERS
337 Winter Street
Weston, Massachusetts   02193
(617) 235-6840
Music
A. Ramon Rivera, Director

NEW ENGLAND CONSERVATORY OF MUSIC EXTENSION
    DIVISION
295 Huntington Avenue
Boston, Massachusetts   02115
(617) 262-1133
Music
Mark Churchill, Director

THE NEW SCHOOL OF MUSIC
25 Lowell Street
Cambridge, Massachusetts   02138
(617) 492-8105
Music
David Deveau, Director

NORTH SHORE COMMUNITY COLLEGE CENTER FOR THE ARTS
P.O. Box 17
Beverly, Massachusetts   01915
(617) 927-4850 (Ext. 334)
Music, Dance, Theatre, Visual Arts, Photography
Ernest M. Clark, Director

PAKACHOAG COMMUNITY MUSIC SCHOOL
191 Pakachoag Street

Auburn, Massachusetts   01501
(617) 791-8159
Music
Peggy Kelley Reinburg, Director

PERFORMING ARTS CENTER OF METRO WEST
McCarthy Center
Framingham State College
100 State Street
Framingham, Massachusetts   01701
(617) 875-5554
Music, Dance, Theatre
Deborah Williamson, Director, Music Division
Lynn Johnson, Director, Dance Division

PERFORMING ARTS SCHOOL OF WORCESTER
29 High Street
Worcester, Massachusetts   01608
(617) 755-8246
Music, Dance
Shirley N. Benjamin, Executive Director

PITTSFIELD COMMUNITY MUSIC SCHOOL
30 Wendell Avenue
Pittsfield, Massachusetts   01201
(413) 442-1411
Music
Marion Maby Wells, Director

SOUTH SHORE CONSERVATORY OF MUSIC
Cedar Hill off Fort Hill Street
Hingham, Massachusetts   02043
(617) 749-7565
Music, Dance
James C. Simpson, Jr., Director

WESTFIELD COMMUNITY MUSIC PROGRAM
Westfield State College
Western Avenue
Westfield, Massachusetts   01086
(413) 562-0606
Music
Patrice Donald, Director

WINCHESTER COMMUNITY MUSIC SCHOOL
P.O. Box 24

Winchester, Massachusetts   01890
(617) 729-7446
Music
Corie Nichols, Director

Michigan

BLUE LAKE COMMUNITY SCHOOL OF THE ARTS
136 West Webster
Muskegon, Michigan   49440
(616) 728-0440 Branch: (616) 894-9024
Music, Dance, Theatre, Visual Arts
Julie S. Anderson, Director

CENTER FOR CREATIVE STUDIES INSTITUTE OF MUSIC AND
    DANCE
200 East Kirby
Detroit, Michigan   48202
(313) 831-2870
Music, Dance
Steven J. Nelson, President

COMMUNITY SCHOOL OF THE ARTS
292 Bellview
Benton Harbor, Michigan   49022
(616) 925-7746
Music, Dance, Theatre
Merry Stover, Executive Director

CROOKED TREE ARTS COUNCIL
Virginia McCune Arts Center
461 East Mitchell
Petoskey, Michigan   49770
(616) 347-4337
Music, Dance, Theatre, Visual Arts
Sean Ley, Director

EAST LANSING ARTS WORKSHOP
693 North Hagadorn
East Lansing, Michigan   48823
(517) 332-2565
Music, Dance, Theatre, Visual Arts, Literature
Madelyn Schrey, Director

FLINT SCHOOL OF PERFORMING ARTS
1025 East Kearsley Street
Flint, Michigan   48503
(313) 238-9651
Music, Dance
Paul Torre, Director

Minnesota

MACPHAIL CENTER FOR THE ARTS
1128 LaSalle Avenue
Minneapolis, Minnesota   55403
(612) 627-4020
Music
Gary L. Zeller, Director

Missouri

SAINT LOUIS CONSERVATORY AND SCHOOLS FOR THE ARTS
560 Trinity at Delmar
St. Louis, Missouri   63130
(314) 863-3033
Music, Dance, Theatre, Visual Arts
Shirley Bartzen, Dean

Nevada

NEVADA SCHOOL OF THE ARTS
University of Nevada - Las Vegas
4505 South Maryland Parkway
Las Vegas, Nevada   89154
(702) 739-3502
Music, Visual Arts
John A. Smith, Executive Director
Carol H. Blanton, Associate Director

New Hampshire

CONCORD COMMUNITY MUSIC SCHOOL
P.O. Box 1725
Concord, New Hampshire   03301

(603) 228-1196
Music
Margaret Senter, Director

GREATER MANCHESTER CENTER FOR ARTS AND MUSIC
79 Dow Street
Manchester, New Hampshire 03101
(603) 644-4548
Music, Dance, Visual Arts
Bernice Krauzer, Program Director
Ruth B. Yegerman, Community Relations Director
Stephen H. Smith, Artistic Director

New Jersey

APPEL FARM ARTS AND MUSIC CENTER
P.O. Box 770
Elmer, New Jersey 08318
(609) 358-2472
Susan Whitehouse, Executive Director

THE ARTS FOUNDATION OF NEW JERSEY SUMMER ARTS
    INSTITUTE
P.O. Box 352
New Brunswick, New Jersey 08903
(201) 463-3640
Music, Theatre, Visual Arts, Writing
Carol Dickert, Director

CENTER FOR MODERN DANCE EDUCATION
84 Euclid Avenue
Hackensack, New Jersey 07601
(201) 342-2989
Dance
Shirley Ubell, Artistic/Executive Director

FAIRLEIGH DICKINSEN UNIVERSITY
Music Preparatory Division
West Passaic and Montross Avenues
Rutherford, New Jersey 07070
(201) 460-5045
Music
Michele A. Flagg, Director

THE HADDONFIELD SCHOOL OF CREATIVE & PERFORMING ARTS
29 Warwick Road
Haddonfield, New Jersey   08033
(609) 429-9327
Carol Corbin, Director

INNER CITY ENSEMBLE THEATRE AND DANCE COMPANY
137 Ellison Street
Paterson, New Jersey   07505
(201) 279-9191
Theatre, Dance
Ralph Gomez, Executive/Artistic Director
Stephen Shiman, Director of Development/Administration

THE J.C.C. SCHOOL OF MUSIC
411 East Clinton Avenue
Tenafly, New Jersey   07670
(201) 569-7900
Music
Dorothy Kaplan Roffman, Director

LONG HILL CHAPEL MUSIC CENTER
525 Shunpike Road
Chatham, New Jersey   07922
(201) 665-9721
Leigh Seibert, Director

MADISON AREA YMCA DANCE DEPARTMENT
1 Ralph Stoddard Drive
Madison, New Jersey   07940
(201) 377-6200
Dance
Susan Brody, Director

MONTCLAIR STATE COLLEGE MUSIC PREPARATORY DIVISION
Upper Montclair, New Jersey   07043
(201) 893-4443
Music
Sheila McKenna, Director

NEIGHBORHOOD HOUSE MUSIC SCHOOL
12 Flagler Street
Morristown, New Jersey   07960
(201) 538-1229
Music
Madelyn H. Aubin, Director

NEWARK COMMUNITY SCHOOL OF THE ARTS
89 Lincoln Park
Newark, New Jersey   07102
(201) 642-0133
Music, Dance, Theatre, Visual Arts
William F. Reeder, Executive Director

THE NEW SCHOOL FOR MUSIC STUDY
P.O. Box 407
Princeton, New Jersey   08542
(609) 921-2900
Music
Samuel S. Holland, Director

SUBURBAN COMMUNITY MUSIC CENTER AT THE MADISON
    AREA YMCA
1 Ralph Stoddard Drive
Madison, New Jersey   07940
(201) 377-6599
Music
Judith G. Wharton, Executive Director

WESTMINSTER CONSERVATORY OF MUSIC
Hamilton Avenue & Walnut Lane
Princeton, New Jersey   08540
(609) 921-7104
Music
Martha Cook Davidson, Director

<u>New York</u>

BLOOMINGDALE HOUSE OF MUSIC
323 West 108 Street
New York, New York   10025
(212) 663-6021
Music, Dance
David D. Greer, Director

BOYS' CHOIR OF HARLEM
550 West 155th Street
New York, New York   10032
(212) 690-3333
Music
Walter J. Turnbull, Director

BROOKLYN COLLEGE PREPARATORY CENTER FOR THE
    PERFORMING ARTS
Roosevelt Hall (Room 114)
Bedford Avenue & Avenue H
Brooklyn, New York   11210
(718) 780-4111
Music, Dance, Theatre, Visual Arts
Ronald Banyay, Director

BROOKLYN CONSERVATORY OF MUSIC
58 Seventh Avenue
Brooklyn, New York   11217
(718) 622-3300
Music, Dance
Jess Smith, President/Director

BROOKLYN MUSIC SCHOOL
126 St. Felix Street
Brooklyn, New York   11217
(718) 638-5660
Music, Dance, Theatre
Donna Merris, Director

CHILDREN'S ART CARNIVAL
62 Hamilton Terrace
New York, New York   10031
(212) 234-4093
Visual Arts, Writing
Betty Blayton-Taylor, President/Director

COMMUNITY MUSIC SCHOOL
185 North Main Street
Spring Valley, New York   10977
(914) EL6-1522
Music
Edward Simons, Artistic Director
Janet Simons, Executive Director

COMMUNITY MUSIC SCHOOL OF BUFFALO
415 Elmwood Avenue
Buffalo, New York   14222
(716) 884-4887
Music
Linda Mabry, Executive Director

COMMUNITY SCHOOL OF MUSIC AND ARTS
Whiton House, Terrace Hill
Aurora & Prospect Streets
Ithaca, New York   14850
(607) 272-1474
Music, Visual Arts, Language Arts, Dance
Mary Trochim, Director

DILLER QUAILE SCHOOL OF MUSIC
24 East 95th Street
New York, New York   10028
(212) 369-1484
Music, Visual Arts
Marjory Duncalfe, Director

EASTERN SUFFOLK SCHOOL OF MUSIC
141 East Main Street
Riverhead, New York   11901
Music, Dance, Theatre
Ann Hirsch, Executive Director

GREENWICH HOUSE MUSIC SCHOOL
46 Barrow Street
New York, New York   10014
(212) 242-4770
Music, Dance
B.C. Vermeersch, Director

HARLEM SCHOOL OF THE ARTS
645 St. Nicholas Avenue
New York, New York   10030
(212) 926-4100
Music, Dance, Theatre, Visual Arts
Betty Allen, Executive Director

HENRY STREET SETTLEMENT/ARTS FOR LIVING CENTER
466 Grand Street
New York, New York   10002
(212) 598-0400
Music, Dance, Theatre, Visual Arts
Barbara Tate, Executive Director

DAVID HOCHSTEIN MEMORIAL MUSIC SCHOOL
50 North Plymouth Avenue
Rochester, New York   14614
(716) 454-4596

Music, Dance
Dr. Carl Atkins, President

HOFF-BARTHELSON MUSIC SCHOOL
25 School Lane
Scarsdale, New York   10583
(914) SC3-1169
Music
Mary Helton, Director

HUDSON VALLEY PHILHARMONIC MUSIC SCHOOL
P.O. Box 191
Poughkeepsie, New York   12602
(914) 454-1222
Music
Arlene Gould, Director of Education
Jody Silverberg, Music School Administrator

LEFFERTS GARDENS COMMUNITY MUSIC CENTER
1800 Bedford Avenue
Brooklyn, New York   11225
(718) 462-0948
Music
Dr. Pandora Hopkins, Director

LIGHTHOUSE MUSIC SCHOOL
New York Association for the Blind
111 East 59th Street
New York, New York   10022
(212) 355-2200
Music, Theatre
George Bennette, Director

MANNA HOUSE WORKSHOPS
338 East 106th Street
New York, New York   10029
(212) 722-8223
Music
Gloria DeNard, President

METROPOLITAN SCHOOL FOR THE ARTS
320 Montgomery Street
Syracuse, New York   13202
(315) 475-5414
Music, Dance, Theatre, Visual Arts
Annetta Kaplan, Director

MID-WESTCHESTER YM-YWHA MUSIC SCHOOL
999 Wilmot Road
Scarsdale, New York   10583
(914) 472-3300
Music
Aviva Domb, Director

MUSIC INSTITUTE OF THE JEWISH COMMUNITY CENTER OF
    STATEN ISLAND
475 Victory Boulevard
Staten Island, New York   10301
(718) 981-1500
Music
Saul Rosenfeld, Music Director

92nd STREET Y DANCE CENTER
1395 Lexington Avenue
New York, New York   10028
(212) 427-6000 (Ext. 170)
Dance

92nd STREET Y SCHOOL OF MUSIC
1395 Lexington Avenue
New York, New York   10028
(212) 427-6000 (Ext. 129)
Music
Hadassah B. Markson, Director

QUEENS COLLEGE - THE AARON COPLAND SCHOOL OF
    MUSIC: CENTER FOR PREPARATORY STUDIES IN MUSIC
Queens College, CUNY
Flushing, New York   11367-0904
(718) 520-7745
Music
Lawrence Eisman, Director
Edward Smaldone, Associate Director

ROOSA SCHOOL OF MUSIC
26 Columbia Place
Brooklyn, New York   11201
(718) 875-7371
Music
Clive Lythgoe, Executive Director

THE SCHOOL FOR STRINGS
419 West 54 Street

New York, New York   10019
(212) 315-0915
Music
Louise Behrend, Director

SHUMIATCHER SCHOOL OF MUSIC
69 Vine Road
Larchmont, New York   10538
(914) 698-7557
Music
Bella Shumiatcher, Director

SOUTHEAST QUEENS HOUSE OF MUSIC
116th Avenue & 166th Street
Jamaica, New York   11434
(212) 657-4760
Music
Ralph Satterthwaite, President

SUNSET PARK SCHOOL OF MUSIC
4520 4th Avenue, Box MH-9
Brooklyn, New York   11220
(718) 748-7860
Music
Anthony Masiello, Executive Director

THIRD STREET MUSIC SCHOOL SETTLEMENT
235 East 11th Street
New York, New York   10003
(212) 777-3240
Music, Dance, Theatre, Visual Arts
Barbara Field, Director

TURTLE BAY MUSIC SCHOOL
244 East 52nd Street
New York, New York   10022
(212) 753-8811
Music
Catherine M. Campbell, Director

WESTCHESTER CONSERVATORY OF MUSIC
20 Soundview Avenue
White Plains, New York   10606
(914) 761-3715
Music
Laura Calzolari, Director

North Carolina

COMMUNITY SCHOOL OF THE ARTS
200 West Trade Street
Charlotte, North Carolina   28202
(704) 377-4178
Music, Dance, Visual Arts
Jenni Harrison, Interim Executive Director

NORTH CAROLINA SCHOOL OF THE ARTS
Community Music School
405 West 4th Street
Winston-Salem, North Carolina
(919) 784-7170
Music
James Houlik, Director

PENLAND SCHOOL OF CRAFTS
Penland Road
Penland, North Carolina   28765
(704) 765-2359
Visual Arts
Verne Stanford, Director

SALEM COLLEGE MUSIC SCHOOL
Fine Arts Center
Winston-Salem, North Carolina   27108
(919) 721-2636
Barbara Lister-Sink, Director

SAWTOOTH CENTER FOR VISUAL DESIGN
226 North Marshall Street
Winston-Salem, North Carolina   27101
(919) 723-7395
Visual Arts
Ray Pierotti, Executive Director

UNIVERSITY OF NORTH CAROLINA AT GREENSBORO
Community Music School
School of Music, UNCG
Greensboro, North Carolina   27412-5001
(919) 379-5889
Music
Dr. James C. Prodan, Director

Ohio

BALDWIN-WALLACE COLLEGE CONSERVATORY OF MUSIC
Preparatory/Adult Education Department
M-P Hall
Baldwin-Wallace College
Berea, Ohio   44017
(216) 826-2365
Music
Mary Lou Hunger, Director

BOWLING GREEN STATE UNIVERSITY COLLEGE OF MUSICAL
   ARTS - CREATIVE ARTS PROGRAM
Bowling Green, Ohio   43403
(419) 352-6328
Music, Dance
Martin Porter, Director

THE BROADWAY SCHOOL OF MUSIC & THE ARTS
5415 Broadway Avenue
P.O. Box 27339
Cleveland, Ohio   44127
(216) 641-0630
Music, Dance, Theatre, Visual Arts
David R. Pierce, Director

CAPITAL UNIVERSITY - COMMUNITY MUSIC SCHOOL
2199 East Main Street
Columbus, Ohio   43209-2394
(614) 236-6412
Eric E. Anderson, Director

CLEVELAND MUSIC SCHOOL SETTLEMENT
11125 Magnolia Drive
Cleveland, Ohio   44106
(216) 421-5806
Director: To be announced

FAIRMOUNT CENTER FOR CREATIVE AND PERFORMING ARTS
8400 Fairmount Boulevard
P.O. Box 80
Novelty, Ohio   44072
(216) 338-3171
Dance, Crafts and Visual Arts, Gymnastics, Fencing, Karate
Marsha L. Carl, Executive Director

KARAMU HOUSE
2355 East 89th Street
Cleveland, Ohio   44106
(216) 795-7070
Music, Dance, Theatre, Visual Arts
Milton C. Morris, Director

SCHOOL OF FINE ARTS
38660 Mentor Avenue
Willoughby, Ohio   44094
(216) 951-7500
Music, Dance, Theatre, Visual Arts
James J. Savage, Executive Director

SUTPHEN SCHOOL OF MUSIC
Phyllis Wheatley Assn.
4450 Cedar Avenue
Cleveland, Ohio   44103
(216) 391-4443
Music, Dance
Lavert Stuart, Director

U. OF CINCINNATI COLLEGE – CONSERVATORY OF MUSIC
    PREPARATORY DEPARTMENT
Cincinnati, Ohio   45221
(513) 475-2883
Music, Dance, Theatre
Patricia Borger, Director

Oregon

COMMUNITY MUSIC CENTER
3350 S.E. Francis
Portland, Oregon   97202
(503) 231-1955 (Director: 231-1956)
Music
Charles Farmer, Director

Pennsylvania

ACADEMY OF CHILDREN'S MUSIC
601 Bethlehem Pike
Fort Washington, Pennsylvania   19034
(215) 233-2133

Music
Ellen Fisher, Executive Director
Robert dePasquale, Music Director

BAUM SCHOOL OF ART
31 North 5th Street (P.O. Box 653)
Allentown, Pennsylvania   18105
(215) 433-0032 or 967-1005
Visual Arts
Rudy S. Ackerman, Director

COMMUNITY MUSIC SCHOOL
32 South 5th Street
Allentown, Pennsylvania   18101
(215) 435-7725
Music, Dance
Martha Maletz, Executive Director

DARLINGTON FINE ARTS CENTER
Baltimore Pike
Wawa, Pennsylvania   19063
(215) 358-3632
Music, Dance, Theatre, Visual Arts
Athena M. Sophocles, Acting Director

THE HEGVIK SCHOOL OF MUSIC
101 East Lancaster Avenue
Wayne, Pennsylvania   19087
(215) 687-6058
Music
Dr. Robin L. Hegvik, Director

MUSIC ACADEMY
519 West College Avenue
State College, Pennsylvania   16801
(814) 238-3451
Music
Chris A. Truax, Director

ANNA L. PERLOW MUSIC SCHOOL OF THE JEWISH COMMUNITY
    CENTER
5738 Forbes Avenue
Pittsburgh, Pennsylvania   15217
(412) 521-8010
Music
Allen Sher, Director

SETTLEMENT MUSIC SCHOOL
P.O. Box 25120 (416 Queen Street)
Philadelphia, Pennsylvania   19147
(215) 336-0400
Music, Dance, Theatre
Robert Capanna, Executive Director

SUBURBAN MUSIC SCHOOL
P.O. Box 1332
Media, Pennsylvania   19063
(215) 566-4215
Music
Beatrice Wernick, Founder/Executive Director

TEMPLE UNIVERSITY COLLEGE OF MUSIC PREPARATORY &
   EXTENSION DIVISION
1619 Walnut Street
Philadelphia, Pennsylvania   19103
(215) 787-1512
Music
Nancy W. Hess, Director

WEST CHESTER UNIVERSITY COMMUNITY MUSIC SCHOOL
Swope Hall
West Chester University
West Chester, Pennsylvania   19383
(215) 436-2530
Music
Dr. Robert Lucas, Director

Rhode Island

CENTER SCHOOL FOR THE ARTS
119 High Street
Westerly, Rhode Island   02891
(401) 596-2854
Music, Dance, Theatre, Visual Arts
Betsy Dottolo, President

South Carolina

ANDERSON COLLEGE ACADEMY OF MUSIC
316 Boulevard

Anderson, South Carolina   29621
(803) 231-2127
Karilyn Slice, Director

CONVERSE COLLEGE DEPARTMENT OF PRE-COLLEGE & ADULT
    MUSIC
151 North Fairview
Spartanburg, South Carolina   29301
(803) 596-9159
Music, Dance
Dr. Irene Grau, Director

                        Tennessee

W. O. SMITH COMMUNITY MUSIC SCHOOL
1416 Edgehill Avenue
Nashville, Tennessee   37212
(615) 255-8355
Music
Dr. Kenneth Wendrich, Director

UNIVERSITY OF TENNESSEE AT CHATTANOOGA
    CADEK CONSERVATORY OF MUSIC
725 Oak Street
Chattanooga, Tennessee   37403
(615) 755-4624
Music
Dr. Peter E. Gerschefski, Director

VANDERBILT U. BLAIR SCHOOL OF MUSIC PRE-COLLEGE &
    ADULT PROGRAMS
2400 Blakemore Avenue
Nashville, Tennessee   37212
(615) 322-7651
Music
John F. Sawyer, Director

                          Utah

U.S.U. DEPARTMENT OF MUSIC YOUTH CONSERVATORY
Utah State University
Logan, Utah   84322-4015

(801) 750-3018
Edward McCallson, Director

Vermont

MUSIC SCHOOL OF BRATTLEBORO MUSIC CENTER
15 Walnut Street
Brattleboro, Vermont 05301
(802) 257-4523
Music
Catherine Stockman, Director

Virginia

ROANOKE COLLEGE PREPARATORY DIVISION OF MUSIC
Salem, Virginia 24153
(703) 389-2351 (Ext. 354)
Music, Theatre, Visual Arts
Judith W. Clark, Director

SHENANDOAH COLLEGE & CONSERVATORY COMMUNITY ARTS
    PROGRAM
Winchester, Virginia 22601
(703) 665-0960
Music, Dance, Theatre, Visual Arts
Jeffrey Schleifer, Director

VIRGINIA COMMONWEALTH UNIVERSITY COMMUNITY SCHOOL
    OF PERFORMING ARTS
1015 Grove Avenue
Richmond, Virginia 23284
(804) 257-1166
Music, Dance, Theatre
Gailyn D. Parks, Director

Washington

UNIVERSITY OF PUGET SOUND SCHOOL OF MUSIC COM-
    MUNITY MUSIC AND DANCE DEPARTMENT
Tacoma, Washington 98416
(206) 756-3575
Music, Dance
Dr. James Sorensen, Director

Wisconsin

ALVERNO COLLEGE COMMUNITY ARTS DEPARTMENT
3401 South 39th Street
Milwaukee, Wisconsin   53215
(414) 647-3906
Music, Dance, Theatre, Visual Arts
Sister Maria Teresa Patterson, Department Coordinator

UNIVERSITY OF WISCONSIN
Music for Everybody Program
Green Bay, Wisconsin   54301-7001
(414) 465-2635
Music
Lois Hahn, Director

WAUSAU CONSERVATORY OF MUSIC
P.O. Box 783
Wausau, Wisconsin   54401
(715) 845-6279
Music
John Martin, Director

WISCONSIN CONSERVATORY OF MUSIC
1584 North Prospect Avenue
Milwaukee, Wisconsin   53202
(414) 276-5760
Music
Patricia Jones, President/Director

Canada

JOHANNESEN INTERNATIONAL SCHOOL OF THE ARTS
3737 Oak Street
Vancouver, B.C.   V6H 2M4
CANADA
(604) 736-1611
Music
J.J. Johannesen, Director

MUSIC SCHOOL OF THE ST. CHRISTOPHER HOUSE
c/o Ryerson Public School
96 Denison Avenue
Toronto, Ont.   M5T 2L1
CANADA

(416) 366-3571
Mary P. Leggatt, Director

NEPEAN SCHOOL OF MUSIC
25 Esquimault Avenue
Nepean, Ont. K2H 6Z5
CANADA
(613) 820-7482
Music
James Wegg, Music Director
Peter Morris, Program Director

UNIVERSITY SETTLEMENT MUSIC SCHOOL
23 Grange Road
Toronto, Ont. M5T 1C3
CANADA
(416) 598-3444
Music
Helen Yap, Director[6]

ARTS MANAGEMENT IN COMMUNITY INSTITUTIONS (AMICI)

A Project of the National Guild of
Community Schools of the Arts

There were nine of them. They came from large
cities, suburban areas and even rural communities
in California, New England, Pennsylvania, Kentucky,
and the New York Metropolitan area. They were
community arts school administrators, as well as teachers and artists, linked in an unusual first-time effort.

It began on July 17, 1985, and when it was over
two weeks later, the graduates of the Arts Management in Community Institutions (AMICI) Project of the
National Guild of Community Schools of the Arts were
no longer strangers but close colleagues. They were
partners in a shared experience that had involved
them in learning new management skills and developing
a deeper awareness of the real and potential role that
the arts and their institutions could play in the society
around them.

The program, a training effort to involve community
arts school administrators from institutions less than
five years old in the spectrum of arts administration

concerns, made the case much larger than each
participant's specific interest. It was planned to
help broaden their frame of reference and to allow
them to experience new concepts and subject areas
from a larger perspective. At the same time, participants gained practical hands-on involvement with such
everyday areas of concern as promotion, fundraising,
organizational development, computerization and business management.

The program was organized for the National Guild
by one of its trustees, Alvin H. Reiss, editor of Arts
Management, director of the Performing Arts Management Institute and, at the time, director of Adelphi
University's graduate arts management program. Reiss,
who also handled the bulk of the teaching load, tried
to develop a program framework in which each new
element related to the sessions that preceded it. It
began with a look at the social history of the arts
in America and moved then to look at the arts industry
and how it developed within the context of American
society. The progress examined components of the
arts industry and looked at individual arts organizations, how they are organized and function, and
what roles their internal and external publics play
within them.

To make the experience richer, classroom sessions,
held at the Turtle Bay Music School in New York
City, were supplemented with three field visits, each
lasting from three to four hours. The visits--to the
New York Shakespeare Festival, to learn about its
program and have a hands-on involvement with computers; to Affiliate Artists, Inc., to discuss its program with staff members and one of the involved
artists; and to the New York State Council on the
Arts, for a tour of the facilities and a work session
with the public relations director and one of the
program directors--gave AMICI participants firsthand
involvement with top arts professionals and helped
to animate some of the abstract topics discussed in
the classroom.

Because the program was limited to only nine par-
ticipants--seven interns and two observers--everyone
was deeply involved in the learning process. Classes
were taught seminar style and discussions were spirited,
and provocative questions were raised frequently.
Students were given overnight assignments on several

occasions, and a number of sessions opened with
discussions of national events in and outside of the
arts that related to the arts, based on students reading every section of the New York Times. A range
of materials was given to students--sample budgets,
marketing plans, fundraising proposals--selected by
the top arts professionals who taught their subject
specialities: Harris Goldman of the Stamford, CT,
Hartman Theatre, on financial management and budgets; Alan Toman, former marketing director of the
New York City Opera, on marketing; and Ilene Lie-
berman, of the Queens Symphony, on fundraising.
In addition, a special panel of top community arts
school administrators, joined by Lolita Mayadas, Executive Director of the National Guild of Community
Schools of the Arts, presented a panel session dealing
specifically with the organization and operation of
a community school of the arts.

As the program continued, a special camaraderie
developed among the participants both in and out
of the classroom, and many went to dinner and to
evening events together. One participant, a New
York City resident, even organized a walking tour
of Greenwich Village for her colleagues. Although
the program held to its overall agenda of time and
topics, flexibility was deliberately built into it because
of the demanding work load and the study assignments.

The program, which concluded its New York portion
with a final gala luncheon at a nearby restaurant,
didn't end then, however. Each participant was
asked to prepare a special assignment and return it
within three to four months. Furthermore, the experience will be enhanced even further when, later
in the 1985-86 season, all of the seven interns will
participate in a four-week work internship at a major
National Guild school, in their specified area of management interest.

Because each of the students came from a different
background and level of experience, the specific
benefits of the program varied among them. What
seemed to be uniform, however, was agreement on
their involvement in a rich and unique experience
and their common interest in continuing and broadening
their activities in the arts.

One called the AMICI program "a real shot in the
arm of inspiration for me, and as a result, my school."

Another claimed to have gained "a much broader
sense of the meaning of the arts in the nation as a
whole and in the local communities as segments of the
whole." Another spoke of "the profound impact on
the way I think about my work. I'm now looking for
and working with ideas on a much broader basis than
before."

Perhaps the best indication of the program's success is the fact that many of the attendees immediately
began to apply much of what they had learned to
their respective schools, organizing board retreats
and special planning sessions. The AMICI program,
which is planned as an annual event, was presented
with support from the National Endowment for the Arts.
This enabled the National Guild not only to offer it
without charge to interns but to provide them with
stipends of $150 a week during the two-week training
session and the four-week on-site internships.[7]

Reprinted from "1984-85
Annual Report" of the
National Guild. Written
by Alvin H. Reiss Dated
October 1985

Many special projects have been undertaken by the
National Guild over the years which had their roots firmly
planted in the community. One of the notable examples is
the program known as the ALPINES. A clear description of
the ALPINES is presented in the National Guild's "1985-86
Annual Report" which also shows how the acronym was derived:

ARTS LITERACY PROGRAM IN NEIGHBORHOOD

ELEMENTARY SCHOOLS (ALPINES)

The ALPINES Project is an in-service training program
that utilizes arts specialists to enhance and expand the
technical skills of elementary classroom teachers for
the purpose of reintroducing the arts into the regular
school curriculum on a continuing basis.

As a result of such training, the project enables
the classroom teachers, with the assistance of arts
specialists, to practice the arts with their students

on a daily basis in the classroom, not just as a once-a-week "frill." Throughout, the accent is on non-competitive development of skills and how they relate to the skills required in the other disciplines. Using this methodology consistently the arts become an integral part of the learning process, absorbed in both student and teacher alike. The conceptual framework was based upon Dr. Zipper's prototype established with the cooperation of the Los Angeles Unified School District under the aegis of the University of Southern California in 1974.

The model ALPINES Project at Newark, New Jersey, was implemented at the Louise Spence Elementary School through the mutual cooperation and support of the National Guild of Community Schools of the Arts, the Newark Board of Education, the National Endowment for the Arts, and the Victoria Foundation. Although the program was intended to be self-perpetuating after a period of 4 years, it has been terminated after a period of 2 years due to several factors. The primary reason, however, is the lack of multi-year grants and the inability of the Newark Board of Education to commit the annual costs involved in supporting the program on an ongoing basis.

Several member institutions have expressed some interest in replicating this project. While the Guild is prepared to provide its services, documentation and materials, sufficient private and public funds for at least 4 years, together with the ongoing commitment of participating school boards, must be obtained prior to implementation of ALPINES in other districts.[8]

This represents a classic example of arts education in the community. Many special groups, organizations and funding agencies are brought together to establish a worthwhile and imaginative arts education program. Perhaps this experiment will motivate other communities to accept the results of the program in Newark, and encourage those communities to learn from the recent past and to take the project through further, valid, experimental techniques.

YOUNG COMPOSERS AWARDS

Annually the National Guild of Community Schools of the

Arts undertakes special projects designed to bring the arts
and creativity into the communities that Guild schools serve.
One of the projects begun in 1983 is The Young Composers
Awards. At the 1983 Guild Conference held in Philadelphia,
Dr. Herbert Zipper announced a gift of $10,000 to establish
an annual award of $1,000 in perpetuity for the best musical
competition written by a teenager who was being instructed
at a member school of the National Guild. Dr. Zipper's generosity was lauded at the meeting of the Board of Directors
on February 2, 1984, and a new committee was formed to
formulate the rules and procedures under which the award
would be presented for the first time during the 1984-85 school
year.

Subsequently, Dr. Zipper also obtained the support of
the Rockefeller Foundation which pledged annual awards of
$750, $500, and $250 respectively for a period of three years
from 1984-1987. Although the Young Composers Awards were
initially open to students at Guild schools only, the Board
made a decision in June, 1984 with the support of Dr. Zipper,
to open this competition to all students of junior high and
high school age, whether or not they were enrolled as students
at a National Guild school. The competition entered its third
year in 1986.

In the announcement brochure for the 1986-87 award,
Dr. Zipper included the following letter announcing the competition to the public:

DEAR FELLOW MUSIC TEACHERS, INSTRUMENTAL,
VOCAL, THEORY AND ALL:

This is an appeal for your cooperation. Three years
ago I established an endowment that enables the
National Guild of Community Schools of the Arts to
award an annual prize of $1,000 to a promising young
composer. The Rockefeller Foundation, recognizing
the merits of this program, added a grant for three
additional prizes. An independent jury of renowned
musicians judges all submitted entries.
Unfortunately, composing serious music today is
not in the center of music education at the pre-college
level. Performing and preparing for the many national
and international competitions overshadow the concern
for the creative aspect of music which is, afterall,

the lifeblood of the art. This situation is what moti-
vated me to initiate "The Young Composers Awards."

In the long range, the purpose of this competition
can be achieved only if all music students from the
elementary level on would be encouraged by their
teachers to try their hand at writing music, beginning
with little pieces for the instrument they are learning,
simple songs, etc. The award competition, I believe,
may become a compelling incentive. If more emphasis
would be focused on the inventiveness of many students, genuine creative talents could eventually be
discovered. It takes tons of ore to extract one ounce
of gold.

I should like to invite you all to join in the effort
by encouraging your students to write music, in the
hope that in the years to come the act of composition
will again occupy the place in the center of music
education where it belongs.

Cordially,

Dr. Herbert Zipper,
Honorary Trustee[9]

The application form carried ample space for information
about the student, where he studied, etc., and a place
to identify the composition he had written and for what it was
scored, his date of birth and a proper place for him to sign
his name, and a place for his teacher to sign verifying the
application. The form also boldly announced the following
information:

THE HERBERT ZIPPER PRIZE

$1,000

THE ROCKEFELLER FOUNDATION AWARDS

$750
$500
$250[10]

The competition was underway!

INTERNATIONAL EXCHANGE

As a result of meetings held between representatives of the National Guild and the German Association of Music Schools (Verband deutscher Musikschulen--VdM) 225 students from eight Guild schools' ensembles were invited to perform during the European Youth Festival of Music in West Germany during May, 1985. No other groups from the United States of America were invited to participate in the Festival which marked the International Year of Youth and the tercentenaries of the births of J. S. Bach, G. F. Handel and D. Scarlatti. The Guild students joined some 9,000 young people who gave performances around the country and in the closing event at the Olympiahalle at Munich, in the presence of the President, Richard von Weizacker.

Prior to that event, representatives of the National Guild attended a conference of the European Music Union at which a joint declaration was signed calling for cooperation for the purpose of promoting music (and performing arts) education in both continents wherever financially possible. The joint declaration included the pursuit of common interests, exchanges of experiences in music education and performance, exchanges of information and ideas, exchanges of student and teacher delegations and ensembles, and the holding of common meetings and congresses.

The exchanges continued in 1986 with two student ensembles from West Germany visiting the United States (Minneapolis, MN and Montclair, NJ). A delegation of six music school directors and officials from the Federal Republic of Germany also attended the National Guild's 49th Conference in Washington, and further plans were made to invite six to eight student groups to this country during the spring and summer of 1987 as part of the 50th Anniversary Celebration.[11]

DISTINGUISHED FACULTY MEMBERS PAST AND PRESENT

The Community Schools of the Arts have attracted distinguished musical performers, conductors and composers in areas throughout the country where such schools existed. A partial list of such faculty members is presented below.

PIANISTS: Bruce Simonds was a faculty member of the Hartford Conservatory of Music and Dance; Isabella Vengerova
joined the faculty of the Music School of the Henry Street
Settlement when she first came to this country and remained
on the faculty until her death; Leonard Shure was chairman
of the piano faculty at Cleveland Music School Settlement for
many years; Gary Graffman has given Master Classes at the
Settlement Music School in Philadelphia; Clyde Lythogoe
served as department chairman at the Cleveland Music School
Settlement and now is the director of Roosa School of Music
in Brooklyn, NY; Guy Duckworth served on the faculty of
the MacPhail Center for the Arts in Minneapolis; and Theodore
Letvin served as department chairman at the Cleveland Music
School Settlement.

SINGERS: The distinguished American soprano, Dorothy
Maynor, earned an outstanding reputation as a recitalist
around the world and later founded the Harlem School of the
Arts in New York City where she was the director for many
years and also taught advanced voice students. Miss Maynor
also served as the president of the National Guild from 1971
to 1974; Rose Bampton, the internationally known Metropolitan
Opera soprano, joined the voice faculty of the Henry Street
Settlement Music School where she successfully prepared two
young singers for their Town Hall debuts in New York. They
were Billie Lynn Daniel, soprano, and Thomas Carey, bari-
tone; Judith Raskin, soprano, and Joanna Simon, mezzo-
soprano, have each served on the faculty of the 92nd Street
YM/YWHA in New York City; and Giovanni Martinelli, the
famed Metropolitan Opera tenor, taught for many years at the
Third Street Music School Settlement.

VIOLINISTS: Louis Persinger and Ivan Galamian, two world-
renowned violin pedagogues, each taught at a settlement
music school in New York City, Persinger at the Third Street
Music School Settlement and Galamian at the Music School
of the Henry Street Settlement; Berl Senofsky was as a child
a student at Henry Street and, as an adult, he has become
a faculty member of the Peabody Institute as well as the
Peabody Prep; Dorothy DeLay, the prominent violin teacher,
was a faculty member of the New England Conservatory Extension Division. She is currently on the faculty of the
Juilliard School of Music also; Joseph Gingold is an alumnus
of the Third Street Music School Settlement and later he
taught at the Cleveland Music School Settlement when he was

the concertmaster of the Cleveland Symphony Orchestra. One
of his pupils at the Cleveland School was Jaime Laredo. Mr.
Gingold is now on the faculty of the Indiana University School
of Music in Bloomington; Helen Kwalwasser was a child prodigy
playing the violin, and she later studied with Ivan Galamian
at the Henry Street Settlement Music School where she also
became a faculty member and taught for many years. Miss
Kwalwasser is currently on the music faculty of Temple University and is frequently heard as a soloist and concertmistress
with several chamber orchestras and ensembles; Louise Behrend,
who had been a scholarship student studying with Mr. Persinger at the Juilliard School of Music, was a recognized
concert violinist when she began to teach at the Henry Street
Music School. It was she who later introduced the Suzuki
method to pre-school aged children at Henry Street. She
founded her own School for Strings in 1970 in New York City.

CONDUCTORS: David Mannes began training the orchestra
of young players at the Third Street Music School Settlement
and later became the director of that school. Subsequently
he established the Mannes College of Music in New York City;
Lehman Engel taught at the Henry Street Settlement Music
School and was the conductor of the premier performance of
Aaron Copland's play opera, The Second Hurricane, when it
was presented at that school in 1937; Arnold Gamson, conductor
of the American Chamber Opera Co., trained the Henry
Street Orchestra for one season; Robert Scholz formed and
conducted the Henry Street Music School's Mozart Orchestra
which included students and faculty members of that School,
and subsequently he established the American Chamber Orchestra which he conducted for several seasons; Felix Popper,
who is currently with the New York City Center Opera, trained
the Opera Workshop at Henry Street and also its orchestra
for several seasons; Paul Vermel, now at the University of
Illinois, conducted the Henry Street Music School Orchestra
from 1956 through 1959 when he left to become the conductor
of the Fresno Symphony Orchestra in California.

OTHER INSTRUMENTS: Flautists included Samuel Baron who
was first a student at Henry Street and then a faculty member; Julius Baker, who is known for his teaching at Juilliard,
was also a faculty member of the 92nd Street YM/YWHA Music
School. Bernard Goldberg taught at the Cleveland Music
School Settlement when he was a member of the Cleveland
Symphony Orchestra. He has been the first flautist with the

Pittsburgh Symphony Orchestra for many years, and for many years he was on the faculty of the Duquesne University School of Music. Oboists who were faculty members at Guild schools include Lois Wann who taught at Henry Street where she was the instructor of Ronald Roseman who later joined the faculty there also. Bassoonists included Stephen Maxym, one of the first bassoonists of the Metropolitan Opera Orchestra, who trained Leonard Hindell at the Henry Street Music School and later at the Manhattan School of Music. After his graduation from the Manhattan School of Music, Mr. Hindell joined the orchestra at the Metropolitan Opera also.

A very special recognition must be given here to Sol Schoenbach, bassoonist of most unusual abilities both in performance and in teaching of the instrument. He was for many years the first bassoonist of the Philadelphia Orchestra. He resigned from that position to assume the post as director of the Settlement Music School in Philadelphia, a position he held for more than twenty years. His interest in the students and their problems, his dedication to the School, and his support of his faculty and staff made him outstanding in every way. At the time of this writing he is frequently called to all parts of the world for advice on both playing and teaching bassoon. He was the winner of the Guild's Rosenbaum Memorial Award in 1983 in recognition of his outstanding service to his school, the National Guild and the music profession.

COMPOSERS: Composers of outstanding reputations have been faculty members of National Guild Schools. The list includes Stephan Wolpe, who taught at the 92nd Street YM/YWHA; Herbert Elwell who was affiliated with the Cleveland Music School Settlement, and Howard Whittaker, who was its director for many years; and in alphabetical order Aaron Copland, Paul Creston, Roy Harris, Robert Starer and Robert Ward were all on the faculty of the Music School of the Henry Street Settlement at some time in that School's sixty year history.

DANCERS: Arthur Mitchell, who was a dancer with the New York City Center Ballet taught at the Harlem School of the Arts and has since formed his own dance company in Harlem; Alwin Nikolais was on the faculty of the Playhouse of the Henry Street Settlement and is outstanding for his creativity and imagination as well as his musical abilities and choreography. He and Murray Louis, each of whom has his own professional dance company at the time of this writing, were on the staff of the Playhouse from 1948 to 1970. During that period of time they presented many brilliant dance performances; Edward Villella was also an important member of the New York City Center Dance Company and has been on the faculty of the Cape Cod Conservatory.

This impressive list of artist teachers is only partial.

DISTINGUISHED ALUMNI OF MEMBER SCHOOLS (partial list)

Alumnus or Alumna	Member School and Location
Larry Adler, Harmonica Virtuoso	Peabody Institute, Preparatory, Baltimore, MD
Lucine Amara, Operatic Soprano	Community Music Center, San Francisco, CA
Samuel Baron, Flautist	Henry Street Settlement Music School, New York
Leon Bates, Jazz Pianist	Settlement Music School, Philadelphia, PA
Abba Bogin, Pianist	Henry Street Settlement Music School, New York
Martin Canin, Pianist	Henry Street Settlement Music School, New York
Stuart Canin, Violinist	Henry Street Settlement Music School, New York
Thomas Carey, Baritone	Henry Street Settlement Music School, New York
Chubby Checker, Pop Artist	Settlement Music School, Philadelphia, PA
Clamma Dale, Soprano	Settlement Music School, Philadelphia, PA
Billie Lynn Daniel, Soprano	Henry Street Settlement Music School, New York
Anthony di Bonaventura, Pianist	Third Street Music School Settlement, New York
Mario di Bonaventura, Conductor	Third Street Music School Settlement, New York
Samuel di Bonaventura, Historian	Third Street Music School Settlement, New York
Armand DiCamillo, Violinist	Settlement Music School, Philadelphia, PA
Jacob Druckman, Composer	Settlement Music School, Philadelphia, PA

Alumnus or Alumna (cont'd)	Member School and Location
Samuel Dushkin, Violinist	Third Street Music School Settlement, New York
Bayard Edwards, Violist	Settlement Music School, Philadelphia, PA
Akiro Ende, Conductor	USC, Los Angeles, Los Angeles, CA
Jules Eskin, Violoncellist	Settlement Music School, Philadelphia, PA
Morton Feldman, Composer	Third Street Music School Settlement, New York
Jose Feliciano, Pop Singer, Guitarist	Lighthouse Music School, New York, NY
Lilit Gampel, Violinist	USC, Los Angeles, Los Angeles, CA
Joseph Gingold, Violinist	Third Street Music School Settlement, New York
Anthony Gigliotti, Clarinetist	Settlement Music School, Philadelphia, PA
Benny Goodman, Clarinetist, "King of Swing"	Hull-House Music School, Chicago, IL
Martha Graham, Dancer, Choreographer	Henry Street Settlement Playhouse, New York
Gideon Grau, Violinist/Conductor	Henry Street Settlement Music School, New York
Buddy Green, Jazz Musician	Settlement Music School, Philadelphia, PA
Sidney Harth, Violinist	Third Street Music School Settlement, New York
Helen Hayes, Actress	Henry Street Settlement Playhouse, New York
Kathleen Hegierski, Opera Singer	Community Music School of Buffalo, Buffalo, NY
Leonard Hindell, Bassoonist	Henry Street Settlement Music School, New York
Randall Hodgkinson, Pianist	Settlement Music School, Philadelphia, PA
Robert Jordan, Pianist	Wilmington Music School, Wilmington, DE
Doris Jung, Soprano	Henry Street Settlement Music School, New York
Jon Klibonoff, Pianist	Spring Valley Music School, Spring Valley, NY
Helen Kwalwasser, Violinist	Henry Street Settlement Music School, New York

Alumnus or Alumna (cont'd)	Member School and Location
Ezra Laderman, Composer	Brooklyn Music School Settlement, Brooklyn, NY
Mario Lanza, Tenor	Settlement Music School, Philadelphia, PA
Jaime Laredo, Violinist	Cleveland Music School Settlement, Cleveland, OH
Isadore Lateiner, Violinist	Henry Street Settlement Music School, New York
Jacob Lateiner, Pianist	Henry Street Settlement Music School, New York
Jerome Lowenthal, Pianist	Settlement Music School, Philadelphia, PA
Irving Ludwig, Violinist	Settlement Music School, Philadelphia, PA
Chuck Mangione, Pop Artist	Hochstein Memorial Music School, Rochester, NY
Johnny Mathis, Pop Singing Artist	Community Music Center, San Francisco, CA
Phyllis McKinney, Violinist	Wilmington Music School, Wilmington, DE
Theresa Merrit, Actress	Settlement Music School, Philadelphia, PA
Horatio Miller, Pianist	Settlement Music School, Philadelphia, PA
Mitch Miller, Oboist/Conductor	Hochstein Memorial Music School, Rochester, NY
David Nadien, Violinist	Henry Street Settlement Music School, New York
Alex North, Pianist	Settlement Music School, Philadelphia, PA
Garrick Ohlsson, Pianist	Westchester Conservatory of Music, Westchester, NY
Leonard Pennario, Pianist	Community Music School of Buffalo, Buffalo, NY
William Preucil, Jr., Violinist	Preucil School of Music, Iowa City, IA
Judith Raskin, Soprano	92nd Street YM/YWHA Music School, New York
Ronald Roseman, Oboist	Henry Street Settlement Music School, New York
Booker Rowe, Violinist	Settlement Music School, Philadelphia, PA
Patricia Rushen, Jazz Pianist	USC, Los Angeles, Los Angeles, CA

Alumnus or Alumna (cont'd)	Member School and Location
Evelyn Sachs, Mezzo-Soprano	Henry Street Settlement Music School, New York
Jeannette Scovotti, Soprano	Third Street Music School Settlement, New York
Berl Senofsky, Violinist	Henry Street Settlement Music School, New York
Ralph Shapey, Composer	Settlement Music School, Philadelphia, PA
Murray Sidlin, Conductor	Peabody Institute, Preparatory, Baltimore, MD
Gerald Tarack, Violin	Henry Street Settlement Music School, New York
Michael Tilson Thomas, Conduc.	USC, Los Angeles, Los Angeles, CA
Tatiana Troyanos, Mezzo-Sopr.	Brooklyn Music School Settlement, Brooklyn, NY
Dionne Warwick, Pop Singer	Univ. of Hartford, Hartt School of Music, Community Division, Hartford, CT
Kathleen Winkler, Violinist	Settlement Music School, Philadelphia, PA

THE COLONEL SAMUEL ROSENBAUM MEMORIAL AWARD

Annually the National Guild of Community Schools of the Arts presents its Colonel Samuel Rosenbaum Memorial Award in honor of the Guild's longtime friend and supporter, Col. Samuel Rosenbaum. The Award is given each year to an individual whose work is nationally recognized as exemplifying and promoting the ideals to which the National Guild and its membership are dedicated. Past recipients are listed below:

1973 Paul Rosenbaum	Generous supporter of Guild School and relative of the Colonel
1974 Donald MacNaughton	Chairman, Chief Executive Officer of the Prudential Life Insurance Company of America

1975 David Rockefeller, Jr.   Nationally recognized arts
                                    education advocate

1976 Roger L. Stevens   Chairman, Board of Trust-
                                    ees, John F. Kennedy Cen-
                                    ter for the Performing Arts

1977 Dr. Herbert Zipper   Project Director, University
                                    of Southern California
                                    School of Performing Arts;
                                    "Prime Mover" of the Com-
                                    munity School Movement

1978 Dr. George Tatham   President, University Settle-
                                    ment, Toronto Canada; active
                                    supporter of the Movement

1979 Dr. Kenneth Brown Billups   Chairman, NEA's Expansion
                                    Arts Panel; Member, Mis-
                                    souri State Arts Council
                                    and civic committees

1980 Philip K. Allen   Chairman, Board of Trus-
                                    tees, Community Music
                                    Center of Boston

1981 A. B. Spellman   Director, Expansion Arts
                                    Program, NEA

1982 Hon. Livingston Biddle, Jr. Retired Chairman, NEA

1983 Dr. Sol Schoenbach   Retired Director, Settlement
                                    Music School, Philadelphia;
                                    long-time supporter of the
                                    Movement

1984 Dr. Lester Glick   Retired President of the
                                    Guild; President, Cleveland
                                    Music School Settlement;
                                    long-time supporter of the
                                    Movement

1985 Richard Colburn   Board Member, Community
                                    School of Performing Arts;
                                    advocate of arts education
                                    for the young

1986 Marta Casals Istomin

Artistic Director, Kennedy
Center for the Performing
Arts; advocate for arts
education

1987 Joseph Gingold

Outstanding violinist and
supporter of the Music
School Settlement Movement[12]

TRUSTEES, PRESIDENTS, DIRECTORS

Honorary Trustees

Dr. Allen Sapp   Dr. Robert Suderburg
James J. Savage   Eloise Sutton
Stephen Shiman   Daniel Windham
John A. Smith

Presidents

Janet D. Schenck	1939-1941
Johan Grolle	1942-1949
Howard Whittaker	1949-1955
Ruth Kemper	1955-1957
Dr.Herbert Zipper	1957-1961
Dr. Robert F. Egan	1961-1965
Harris Danziger	1966-1971
Dorothy Maynor	1971-1974
Dr. Kenneth Wendrich (Acting)	1975
Dr. Lester Glick	1975-1979
Dr. Allen Sapp	1979-1981
Henry Bridges	1981-1983
Monroe Levin	1983-1987

Directors

Dr. Herbert Zipper	1967-1972
Charles Mark	1972-1973
Dorothy Amarandos	1973-1977
Marcie Horwitz	1977-1981
Lolita Mayadas	1981-[13]

50th ANNIVERSARY CELEBRATION

November 7-10, 1987
Penta Hotel, New York City

The 50th Anniversary of the National Guild of Community
Schools of the Arts, which was celebrated at the Guild's
annual conference in 1987, marked a milestone in the history
of this long established community arts organization. As a
firmly founded professional and service association, the Guild
is recognized throughout the United States and Canada. At
the time of this writing the Guild represents 170 certified
member schools. The membership of the National Guild was

projected to be 200 schools by the time of the Fall, 1987 conference. This book had been planned to be completed in time for the gala celebration in New York City, the home of the first Settlement Music School.

Currently the member schools have a combined annual budget over $37,000,000 and serve almost 280,000 students in regular classes and in outreach programs in cooperation with public schools, orchestras, and other cultural and social service agencies in communities around the country.

In recognition of this half-century of service in the arts, the Guild presented a program of celebration which reflected the diversity of these schools as well as the unity of their central mission. The program also recognized the achievements of distinguished alumni from Guild schools, showcased young, talented musicians and artists, presented activities in fine and performing arts, and built a national visibility and awareness.

Because the National Guild was founded in New York City and was later incorporated in the state of New York, many of these jubilee events were held in New York City to coincide with the 50th national convention co-hosted by the New York Metropolitan Chapter (with 43 member schools, it is the largest in the Guild). Zubin Menta was honorary chairman of the celebration.

RECOMMENDED STRUCTURE FOR A COMMUNITY SCHOOL OF

THE ARTS

At this point it seems wise to look closely at how a community school of the arts is actually structured. Many schools have been organized and opened for business in a rather hit-or-miss fashion (which was also true of some of the early Community Music Schools). Since this is never an advisable procedure to adopt, the following information and materials are intended for those who are interested in forming a fledgling school or schools in their own communities, or for those who might wish to re-structure their present institutions or perhaps to expand them. There are no set rules that must be followed in the organizing of a community school of the arts, but these are guidelines or suggestions which may be helpful:

Philosophy

As has been stated earlier in this document, it is essential for a community school of the arts to have a fully
developed and understood philosophy which ultimately must
be accepted by the Board of Directors, the administrators
and the faculty members and staff. Several examples of
philosophical statements from various schools have been presented earlier (see chapter III), and the National Guild's
philosophy has been presented in full. It is, therefore, sufficient to say that a firm philosophy is a requirement in order
to structure a school of the arts.

Board of Directors, Trustees, or Governors

The governing body of a Community School of the Arts
usually consists of a Board of Directors, Trustees, or Governors, which is the group fundamentally responsible for successful operation of the school. The title is really a matter
of choice and makes little difference. The Board's main
responsibilities are 1) to approve and accept the school's
philosophy and to see to it that it is observed; 2) to select
the chief administrative officer, director or whatever is the
chosen title; 3) to approve and to be responsible for the
School's budget and its support.

The members of the Board must be selected with great
discernment. They should have a genuine interest in the
arts that are being taught at the School. Since the needs
of the organization are vast, it is wise to choose Board members from different areas of expertise such as the following:

1) a lawyer, to advise on necessary legal matters;

2) an accountant or banker, to help organize and to
   supervise the bookkeeping system of the School
   and to advise on matters of taxes, investments,
   etc.;

3) a realtor or an architect, to advise on land values
   and building codes;

4) a public official, to advise on current trends in
   city planning, road construction, etc.:

5) a prominent educator, to suggest and support the educational policies of the School;

6) an eminent musician, to evaluate and guide the School's musical standards;

7) a public relations or advertising executive, to give advice on the School's publicity campaign;

8) people from other professions and industry, to add vitality to the School;

9) a faculty representative (chosen by the faculty);

10) a community representative (selected by the community). Other categories can certainly be added according to the School's needs.

It is always prudent to have Board members who can raise funds and/or contribute themselves in generous amounts, and other Board members who have those special skills which are needed by the School. All Board members should contribute something, be it money, time and/or service or a combination of the three to the School. Inactive Board members are of little value.

An exceedingly large number of Board members can become unwieldy. Many schools find that eleven to twenty-five Board members are adequate for their needs. An uneven number of Board members is desirable. Particularly when voting on important issues, the uneven number can show a clear majority and avoid the often difficult and time-consuming ties during voting procedures.

Board meetings should be held at least once every other month, preferably monthly. An arrangement can be made, however, to have the Executive Committee of the Board meet alternately with the full board. For example:

Month	Meeting	Month	Meeting
Sept.	Full Board	Oct.	Exec. Committee
Nov.	Full Board	Dec.	Exec. Committee, etc.

Length of terms for both Board members and officers should be determined carefully from the beginning. Many

Boards use a rotation system for the election of members and officers of the Board. In such a case each term of office is for two or three years, with an option of being elected to a second and consecutive term. The procedure to be followed should be clearly explained in the By-laws of the institution.

Ordinarily Board members should not be involved in the daily operations of the school or in the formation of curricula, etc., except in special or unusual situations. These matters are the tasks of the faculty members and administrators.

In order to be considered a not-for-profit organization, the school should be incorporated in the state in which it exists. The By-laws of the institution should define all of the procedures expressed above. Individual states will have their own requirements and procedures for incorporation. Information can be obtained from the State Capitol. Institutions should treat these matters with great care and caution.

The Music Advisory Committee, Art Advisory, Dance, etc.
An expecially valuable body comes in the form of the Music Advisory Committee, or the Art Advisory Committee, or the Dance Advisory Committee, etc., particularly when the art form taught is housed as a department of the larger institution, e.g. a settlement house, a YM/YWHA, a community center, etc. In this case the Board of Directors governs the entire organization, and many Board members feel that it is wise to have an Advisory Committee in the specialized field, consisting of professionals in the indicated area or areas. Often the chairman of such an advisory committee is also voted to the Board of Directors, where his specific responsibility is to represent the program of that specified artistic endeavor. This arrangement works very satisfactorily, and many Board members consider it a necessity to have this kind of arrangement, since they themselves know little or nothing about the artistic field in question, but they are very interested in furthering the development of the arts in the total program.

The Honorary Music Committee, Honorary Art Committee, etc.
Many Schools have found it constructive and helpful to create an Honorary Music Committee, or an Honorary Art Committee, etc., which seldom functions as a committee, but consists of prominent artists in the various fields who are willing to lend their prestige to advance the cause of a community

school of the arts. Such committees have occasionally proved themselves to be very helpful, but they should not be confused with the more action-oriented Music or Art Advisory Committee.

Musical Director and Executive Director

Some schools have found the pressure so great that it is necessary and desirable to split the position of director into two, classifying them as musical director and executive director. The administration then divides its responsibilities. All dealings with the faculty, problems with curriculum, program planning, music problems with students, etc., are handled by the musical director. All other details: supervision of the office, schedules, payment of bills, collection of fees, etc., are handled by the executive director. This system works in some schools, but it is obvious that the two directors must be cooperative and compatible, otherwise this system cannot work at all.

The Faculty

The teaching staff is the backbone of the school. A school is quite naturally measured by the calibre of its faculty members. Therefore, the hiring and retaining of teachers should be done cautiously. It is understood that the people being considered should have the best artistic backgrounds available in the community. For some schools in smaller communities this poses a difficult problem.

The teacher must also have a true sense of social consciousness. The people with whom he/she deals are of prime importance, and art is the means by which to reach them. This must be keenly felt by each teacher. This does not imply that the teacher lowers his artistic standards. Rather, he strives to elevate the student's musical or artistic taste and to cultivate the interest of the pupil to its full capacity.

It has not been the usual practice to require that the teacher have a degree, but this requirement is being adopted by many schools, particularly if the schools are hiring young or inexperienced faculty members. In lieu of a degree, a satisfactory art education and teaching experience can be

accepted. Some music schools require performance ability,
others do not.   Discretion must be used in establishing any
kind of rigid regulation, but a thorough investigation of the
prospective faculty member's background and abilities should
be made before he is hired. At the time he joins the staff,
the teacher must be informed of pay rates, methods of payment to faculty members, school policies and procedures,
specific faculty responsibilities, length of school year, the
school's calendar, etc. Often a faculty handbook is presented
which gives all such information.

Should there be a conflict with other employment of the
prospective teacher, such as his being a member of a professional performing symphony orchestra, will he experience
time conflicts with his school schedule? Does the orchestra
go on tour for six to eight weeks in the middle of the school's
teaching year? How will this affect the students he teaches?
Are his talents so great that, even though the conflict exists,
he is needed and wanted at the school? Many schools do face
such problems and solve them successfully. Those problems,
however, must be addressed before the new faculty member
is hired.

The Student Body

Numerically speaking, the largest group or classification
in any school is the student body. Most community schools
of the arts will find that their student bodies are quite
diversified as to musical or artistic abilities, length of time
in previous study, interest and aims with the art form, financial situation, etc. It is the responsibility of the community
school of the arts to absorb these different backgrounds into
its composite picture. The implications of this are vast.

A student who is ready for public performances or continuation of a performance career should be able to find an
instructor who can lead him further, and the absolute be-
ginner needs an instructor sufficiently experienced to start
him successfully on his musical or his artistic study. Students
who come from financially secure backgrounds can pay the
full established fee, while those who come from modest means
pay a commensurate amount.

The majority of students come primarily from the local

community or the neighborhood, but as the school establishes itself and builds a good reputation, students may come from distant points. Whenever possible, those newcomers should be absorbed into the school program, for they often bring to the school new life and interest.

There follow some visual examples (pp. 388-89) to clarify some aspects and relationships of a community school of the arts.

1. STRUCTURE OF A COMMUNITY SCHOOL OF THE ARTS

   As in many other not-for-profit organizations, the Board of Directors, Trustees, or Governors is the chief body responsible for the operations of the school, both philosophically and financially.

   The daily operations of the school, its selection of faculty members, and its contact with the Board are channeled through the office of the school's director, who in turn supervises the administrative and clerical staff as well as the faculty. The director also has great obligations and responsibilities to the student body without which the school would not exist.

   Formal structure and procedures can facilitate the smooth operation of the institution.

2. PUBLIC RELATIONS

   Good informational coverage of the local community is essential and must of necessity be a two-way street: information sent out and information brought in through various informational media-- direct mailing, newspapers, periodicals, radio, and television.

   Clear and effective job descriptions can be of great value to all parties concerned. Each employee knows his responsibilities, and each supervisor knows who is responsible for each operation of the school. In written form these become invaluable.

THE STRUCTURE OF A COMMUNITY SCHOOL OF THE ARTS

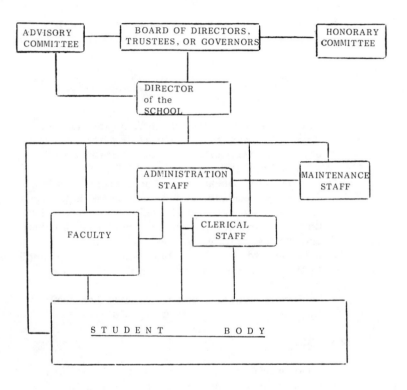

In some cases the Director may be divided into two positions, the Executive Director and the Musical Director.

Where the School of the Arts is a function of a larger organization, the Board of Directors works through the Director of the larger organization to the head of the School of the Arts. In this case the Music and Arts Advisory Committee is required to advise and report to the Board of Directors.[14]

PUBLIC RELATIONS[15]

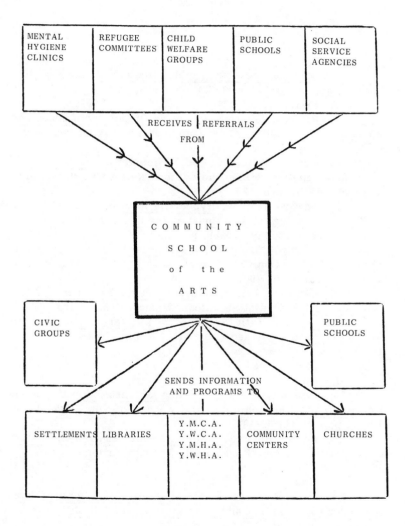

NOTES *

CHAPTER 1

1. Webster's New Biographies Dictionary (Springfield,
Mass.: Merriam-Webster, 1983), p. 790.
2. Ibid., p. 127.
3. H. C. Colles (ed.), Grove's Dictionary of Music and
Musicians, third edition (New York: The Macmillan Company,
1935), pp. 391, 392.
4. Jean L. McKechnie (ed.), Webster's New Universal
Unabridged Dictionary, second edition (New York: Simon and
Schuster, 1979), p. 1120.
5. Edward Winslow, Hypocrisie Unmasked (1646). Quoted
in Waldo Seldon Pratt, The Music of the Pilgrims (Boston:
Oliver Ditson Company, 1921), p. 6.
6. Luman H. Long (ed.), The World Almanac and Book
of Facts, 1971 edition (New York: Newspaper Enterprise Association, 1971), p. 700.
7. Henry C. Lahee, Annals of Music in America: A
Chronological Record of Significant Musical Events, from 1640
to the Present Day, with Comments on the Various Periods into
Which the Work Is Divided (Boston: Marshall Jones Company,
1922), p. 3.
8. Ibid.
9. Ibid.
10. James A. Keene, A History of Music Education in the
United States (Hanover: University Press of New England,
1982), pp. 15-31, 32-58.
11. Romain Rolland, A Musical Tour Through the Land
of the Past (London: Kegan Paul, Trench, Trubner & Co.,
1922), pp. 171, 172.
12. Ibid.
13. Janet D. Schenck, Music, Youth, and Opportunity:
A Survey of Settlement and Community Music Schools (Boston:
National Federation of Settlements, 1926), p. 15.

---

*Correspondence cited in notes is part of author's personal file.

14. Oscar G. T. Sonneck, Francis Hopkinson: The First American Poet-Composer (1737-1791) and James Lyon, Patriot, Preacher, Psalmodist (1735-1794) (New York: Da Capo Press, 1967), p. X.

15. Ibid., p. XI.

16. Ibid.

17. Lucy E. Carroll, "Three Centuries of Song: Pennsylvania's Choral Composers, 1681 to 1981" (doctoral dissertation, Combs College of Music, 1982).

18. Samuel Preston Bayard, Hill Country Tunes Instrumental Folk Music of Southwestern Pennsylvania (Philadelphia: American Folklore Society, 1944).

19. Jane Campbell, Old Philadelphia Music (Philadelphia: City History Society of Philadelphia, 1926).

20. William Armes Fisher, Notes on Music in Old Boston (Boston: Oliver Ditson Company, 1918).

21. Robert A. Gerson, Music in Philadelphia (Westport, Conn.: Greenwood Press Publishers, 1970).

22. Philip Hart, Orpheus in the New World: The Symphony Orchestra as an American Institution (New York: W. W. Norton & Company, 1979).

23. Ernest MacMillan (ed.), Music in Canada (St. Clair Shores, Mich.: Scholarly Press, Inc., 1978).

24. Joyce Ellen Mangler, Rhode Island Music and Musicians, 1722-1850 (Detroit: Information Service, 1965).

25. Ethel Peyser, The House That Music Built: Carnegie Hall (New York: Robert M. McBride & Company, 1936).

26. Louis Pichieri, Music in New Hampshire, 1623-1800 (New York: Columbia University Press, 1960).

27. Gertrude Martin Rohrer, Music and Musicians of Pennsylvania (Port Washington, N.Y.: Kennikat Press, Ira J. Friedman Division, 1940).

28. John Anthony Scott, The Ballad of America: The History of the United States in Song and Story (New York: Grosset & Dunlap Publishers, 1967).

29. Louis Snyder, Community of Sound Boston Symphony and Its World of Players (Boston: Beacon Press, 1979).

30. Walter Raymond Spalding, Music at Harvard (New York: Coward-McCann, 1935).

31. Richard D. Wetzel, Frontier Musicians on the Connoquenessing, Wabash, and Ohio (Athens, Ohio: Ohio University Press, 1976).

32. Grace D. Yerbury, Song in America from Early Times to about 1950 (Metuchen: Scarecrow Press, 1971).

33. John Tasker Howard (ed.), The Music of George Washington's Time (Washington, D.C.: United States George Washington Bicentennial Commission, 1931).

34. Ibid., p. 3.

35. Ibid., p. 5.

36. Ibid.

37. Ibid., pp. 5, 6.

38. James A. Keene, A History of Music Education in the United States (Hanover: University Press of New England, 1982), p. 106.

39. Ibid.

40. Ibid., pp. 107, 108.

41. Walter Raymond Spalding, Music at Harvard: A Historical Review of Men and Events (New York: Da Capo Press, 1977), pp. xi-xiii.

42. Ibid., pp. 1, 2.

43. Stanley Sadie (ed.), The New Grove Dictionary of Music and Musicians, sixth edition (London: Macmillan Publishers, 1980), volume 13, pp. 179-80.

44. Ibid., p. 181.

45. Ibid., volume 3, pp. 82, 83.

46. Ibid., volume 2, pp. 578, 579.

CHAPTER 2

1. The college missions were charitable or educational organizations doing welfare work for the needy of a city or district. The missions often had a religious affiliation.

2. In England the term "warden" meant a governing officer in certain colleges, guilds, hospitals, etc. In the days of Jane Addams, Lillian D. Wald, Helen Hall, etc., the term was the equivalent of headworker.

3. Robert A. Woods and Albert J. Kennedy (eds.), Handbook of Settlements (New York: Charities Publications Committee, 1911), p. ix. [Reprinted by Arno Press, 1970.]

4. Henrietta Barnett and Samuel Barnett, Towards Social Reform (London: T. Fisher Unwin, 1909), pp. 246, 247.

5. Jane Addams, Twenty Years at Hull-House (New York: The Macmillan Company, 1910), p. 87.

6. Ibid., p. 89.

7. Robert A. Woods and Albert J. Kennedy, The Zone of Emergence, with a preface by Sam B. Werner, Jr. (Cambridge, Mass.: Harvard University Press, 1962), p. 10.

8. Addams, p. 371.

9. Ibid., p. 378.

10. Janet D. Schenck, Music Schools and Settlement Music Departments (Boston: National Federation of Settlement, 1923), p. 18.

11. Ibid., see footnote.

12. Woods and Kennedy, Handbook of Settlements, p. 125.

13. Woods and Kennedy, loc. cit., Zone of Emergence.

14. Lorene M. Pacey (ed.), Readings in the Development of Settlement Work (New York: W. W. Norton and Company, 1950), p. 91.

15. Mary K. Simkhovitch, Neighborhood: My Story of Greenwich House (New York: W. W. Norton and Company, 1938), pp. 86, 87.

16. Ibid., p. 70.

17. Woods and Kennedy, Handbook of Settlements, p. 219.

18. First Annual Report of the Music School of the University and College Settlements, 1901-02, dated March 4, 1902. [In the files of the Third Street Music School, Settlement.]

19. Ibid.

20. Ibid.

21. Ibid.

22. National Guild of Community Schools of the Arts, Membership Directory 1985.

23. The Peabody Institute of the Johns Hopkins University (Baltimore), The Preparatory (1984-85 bulletin), p. 3.

24. Harold C. Livesay, Samuel Gompers and Organized Labor (Boston: Little, Brown and Company, 1978), p. 1.

25. Ibid., p. 2.

26. Ibid., p. 75.

27. Alice Taylor, New York City (Garden City, N.Y.: Nelson Doubleday, 1963), p. 25. [Prepared with the cooperation of the American Geographic Society.]

28. Vincent Jones, Music Education in the College (Boston: C. C. Birchard and Company, 1949), pp. 4-6.

29. Ibid.

30. Ibid.

31. Walter Raymond Spalding, Music at Harvard: A Historical Review of Men and Events (New York: Da Capo Press, 1977), p. 93.

32. Jean L. McKechnie (ed.), Webster's New Universal Unabridged Dictionary, second edition (New York: Simon & Schuster, 1979), p. 624.

33. Eastman School of Music 1984-85 Catalog, p. 3.

34. Woods and Kennedy, Handbook of Settlements, p. 193.

35. Ibid.

36. Daniel Levine, Jane Addams and the Liberal Tradition (Madison: State Historical Society of Wisconsin, 1971), p. 40.

37. Woods and Kennedy, Handbook of Settlements, p. 53.

38. Ibid., p. 58.

39. Addams, loc. cit.

40. Jane Addams, The Second Twenty Years at Hull House (New York: The Macmillan Company, 1930), p. 373.

41. B. C. Colles (ed.), Grove's Dictionary of Music and Musicians, third edition (New York: The Macmillan Company, 1935), p. 127.

42.ᴸ Lillian D. Wald, The House on Henry Street (New York: Henry Holt and Company, 1915), pp. 9, 10.

43. Ibid., pp. 10, 11.

44. Ibid., p. 24.

45. Ibid., pp. 179, 180.

46. Lillian D. Wald, Windows on Henry Street, pp. 156, 157.

47. Ibid., p. 164.

48. Ibid., p. 165.

49. Ibid.

50. Helen Hall, Unfinished Business (New York: The Macmillan Company, 1971), p. 174.

51. Wald, p. 174.

52. Simkhovitch, pp. 58, 59.

53. Ibid., p. 60.

54. Ibid., p. 61.

55. Ibid., p. 63.

56. Ibid., p. 89.

57. Ibid., p. 88.

58. Ibid., p. 89.

59. Ibid., pp. 256, 257.

60. Stanley Sadie (ed.), The New Grove Dictionary of Music and Musicians, sixth edition (London: Macmillan Publishers, 1980), volume 14, p. 186.

61. Simkhovitch, p. 301.

CHAPTER 3

1. Janet D. Schenck, Music, Youth, and Opportunity: A Survey of Settlement and Community Music Schools (Boston: National Federation of Settlements, 1926), pp. 15, 16.

2. Robert F. Egan, "The History of the Music School of the Henry Street Settlement Music School" (doctoral dissertation, New York University, 1967), p. 2.

3. Robert F. Egan (ed.), "Manual: A Guide for the
Establishment and Administration of a Community Music School"
(New York: National Guild of Community Music Schools, 1958),
pp. 1, 2.
     4. Lillian D. Wald, The House on Henry Street (New
York: Henry Holt and Company, 1915), p. 6.
     5. Ibid., pp. 11, 12.
     6. National Guild of Community Music Schools, The
Quarterly 1 (May 1940): 5.
     7. Schenck, pp. 26, 27.
     8. Robert A. Woods and Albert J. Kennedy (eds.),
Handbook of Settlements (New York: Charities Publications
Committee, 1911), p. 220. [Reprinted by Arno Press, 1970.]
     9. Ibid., p. 131.
     10. Ibid., p. 107.
     11. South End Music Centre,Vol. VIII, No. 1 (Sept.
1963), p. 1.
     12. National Guild of Community Schools of the Arts,
Membership Directory 1985, p. 19.
     13. Stanley Sadie (ed.), The New Grove Dictionary of
Music and Musicians, sixth edition (London: Macmillan Pub-
lishers, 1980), volume 6, pp. 701, 702.
     14. Clarence A. Grimes, They Who Speak in Music: The
History of the Neighborhood Music School (New Haven: The
Neighborhood Music School, 1957), "Foreword."
     15. Neighborhood Music School Brochure (New Haven:
The Neighborhood Music School, 1978-1979), p. 1
     16. Ibid.
     17. Grimes, p. 22.
     18. Janet D. Schenck, Music Schools and Settlement
Music Departments (Boston: National Federation of Settlements,
1923), p. 9.
     19. Ibid.
     20. Ibid., p. 32.
     21. Ibid.
     22. Paul Rolland, "Public MUSIC Schools: A new pattern
for American Music Instruction," Music Educators Journal
(November-December 1965).
     23. "Thoughts of the General Establishment of Public
Music Schools Throughout the Country." Speech delivered
at the National Music Council Meeting in New York City at
the Plaza Hotel on May 11, 1966. [Later printed in the National
Music Council Bulletin.]
     24. Ibid.
     25. "Bronx House Music School, 1978-1979" [Bronx, N.Y.:
The Bronx House Music School, 1978), p. 1.

26. "The Lighthouse Music School" (New York: The
New York Association for the Blind, undated), p. 4.
27. Ibid., p. 5.
28. Ibid., p. 6.
29. Ibid., p. 9.
30. "The Cleveland Music School Settlement, 1978-1979"
(Cleveland: The Cleveland Music School Settlement, 1978),
p. 26.
31. "The Cleveland Music School Settlement, 1984-1985"
(Cleveland: The Cleveland Music School Settlement, 1984). p. 4.
32. Response to questionnaire question 14, section a,
mailed to all member schools of the Guild for information concerning the member schools.   (Responses to the questionnaire
are in the author's files.)
33. Ibid., question 4.
34. "Pre-School at the Cleveland Music School Settlement," undated.
35. Ibid.
36. Ibid.
37. "Teens in Training" (Cleveland: The Cleveland
Music School Settlement, undated).
38. "Music Therapy at the Cleveland Music School
Settlement," undated.
39. Ibid.
40. "Cleveland Music School Settlement Self-Study"
(February 1985):3.
41. Ibid.
42. "Purchase of Service Contracts" (music therapy
flier): undated, p. 5.
43. "Cleveland Music School Settlement Self-Study"
(February 1983): p. 20.
44. Parent/Teacher Handbook (Harlem School of the
Arts, 1984-85).
45. "Architectural Record" (New York: McGraw-Hill),
1979), unpaginated, May 1979.
46. Parent/Student Handbook.
47. "Louise Behrend Scores in Town Hall Recital,"
New York World Telegram and Sun, March 30, 1950.
48. Louise Behrend, "No Shortage of String Players
in Japan." (New York: Henry Street Settlement Music
School), December 1, 1965. [Manuscript]
49. "National Guild of Community Schools of the Arts
Membership Directory, 1986" (Englewood, N.J., 1986), p. 61.
50. "Baum School of Art, Spring, 1984" (Allentown,
Pa.: Baum School of Art, Spring 1984), unpaginated.
51. Ibid.

52. "Baum School of Art Fiftieth Anniversary, 1926-1976" (Allentown, Pa.: Baum School of Art, 1976), unpaginated.
53. Ibid.
54. Ibid.
55. Letter to the author from Emily Franz.

CHAPTER 4

1. Cabell Phillips, From the Crash to the Blitz, 1919-1939 (London: The Macmillan Company, Collier-Macmillan), p. 57.
2. Janet D. Schenck, Music Schools and Settlement Music Departments (Boston: National Federation of Settlements, 1923), p. 51.
3. Ibid.
4. Ibid.
5. Ibid., p. 53.
6. Ibid.
7. Ibid.
8. Ibid., pp. 53-54.
9. Robert A. Woods and Albert J. Kennedy, The Settlement Horizon (quoted in Janet D. Schenck, Music, Youth, and Opportunity) (Boston: National Federation of Settlements, 1926), p. 67.
10. Ibid.
11. Ibid.
12. Ibid.
13. Ibid., pp. 67, 68.
14. Ibid., p. 68.
15. Ibid.
16. "National Guild of Community Schools of the Arts, Inc. Membership Directory 1985," p. 51.
17. Robert F. Egan, "The History of the Music School of the Henry Street Settlement" (doctoral dissertation, New York University, 1967), p. 2.
18. Ibid., p. 120.
19. Ibid., p. 122.
20. The Encyclopedia Americana (Danbury, Conn.: Grolier, 1986), pp. 67, 68.
21. Nikolai Sokoloff, director, "Federal Music Project" (Washington, D.C.: Works Progress Administration, Harry L. Hopkins, administrator, 1936), p. 3.
22. Ibid., p. 5.
23. Ibid., p. 7.
24. Ibid., p. 19.

25. Ibid.
26. Memo from Ashley Pettis, unit manager, Music Education Division of the Federal Music Project of the WPA to "All Supervisors and Head Teachers of New York City," July 22, 1937.
27. Letter from Ashley Pettis to Ruth Kemper, July 20, 1937.
28. Letter from Ashley Pettis to Ruth Kemper, July 22, 1937.
29. Letter from William Haddon, state director of the Federal Music Project in Boston, to Ruth Kemper, undated.

CHAPTER 5

1. "Statement: The Community Music School Movement" (Original manuscript document in the files of the National Guild of Community Schools of the Arts), p. 1.
2. Ibid., "Design."
3. Ibid., "Purpose."
4. National Guild of Community Music Schools, The Quarterly (May 1940):1.
5. Ibid., p. 3.
6. Ibid., p. 2.
7. Ibid., p. 1.
8. Fletcher Hodges, Jr., The Swanee River and a Biography of Stephen C. Foster (Orlando, Fl.: Robinson Inc., 1958), p. 2.
9. Ibid., p. 11.
10. The Stephen Collins Foster Memorial of the University of Pittsburgh: A Tribute to the Composer Whose Melodies Have Become the Heart Songs of the American People. Dedicated June 2, 1937 (Pittsburgh: Stephen Foster Dedication Committee, 1937). pp. 3, 4.
11. Robert F. Egan, "The History of the Music School of the Henry Street Settlement" (doctoral dissertation, New York University, 1967), p. 175.
12. Ibid., p. 176.
13. Ibid., p. 177.
14. National Guild of Community Music Schools, The Quarterly 1 (March 1941):1.
15. Ibid.
16. Ibid., p. 5.
17. Ibid.

18. National Guild of Community Music Schools, The Quarterly 4 (June 1944):1.

19. Letter from Johan Grolle to Eleanor Stanley White, March 5, 1944.

20. Letter from Winifred M. Jacobson to Eleanor Stanley White, June 12, 1941.

21. Letter from Johan Grolle to Eleanor Stanley White, February 3, 1944.

22. Letter from Mabel B. Worth to Eleanor Stanley White, February 3, 1944.

23. George Martin. The Damrosch Dynasty: America's First Family of Music (Boston: Houghton Miflin Company, 1983), pp. 213, 214.

24. Ibid.

25. Letter from Johan Grolle to all members of the Executive Committee of the National Guild of Community Music Schools, May 25, 1944.

26. Letter from Johan Grolle to Edna Lieber, May 10, 1944.

27. Jeannine Cossitt (ed.), "Music and Leisure," National Federation of Settlements, Music Division Report, June 1944.

28. Ibid., p. 3.

29. Ibid.

30. Ibid., p. 10.

31. National Guild of Community Music Schools, The Quarterly 2 (June 1942):1.

32. Ibid., p. 2.

33. National Guild of Community Music Schools, The Quarterly 3 (February 1943):2.

34. Ibid., p. 6.

35. National Guild of Community Music Schools, The Quarterly 4 (December 1944):1.

36. Ibid.

37. Ibid., p. 2.

38. Ibid.

39. Letter from Johan Grolle to the members of the Executive Committee of the National Guild, May 17, 1945.

40. National Guild of Community Music Schools Booklet, 1946.

41. Ibid.

42. Ibid.

43. Ibid.

CHAPTER 6

    1. "Music Off the Beaten Path," Musical America (September 1946). Under "Radio for Record: A Sounder Pattern."
    2. "Music for the Connoisseur," Daily Worker, New York, May 20, 1949, p. 13.
    3. Letter: Howard Whittaker to Ruth Kemper, June 29, 1949.
    4. Letter: Whittaker to James C. Petrillo, July 5, 1949.
    5. Letter: Petrillo to Whittaker, July 8, 1949.
    6. Letter: Ruth Kemper to Julius Rudel, July 20, 1949.
    7. Letter: David Randolph to Whittaker, August 25, 1949.
    8. Letter: Kemper to Whittaker, August 26, 1949.
    9. Letter: Whittaker to Randolph, August 30, 1949.
    10. Letter: Clarence Worden to Kemper received by her August 30, 1949.
    11. Letter: Maxwell Powers to Julius Rudel, September 21, 1949.
    12. Letter: Whittaker to Powers, November 28, 1949.
    13. Letter: Whittaker to Grace Spofford, November 29, 1949.
    14. Letter: Spofford to Whittaker, December 21, 1949.
    15. Letter: Kemper to Whittaker, September 8, 1949.
    16. Letter: Kemper to Whittaker, September 15, 1949.
    17. Telegram: Kemper to Whittaker, September 15, 1949.
    18. Telegram: Whittaker to Kemper, September 15, 1949.
    19. Letter: Kemper to Whittaker, October 3, 1949.
    20. Letter: Whittaker to Kemper, October 5, 1949.
    21. Letter: Kemper to Whittaker, October 18, 1949.
    22. Letter: Kemper to Whittaker, October 19, 1949.
    23. Letter: Randolph to Whittaker, October 19, 1949.
    24. Letter: Randolph to Whittaker, October 19, 1949.
    25. Letter: Whittaker to Kemper, October 20, 1949.
    26. Letter: Whittaker to Swift, October 20, 1949.
    27. Letter: Whittaker to Randolph, October 21, 1949.
    28. Letter: Kemper to Whittaker, November 4, 1949.
    29. Letter: Randolph to Whittaker, November 10, 1949.
    30. Script for Musical Notebook with David Randolph (new title, formerly Music for the Connoisseur). WCBS,

Sunday, November 6, 1949, 1:30-2:00 p.m. (Copy in the files of the National Guild of Community Schools of the Arts.)

31. Ibid.

32. Publicity materials sent with the script. (In the files of the National Guild.)

33. Ibid.

34. Ralph Hays to Whittaker, August 4, 1950.

35. Letter: John Marshall to Whittaker, August 15, 1950.

36. Letter: John McDowell to Whittaker, November 15, 1950.

37. Letter: Whittaker to McDowell, March 29, 1951.

38. Letter: Whittaker to Grace Spofford, June 27, 1951.

39. Ibid.

40. Letter: Spofford to Whittaker, September 13, 1951.

41. Telegram: Whittaker to Spofford, September 17, 1951 (12:28 p.m.).

42. Letter: Spofford to Whittaker, September 25, 1951.

43. Letter: Whittaker to Spofford, September 29, 1951.

44. Letter: Powers to Whittaker, December 26, 1951.

45. Nicholas John Cords, "Music in Social Settlement and Community Music Schools, 1893-1939: A Democratic-Esthetic Approach to Music Culture" (doctoral dissertation, University of Minnesota at Minneapolis, 1970), p. 72.

46. Letter: Powers to Whittaker, January 17, 1952.

47. Ibid.

48. Speech delivered by Howard Whittaker to the National Federation of Settlements' Annual Conference in Milwaukee, Wisconsin, May, 1952. (Copy in the files of the National Guild of Community Schools of the Arts.)

49. Ibid.

50. Letter: Powers to Whittaker, May 26, 1952.

51. Letter: Whittaker to Powers, June 19, 1952.

52. Ibid.

53. Letter: Powers to Whittaker, October 20, 1954.

54. Howard Whittaker, "A Plan for the Future," presented at the Annual Conference of the National Guild of Community Music Schools, 1955.

55. Ibid.

56. Robert F. Egan (ed.), "Manual: A Guide for the Establishment and Administration of a Community Music School" (New York: National Guild of Community Music Schools, 1958), "Foreword."

57. Alice Conway (ed.), "Guild Notes." (Rochester, May, 1965), p. 2.

58. Ibid., pp. 3, 4.

59. Max Kaplan, "National Guild of Community Music Schools Observations and Recommendations." (Brookline, Mass., May 1, 1966).

60. Ibid., pp. 80-89.

61. Letter from Porter McCray, director of the JDR III Fund, to Dr. Herbert Zipper, dated October 31, 1967.

62. Memorandum read on August 17, 1970, at a meeting of the representatives of participating institutions in Seoul, Korea.

63. Ibid.

CHAPTER 7

1. "Arts for All." A Mobile Academy of the Performing Arts for Children of Rural South East Arkansas (Evanston, Ill.: National Guild of Community Music Schools, 1969), unpaginated.

2. Ibid.

3. Ibid.

4. Ibid.

5. Ibid.

6. Janice Clark, "Performing Arts' Project a Hit in Southeast Arkansas," Arkansas Gazette, July 27, 1969, p. 4E.

7. Ibid.

8. Ibid.

9. Herbert Zipper, "Executive Office Report" presented at the annual conference, 1969.

10. Ibid.

11. Allegro (July 1969). Publication of the American Federation of Musicians, Local 802, New York City.

12. The Arts Reporting Service, number 7, November 30, 1970.

13. The first grant from the National Endowment for the Arts was granted to the National Guild of Community Music Schools in 1967, the first of several that were to follow annually.

14. The Arts Reporting Service, volume 2, number 9, December 17, 1971.

15. Letter: Robert T. Adams, executive director, Hull House in Chicago, to Herbert Zipper, read at the National Guild Conference in New York City, November 1969.

16. Minutes of the National Guild meeting, November 8, 1969, 8:00 p.m.

17. Resolution submitted to the Hull House Association, November 11, 1969.

18. Harry Golden, "The Neighborhood Is Different and so Are the People," in In a Proud Tradition (New York: Society of the Third Street Music School Settlement, 1969), pp. 1, 2.

19. Letter: from Herbert Zipper to all Guild members, December 1, 1969.

20. Ibid.

21. Ibid.

22. Letter: from Herbert Zipper to all member schools, December 17, 1969.

23. Ibid.

24. Letter: from Herbert Zipper to all member schools, March 8, 1970.

25. "Arts for All Fund of the National Guild of Community Music Schools," p. 1.

26. Ibid., p. 2.

27. Ibid., p. 3.

28. Ibid.

29. Ibid., p. 5.

30. "Report on the Activities of the Executive Office of the National Guild ...," October 1, 1969-September 30, 1970, p. 1.

31. Ibid., p. 2.

32. Ibid., p. 3.

33. Ibid.

34. Ibid., p. 4.

35. Letter: from Herbert Zipper to all the Guild member schools, January 21, 1972.

36. Letter: from Harris Danziger to directors of Guild schools, January 31, 1972.

37. Ibid.

38. "National Guild of Community Schools of the Arts Membership Directory, 1985" pp. 88-92.

39. Letter: Herbert Zipper to members, January 31, 1972.

40. Letter: Herbert Zipper to members, May 16, 1972.

41. Letter: Charles C. Mark to all member schools, undated. (Received by member schools September 5, 1972.)

42. Letter: Charles C. Mark to the members, May 10, 1973.

43. Recommendations from the task force approved by the Board of Directors, February 9, 1975.

44. Ibid.

45. Letter: Charles C. Mark to members, August 24, 1973.

46. Letter: from the National Endowment for the Arts to Dorothy Maynor, president of the National Guild of Community Music Schools, May 15, 1974.

47. Report of the National Guild Board Meeting, May 15, 1974.

48. Guildletter, December 12, 1974.

49. "Code of Regulations" of the National Guild of Community Schools of the Arts, as amended October 1979.

50. Ibid., p. 11.

51. "Administrative Internship Program, 1976-1977, Summary," p. 1.

52. Ibid., p. 12.

53. Ibid., pp. 2, 3.

54. Ibid., pp. 4-7.

55. Ibid., pp. 7, 8.

56. Ibid., p. 11.

57. Guildletter, January, 1977. p. 1.

58. Ibid.

59. Marcy Horwitz and Sandie Kaplan (eds.), "The Washington Connection." Report of the proceedings of the 39th Annual Conference, National Guild of Community Schools of the Arts, held in Washington, D.C., November 7-10, 1976. "The President's Welcome," p. 4. [Manuscript]

60. Ibid., pp. 1-3.

61. Ibid., p. 54.

62. Marcy Horwitz and Sandie Kaplan (eds.), "Explo! '77: Arts Education and Human Development." Report of the proceedings of the 40th Annual Conference, National Guild of Community Schools of the Arts, held in San Francisco, November 27-30, 1977, p. i. [Manuscript]

63. Ibid., pp. 11-27.

64. Ibid., pp. 27, 28.

65. Marcy Horwitz and Sandie Kaplan (eds.), "Arts in a Troubled Society." Report of the proceedings of the 41st Annual Conference, National Guild of Community Schools of the Arts, held in Toronto, Ontario, Canada, November 12-15, 1978. [Manuscript]

66. Ibid.

67. Ibid., p. i.

68. Marcy Horwitz and Sandie Kaplan (eds.), "A B C: Arts--Basic to the Child." Report of the proceedings of the 42nd Annual Conference, National Guild of Community Schools of the Arts, held in St. Louis, October 27-30, 1979). [Manuscript]

69. Marcy Horwitz and Sandie Kaplan (eds.), "Putting It All Together (So It Works!)." Report of the proceedings of the 43rd Annual Conference, National Guild of Community Schools of the Arts, held in Boston, November 9-12, 1980. [Manuscript]

70. Stanley Sadie (ed.), The New Grove Dictionary of Music and Musicians, sixth edition (London: Macmillan Publishers, 1980), volume 1, p. 400.

71. Horwitz and Kaplan, "Putting It All Together (So It Works!)," p. i.

72. Ibid., "Table of Contents."

73. Letter: Marcy Horwitz to directors of member schools, February 13, 1981.

74. Letter: Lolita Mayadas to the Board of Directors of the National Guild, February 3, 1982.

75. Alfred D. Andreychuk, E. Arthur Prieve, and Sharon Leslie. A Study of the National Guild of Community Schools of the Arts, made by the Center for Arts Administration of the University of Wisconsin-Madison, 1982. p. 1.

CHAPTER 8

1. National Guild of Community Schools of the Arts, "Annual Report, July 1983--June 1984" p. 20.

2. National Guild of Community Schools of the Arts, "Annual Report, 1984-85," p. 22.

3. National Guild of Community Schools of the Arts, "Membership Directory 1986."

4. National Guild of Community Schools of the Arts, "Annual Report 1984-85" p. 16.

5. Ibid., p. 25.

6. "Membership Directory 1986" pp. 1-93.

7. "Annual Report 1984-85," p. 38.

8. Ibid., p. 12.

9. "Young Composers Awards, 1986-87." [Brochure]

10. Ibid.

11. "Annual Report 1985-1986," p. 11.

12. "Membership Directory 1986," p. ix.

13. Ibid., p. x.

14. Robert F. Egan (ed.), "Manual: A Guide for the Establishment and Administration of a Community Music School," National Guild of Community Music Schools., p. 3.

15. Ibid., p. 12.

BIBLIOGRAPHY

ARTS AND CULTURE

Advisory Committee on the Arts. Cultural Presentation of the
    U.S. Department of State, July 1, 1963-June 30, 1964.
    A report to the Congress and the public. Washington,
    D.C.: The Advisory Committee on the Arts, 1964.
    _____. Cultural Presentation USA, 1967-1968. A report
    to the Congress and the public. Washington, D.C.:
    The Advisory Committee on the Arts, 1969.
American Council for the Arts. A Guide to Corporate Giving
    in the Arts. New York: American Council for the
    Arts, 1978.
    _____. Americans and the Arts: A Survey of Public Opin-
    ion. New York: American Council for the Arts, 1974.
    _____. Arts Administration Compensation: 1978 Survey.
    New York: American Council for the Arts, 1979.
    _____. Arts Administration Training (A Survey of Arts
    Administration in the United States and Canada: 1979-
    1980). New York: American Council for the Arts, 1981.
    _____. Arts Advocacy: A Citizen Action Manual. New
    York: American Council for the Arts.
    _____. United Arts Fundraising Policybook. New York:
    American Council for the Arts.
    _____. United Arts Fundraising, 1979. New York: Ameri-
    can Council for the Arts.
    _____. United Arts Fundraising Manual. New York:
    American Council for the Arts.
American Music Conference. The Role of Music in the Life
    of Man: An Inquiry into the Significance of Music.
    Wilmette, Ill.: American Music Conference, 1978.
Associated Councils for the Arts. Americans and the Arts.
    New York: Associated Councils for the Arts, 1975.
    (Research conducted by the National Research Center
    of the Arts.)

Ayers, Christine Merrick. Contributions to the Art of Music in America by the Music Industries of Boston, 1640-1936. New York: The H. W. Wilson Company, 1937. [Reprints: Johnson Reprint Corp., 1969.]

Barnes, Edwin Ninyon Chaloner. American Music from Plymouth Rock to Tin Pan Alley. Washington, D.C.: Music Education Publications, 1936.

Baumol, William, and William C. Bowman. Performing Arts: The Economic Dilemma. New York: The Twentieth Century Fund, 1966.

Browne, Ray B. (ed.). Popular Culture and the Expanding Consciousness. New York: John Wiley & Sons, 1973.

Coe, Linda, Rebecca Denny, and Anne Rogers. Cultural Directory II. New York: American Council for the Arts. Published by the Smithsonian Institution Press.

Falk, Robert, and Timothy Rice. Cross-Cultural Perspectives on Music. Toronto: University of Toronto Press, 1982.

Hart, Philip. Orpheus in the New World: The Symphony Orchestra as an American Institution. New York: W. W. Norton & Company, 1979.

Kreisberg, Louisa. Local Government and the Arts. New York: American Council for the Arts, 1979.

Meyer, Leonard B. Music, the Arts, and Ideas: Patterns and Predictions in Twentieth-Century Culture. Chicago: The University of Chicago Press, 1967.

Reiss, Alvin H. The Arts Management Handbook: A Guide for Those Interested in or Involved with the Administration of Cultural Institutions. Law-Arts Publishers, 1970.

AUTOBIOGRAPHIES AND BIOGRAPHIES OF PROMINENT
AMERICANS IN THE ARTS AND SOCIAL WORK

Addams, Jane. My Friend, Julia Lathrop. New York: The Macmillan Company, 1935.

Carnegie, Andrew. Autobiography of Andrew Carnegie. Boston and New York: The Houghton Mifflin Company, 1920.

Davis, Allen. American Heroine: The Life and Legend of Jane Addams. New York: Oxford University Press, 1973.

Duffus, R. L. Lillian Wald: Neighbor and Crusader. New York: The Macmillan Company, 1939.

Gaul, Harvey. The Minstrel of the Alleghenies. Pittsburgh, Pa.: Friends of Harvey Gaul, 1934.

George, Don. Sweet Man: The Real Duke Ellington. New
    York: G. P. Putnam's Sons, 1981.
Hodges, Fletcher, Jr. Swanee Ribber and a Biography of
    Stephen C. Foster. Orlando, Fl: Robinsons, 1938.
Howard, John Tasker. Stephen Foster, America's Troubadour.
    New York: Thomas Y. Crowell Company, 1953.
Levine, Daniel. Jane Addams and the Liberal Tradition.
    Madison, Wis.: State Historical Society of Wisconsin,
    1971.
Linn, James Weber. Jane Addams: A Biography. New York:
    D. Appleton-Century Company, 1937.
Mannes, David. Music Is My Faith: An Autobiography.
    New York: Da Capo Press, 1978. (Reprint of 1936
    edition, published by Norton, New York.)
Moreland, Faye Witt. Green Fields and Fairer Lanes: Music
    in the Life of Henry Ford. Tupelo, Miss.: Five Star
    Publishers, 1969.
Morneweck, Evelyn Foster. Chronicles of Stephen Foster's
    Family. Pittsburgh, Pa.: University of Pittsburgh
    Press, 1944. Volume 1.
Schwartz, Charles. Gershwin: His Life and Music. Indian-
    apolis, Ind.: The Bobbs-Merrill Company, 1973.
Siegel, Beatrice. Lillian Wald of Henry Street. New York:
    Macmillan Publishing Co., 1983.
Simkhovitch, Mary Kingsbury. Neighborhood: My Story of
    Greenwich House. New York: W. W. Norton & Company,
    1938.
Smith, Julia. Aaron Copland: His Work and Contributions
    to American Music. New York: E. P. Dutton and
    Company, 1955.
Ware, Louise. Jacob A. Riis: Police Reporter, Reformer,
    Useful Citizen. New York: D. Appleton Century
    Company, 1938.
Williams, Beryl. Lillian Wald: Angel of Henry Street. New
    York: Julian Messner, 1948.
Wise, Winifred E. Jane Addams of Hull-House. New York:
    Harcourt, Brace and Company, 1935.

CHURCH MUSIC IN AMERICA

David, Hans T. Musical Life in the Pennsylvania Settlements
    of the Unitas Fratrum. Winston-Salem, N.C.: The
    Moravian Music Foundation, 1959. (Reprinted from
    Transactions of the Moravian Music Foundation Society,
    volume 13, 1942.)

Gould, Nathaniel D. The History of Church Music in America. Boston: A. N. Johnson, 1953.

McCorkle, Donald M. The Collegium Musicum Salem: Its Music, Musicians and Importance. Winston-Salem, N.C.: The Moravian Music Foundation, 1956. (Reprinted from the North Carolina Historical Review, October 1956.)

McCorkle, Donald M. The Moravian Contribution to American Music. Winston-Salem, N.C.: The Moravian Music Foundation, 1956. (Reprinted from Music Library Association Notes, September 1956.)

Rau, Albert G., and Hans T. David (eds.). A Catalog of Music by American Moravians, 1742-1842. From the Archives of the Moravian Church at Bethlehem, Pa. New York: AMS Press, 1970.

Sweet, William Warren. Religion in the Development of American Culture, 1765-1840. New York: Charles Scribner's Sons, 1952.

DEMOCRACY AND THE ARTS

Canon, Cornelius B. "The Federal Music Project of the Works in a Democracy". Ph.D. dissertation, University of Minnesota, 1963.

Carnegie, Andrew. Triumphant Democracy. New York: Charles Scribner's Sons, 1886.

Clark, Kenneth S. Music in Industry. New York: National Bureau for the Advancement of Music, 1929.

EDUCATION, MUSIC EDUCATION, AND MUSIC THERAPY

Barnes, Stephen . A Cross-section of Research in Music Education. Lanham, Mo.: University Press of America, 1982.

Bloom, Kathryn, Junius Eddy, Charles Fowler, Jane Homer, and Nancy Shuker. An Arts in Education Source Book: A View from the JDR 3rd Fund. New York: American Council for the Arts, 1979.

Burk, Cassie, Virginia Meierhoffer, and Claud Anderson Phillips. America's Musical Heritage. New York: Laidlaw Brothers Publishers, 1942.

Choksy, Lois. The Kodaly Method: Comprehensive Music Education from Infant to Adult. Englewood Cliffs, N.J.: Prentice-Hall, 1974.

Cook, Clifford A. Essays of a String Teacher: Come Let Us Rosin Together. New York: Exposition Press, 1973.
Crist, Christine Myers. An Unprecedented Conference: Arts and Education at Little Rock. New York: American Council for the Arts, 1980.
Cross, Patricia. Adults as Learners. San Francisco: The Josey-Bass Series in Higher Education. August 1981.
Davis, Allen F. Spearheads for Reform. New York: Oxford University Press, 1967.
Feier, Elaine, and Bernard Feier. The Expressive Arts Therapies. Englewood Cliffs, N.J.: Prentice-Hall, 1981.
Glenn, Neal E., and Edgar M. Turrentine. Introduction to Advanced Study in Music Education. Dubuque, Iowa: Wm. C. Brown Company Publishers, 1958.
Graham, Richard M. (ed.). Music for the Exceptional Child. Reston, Va.: Music Educators National Conference, 1975.
Harris, Ernest E. Music Education: A Guide to Information Sources (volume I in the Education Information Guide Series.) Detroit: Gale Research Company, 1978.
Hollander, Patricia A., J.D. Legal Handbook for Educators. Boulder, Colo.: Westview Press, 1978.
Howsman, Robert B., Dean C. Corrigan, George W. Denmark, and Robert J. Nash. Educating a Profession. Washington, D.C.: American Association of Colleges for Teacher Education, 1976.
Jones, Vincent. Music Education in the College. Boston: C. C. Birchard and Company, 1949.
Keene, James A. A History of Music Education in the United States. Hanover, N.H.: University Press of New England, 1982.
Kowall, Bonnie C. (ed.). Perspectives in Music Education; Source Book III. Washington, D.C.: Music Educators National Conference, 1966.
Landon, Joseph W. Leadership for Learning in Music Education. Costa Mesa, Calif.: Educational Media Press, 1975.
Machlis, Joseph. The Enjoyment of Music. New York: W. W. Norton & Company, 1977. (An Introduction to Perceptive Listening, fourth edition.)
National Endowment for the Humanities. Education Program, 1977-1978. Washington, D.C.: National Endowment for the Humanities, 1979.
Neidig, Kenneth E. Music Director's Complete Handbook of Forms. West Nyack, N.Y.: Parker Publishing Company, 1973.

Reimer, Bennett. A Philosophy of Music Education. Engle-
wood Cliffs, N.J.: Prentice-Hall, 1970.
Shemel, Sidney, and M. William Krasilovsky. More About This
Business of Music. New York: Billboard Publishing
Company, 1967.
Suzuki, Shinichi. Nurtured by Love: A New Approach to
Education. Translated by Waltraud Suzuki. New York:
Exposition Press, 1969.
Wadsworth, Barry J. Piaget's Theory of Cognitive Develop-
ment: An Introduction for Students of Psychology and
Education. New York: Longman, 1979. Second edition.
Wendrich, Kenneth. Essays on Music in American Education
and Society. Washington, D.C.: University Press of
America, 1982.

FUND RAISING AND THE ARTS

Brownrigg, W. Grant. Corporate Fundraising: A Practical
Plan of Action. New York: American Council for the
Arts, n. d.
Carmen, William I. Long-Range Planning for Non-Profit
Organizations. Philadelphia: Levanthol & Horwath,
Certified Public Accountants, n. d.
Millsaps, Daniel, et al. (eds.). The National Directory of
Grants and Aid to Individuals in the Arts, International.
Third edition. Washington, D.C., 1970.
Nelson, Charles A., and Frederick J. Turk. Financial Man-
agement for the Arts: A Guidebook for Arts Organiza-
tions. New York: American Council for the Arts, n. d.
Shaver, G. W. & Company. Funding Guidelines. A financial
and fundraising planning and action manual for trustees
and executives of community schools of music and the
arts. New York: C. W. Shaver & Company, 1973.

MUSIC HISTORY

Elson, Louis C. The History of American Music. New York:
The Macmillan Company, 1925.
Hood, George. The History of Music in New England. Boston:
Wilkins, Carter and Company, 1846.
Howard, John Tasker (ed.). The Music of George Washington's
Time. Washington, D.C.: United States George Wash-
ington Bicentennial Commission, 1931.

_____, and George Kent Bellows. A Short History of Music
in America. New York: Thomas Y. Crowell Company,
1957.
Hubbard, W. L. (ed.). History of American Music. Volume
8 of The American History and Encyclopedia of Music.
Toledo, Ohio: Irving Squire, 1908-1910.
Institute for Studies in American Music. American Music 1865
in Print and Records, a Biblio-Discography. Brooklyn,
N.Y.: Department of Music, School of Performing Arts,
Brooklyn College of the City University of New York,
1976.
Lang, Paul Henry (ed.). The Creative World of Mozart.
New York: W. W. Norton & Company, 1963.
_____. Problems of Modern Music. New York: W. W.
Norton & Company, 1960.
McKinney, Howard D., and W. R. Anderson. Music in History:
The Evolution of an Art. New York: American Book
Company, 1940.
Morley, Thomas. A Plain and Easy Introduction to Practical
Music. Second edition, ed. R. Alec Harman. New York:
W. W. Norton & Company, 1973.
Pauly, Reinhard G. Music in the Classic Period. Ed. H.
Wiley Hitchcock. Englewood Cliffs, N.J.: Prentice-Hall,
1973.
Pratt, Waldo Selden. The Music of the French Psalter of 1562.
New York: Columbia University Press, 1939.
Rolland, Romain. A Musical Tour through the Land of the
Past. London: Kegan Paul, Trench, Trubner & Co.,
1922.
Scholes, Percy A. The Puritans and Music in England and
New England. New York: Oxford University Press,
1934.
Schwartz, Boris. Music and Musical Life in Soviet Russia.
New York: W. W. Norton & Company, 1972.
Slonimsky. Music Since 1900. Third edition, revised and en-
larged. New York: Coleman-Ross Co., 1949.
Stuckenschmidt, H. H. Twentieth-Century Composers.
Volume 2, Germany and Central Europe. New York:
Holt, Rinehart and Winston, 1970.

MUSIC AND MUSICAL LIFE IN AMERICA

Aldrich, Richard. Concert Life in New York, 1902-1923.
Freeport, N.Y.: Books for Libraries Press, 1973.
(first published 1941).

Barzun, Jacques. Music in American Life. New edition.
    Bloomington: Indiana University Press, 1962.
Bayard, Samuel Preston. Hill Country Tunes: Instrumental
    Folk Music of Southwestern Pennsylvania. Philadelphia:
    American Folklore Society, 1944. (Kraus Reprint Co.,
    New York, 1969.)
Bio-bibliographical Index of Musicians in the United States
    of America from Colonial Times. New edition. Washington,
    D.C.: Music Division, Pan American Union, 1956.
Boretz, Benjamin, and Edward T. Cone (eds.). Perspectives
    on American Composers. New York: W. W. Norton &
    Company, 1971.
Burke, James Francis. Stephen Collins Foster. Address of
    Honorable James Francis Burke--Dedicating the Foster
    Memorial at Bardstown, Kentucky, on July 4th, 1923.
Campbell, Jane. Old Philadelphia Music. Philadelphia: City
    History Society of Philadelphia, 1926.
Carroll, Lucy Ellen. "Three Centuries of Song: Pennsylvania's
    Choral Composers, 1681-1981." D.M.A. dissertation,
    Combs College of Music, 1982.
Cazden, Norman, Herbert Haufrecht, and Norman Studer
    (eds.). Folk Songs of the Catskills. Albany: State
    University of New York Press, 1982.
Chase, Gilbert (ed.). The American Composer Speaks (A
    Historical Anthology, 1790-1965). Baton Rouge: Louisiana
    State University Press, 1966.
_____. America's Music from the Pilgrims to the Present.
    Revised second edition. New York: McGraw-Hill Book
    Company, 1966.
Cole, Hugo. The Changing Face of Music. London: Victor
    Gollanz, 1978.
Cope, David H. New Directions in Music. Fourth edition.
    Dubuque, Iowa: Wm. C. Brown Company Publishers,
    1971.
Copland, Aaron. Copland on Music. Garden City, N.Y.:
    Doubleday & Co., 1960.
Cowell, Henry (ed.). American Composers on American Music.
    A symposium with a new introduction by the author.
    New edition. New York: Frederick Ungar Publishing
    Company, 1962. (Originally published in 1933.)
Crawford, Richard A. (ed.). The Core Repertory of Early
    American Psalmody. Recent researches in American
    Music, volumes XI and XII. Madison, Wis.: A-B
    Educations, 1984.
Dietz, Robert J. "The Operatic Style of Marc Blitzstein in

the American 'Agit-Prop Era.'" Doctoral dissertation,
University of Iowa, 1970.

Edwards, Arthur C., and W. Thomas Marrocco. Music in the
United States. Dubuque, Iowa: Wm. C. Brown Company
Publishers, 1968.

Edwards, George Thornton. Music and Musicians of Maine.
New York: AMS Press, 1970.

Ewen, David. Music Comes to America. New York: Allen,
Towne & Heath, 1947.

Fisher, William Armes. Notes on Music in Old Boston. Boston:
Oliver Ditson Company, 1918.

_____. One Hundred and Fifty Years of Music Publishing
in the United States. Boston: Oliver Ditson Company,
1933. (A revision and extension of the author's Notes
on Music in Old Boston, 1918.)

Foster, George. Music. Volume 7 of Works Progress Administration: Record of Program Operation and Accomplishment, 1935-1943.

Foster, Stephen Collins. The Stephen Collins Foster Memorial
of the University of Pittsburgh. Dedicated June 2,
1937.

Franzen, Ulrich, and Associates. "The Harlem School of the
Arts Program Study." New York: Ulrich Franzen and
Associates. (Mimeographed. In the files of the author.)

Gerson, Robert A. Music in Philadelphia. Westport, Conn.:
Greenwood Press Publishers, 1970.

Gleason, Harold, and Warren Becker. Early American Music
in America from 1620 to 1920. Bloomington, Ind.:
Frangipane Press, 1981.

Goldman, Richard Franko (ed.). Landmarks of Early American
Music, 1760-1800. New York: G. Schirmer, 1943.

Gombosi, Marilyn. A Day of Solemn Thanksgiving--Moravian
Music for the Fourth of July, 1783, in Salem, North
Carolina. Chapel Hill: The University of North Carolina
Press, 1977.

Good, Marian Bigler. Some Musical Backgrounds of Pennsylvania. Carrolltown, Pa.: Carrolltown News Press, 1932.

Hamm, Charles. Music in the New World. New York: W. W.
Norton and Company, 1983.

_____. Yesterday's Popular Song in America. New York:
W. W. Norton and Company, 1983.

_____, Bruno Nettl, and Ronald Byrnside. Contemporary
Music and Cultures. Englewood Cliffs, N.J.: Prentice-
Hall, 1975.

Hitchcock, H. Wiley. Music in the United States: A Historical
    Introduction. Englewood Cliffs, N.J.: Prentice-Hall,
    1969.
Hodges, Fletcher, Jr. A Pittsburgh Composer and His Memorial.
    Pittsburgh: The Historical Society of Western Pennsyl-
    vania, 1938.
Howe, M. A. DeWolfe. The Boston Symphony Orchestra,
    1881-1931. Boston and New York: Houghton Mifflin
    Company, 1931.
Johnson, Frances Hall. Musical Memories of Hartford. New
    York: AMS Press, 1970. (Reprinted from the 1951
    edition, Hartford, CT.: Witlcower's).
Johnson, H. Earle. Musical Interludes in Boston. New York:
    Columbia University Press, 1943.
_____. Symphony Hall, Boston. Boston: Little, Brown
    and Company, 1950.
Juhasz, Vilmos. Bartok's Years in America. Washington,
    D.C.: Occidental Press, 1981.
Kroeger, Karl (ed.). Pelissier's Columbian Melodies Music
    for the New York and Philadelphia Theatres. Recent
    Researches in American Music, volumes XIII and XIV.
    Madison, Wis.: A-R Editions, 1984.
Krueger, Karl. The Musical Heritage of the United States:
    The Unknown Portion. New York: The Society for
    Preservation of Musical Heritage, 1973.
Lahee, H. Annals of Music in America: A chronological
    record of significant music events, from 1640 to the
    present ... Boston: Marshall Jones Company, 1922.
Lang, Paul Henry (ed.). One Hundred Years of Music in
    America. New York: G. Schirmer, 1961. (A Centennial
    Publication. Grosset & Dunlap distributor to the book
    trade.)
Lowens, Irving. "John Tuft's Introduction to the Singing of
    Psalm-Tunes (1721-44): The First American Textbook."
    In Music and Musicians in Early America.
_____. Music in America and American Music. New York:
    Institute in American Music, School of Performing Arts,
    Brooklyn College of the City University of New York,
    1978. (ISAM Monographs number 8.)
_____. Music and Musicians in Early America. New York:
    W. W. Norton and Company, 1964.
MacMillan, Ernest (ed.). Music in Canada. St. Clair, Mich.:
    Scholarly Press, 1978.

Mangler, Joyce Ellen. Rhode Island Music and Musicians, 1722-1850. Detroit: Information Service, 1965. (Detroit Information Service, 1965. (Detroit Studies in Music Bibliography-7.)

Marrocco, W. Thomas, and Harold Gleason. Music in America: An Anthology from the Landing of the Pilgrims to the Close of the Civil War, 1620-1865. W. W. Norton and Company, 1964.

Mason, Daniel Gregory. The Dilemma of American Music. New York: The Macmillan Company, 1928.

_____. Music in My Time. New York: The Macmillan Company, 1938.

_____. Tune In, America! A Study of Our Coming Musical Independence. New York: Alfred A. Knopf, 1931.

Mellers, Wilfrid. Music in a New Found Land: Themes and Developments in the History of American Music. New York: Alfred A. Knopf, 1965.

Peyser, Ethel. The House that Music Built: Carnegie Hall. New York: Robert W. McBride & Company, 1936.

Pichierri, Louise. Music in New Hampshire, 1623-1800. New York: Columbia University Press, 1960.

Pratt, Waldo Selden. (Copyright 1921 by Oliver Ditson Company: Copyright renewed by Oliver Ditson Company, 1949.)

Rockefeller Panel Report. Coming to Our Senses. David Rockefeller, chairman. New York: McGraw-Hill Book Company, 1977.

Rockefeller Panel Report. The Performing Arts: Problems and Prospects. Report on the future of theatre, dance, and music in America. Rockefeller Brothers Fund. New York: McGraw-Hill Company, 1965.

Rockwell, John. All-American Music: Composition in the Late Twentieth Century. New York: Alfred A. Knopf, 1983.

Rohrer, Gertrude Martin. Music and Musicians of Pennsylvania. Port Washington, N.Y.: Kennikat Press, Ira J. Friedman Division, 1940.

Sabolsky, Irving. American Music. Chicago: The University of Chicago Press, 1969.

Scott, John Anthony. The Ballad of America: The History of the United States in Song and Story. New York: Grosset & Dunlap Publishers, 1967.

Sessions, Roger. Reflections on the Music Life in the United States. New York: Merlin Press, 1956.

Shaffer, Helen B. Music in America. Volume II. Washington, D.C.: Editorial Research Reports, 1956.

Snyder, Louis. Community of Sound: Boston Symphony and Its World of Players. Boston: Beacon Press, 1979.

Sonneck, Oscar G. Bibliography of Early American Secular Music. Revised and enlarged by William Treat Upton. New edition with preface by Irving Lowens. New York: Da Capo Press, 1964.

_____. Early Concert Life in America. Leipzig: Breitkopf & Hartel, 1907. (Reprinted by Misurgis, New York, 1949.)

_____. Early Opera in America. New York: G. Schirmer, Inc., 1915. (Reprinted by B. Blom, New York, 1963.)

_____. Francis Hopkinson and James Lyon. New York: Da Capo Press, 1967.

Southern Eileen. The Music of Black Americans. New York: W. W. Norton & Company, 1971.

Spaeth, Sigmund. Music and Dance in Pennsylvania, New Jersey, and Delaware. New York: Bureau of Musical Research, 1956.

Spalding, Walter Raymond. Music at Harvard. New York: Da Capo Press, 1977.

Thomson, Virgil. American Music Since 1910. New York: Holt, Rinehart and Winston, 1970.

Tirro, Frank. Jazz: A History. New York: W. W. Norton & Company, 1977.

Tufts, John. A Very Plain and Easy Introduction to the Singing of Psalm Tunes. Boston: 1721. (Facsimile edition published by Harry Dichter. Philadelphia, Musical Americana, 1954.)

Vinson, Lee (ed.). The Early American Songbook. Englewood Cliffs, N.J.: Prentice-Hall, 1974.

Westrup, (Sir) Jack. Music: Its Past and Its Present. A lecture delivered by Sir Jack Allan Westrup in the Whittall Pavilion of the Library of Congress, September 3, 1963. Washington, D.C.: The Library of Congress, 1964.

Wetzel, Richard D. Frontier Musicians on the Connoquenessing, Wabash and Ohio. Athens: Ohio University Press, 1976.

Yeabury, Grace D. Song in America from Early Times to About 1950. Metuchen, N.J.: The Scarecrow Press, 1971.

Zuck, Barbara A. A History of Musical Americanism. Ann Arbor, Mich.: University of Microfilms International, 1978.

SETTLEMENT HOUSES AND THEIR WORK IN THE ARTS

Addams, Jane. A Centennial Reader. New York: The
        Macmillan Company, 1960.
_____. Democracy and Social Ethics. Cambridge, Mass.:
        The Belknap Press of Harvard University Press, 1961.
_____. The Long Road of Woman's Memory. New York:
        The Macmillan Company, 1916.
_____. The Second Twenty Years at Hull-House. New York:
        The Macmillan Company, 1930.
_____. The Spirit of Youth and the City Streets. New
        York: The Macmillan Company, 1937.
_____. Addams, Jane. Twenty Years at Hull-House.
        New York: The Macmillan Company, 1910.
_____, and Others. Philanthropy and Social Progress.
        College Park, Md.: McGrath Publishing Company, 1893.
        (Reprint by Arno Press, New York, 1969.)
Egan, Robert F. "The History of the Music School of the
        Henry Street Settlement." Ph.D. dissertation, New
        York University, 1967.
_____ (ed.). "Manual: A Guide for the Establishment
        and Administration of a Community Music School." The
        National Guild of Community Music Schools, 1958.
Grimes, Clarence L. They Who Speak in Music. New Haven,
        Conn.: The Neighborhood Music School, 1957.
Hall, Helen. Unfinished Business in Neighborhood and Nation.
        New York: The Macmillan Company, 1971.
Hull-House Maps and Papers. Residents of Hull-House. New
        York: Arno Press & The New York Times, 1970.
Pacey, Lorene M. Readings in the Development of Settlement
        Work. New York: Association Press, 1950.
Schenck, Janet D. Music Schools and Settlement Music Depart-
        ments. Boston: National Federation of Settlements,
        1923.
_____. Music, Youth & Opportunity. Boston: National
        Federation of Settlements, 1926.
Simkhovitch, Mary K. Group Life. New York: Association
        Press, 1940.
Wald, Lillian D. The House on Henry Street. New York:
        Henry Holt and Company, 1915.
_____. Windows on Henry Street. Boston: Little, Brown,
        and Company, 1934.
Woods, Robert A. The City of Wilderness. New York: Gar-
        rett Press, 1970.

_____, and Albert J. Kennedy (eds.). Handbook of Settle-
ments. New York: The Russell Sage Foundation.
(Reprint Edition by Arno Press, 1970.)
_____, and _____. The Zone of Emergence. Abridged
and edited with a preface by Sam B. Warner, Jr.
Cambridge, Mass.: The Harvard University Press,
1962.
Woods, Robert A., W. W. Elsing, et al. The Poor in Great
Cities (Their Problems and What Is Being Done to Solve
Them). Kegan, Trench, Trubner & Co., 1896.
Wright, Richardson. Hawkers and Walkers in Early America.
Philadelphia: J. B. Lippincott Company, 1927.

OTHER ART FORMS

Dunlap, William. History of the Rise and Progress of the Arts
of Design in the United States. New York: Benjamin
Blom, 1965. New edition, revised and edited by Alex-
ander Wyckoff with preface by William P. Campbell.
Volumes I, II, III.
Horwitz, Marcy, and Sandie Kaplan (eds.). Explo! Arts
Education and Human Development. Report of the Pro-
ceedings of the 40th Annual Conference. New York:
National Guild of Community Schools of the Arts, 1978.
(Mimeographed.)
_____, and _____ (eds.). Putting It All Together (So
It Works!). New York: National Guild of Community
Schools of the Arts, 1981.
Houseman, John. Run-Through. New York: Simon and
Schuster, 1972. [Houseman headed first the Negro
Theatre Project and thereafter Project #891 of New York
City's Federal Theatre, the latter being the designation
of the classical theatre program.]
Mather, Frank Jewett, Jr., Charles Rufus Morey, and William
James Henderson. The American Spirit in Art. New
Haven, Conn.: Yale University Press, 1927.
Miller, Lillian B. Patrons and Patriotism. Chicago: The
University of Chicago Press, 1966.
Mumford, Lewis. The Brown Decades: A Study of the Arts
in America (1865-1895). New York: Dover Publications,
1955. (Original copyright 1931 by Mumford.)
Porter, Robert (ed.). The Arts and City Planning. New York:
American Council for the Arts, 1980. [City planners
and arts administrators join together to discuss coopera-
tive efforts in making cities livable].

Robb, David M., and J. J. Garrison. Art in the Western
     World. New York: Harper & Brothers Publishers, 1942.
Silverman, Kenneth. A Cultural History of the American
     Revolution. (Painting, Music, Literature, and the
     Theatre in the Colonies and the United States from the
     Treaty of Paris to the Inauguration of George Washington,
     1763-1789.) New York: Thomas Y. Crowell Company,
     1976.
Ulanov, Barry. The Two Worlds of American Art, the Private
     and the Popular. New York: The Macmillan Company,
     1965.

SOCIOLOGY AND THE ARTS

Ballantine, Christopher. Music and Its Social Meanings.
     New York: Gordon and Breach Science Publishers,
     1984.
Bernard, Kenneth A. Lincoln and the Music of the Civil War.
     Caldwell, Idaho: The Canton Printers, 1966.
Birmingham, Stephen. "Our Crowd": The Great Jewish
     Families of New York. Dell Publishing Co., 1967.
_____. "The Rest of Us": The Rise of America's Eastern
     European Jews. Boston: Little, Brown and Company,
     1984.
Division Federal Administrator of WPA. "A Report on the
     Music Project." Government Aid During the Depression
     to Professional, Technical, and Other Service Workers.
     WPA, 1936.
Durant, Alan. Conditions of Music. Albany, New York:
     State University of New York Press, 1984.
Gutman, Robert, and David Popenoe (eds.). Neighborhood,
     City, and Metropolis: An Integrated Reader in Urban
     Sociology. New York: Random House, 1970.
Hauser, Arnold. The Sociology of Art. Translated by Kenneth
     J. Northcott. London: Routledge & Kegan Paul, 1982.
Hopkins, Harry. Spending to Save. New York: W. W.
     Norton & Company, 1936.
Howe, Irving. World of Our Fathers. New York: Harcourt
     Brace Jovanovich, 1976.
Kaplan, Max. National Guild of Community Music Schools
     Observations and Recommendations. Brookline, Mass.:
     National Guild of Community Music Schools, 1966.
     (Mimeographed. In the files of the author.)
Livesay, Harold C. Samuel Gompers and Organized Labor in
     America. Boston: Little, Brown and Company, 1978.

Mussulman, Joseph Agee. Music in the Cultured Generation:
    A Social History of Music in America, 1870-1900.
    Chicago: Northwestern University Press, 1971.
National Conference of State Legislatures. Arts and the
    States: A Report of the Arts Taskforce. Compiled by
    Larry Briskin. Denver: The National Conference of
    State Legislatures, 1981.
Neidle, Cecyle S. (ed.). America's Immigrant Women. Boston:
    Twayne Publishers, a Division of G. K. Hall & Co., 1975.
Phillips, Cabell. From the Crash to the Blitz, 1929-1939.
    London: The Macmillan Company, 1969.
Raynor, Henry. A Social History of Music from the Middle
    Ages to Beethoven: Music & Society Since 1815. Two
    volumes in one unabridged. New York: Taplinger
    Publishing Company (A Crescendo Book), 1978.
Smith, David Messner. The Community Music Association:
    Principles and Practices Suggested by a Study of The
    Flint Community Music Association. New York: Bureau
    of Publications, Teachers College, Columbia University,
    1954.
Stalcup, Robert J. Sociology and Education. Columbus, Ohio:
    Charles E. Merrill Publishing Company, A Bell & Howell
    Company, 1968.
Urban Innovations Group. The Arts in the Economic Life of
    the City. New York: American Council for the Arts,
    1979.
Wilensky, Harold L. Industrial Society and Social Welfare.
    New York: Russell Sage Foundation, 1958.

HISTORY OF THE UNITED STATES OF AMERICA

Gabriel, Ralph Henry (ed.). The Pageant of America: The
    American Spirit in Art.
Gunther, John. Inside U.S.A. New York: Harper & Brothers,
    1951.
Hoffman, Charles. The Depression of the Nineties. Westport,
    Conn.: Greenwood Publishing Corporation, 1970.
Morison, Samual Elliot, and Henry Steele Commager. The
    Growth of the American Republic. Volumes 1 and 2.
    New York: Oxford University Press, 1942.
Taylor, Alice. New York City. Garden City, N.Y.: Nelson
    Doubleday, 1963.

MISCELLANEOUS

Cords, Nicholas John. "Music in Social Settlement and Community Music Schools, 1893-1939: A Democratic-Esthetic Approach to Music Culture." Ph.D. dissertation, University of Minnesota at Minneapolis, 1970.

Mayer, Martin. The Met: One Hundred Years of Grand Opera. New York: Simon and Schuster, 1928.

Merkling, Frank, John W. Freeman, et al. (eds.). The Golden Horseshoe: The Life and Times of the Metropolitan Opera House. New York: Viking Press, 1965.

INDEX

DA